Silvia Ronchey
Hypatia

Silvia Ronchey

Hypatia

The True Story

English Translation by
Nicolò Sassi

With the Collaboration of
Giulia Maria Paoletti

2nd rev. edition

DE GRUYTER

ISBN 978-3-11-124553-9
e-ISBN (PDF) 978-3-11-124575-1
e-ISBN (EPUB) 978-3-11-124581-2

Library of Congress Control Number: 2023941021

Bibliographic information published by the Deutsche Nationalbibliothek
The Deutsche Nationalbibliothek lists this publication in the Deutsche Nationalbibliografie;
detailed bibliographic data are available on the Internet at http://dnb.dnb.de.

© 2023 Walter de Gruyter GmbH, Berlin/Boston
Cover image: John William Godward, Contemplation (1903). Peter Nahum Private Collection at
The Leicester Galleries, London.
Printing and binding: CPI books GmbH, Leck

www.degruyter.com

To Theon

Author's Note

Putting together this book would have been more difficult without the knowledge and assistance of Pia Carolla (and not just for her help with the bibliographical update) and without the insightful contributions of Davide Baldi and Francesco Monticini. I also thank here Sergio Basso and Laura Borghetti for their aid with the bibliography; Silvia Pedone for her precious insights on iconography; Peter Schreiner for reading the new manuscript and providing advice. Nicolò Sassi, with the collaboration of Giulia Maria Paoletti, not only translated the majority of the sections written *ex novo* by the author for the second enlarged edition, but has also reviewed and fundamentally reformulated the previous English translation drafted by Katherine Clifton and Elisabeth Giansiracusa. To both translators-reviewers goes my gratitude. However, I must extend my final thanks to Judith Ryder for her strenuous work in revising the English style, which she greatly improved, as well as in ensuring the correct rendering of technical terminology.

Preface

The present work reconstructs Hypatia's life, intellectual work, and modern *Nachleben* through a sustained philological and literary analysis. The ultimate goal of this analysis is to bring to light the intrinsically political dimension of Hypatia's murder, caused by the *phthonos* (violent envy) of the Christian bishop Cyril of Alexandria. The book is addressed to an educated, non-specialist readership, as well as research scholars and students, and the intentionally provocative title relates to the contemporary historiographical concept of "false" or "fake history," as does the overall conceptual and methodological treatment.

In the first section (*Clarifying the Facts*) I compare and apply philological analysis to all extant evidence on Hypatia's life and death gleaned from all available ancient sources, both Pagan and Christian. Originally, two versions of Hypatia's assassination, one Pagan and one Christian, must have co-existed, each available in two variants, one moderate and one radical.

In the three centuries between the life and death of Hypatia and the evolution of the Byzantine historical tradition after the Arab conquest, one of the Christian narratives, John of Nikiu's *Chronicle*, derived from one or more older, possibly vernacular versions produced in favour of Cyril of Alexandria within the Coptic Church, was lost to the West. Nonetheless, this version was preserved in the Eastern tradition in a late Ethiopic version, which appears as the most radically pro-Cyril among ancient Christian sources. The other, more moderate Christian version, eschewed by dominant Western ecclesiastical opinion, is by Socrates Scholasticus, whose narrative regarding the case in question probably conforms to the point of view of the central Byzantine Church.

The Byzantine author Suidas transmitted both of the Pagan narratives, by Hesychius of Miletus and Damascius. In addition, the version by Philostorgius (an Arian Christian, and as such an opponent of Cyril), whose text is preserved in numerous fragments from Photius' *Library*, was appended to Damascius' variant of the Pagan version from the beginning of the manuscript tradition. Another source from the time of Justinian, the *Chronicle* of John Malalas, seems to be derived from another Byzantine tradition close to the court clergy but especially to the Church of Antioch, which was traditionally at odds with the Church of Alexandria. The account offered by Malalas identifies Cyril, as does Socrates, as prime instigator of, and morally responsible for, Hypatia's assassination. Malalas probably draws on his own, independent sources, which appear in agreement with Socrates on the bishop's guilt but are also aware of details lacking in the accounts of Socrates and Suidas-Damascius. The most well-known version in Byzantium would remain that of Socrates, an Orthodox Christian, more cautious than the Pagan and Arian-Christian accounts and slightly different from the one Malalas draws on, but equally anti-Cyril.

The same orientation would emanate from subsequent Byzantine sources which would gradually add useful features from Pagan sources. From 5th and 6th century information, influence, and manuscript tradition, which appears more ramified than generally thought, derives during iconoclasm the succinct mention of the assassination found in Theophanes' *Chronicle*. In the 9th century, Photius, clearly believing in Cyril's guilt, reprises Damascius as well as Philostorgius. As mentioned above, in the 10th century Suidas follows at least Damascius and Hesychius. In the 14th century, Nikephoros Kallistos Xanthopoulos draws directly on Socrates Scholasticus.

From the examination of these sources, together with other contemporary evidence as well as Synesius' letter collection, emerges a complex picture of the tensions and social and political conflicts in 4th to 5th century Alexandria, which makes it impossible to reduce the issue of Hypatia's assassination to a clash between Paganism and Christianity. However, precisely this ideological simplification, this polarity between Hypatia "Pagan martyr" and Cyril "bishop-executioner," has dominated European thought for so long.

The second section of the work (*Betraying the Facts*) is devoted to the afterlife of the figure of Hypatia, modernised, falsified, and transformed, according to the period and its cultural and religious trends, into a secular icon, a romantic heroine, or even a Christian martyr. Yet, perhaps even more revealing for the history of political thought has been the reception of the figure of Cyril. If ecclesiastical authority tended to interfere constantly in the jurisdiction of the prefect Orestes and the Roman-Constantinopolitan central government – the very erosion of State power by the Church dreaded by the Alexandrian aristocracy (Pagan as well as moderate Christian) of which Hypatia was a spokesperson –, the conviction or exaltation of the feared bishop is a litmus test of the position that every historian or literary interpreter assumes with respect to relations between Church and State. This appears from the first ancient sources through Hypatia's entire historiographical afterlife: from the Counter-Reformation, which would even discredit a primary source like Socrates Scholasticus to save Cyril, up until 18th and 19th century lay literature, when the fabrication of Hypatia as a secular icon would be interwoven with the debate concerning Papal temporal authority.

The third section (*Interpreting the Facts*) responds to the more or less conscious distortions built up by scholarship over the centuries. Hypatia was not a "secular martyr," nor a "Galileo in a skirt" punished by the Church for her scientific discoveries, let alone a Proto-Feminist icon. It is true that the conflict she found herself involved in – eternal, and cutting across the very same Pagan upper classes, in large part christianised, especially after the Theodosian Decrees – was between fundamentalism and moderation, dogmatism and open-mindedness. It is also true, however, that Hypatia was a charismatic, priestly figure, a mentor of consciences and an "initiator" in the esoteric teachings of Platonism: a "woman-philosopher," as long as we understand her *philosophia* as that particular relationship between the female and the sphere of the sacred, of the super-rational, that is typical of the spirituality of Late Antiquity.

Hypatia is the symbol of the intellectual fervor of the "Eclectic" Platonism that dominated 5th century Alexandria and continued after her "martyrdom", and was indeed the prerequisite and threshold for a flourishing that would continue for the entire Byzantine millennium.

To the Reader

I have been working on Hypatia for over twenty years (an early essay of mine on the topic was published in 2001 by The University of Chicago Press)[1]. *Hypatia. The True Story* was conceived both as a scholarly contribution to the debate on the fate of the philosopher/mathematician and as a treatment accessible to an educated, yet non-academic audience. This has already been partially achieved, considering that the book's first edition, published by Rizzoli in 2010, is in its 6th reprint in Italy. This is the first reason why I have decided to produce, ten years later, a revised, updated, and enlarged English edition. The second, more pressing reason is that never before has there been such an explosion of interest in Hypatia as there has been in the last ten years: scholarly articles, fiction, hybrid contributions bridging the former and the latter; events, conferences, performances, theatrical plays; blog posts, historical summaries, biographical sketches, often multiplied and scattered across the web in a game of reflections and distortions.

Such multiplication of opinions about Hypatia is an interesting, important, positive phenomenon. This rich, sometimes cacophonous polyphony of voices, however, has also made even less clear the truth about her life and death, a truth that has been, since its very beginning, at the core of my book. My goal in the following pages is to bring order to our sources, to clear the confessional and historiographical prejudice of literary and popular legends, and to correct the outright mistakes caused by ideological infiltrations or, more simply, by a lack of historical and philological proficiency in reading and interpreting ancient sources.

* * *

As mentioned above, this book was intended from the beginning to be read and enjoyed by both a relatively wide public and by specifically academic readers. In the first Italian edition, an annotated documentation – including the references regarding the main text plus various detailed additions, materials, and comments printed in a smaller font, but of a length equal to that of the main text – followed the text and occupied a second and distinct section of the book, destined for a more markedly specialist readership. In the English version hereby offered to the reader, each chapter is followed by this part of the work (the *Appendix*). Besides, I felt that in this new, more comprehensive edition at least some of the references in the documentation should be anticipated in the form of footnotes. I have therefore included in the book both forms of documentation: the information provided by the footnotes, basic and brief, and a wider documentation and discussion in the Appendix following each chapter.

---

[1] S. RONCHEY, *Hypatia the Intellectual*, in A. FRASCHETTI (ed.), *Roman Women*, Chicago & London: The University of Chicago Press, 2001, pp. 160–189, English translation of S. RONCHEY, *Ipazia, l'intellettuale*, in A. FRASCHETTI (ed.), *Roma al femminile*, Roma: Laterza, 1994, pp. 213–258.

I hope that while reading the main body of the text, the reader will take into account that it represents the 'thread' of the narrative, and therefore gives a clear idea of the book's cultural formulation and essential content, but does not include the more scholarly part of it, which specialists or simply more curious readers will find in the Appendix.

Contents

Introduction — 1

Part I: Setting out the Facts

1 Once there was a Woman — 5

2 The Destruction of the Serapeum — 12

3 Elegant Insolence — 18

4 The Terrible Patriarch of Alexandria — 23

5 Good Use of Power — 30

6 Treacherous Zeal — 34

7 The Bishop of Nikiu — 38

8 A Three-Handed Game — 41

9 The Intimidation of Orestes — 45

10 Mortal Envy — 51

11 The Cover-Up — 59

Part II: Betraying the Facts

12 The Glory of Her Own Sex and the Wonder of Ours — 65

13 The Excesses of Fanaticism — 69

14 A Very Beautiful and Well-educated Woman is Torn Asunder — 74

15 From Fielding to Gibbon Passing Through the Shadow of a Donkey — 79

16 The Catholic Wing — 83

17 Refreshing Exceptions —— 89

18 Uncontrolled Effects on the Poets —— 94

19 New Faces For Old Foes —— 100

20 *Kulturkampf.* Hypatia *à la Bismarck* —— 104

21 Celestial Virgin —— 108

22 Miraculous Devotion. Chateaubriand, Péguy and the Flourishing of Feminist Literature —— 114

23 Superfluous Heroisms —— 121

24 The Forces of the Universe —— 125

25 A Name, a Mantra —— 127

Part III: Interpreting the Facts

26 May the Witnesses Return to the Court —— 133

27 The DNA of the Ancient Tradition —— 137

28 Church and State —— 141

29 An Age of Anxiety —— 144

30 Hypatia in All Her States of Being —— 149

31 What Did Hypatia Teach? —— 157

32 All Synesius' Mysteries —— 167

33 Synesius, Hypatia and *Philosophia* —— 173

34 Women Who Philosophised —— 180

35 The Power of Hypatia —— 185

36 *Dramatis Personae* —— 191

37 Hypatia's Sacrifice —— 195

38 The Martyrdom of Hypatia —— 200

39 A Question of Method —— 203

40 The Eminence of Hypatia —— 205

Aftershock: And What If… —— 211

Bibliography —— 217

Index of Names —— 250

Introduction

In the 5th century A.D., a woman was murdered. We know little of her, except these two things: she was beautiful and she was a philosopher. We know that she was stripped naked and disfigured with potsherds. Her eyes were put out. We know that the remains of her body were scattered throughout the city and then burnt. We also know that all this was done by fanatical Christians.

Since then, she has become a symbol, an 'icon', of whom, however, there are no extant visual portrayals. We do not know whether she was dark-haired with penetrating brown eyes like a Fayum, or blonde and diaphanous like a Victorian portrait. We know that her students fell in love with her, and that she rejected them. We know that she was an aristocrat, from every point of view. We know that her assassination was a scandal that has echoed down through fifteen centuries, though the Catholic Church, that is to say the 'Church of the Popes', has quashed it as much as it could, turning her, for this precise reason, into a banner of secularism. What exactly this banner means, however, is not clear.

According to some, her assassination was a political matter. According to others, it was the expression of ancient extremist monks' own religious intolerance, whose violence reflected their extremist vocation and the integralist excesses of the Church during the genesis of its climb to power.

According to some, her assassination was unplanned collateral damage caused by the battle against Judaism engaged in by newly born Christianity, which was born as its heresy; grown up in the shadow of the synagogues, Christianity finally became Judaism's worst enemy. According to others – including ancient sources – there was, on the contrary, a precise individual hostility behind the commission, that of a young, choleric and ambitious bishop.

According to some, this murdered woman was a scientist, "the most important until Madame Curie". According to others, a philosopher, "Pupil of Plotinus". Yet others say that she was a priestess and a theurgist.

Some have crowned her as a Proto-Feminist heroine, others as a martyr of freedom of thought. Some have commemorated her as the sacrificial lamb of Paganism's last vestiges; yet others considered her as the first witch burnt at the stake of the ecclesiastical inquisition.

She incarnated the superiority of Paganism, with its pluralism and its openness, compared with the dogmatic narrowness of Monotheisms. Or else she has become an allegory of the battle against secular fundamentalisms, the symbol of the radical refusal of the all-pervasive faiths and ideologies.

While historiography has rather exploited her, literature, on the other hand, transformed and betrayed her to a great extent. She was an Enlightenment figure and a Romantic, Decadent and Parnassian, a Freethinker and a Socialist, a Protestant, a Freemason, an Agnostic, a Neo-Pagan vestal virgin and even a Christian saint. She has been a female Galileo and a Mademoiselle de Maupin, a George Sand and an Odette, an asteroid and an invisible star with a prodigious attractive force, a black hole.

What is, however, hidden behind all these masks and visions? To understand this, an inquiry must be set up. Not to add traits, but to prune away, from those few that ancient traditions have handed down, those which the analysis of the slim dossier of original testimonies about her suggest are false or distorted.

We are certain, or almost certain, of what this woman was not. She was not a Cynic philosopher, nor a Crypto-Christian, nor a scientist persecuted by the Church for her astronomical discoveries, let alone a Proto-Feminist. In general, she was none of what she was deemed to be, with more or less conscious or deliberate sublimation or misrepresentation, by the historians and scholars who have sketched her posthumous fortune.

Something else, I would argue, is almost certain: she sought the truth, she loved doubt and she detested manipulation. We believe that a methodical diffidence towards what has been said about her, and a systematic dismantling of her literary myth and her political-ecclesiastical and historiographical re-invention, could only please her.

Everyone wants to accommodate her, to know this mysterious martyr of knowledge. Yet, to speak of her demands a certain level of initiation. Not of Platonic initiation, such as that of her pupils or her Byzantine and modern continuators. An initiation into other and more ancient mysteries, truths that it is neither easy nor immediate to know or recognise: the propagandistic nature of history, the inevitability of literary distortion, the near impossibility of issuing a fair judgement on the past free from the present and from all those sedimentary layers deposited by recent pasts that, when added to the most ancient testimonies, shape the historical object of study.

These ideas about the nature of history, and about the almost insurmountable difficulty of its reconstruction, are esoteric, intended for a select few, because they could lead many to become discouraged, to transform their disenchantment into scepticism or cynicism, to transform the absence of biases with which the versions of sources are evaluated into interpretative frivolity, or even into the temptation to manipulate them in turn.

Perplexity, disenchantment, and doubt are tools to be handled with care, so that the conclusions of those who exercise historical criticism are not distorted by the present, and subliminally manipulated by its propaganda, thereby becoming guilty of that same ideological subjugation which the ancient philosopher Hypatia should represent the negation of.

If we truly wish to pay her homage, we must not waste the opportunity to identify her true nature and her sacrifice, which are so important in the world of politics and thinking, in a non-sectarian manner. We must read her story in a truly secular and free manner, that is to say, as far as possible, true.

Part I: Setting out the Facts

> No wild beasts are so deadly to humans
> as most Christians are to each other.
> 						AMMIANUS MARCELLINUS

1 Once there was a Woman

Fifteen centuries ago there was a woman in Alexandria, Egypt, whose name was Hypatia. In the Greek spoken at that time, this name evoked an idea of 'eminence', 'acuity', 'supremeness'. It was given to her by her father, a renowned scholar, who planned an academic career for his daughter. No one could imagine that fate, or chance, which rules the world, would make Hypatia a martyr to reason. That this daughter of a peaceful professor in civilised Alexandria would meet a violent death. That she would be the victim of an atrocious slaying, one of the most deplored in cultural history.

> There was a woman then in Alexandria, whose name was Hypatia. She was the daughter of Theon, philosopher of the school of Alexandria, and she had reached such a high level of knowledge that she surpassed by far all the philosophers of her circle[2] [...]

says a Christian historian, her contemporary, Socrates Scholasticus, a lawyer at the court of Constantinople.

From a young age, say the ancient historical sources, Hypatia was accustomed to studying. Theon taught her everything he could; yet, she was not satisfied with her father's teachings; she wanted to learn more. Thus, she gained an even wider knowledge including different disciplines to those to which Theon had introduced her. The fact was, say these historical sources, that the pupil was actually smarter than the teacher:

> being by nature more gifted than her father, she did not stop at the technical-mathematical teachings he practised, but dedicated herself to pure philosophy, and with merit[3] [...]

reports Suidas, a 10th century Byzantine intellectual, in the lengthy entry *Hypatia, or the factiousness of the Alexandrians* in his encyclopaedia. His information comes from two accounts, now lost, from the century following those events; namely, that – real, or at least presumed to be so – of Hesychius of Miletus, and *The Life of Isidorus*, the last priest of the temple of Serapis, which was composed by the Neoplatonist Damascius, the last scholarch of the School of Athens before it was closed down by Justinian. Both texts only survive in fragments. Suidas possibly draws from the latter of these sources the statement above, which is also confirmed by the *Church History* by Philostorgius, an ancient testimony largely lost to us but written only a few years following Hypatia's death. It is possible that Philostorgius attended her lessons:

> Hypatia outshone her master, particularly in astronomy, and it came to pass that she was the teacher for many in mathematical sciences[4] [...]

---

2 SOCRATES VII 15, 1, p. 360, 19–21 Hansen; HARICH-SCHWARZBAUER 2011, p. 188.
3 DAMASCIUS, *Vita Isidori* fr. *102, p. 77,1–3 Zintzen = fr. 43A, p. 128, 2–4 Athanassiadi = SUIDAS Y 166, IV, p. 644, 13–15 Adler (HARICH-SCHWARZBAUER 2011, p. 246).
4 PHILOSTORGIUS 8, 9, p. 111 Bidez = 8, 9, p. 366, 1–5 Bleckmann – Stein (HARICH-SCHWARZBAUER 2011, p. 318); see also PHILOSTORGIUS, pp. 28–29 Bleckmann – Stein, according to whom Philostorgius's ac-

An encyclopaedist writing eight centuries after Suidas, Denis Diderot, punctilious interpreter of his Byzantine predecessor, in the two columns of the *Encyclopédie* devoted to Hypatia, says: "Nature had never granted to anyone a superior soul or a more felicitous genius than that of Theon's daughter. Education made her a prodigy" because "she drew on the fundamental principles of other sciences" learned from her father "in the conversations and the schools of the renowned *philosophes* then flourishing in Alexandria." And he concludes: "What can be denied to such a penetrating intelligence and a true passion for study?"[5]

After years of study, Hypatia had acquired a reputation amongst the intellectuals of her time. A reputation for connoisseurs, which was not limited to her city, but had spread amongst the international community of scholars of Late Antiquity. Although the Western Roman empire was about to fall into the hands of the barbarians, another empire was flourishing in the East, the Byzantine empire, its glorious continuation. Although that century, the 5th after Christ, may seem an epoch of decadence, love of culture was everywhere greater than ever. In fact, it was more alive than the academic culture, which outside Alexandria was entrusted, we are told[6], to sterile professors incapable of transmitting knowledge in a charismatic manner. Hypatia was, thus, seen by all as a luminous exception, and from all corners of the Greek and Roman world lovers of knowledge came to attend her academic lessons, in which the tradition of the ancient Platonic school was carried forward.

> She inherited (*diadoche*, διαδοχή) the legacy of the teachings of the Platonic school derived from Plotinus and expounded to a free audience all the philosophical disciplines [...]. From all parts, they came to hear her those who wanted to study philosophy [...][7]

says Socrates Scholasticus in his *Ecclesiastical History*.

Hypatia had a particularly efficacious way of teaching and a fluid eloquence:

> She had reached an excellent level in the practice of teaching,

states Suidas, who here reports the words of Damascius, and

> in speaking, she was fluent and dialectical.[8]

---

count may have been transmitted to Suidas either through Hesychius or through the *Excerpta Constantiniana:* see below Appendix.

5 Diderot.
6 Synesius, *Ep.* 136, 16–17, p. 275 Roques. See below, Appendix *ad loc.*
7 Socrates VII 15, 1, p. 360, 21–24 Hansen (Harich-Schwarzbauer 2011, p. 188).
8 Damascius, *Vita Isidori* fr. *104, p. 79, 12 Zintzen = fr. 43E, p. 130, 1–3 Athanassiadi = Suidas Y 166, IV, p. 644, 18–19 and 30 Adler (Harich-Schwarzbauer 2011, p. 247).

Moreover, according to Damascius, "although she was a woman, she wore the *tribon* (τρίβων)", a term that at the time of Hypatia indicated the eminent garment of the philosopher more than the rough cloak of the Cynic street preachers,

> [...] and she made her public appearances in the centre of the city to explain, to anyone who wanted to listen to her, Plato, Aristotle or any other philosopher.[9]

And the 18th century encyclopaedist Diderot concludes:

> All the knowledge available to the human spirit, gathered in this woman of enchanting eloquence, made her a surprising phenomenon, and I do not mean merely for the people, who will wonder at anything, but for the philosophers themselves, whom it is difficult to astound.[10]

---

9 DAMASCIUS, *Vita Isidori* fr. *102, p. 77, 5–7 Zintzen = fr. 43A, p. 128, 6 Athanassiadi = SUIDAS Y 166, IV, p. 644, 16–18 Adler (HARICH-SCHWARZBAUER 2011, p. 246).
10 DIDEROT.

Appendix
Setting out the Facts

The quotation in exergo is taken from Ammianus Marcellinus, *Res gestae*, XXII 5, 4: "[...] nullas infestas hominibus bestias, ut sunt sibi ferales plerique Christianorum".

Once there was a Woman

On the etymological meaning of the name Hypatia see below, part II, chapter "A Name, a Mantra". For its rare occurrences in Late Antiquity see the bibliography in DZIELSKA 1993 = DZIELSKA 1995, pp. 137–138, n. 5; see also HOCHE, p. 440 with n. 22; MEYER, p. 8.

The name of Hypatia's father, according to recent studies, was not Theon, but Theoteknos, "son of God". However, the theory advanced by ROQUES 1995 and ROQUES 1998 that in Synesius' *Eps.* 4 and 16 (SYNESIUS, tom. I Garzya – Roques) the names of Theoteknos – of which Theon could be considered the diminutive – and Athanasius respectively indicate the father and the brother of Hypatia, is mistaken: see the counter-arguments of MASSON and of SCHMITT, according to whom the "most blessed father" in question was a Christian priest; a hypothesis that is also contestable. See discussion in DZIELSKA 1995, p. 37, and HARICH-SCHWARZBAUER 2011, pp. 79–80. Most probably the denominations "father" and "brother" that we find in the two epistles of Synesius are those in use in the Neoplatonic *phratria* (φρατρία): see the similar use in the phratry of George Gemistus Plethon, the last Platonic school of the Byzantine empire, with headquarters at the imperial court of Mystras in the Peloponnese, on which see below, part III, chapters "Synesius, Hypatia and *Philosophia*" and "The Eminence of Hypatia", with Appendix *ad loc.* The mistaken theory of Roques was already tentatively advanced by BERETTA 1993, p. 35; and the identification of Theoteknos with Theon was already to be found in BIGONI who, however, correctly considered Athanasius and Synesius to be brethren, that is, Athanasius to be a pupil of the school. Maria Dzielska identifies him as the homonymous sophist of Alexandria, pupil of Hypatia (DZIELSKA 1991).

A *terminus post quem* for the death of Theon (395, the end of the reign of Theodosius I) would seem to be supplied by the encyclopaedia written in the 10th century by Suidas: see SUIDA Θ 205, II, p. 702, 10–16 Adler, which calls him "scholar of geometry and philosophy, particularly dedicated to mathematics and astronomy". Scholars are still debating on the details of Theon's life and death and his intellectual personality. According to the testimony of Suidas, his scientific maturity is to be dated between 379 and 395 and, although some have considered, on the basis of fragile evidence, that his date of birth must be earlier than supposed, and should be placed around 335, it is likely, as argued by NEUGEBAUER, p. 873, that Theon was still alive in the early years of the 5th century.

Given that it is certain that a family called Σουίδας existed in the mid-Byzantine period, as is proved by documents and seals which show that it can be attributed to a family of dignitaries at the Constantinopolitan court, perhaps of Varangian origin, in this book, diverging from the opinion of the majority, but following that of Klaus Alpers, we take as certain that the name *Suidas*, under which the work in question has been transmitted (in this form or in the inferior reading *Souda/Suda*), is that of the author and not the title of the work. It is not possible here to dive into the long and complex specifics of such a topic, nor is this the place to take into account the conundrum the name represents: we refer to KAZHDAN – RONCHEY, reserving the opportunity to give further information in a specific context.

Facts and background to the story of Hypatia are given in chapter 15 of the VII book of the *Ecclesiastical History* by Socrates, which can be read in SOCRATES SCHOLASTICUS, pp. 360–361 Hansen. Other quotations in this book attributed to the same author are taken from this volume.

Socrates, just a few years younger than Hypatia, was writing not many years after her death, and in any case finished his work between 439 and 443: see URBAINCZYK, pp. 19–20. On his political personality and the ideological context of his account of Hypatia's murder in the last book of his *Ecclesiastical History* see URBAINCZYK, pp. 26–28; WALRAFF, pp. 235–257.

The epithet *scholastikos* (σχολαστικός) refers to a specific position at the Constantinopolitan court, which in the 5th century could designate either, generically, a "rhetorician", or, more specifically, a "jurist" or a "lawyer": see LOUKAKI, pp. 50–52; NUFFELEN; CLAUS. And this is what the majority of scholars consider him to have been.

E.J. Watts, H*ypatia. The Life and Legend of an Ancient Philosopher* (WATTS 2017, pp. 22–31), attempts to reconstruct Hypatia's cursus studiorum. According to Watts, Hypatia "could have done her grammatical training in a classroom with boys (and perhaps other girls), probably under the supervision of one of Theon's teaching assistants" and "she likely began" her philosophical and mathematical training "under her father's direction when she was in her late teens or early twenties" (p. 27). Here and elsewhere Watts' syntax is cautiously hypothetical. Nothing of what the author has extensively written on the education of Hypatia is attested in any specific source. Watts bases his reconstruction on his wide knowledge of Late Antique schools, and from this he deduces parallelisms that appear as highly conjectural if not random. His chronological reconstruction of Hypatia's academic career, as we shall see (part III, chapter "Hypatia in All Her States of Being", Appendix *ad loc.*), is based on the questionable backdating of her birth to 355. If this were to be the case, at the moment of her death Hypatia would have been sixty rather than forty five, as hypothesised by a long *lignée* of previous scholars. Such backdating allows Watts to assume, rather arbitrarily, that Hypatia "took over the school in the 380s", that is, "by the time she reached her thirtieth birthday", and that "Theon turned the role of primary instruction over to Hypatia sometime in the early or mid-380s" (pp. 37–38).

The article by SUIDAS Y 166 is dedicated to Hypatia (IV, pp. 644–646 Adler; see also s. v. *Theon* Θ 205, II, p. 702, 10–16 Adler). That Hypatia was "born, raised and educated in Alexandria" we read in SUIDAS Y 166, IV, p. 644, 12–13 Adler.

On the characteristics and the sources of Suidas' article on Hypatia see *in primis* TANNERY 1880.

A German translation and commentary on the Greek text of the parts attributable to Damascius – who says that he was in Alexandria in 485, that is seventy years after Hypatia's death, and writes around 495 – are to be found in ASMUS 1911, pp. 31–33. The fragments of the *Life of Isidore* by Damascius, taken from the article by Suidas and from Code 242 of the *Bibliotheca* (*Myriobiblion*) of Photius (PHOTIUS, vol. VI Henry), were later collected by Clemens Zintzen in *Damascii Vitae Isidori reliquiae*: on Hypatia see DAMASCIUS pp. 76–81 and 218–221 Zintzen; finally, see the bilingual edition (DAMASCIUS Athanassiadi), more accessible to non-specialist readers. For a tentative evaluation of "Damascius's project" see the recent paper by WATTS 2013.

On Hesychius of Miletus and his *Onomatologos*, a collection of biographies of Pagan scholars composed in the 6th century, now lost, but also preserved in fragments from Photius and Suidas, see KALDELLIS; HUNGER, p. 250. All quotations from Hesychius are based on the more recent critical edition of Suidas by Ada Adler rather than the one provided by MÜLLER, pp. 145–177.

The passage from Philostorgius can be read in the epitome of his *Church History*, which survived in the *Bibliotheca* of Photius: PHILOSTORGIUS, p. 111 Bidez; see also the French translation by É. DES PLACES (PHILOSTORGIUS des Places); and the recent critical edition, German translation and commentary by B. BLECKMANN – M. STEIN (PHILOSTORGIUS, pp. 366–368 Bleckmann – Stein). For an English translation see e.g. PHILOSTORGIUS Amidon; PHILOSTORGIUS Walford.

On the role of Photius see BATTIFOL p. 31. According to B. Bleckmann (PHILOSTORGIUS, pp. 28–29 Bleckmann – Stein), Philostorgius may have accessed Suidas either through Hesychius or the *Excerpta Constantiniana*. It has long been known that many terms that appear in Suidas ultimately derive from the *Excerpta:* this has been demonstrated, in particular, by Carl de Boor. According to an expert, namely Pia Carolla, whom I thank here for discussing this matter with me *per litteras*, the Bleckmann-Stein hypothesis is very likely, even if not totally demonstrable because of the lack of the complete text of both Hesychius and the pivotal *Excerpta*.

In the same passage of his *Church History*, in which he discusses the education of Hypatia, Philostorgius states that she had been trained in the μαθήματα. In the Greek of Philostorgius, this term cannot be interpreted as referring specifically to an education in mathematics, see WATTS 2017, p. 163, n. 34.

Philostorgius, born around 368 AD, and therefore contemporary to the facts related here, may have attended Hypatia's lessons, as suggested by Joseph Bidez in the foreword to his edition of the *Church History*, precisely on the basis of the author's praise of her teaching skills, which Bidez suggests is due to direct experience, also because this Christian author, despite being an Arian, was personally interested in astronomy and astrology: see PHILOSTORGIUS, pp. cix-cx Bidez. Luciano Canfora considers that Philostorgius may not only have attended Hypatia's lessons, but have been also present at her death: see CANFORA 2000, pp. 196–203. On the dating of Philostorgius' *Church History* and on the ideological contents of the work see ARGOV, pp. 497–502.

The passage from Diderot, like the others quoted in parts I and II of this book, comes from the article *Éclectisme* in the V volume of the *Encyclopédie* (1755): DIDEROT; below, part II, chapter "The Glory of Her Own Sex and the Wonder of Ours".

On the widespread fame of Hypatia see both Suidas (καί πολλοῖς γνώριμος, HESYCHIUS = SUIDAS Y 166, IV, p. 644, 1–2 Adler [HARICH-SCHWARZBAUER 2011, p. 324]), and SOCRATES VII 15, 1, p. 360, 23–24 Hansen (οἱ πανταχόθεν etc.), in addition to other later Byzantine sources.

On the superiority of Hypatia's teaching and the sterility and decadence of the Athenian lessons, I want to follow what Synesius writes, not without apparent hyperbole, in SYNESIUS, *Ep.* 136, 16–17, p. 275 Roques (Engl. transl. p. 229 Fitzgerald), where on the question of Athens he ironises: "Athens was aforetime the dwelling-place of the wise: today the bee-keepers alone bring it honour. Such is the case of that pair of sophists in Plutarch who draw the young people to the lecture room – not by the fame of their eloquence, but by pots of honey from Hymettus"; and earlier: "Athens today has nothing exceptional, apart from the names of the places. Just as, once the victim has been consumed, the hide remains as a trace of the beast that it was, so, philosophy having migrated from here, all that remains to admire is the Academy, the Lyceum, the Stoa Poikile"; see below, part III, chapter "All Synesius' Mysteries" and Appendix *ad loc.*; some scholars trace the reduction of certain aspects of Hypatia's teaching to that of the "trivial" model of a Cynic preacher, which also seems present in Damascius' account, to the school rivalry witnessed by the aforementioned polemical comments on the Athenian academy present in Synesius; see below, part III, "Hypatia in All Her States of Being", Appendix *ad loc.*

It goes without saying that the situation of the school of Athens was not as bleak as Synesius depicts it, as recently shown by WATTS 2017, p. 53 (cf. also WATTS 2020a). Watts creates a parallel between the "cultural pedigree" of the Platonic education of fourth century Athens and a "degree from Oxbridge or the Ivy League", and compares the acrimony of the students of Alexandria, such as Synesius, against the teachers of Athens to that of the "graduates" of Berkeley against the professors of Harvard: "As one would expect, people who had not attended schools in Athens tended to push back against this in much the same way that a Berkeley graduate pushes against the conceit of Harvard".

On Hypatia's ability as a teacher (τῷ διδασκαλικῷ) and her eloquence "fluent and dialectic" (ἐντρεχῆ καὶ διαλεκτικήν) our primary source is Suidas (DAMASCIUS, *Vita Isidori* fr. *102, *104, pp. 77,7 and 79,12 Zintzen = fr. 43E, p. 130, 1–3 Athanassiadi = SUIDAS Y 166, IV, p. 644, 18–19 and 30 Adler (HARICH-SCHWARZBAUER 2011, p. 247).

On Hypatia's "public appearances" (προόδους) and on the meaning of the term *tribon* (τρίβων), which in the fifth century was no longer associated with the Cynic street preacher, see below, chapter "Mortal Envy", and part III, chapter "Hypatia in All Her States of Being", with discussion in the Appendix *ad loc.*

2 The Destruction of the Serapeum

> Are not we Hellenes in truth already dead?
> Do we but seem alive in our hard times?
> Do we somehow imagine dreams are life?
> Or do we live though life itself is dead?
>
> PALLADAS[11]

Twenty years before Hypatia reached the height of her fame, and one century after the edict of 313 A.D. that granted Christians the right to practise their religion, the tolerance shown by the emperor Constantine had rapidly turned, under his successors, to wholesale intolerance. In 391, a constitution by Theodosius had in fact made Christianity the State religion and in 392, a special law against Pagan cults[12] had been enacted for Egypt, "the cradle of all the gods", according to the early philosophers. Making sacrifices to the gods was now equated to lese-majesty, and anyone who did so risked the death penalty. The policy of the Christian religious leaders of Alexandria, παντοτρόφος[13], "cradle of all thinking", the supreme Greek cultural centre of the Mediterranean Koiné and the epicentre of this ideological earthquake, aimed to annihilate ritual Paganism, the religion of the ancient temples.

> It all occurred as in the myths of the poets, when the Giants dominated the Earth: the religion of the temples of Alexandria and the sanctuary of Serapis itself were both dispersed on the winds, and not only the ceremonies, but the buildings themselves, under the reign of Theodosius[14]

writes the biographer of the last Neoplatonists, Eunapius.

At the time, Theophilus, the Christians' bishop, "reigned over these abominable beings like a sort of Eurymedon over the angry Gigantes," deplores Eunapius.

> And those beings, raging against our sacred places like masons on rugged stone [...], demolished the temple of Serapis [...] and made war on its treasures and its statues, shattering them like adversaries unable to defend themselves[15].

Until that time, a supernatural arcane atmosphere of suspended sacredness had reigned in the great halls and along the magnificent colonnades of the Serapeum. "The statues," wrote Ammianus Marcellinus, the last great historian of antiquity, "seemed to be alive." "There is nothing like it on Earth."[16]

---

11 *AP* X 82, transl. Harold Anthony Lloyd (slightly altered).
12 *Cod. Theod.* 16, 10, 10 and 16, 10, 11, pp. 899–900 Mommsen – Meyer.
13 WILCKEN 1905, p. 552.
14 EUNAPIUS VI 11, 3–5, pp. 38–39 Giangrande.
15 *Ibid.*
16 AMMIANUS MARCELLINUS, *Res gestae* XXII 16, 12.

The statue of Serapis, the enthroned god-demon, had been commissioned by Ptolomy I Soter from Bryaxis, according to some the renowned Greek sculptor, in the opinion of others, a namesake. It incarnated the power of the Hellenistic monarchs and, at the same time, the dominion over the secrets of Hades. Its body was, it seems, in a bluish metal alloy, and its mantle was studded with precious stones representing the celestial bodies, celebrating the astronomical-zodiacal knowledge of the Orient.

According to the Christian theologian Clement of Alexandria,

> Bryaxis, the artist, and not the Athenian, but a namesake, used a variety of metals in making the statue. The body was composed of gold shavings, silver, copper, iron, lead and also tin. And none of the Egyptian stones were lacking, fragments of sapphire, hematite, emerald and also topaz. After pounding the various elements to a powder and mixing them, he coloured them [blue] with cyan. For this reason, the statue is almost black.[17]

According to the ecclesiastical historian Theodoret of Cyrus it was

> [...] an enormous statue that induced fear merely by its size and also for the widespread belief that if anyone approached it, the Earth would quake causing immense damage.[18]

In the general terror, the bishop Theophilus, again according to Theodoret, ordered that the statue be decapitated with an axe:

> When the head of the statue was chopped off, mice fled in great numbers from within: in truth, the Egyptian divinity was an abode for mice[19].

After which the Christians

> [...] chopped the statue into small pieces, burned part of it and dragged the head through the city under the gaze of its venerators, deriding the weakness of that being which had been worshipped. Thus, everywhere, waging war on them on land and on sea, the temples of the idols were razed.[20]

The Serapeum of the hundred steps was a place of pilgrimage not only in the Roman and Greek world, but also in the Oriental realm. According to the descriptions of ancient travellers, which would end up in *The Meadows of Gold and Mines of Gems* by the great Arab encyclopaedist of the 10th century Al Mas'udi, that "gigantic palace, without equal on this Earth" was "five hundred cubits long and two hundred and fifty cubits wide" and inside there were "at least one hundred monolithic columns."

The destruction of this magnificent symbol of Paganism, perpetrated by the bishop Theophilus promptly, in compliance with the Theodosian decrees, which he probably encouraged, was exacerbated by the pillage. Eunapius accuses once more:

---

17 CLEMENS ALEXANDRINUS, *Protrept.* 4, 48.
18 THEODORETUS CYRENSIS 5, 22.
19 *Ibid.*
20 *Ibid.*

[...] of the Serapeum, they left only the floors and this simply because the stones were too heavy[21].

"The perpetual enemy of peace and virtue; a bold, bad man, whose hands were alternately polluted with gold and with blood,"[22] was how Edward Gibbon described Theophilus. According to Socrates Scholasticus, he "did everything he could to offend the mysteries of the Hellenes"[23] and he exposed to the public gaze the precious objects of cult that he had ordered to be plundered, so that their sumptuous beauty and their mysterious power of enchantment should be debased and derided by the crowd of passers-by.

It was an act of intolerance and mortification of cultural life that would remain imprinted in the historical memory of the West like few others, such as the burning of the Ptolemaic library and the closure of the schools of Athens. Erudites of the past have in vain attempted to exculpate Theophilus, attributing to him only the burning of the temple and its furnishings, and postponing the destruction of the Serapeum library to a later date, during the Arab invasion. This narrative famously proved to be wrong, as articulated by, among others, a man of letters such as Gérard de Nerval as early as the mid 19th century, and beautifully expressed in the words of Angélique, the heroine of *Les filles du feu:*

> La bibliothèque d'Alexandrie et le Serapéon, ou maison de secours, qui en faisait partie, avaient été brûlés et détruits au quatrième siècle par les chrétiens.

> The library of Alexandria and the Serapeum, or house of recovery, which was part of it, were burnt down and destroyed in the 4th century by the Christians.

Nerval denounces, in the wake of Gibbon:

> Ce sont là, sans doute, des excès qu'on ne peut reprocher à la religion, mais il est bon de laver du reproche d'ignorance ces malheureux Arabes dont les traductions nous ont conservé les merveilles de la philosophie, de la médecine et des sciences grecques, en y ajoutant leurs propres travaux, qui sans cesse perçaient de vifs rayons la brume obstinée des époques féodales.[24]

> These were undoubtedly excesses that would be unfair to attribute to the religion itself, but it is wise to exonerate from the accusation of ignorance those poor Arabs whose translations have brought to us the wonders of Greek philosophy, medicine and sciences, and whose own works penetrated with their intense rays the persistent gloom of the feudal era.

---

21 EUNAPIUS VI 11, 3–5, pp. 38–39 Giangrande.
22 GIBBON, II, p. 82 (first ed. III, 1781, chapt. XXVIII).
23 SOCRATES V 16, 2, p. 289, 24–26 Hansen.
24 NERVAL, p. 9.

Appendix
The Destruction of the Serapeum

Palladas' epigram *in exergo* can be read in *AP* X 82 (*Anthologia Palatina*, vol. IX, p. 30 Irigoin – Maltomini – Laurens): Ἆρα μὴ θανόντες τῷ δοκεῖν ζῶμεν μόνον,/ Ἕλληνες ἄνδρες, συμφορᾷ πεπτωκότες / ὄνειρον εἰκάζοντες εἶναι τὸν βίον; / ἢ ζῶμεν ἡμεῖς, τοῦ βίου τεθνηκότος;

The constitutions of Theodosius against the Pagan cults of February and June 391 and November 392, that is the so-called "Theodosian decrees", can be read in the *Codex Theodosianus*, 16, 10, 10 (24 February 391), pp. 899–900 Mommsen – Meyer: IDEM AAA. AD ALBINVM P(RAEFECTVM) P(RAETORI)O, and 16, 10, 11 (16 June 391), p. 900 Mommsen – Meyer: IDEM AAA. EVAGRIO P(RAE)F(EC)TO AVGVSTALI ET ROMANO COM(ITI) AEG(YPTI).

That it was Theophilus who personally pushed for the Theodosian decrees is reported by Socrates' *Ecclesiastical History* V 16, 1, in the account of the destruction of the Serapeum (p. 289, 21–24 Hansen).

In general on the anti-Pagan policies of Theodosius see the classic work by BLOCH, pp. 195–210.

For an evaluation of Theodosian legislation and a juridical clarification of the concept of intolerance see GAUDEMET; BUCCI.

For the definition of Alexandria as *pantotrophos* (παντοτρόφος) see WILCKEN 1905, p. 552.

Eunapius' account of the destruction of the Serapeum is to be found in *Life of Eustathius* VI 11, 3–5, pp. 38–39 Giangrande. In my rendering I accept the *constitutio textus* given by Giangrande who, with Lündstrom, supplies an alternative reading for the lacuna at line 22 and further amends the text in various points; but I diverge from the literal translation supplied by M. Civiletti (EUNAPIUS, p. 137 Civiletti).

On the destruction of the Serapeum see also the version of SOZOMENUS 7, 15, pp. 319–322 Hansen; RUFINUS, *Historia Ecclesiastica* XI 23–29 (pp. 1028, 9–1029, 1; see also pp. 1034, 29–1035, 3 Schwartz – Mommsen – Winkelmann); SOCRATES SCHOLASTICUS V 16, pp. 289, 21–290, 29 Hansen, and V 17, pp. 290, 30–291, 29 Hansen.

Even though the versions of EUNAPIUS (*Vitae Sophistarum* VI 11, 3–5, pp. 38–39 Giangrande) and RUFINUS (*Historia Ecclesiastica* XI, 23–29) state that both the temple and the surrounding buildings were completely destroyed, according to other sources such as EVAGRIUS SCHOLASTICUS, *Historia Ecclesiastica* II 5, and the *Life of Peter the Iberian* 72 (as reported by WATTS 2017, p. 172, n. 56; for the edition of the *Life* see also Joannes Rufus in RUFUS Horn – Phenix), the site might have been still partly used in the mid-fifth century.

The militant activity of the Pagan intellectuals, including Olympus, Claudianus and Palladas himself, who barricaded themselves inside the Serapeum and joined those who strenuously defended it against both the government troops and Theophilus' men, is told in the ancient sources and has been widely studied by modern historians, including CHUVIN; CAMERON – LONG; HAAS 1997.

WATTS 2017, p. 61, shows an exceptional indulgence towards the Christian leadership, and attributes *tout court* the destruction of the Serapeum, described with precision by Christian historians and mourned with horror and scandal by the Pagan Eunapius, not to the intolerance of the new wave of Alexandrian ecclesiastical politics ushered in by Theophilus, but to the cultic resistance of the radical faction of the Platonists with Iamblichaean leanings, embodied, according to him, by Olympus and Antoninus (but the latter, we must underscore, abstained from theurgical practices, ἐπεδείκνυτο [...] οὐδὲν θεουργόν, according to EUNAPIUS VI 10, 7, p. 37, 16–17 Giangrande: "The fervor and enthusiasm of the Iamblichans had done real, serious, and irreversible damage to the religious infrastructure of Alexandria"). Such attribution is bewildering and impossible to endorse, considering that the militia of Theophilus comprised the violent and intolerant extremist groups of Egyptian "monasticism", the same groups that will be used later by Cyril.

DZIELSKA 1995, p. 88 speaks curiously of a "harmonious cooperation between civil and military authorities" in putting down the defence of the Serapeum; she, nonetheless rightly, on p. 83, feels that it is possible to exclude that Hypatia and her pupils took part in the resistance. She is followed by CHUVIN – TARDIEU, p. 66.

AMMIANUS MARCELLINUS' description of the Serapeum can be read in *Res gestae* XXII 16: "It is so adorned with atriums with magnificent colonnades, of statues that seem to be alive and works of art of every kind, that there is nothing on Earth more sumptuous except for the Capitol."

Other descriptions of the Serapeum are to be found in EUNAPIUS VI 10, 8, p. 37 Giangrande and in RUFINUS XI 23, pp. 1026, 28–1028, 8 Schwartz – Mommsen – Winkelmann.

On the archaeological evidence see MCKENZIE, pp. 198–203; MCKENZIE – GIBSON – REYES.

The first description of the statue of Serapis, which we quote in the text, is taken from the *Protrepticus* of Clement of Alexandria, 4, 48 (CLEMENS ALEXANDRINUS Butterworth); the second one is in the *Church History* by Theodoret of Cyrus, 5, 22 (THEODORETUS CYRENSIS, p. 321 Parmentier – Scheidweiler).

Neither of the two descriptions is to be taken literally. In particular, scholars warn against the reliability of that of Clement of Alexandria. The *status quaestionis* is summarised in VOLLKOMMER, p. 124, who like the majority of scholars considers the twofold identification of Bryaxis introduced by Clement to be false: the sculptor was most probably the renowned Athenian himself.

The passage by Theodoret on the destruction of the statue is taken from his *Church History:* THEODORETUS CYRENSIS, 5, 22, p. 321 Parmentier – Scheidweiler. Note the affinity between the punishment inflicted on the statue of Serapis and that which Hypatia would suffer: see below, part III, "Hypatia's Sacrifice" and Appendix *ad loc.*, where we also cite the interesting interpretation (or over-interpretation) of this part in the sources, recently provided by HAASE.

For the description of the Serapeum found in al-Mas'udi (9th-10th century), quoted by the later Egyptian historian al-Maqrizi (14th-15th cent.) see BUTLER, p. 387. Al-Mas'udi can be read in the French translation of the 19th-century bilingual edition by C. BARBIER DE MEYNARD and A. PAVET DE COURTEILLE (*non vidi*); the reference edition, in Arabic only, is the one revised and corrected by C. Pellat: AL-MAS'UDI, vol. IV (1973) Pellat.

On Theophilus's personality, thought, and career see the indulgent yet well documented volume by RUSSELL 2007, pp. 3–41, containing an updated bibliography; see also DAVIS 2004, pp. 63–70; HAAS 1997, pp. 159–168. On Theophilus's role in the destruction of Pagan temples see HAHN 2004, pp. 81–105.

The portrait of Theophilus drawn by Gibbon in his *Decline and Fall* is to be found in the first edition's third volume (1781), chapt. XXVIII: see GIBBON, II, p. 82; Gibbon's negative judgment is anticipated by a Christian source, precisely from the monastic environment, namely Palladius, who speaks reprovingly and disdainfully of him in *The Dialogue concerning the Life of St. John Chrysostom* (PALLADIUS Malingrey – Leclerq).

On the statement of SOCRATES SCHOLASTICUS V 16, 2, p. 289, 24–26 Hansen, according to which Theophilus "did everything he could to offend the mysteries of the Hellenists", see HAHN 2004, pp. 91–92.

The comparison between the destruction of the Serapeum, the burning of the Ptolemaic library and the closure of the schools in Athens is in BLOCH, pp. 205–206.

With regard to the scholars who absolve Theophilus of the burning of the Serapeum library and ascribe it to the Arab invasion, an early discussion is found in PARSONS, pp. 356–370. The definitive word on the topic is pronounced by CANFORA 1986, pp. 92–108 and above all 117–121 (on page 108 of his book there is a brief, memorable account of the death of Hypatia in the words of John Philoponus). A revisionist position has been taken by TAKÁCS 1995, p. 54, who once again doubts that the books of the Serapeum library were burnt during the attack by Theophilus.

For a historical framework of the destruction of the Serapeum and the associated events see CHUVIN, pp. 70–74; HAHN 2004, pp. 82–84; HAHN 2008; RUSSELL 2007, pp. 7–11. See also FOWDEN 1978, pp. 69–70. Of the Pagan temples only that of Dionysus, which Theophilus had received as a gift from the emperor, was spared because it was transformed into a church in a similar way to the temple of Augustus or Caesareum years before, which became the most important building for the Christian cult in the city; it was here that Hypatia was assassinated: see below chapter "Mortal Envy" and Appendix *ad loc.*

Considerations on the destruction of the Serapeum library by the Christians and not the Arabs are put forward by NERVAL, p. 9, where we also find mention of Hypatia as the "Pythagorean philosopher": the Christians who destroyed the Serapeum are those "qui, en outre, massacrèrent dans les rues la célèbre Hypatie, philosophe pythagoricienne". The influence of Gibbon's standpoint is evident; however, perhaps Nerval's heroine, and Gibbon himself, were confusing the library of the Serapeum with the royal library: see GIBBON, II, pp. 83–85 (first ed. III, 1781, chapt. XXVIII).

3 Elegant Insolence

Hypatia was as seductive and beautiful as she was little inclined to frivolity, and had an ascetic nature. Austerity of life belonged to the principles of Platonic philosophy. In general, she sternly rejected anyone who believed they could court her; in particular her students, who dangerously confused the platonic love of the pupil for the master with amorous desire. Hypatia tried to explain to them that intellectual eros and physical passion were separate and distinct.

According to the words of Damascius, reported by Suidas, Hypatia once suggested treating with music a student who was incapable of taming his amorous desire, which the Platonists considered a disease. Once it was clear that the therapy would not serve to placate the young man's ardour, she showed him with a theatrical gesture that we are all victims of the instinct to reproduce the species and that physical desire is linked to the fluxes of the body, while the true eros must sublimate and transcend it, becoming a love of knowledge.

> In addition to the art of teaching, she had reached such a level of moral awareness, and she was so poised and austere, that she remained chaste, and at the same time, she was so extraordinarily seductive and beautiful (σφόδρα καλή τε οὖσα καὶ εὐειδής) that one of her pupils fell in love with her. The young man was not capable of keeping his love to himself, but had begun to manifest also to her the signs of passion. The less informed say that she freed him of this disease with music. But the original truth is that the musical therapy failed and so she took to lessons one of those cloths that women use for menstrual blood and showed it to him, as a symbol of the impurity of procreation: "Ultimately, my boy, it is with this that you have fallen in love," she said to him, "nothing sublime."[25]

We do not know if this episode, narrated in the *Life of Isidore* by Damascius and taken up by Suidas, is true or legendary, or somewhere in between, perhaps an exaggeration of the truth, using anecdote to portray the eccentricities of the philosophers following the tradition of paradoxography, which Damascius is not unfamiliar with. However, we know for certain, because all the sources agree in witnessing it, that Hypatia was as sober in life and sentiments as she was direct, almost brutal, in her actions and her speech.

The style of her discourse was so frank as to be, according to some, elegantly insolent. She was often the only woman at meetings generally reserved for men, but the masculine company did not embarrass her, nor did it make her less dispassionate and lucid in her dialectic.

---

[25] DAMASCIUS, *Vita Isidori* fr. *102, p. 77, 7–17 Zintzen = frr. 43A-C, p. 128, 7–20 Athanassiadi = SUIDAS Y 166, IV, p. 644, 18–28 Adler (HARICH-SCHWARZBAUER 2011, p. 247).

> From the Hellenic education (*paideia*) she derived her self-control and frankness in speaking (*parrhesia*, παρρησία) which allowed her to meet face to face, with the same imperturbability, also the powerful,[26]

writes Socrates Scholasticus.

"Let the women keep silent in the assembly",[27] we read in Saint Paul's first letter to the Corinthians. However, she, writes the Christian Socrates admiringly,

> [...] was not afraid to appear at the meetings of the men: given her extraordinary wisdom, the men were all deferent and looked at her, if anything, with amazement and reverential awe.[28]

As Diderot summarises and concludes,

> [...] the Christians and the Pagans who have transmitted to us her story and her misadventures agree on her beauty, culture and virtue; and in their praises, despite the divergence of their beliefs, there is so much unanimity that it would be impossible to imagine, when comparing their accounts, which religion Hypatia followed, if we did not know from other sources that she was a Pagan.[29]

---

26 SOCRATES VII 15, 2, p. 360, 24–26 Hansen (HARICH-SCHWARZBAUER 2011, p. 188).
27 1 *Cor.* 14, 34–36.
28 SOCRATES VII 15, 2, p. 360, 26–28 Hansen (HARICH-SCHWARZBAUER 2011, p. 188).
29 DIDEROT.

Appendix
Elegant Insolence

Damascius insists on the chastity of Hypatia, and after emphasising her asceticism (*sophrosyne*, σωφροσύνη) declares explicitly (and perhaps exaggeratedly, but DZIELSKA 1995, p. 53, takes him literally) that she "remained a virgin" (διετέλει παρθένος): DAMASCIUS, *Vita Isidori* fr. *102, p. 77, 9 Zintzen = fr. 43A, p. 128, 7–11 Athanassiadi = SUIDAS Y 166, IV, p. 644, 18–20 Adler (HARICH-SCHWARZBAUER 2011, p. 247); see also below, part III, chapter "Hypatia's Sacrifice". Clearly misrepresenting his source, Suidas/Hesychius on the other hand considers her to be married, and precisely to Isidore, calling her the "wife of the philosopher Isidore" at the start of the article: SUIDAS Y 166, IV, p. 644, 2–3 Adler (HARICH-SCHWARZBAUER 2011, p. 324); the error would germinate in the poem by DIODATA SALUZZO ROERO, see below, part II, chapter "Uncontrolled Effects on the Poets".

Watts too (WATTS 2017, pp. 74–78) accepts the idea of Hypatia's virginity suggested by Damascius ("Hypatia's philosophical ideal of divine love [...] helps to explain her decision to remain virgin" [p. 75]) by associating "her embrace of a celibate life" with the "ascetism embraced by increasing numbers of elite Christian women in the later fourth and early fifth centuries" (*ibid.*) and, on the basis of the biographical parallelisms, found also in Damascius, of the contemporary Proclus and Marinus, concludes that "Hypatia's decision to refrain from sexual intercourse illustrated a key part of the philosophical system that she taught" (p. 76). Nonetheless it must be underscored that SOCRATES SCHOLASTICUS VII 15, 2, p. 360, 26 Hansen (HARICH–SCHWARZBAUER 2011, pp. 268–270: p. 188 and 201–202 commentary) speaks exclusively, and more generically, of σωφροσύνη.

Hypatia's provocation can be compared to the *aischrourgia* (αἰσχρουργία) of the Cynic philosopher Hipparchia (see below, part III, chapter "Hypatia in All Her States of Being"), rather than to the preceding account – mentioned by numerous scholars, but not pertinent – concerning Sosipatra, the Neoplatonic philosopher who, upon becoming Eustathius' widow, is described by Eunapius (*Vitae Sophistarum* VI 9, 3–8) as rejecting the courtship of her cousin Philometor, but with totally different methods. The most recent feminist reading of Hypatia's aischrourgia is by LEONARD, pp. 171–192; see also below, chapt. "Hypatia in All her States of Being", Appendix *ad loc.* See also GEFFCKEN, p. 199, where, in illustrating the Neoplatonists' detachment from the body and corporeality, the classic example of Hypatia is compared not only to that of Sosipatra, but also to that of Heraiscus, who suffered from terrible headaches every time he approached a menstruating woman. Other parallels are to be found in ASMUS 1907, pp. 15–16; and more recently in CAMERON – LONG, p. 61, where a Christian girl is cited (a case taken from Isidore of Pelusium, *Ep.* 2, 53), who discouraged her suitor by shaving her head, painting her face with a paste of ashes and water and asking him, "is this the ugliness with which you are in love?" The book also suggests, very conjecturally (p. 51), a succession from Sosipatra to Hypatia, in which the latter had her alleged theurgical initiation from Antoninus himself, the son of the former, who was in turn initiated by his mother.

On the initiation of Sosipatra, on her abilities as a medium, and her magical *exploits* as described by Eunapius see PACK; JOHNSTON. On the life and personality of Antoninus as described by Eunapius, his gifts as a clairvoyant, and in particular his prophecy about the fate of the Serapeum, see CHUVIN, chapters 5 and 6; WATTS 2006a, pp. 188–190; on the still debatable *diadoche* (διαδοχή) Sosipatra – Hypatia, see also below, part III, chapter "Women Who Philosophised" and Appendix *ad loc.*

On the other hand, WATTS 2017, pp. 97–100 dwells on the necessary distinctions between the teaching of Hypatia and that of Sosipatra, underscoring rather too emphatically the differences between the two philosophers. Yet it is precisely such traits, which according to Watts distinguish Sosipatra from Hypatia, that can help us fully understand the nature of the teaching of the latter. We are not just referring to the "priestly" elements which, as we shall see (below, part III, chapters "All Synesius' Mysteries", "Synesius, Hypatia, and *Philosophia*", "Women who Philosophised", "The Power of Hypatia" and Appendices *ad loc.*) are in no way alien to the personality of Hypatia (at least as it is depicted in Synesius' epistles), nor the elements that we may consider *topoi*, such as the "ability to resist the charms of male suitors", which as we have seen is celebrated by the sources, but to the fact that Sosipatra "did not teach publicly and her teaching was not open to every student", but "'philosophised in her own home' and opened the space only to those who were members of the inner circle" (p. 98). We shall see how this habit, according to Damascius' account, has a clear and significant parallel in Hypatia: see below, part III, chapter "The Power of Hypatia". As we shall see below, chapters "Hypatia in All her States of Being" and "The Power of Hypatia", Appendices *ad loc.*, we cannot agree with GERTZ, who argues that Hypatia only taught privately.

A comparable episode, although less brutal, but with an ending perfectly analogous to that which we read in Damascius ("shaming" and "spiritual transformation" of the suitor) can be found in a work from the 6th century, which however collects anecdotes already circulating in the Syrian, Palestinian and Egyptian environments for about two centuries: John Moschus' *Spiritual Meadow*, chapter 205 (MOSCHUS, coll. 3096–3097): "'Tell me the truth... have you ever known a woman?' 'No,' answered the monk, 'and that is why I want to try this experience.' 'So, this is why you are so upset! You do not know how nauseating the smell of women is, poor things...' Intending to dampen the monk's passions, she continued to speak with disdain of her own body. 'I am menstruating, and no one can approach me or smell my odour, which is unbearable!' Hearing these words and other similar speech, the monk repented, regained his senses and began to weep", as reported by LACOMBRADE 1951, p. 45, n. 42.

Although accepting as *recta lectio* that given by LIVREA 1995, we diverge from his translation and prefer to translate ἐπ'αὐτοῦ βαλέσθαι as "she presented it to him" rather than, as in Livrea, "she threw it at him".

If we were to accept the testimony of Damascius as entirely historical, the final phrase would restore the only textual words of Hypatia known to us; along with those maliciously quoted from Plato's *Republic*, in which she calls Synesius ἀλλότριον ἀγαθόν, "good" or "salvation of others", alluding to his continual maneuvering for favours for his friends, as exemplified in *Epistle* 81, see below, chapter "Good Use of Power".

As far as the translation is concerned, although substantially agreeing with the version of DZIELSKA 1995, p. 50 ("This is what you really love, my young man, but you do not love beauty for its own sake") and in general her "profoundly Platonic" interpretation of the episode, with direct reference to the philosophical reasons for the celebrated refusal of Alcibiades by Socrates ("Discover in me the invisible beauty," *ibid.*, pp. 51–52 and n. 62) and the perception of eros in Plotinus ("Whenever we see beauty in bodies, we do not need to chase them, but to be aware that they are images, traces, shadows, and move towards that of which they are images" etc., *ibid.*, p. 51 and n. 63), we prefer a more neutral and less interpretative version. See also WATTS 2017, p. 73; Henriette Harich's doctoral thesis, *Hypatia* (Graz), later reworked as HARICH–SCHWARZBAUER 2011, pp. 268–270.

For a discussion of the actual historicity of the so-called *aischrourgia* (αἰσχρουργία) of Hypatia and, in any case, of its unquestionable Cynic connotation, see below, part III, chapter "Hypatia in All Her States of Being" and Appendix *ad loc.*

The quotation from SOCRATES SCHOLASTICUS on Hypatia's *parrhesia* (παρρησία), deriving from her "Hellenic education" is at VII 15, 2, p. 360, 24–26 Hansen (HARICH–SCHWARZBAUER 2011, p. 188).

The phrase from Saint Paul is to be found in *1 Cor.* 14, 34–36; obviously the "assembly" (*ekklesia*, ἐκκλησία) in question is, for Paul, that of the faithful.

4 The Terrible Patriarch of Alexandria

The entire Church of Egypt had taken part in the anti-Pagan mobilisation of the late 4th and early 5th centuries. A climate of civil and religious insurgence accompanied the transition and the transformation of the powers of the megalopolis of Alexandria. The wealth of its Church was such that absolute power was bestowed upon the *papas* (πάπας), the bishop, placing him de facto above the *praefectus augustalis*, the Roman provincial governor (Patlagean). The religious head of Alexandria had immense resources at his disposal, not only economic but also human. In the sense that he knew how to rouse the masses.

To support the actions of Theophilus, monks had swarmed down from the mountains of Wadi el-Natrun, the desert of Nitria, or at least those who went by this name: the extremist and intolerant fringes of Egyptian Christianity.

> They allowed them to enter the sacred places and they called them monks.

writes Eunapius,

> [...] but they were not even men, except in appearance, because their way of life was swinish and they openly carried out and encouraged innumerable and unmentionable crimes[30].

The evolution of monasticism into a mass phenomenon amplified every political act and acted as a sound box throughout the history of the 5th century. At the time of Anthony of Thebaid, the Fathers of the Desert had preached the rejection of society, abstinence from the social rites of food, flight from the world and from nature itself (*anachoresis*, ἀναχώρησις). They practised asceticism and celebrated the inner desert (*eremos*, ἔρημος) by settling in a geographical one. A great spiritual movement, early Egyptian eremitism was still a localised phenomenon, to some extent an elite one, but in any case that of a minority.

Its subversive potential, however, already primed but unexpressed in the 4th century, gave rise to the movements of seditious asceticism that in the 5th century embodied its deviation from the original purposes of eremitism. The militia of monks who had destroyed the Serapeum returned to terrorise the city under the episcopacy of Theophilus' nephew and future saint Cyril, "on whom nature had impressed the same mark of fanaticism."[31]

Zealots, "beings of incandescent spirit" as the Christian Socrates Scholasticus[32] describes them, the often illiterate monks recruited by the bishop, were gangs of violent men, who travelled from city to city, filled with social hatred not only against the Pa-

---

30 EUNAPIUS VI 11, 3–5, pp. 38–39 Giangrande.
31 SOCRATES VII 14, 1, p. 359, 23–24 Hansen (see HARICH-SCHWARZBAUER 2011, p. 188).
32 ID., VII 15, 5, pp. 361, 1–2 Hansen (see HARICH-SCHWARZBAUER 2011, p. 188).

gans, but also against the civilised world as a whole and against the inhabitants of the metropoles.

At the end of 412, almost exactly one hundred years after the proclamation of Constantine's Edict, Cyril succeeded Theophilus to the see of the greatest Christian metropolis in the East. His episcopacy totally contradicted the abstract principle of tolerance that that Edict proposed, as well as the conciliatory tendency of Christianity towards elite Paganism, which Constantine had politically supported and juridically sanctioned.

The bishop nephew intended to complete the violent religious colonisation begun by his bishop uncle with a zeal and an "incandescence of spirit" that appeared excessive even to his co-religionists. For example, in 414, ignoring the wishes of the majority of the population, the new *papas* substituted the healing oracle of Isis at Menouthis, near modern-day Abukir, with the Christian cult of the thaumaturgical saints Cyrus and John, martyrs under Diocletian. Although a late source regarding the event, Sophronius of Jerusalem informs us that the goddess immediately lost her powers, which passed to the Christian saints, causing both the Pagan priests and the stubborn inhabitants of the village to convert to the new religion. Nonetheless, as a punishment for their earlier idolatry, all the inhabitants of the village sank, together with the oracle of Isis and the village itself, into the sands of the desert.[33]

In other cases, certainly not all the sources, not even the Christian ones, endorse Cyril's actions with such adulation. However, history is written by the victorious. Cyril would win his historical contest for reasons other than the brutal methods of his campaign for power and the fundamentalist excesses of his personality. In that heated period of the history of the Church, marked by disputes on the human and/or divine nature of Christ, he supported the papacy of Rome against the Nestorian heresy, elaborating a doctrine on the incarnation that would feed another heresy, Monophysitism, which asserted only the divine nature of Christ.

In whatever way we interpret the intricate ethnic-religious events of Christian Egypt, Cyril's Miaphysitism would certainly offer an unquestionable doctrinal basis for the Egyptian province's claims of independence from the central government of Constantinople. Even though enfranchisement from the Byzantine dogmatic yoke would not be the only and most immediate motivation, it is a fact that in 641, two centuries after the victory of Cyril and of Pope Celestine I against Nestorius at the Council of Ephesus in 431 and the subsequent condemnation of Monophysitism at the Council of Chalcedon in 451, Alexandria opened its doors to the Arab "liberators". The alignment between Cyril and the Roman Church would continue through the centuries, culminating in the 19th century, when the title Doctor of the Church was conferred on him by the Curia for his doctrine of the Incarnation: *Doctor Incarnationis*.

In the meantime, for ten centuries, Christian Egypt, wrested from the political domination of the Byzantine empire, and the Coptic Church, of which Cyrillian heterodoxy would always be a banner, would continue to lend support to the West in the

---

33 Sophronius Hierosolimitanus 3, coll. 3409–3413 and 3416.

political-ecclesiastical battle between Rome and Constantinople and, together, to wage war against other doctrinal break-away groups, such as that of Nestorius, which settled in the Islamised territories and set up their Churches, again in conflict with the central Constantinopolitan Church. A strategic role that would make Cyril of particular interest even to the latter.

The Miaphysite Cyril would be made a saint. His spectre, that of the untouchable heresiarch, would live on implacably in Byzantine iconography, with the dark beard as pointed as the headdress woven with crosses, prerogative of the patriarch of Alexandria.

Appendix
The Terrible Patriarch of Alexandria

The title alludes to the definition of Cyril ("terrible archevêque") provided, many centuries later, by the great Catholic historian Louis Duchesne: DUCHESNE, vol. III, p. 301, n. 1; cf. below, part II, chapter "Refreshing Exceptions" and Appendix *ad loc.*

The considerations on the wealth of the Alexandrian Church, on the absolute power of its *papas* (πάπας) and on its superiority with respect to the *augustalis* himself are taken from PATLAGEAN, p. 979. See also E. WIPSZYCKA 2015, pp. 43–58; 237–269.

As noted above (chapter "The Destruction of the Serapaeum"), WATTS 2017, pp. 56–61, has an oddly irenic view of the relationship between the Egyptian Church and the Alexandrian elites between the end of the 4th and the beginning of the 5th century, and minimises the social impact of the pursuit of political hegemony and of the violent methods of ecclesiastical government ushered in by Theophilus. Watts goes as far as to suggest that the moderate wing of Platonism, led by Hypatia, had a good relationship with Theophilus (p. 8), and brings as evidence the fact that Theophilus officiated at Synesius' wedding (SYNESIUS, *Ep.* 105, 69–70, p. 238 Roques). Yet this is hardly sufficient to prove, after the destruction of the Serapaeum, the kind of "peaceful coexistence and cooperation" between "the bishop, the civic elites, and philosophers", which Watts assumes (p. 107; see also p. 153: "Synesius' close ties to Theophilus suggest that Hypatia may also have at least a working relationship with the bishop"; and p. 113: "She and her students had worked productively with Theophilus in the past"). Moreover, the assumption that Hypatia's circle may have benefited from the "elimination of her Alexandrian Iamblichan competitors" produced by the destruction of the Serapaeum, which would have allowed Hypatia "to draw some of the former students of Olympus into her classes" (p. 61), appears even wilder. At the same time, as Watts himself recognises, "she was unlikely to keep these radicalised Pagan students even if they enrolled initially", considering that "she did not share the Iamblichan idea [...] and she did not teach the rituals". The consequence of all of this, in Watts' reconstruction, is that her teaching, starting from the first half of the nineties of the fourth century, would appear as "a welcome antidote to the violence and division that had gripped Alexandria in the early 390s" (p. 62). Such reconstruction is proven wrong by the prompt escalation of violence, perpetrated by that extremist wing of Egyptian monasticism put together for the first time by Theophilus, during the episcopate of Cyril; see below, chapters "A Three-handed Game" and "The Intimidation of Orestes".

An idea of the extent of the human resources that the *papas* of Alexandria could mobilise, by bringing to the city the monks who lived in the hermitages and monasteries of the Nitrian desert (Wadi el-Natrun), is to be found in the testimony of Palladas, according to whom "five thousand hermits lived in that desert", reported by TAKÁCS 1995, p. 54; see also p. 58, in which we note that the militant monks assembled first by Theophilus and later by Cyril also came from the area of the monastery of Ennaton (Dair al-Hanatun) and the region of Lake Mariout.

In general, on the economic, social, political and religious framework of the Egyptian megalopolis see FRASER, pp. 43–51; HAAS 1997; see also HAAS 2002, pp. 51–52; and in particular, in relation to the story of Hypatia, TAKÁCS 1995, pp. 47–62, where the evocative passage on the immensity of the megalopolis and its human population, which we find in *The Adventures of Leucippe and Clitophon* by Achilles Tatius, is quoted and translated (pp. 48–49).

The quotations from Eunapius's *Life of Eustathius* are taken from EUNAPIUS VI 11, 3–5, pp. 38–39 Giangrande.

The considerations on the role of monasticism, which became a mass movement during the 5th century, are to be found in PATLAGEAN, pp. 979–980; see also TAKÁCS 1995, pp. 58 and 61–62; LOUTH; HEDSTROM – DARLENE.

On early Egyptian eremitism see ATHANASIUS, *Life of Anthony* chapt. 4, 5, 14, 23, 27, 30, 40, 44, 47 (on abstinence); 3, 12, 14, 26, 41, 44, 45, 47, 54 (on *anachoresis*); 3–5, 7–8, 14–16, 18–19, 22, 24–25, 27, 30, 34–37, 40, 44, 46–47, 51, 55, 61, 66, 82, 84, 88 (for asceticism); see also BALDI, pp. 13–16, 19–24, 40 n. 14, 41 nn.18–19, 43 n. 25, 47 n. 32, 49 n. 36, 56 n. 53, 57 n. 57, 71 n. 74, 83–85 and notes.

Amongst the heretical movements born in the ascetic-monastic environment of the second half of the fourth century, which reached their peak in the 5th century, the best known is Messalianism: see ESCOLAN, pp. 91 ff.

The definition of the *parabalaneis* (παραβαλανεῖς) as "creatures of incandescent spirit" is in SOCRATES VII 14, 1, p. 359, 23–24; 15, 5, p. 361, 1–2 Hansen. On them, see below, chapter "A Three-Handed Game" and Appendix *ad loc.*

On Cyril of Alexandria, his biography, his theology, his ecclesiastical action, and for an English translation of some of his writings useful to understand all of the above, see MCGUCKIN.

The account of the substitution, by Cyril, of the healing oracle of Isis at Menouthis, near modern-day Abukir, with the Christian cult of the thaumaturgical saints Cyrus and John, and the subsequent sinking of the village and its oracle into the sands of the desert, can be found in the *Laudes in SS. Cyrum et Ioannem* (SOPHRONIUS HIEROSOLIMITANUS 3, coll. 3409–3413 and 3416); even more detailed is the information in their *Vita*, damaged at the beginning: *Alia vita acephala Sanctorum Martyrum Cyri et Ioannis* (SOPHRONIUS HIEROSOLIMITANUS 2, coll. 3693–3696); see also *Vita Cyri et Ioannis* (SOPHRONIUS HIEROSOLIMITANUS 1). Cyril's initiative, studied by ROUGÉ 1990, and by MCGUCKIN, pp. 16–18, has been analysed in all its political and political-religious implications by TAKÁCS 1994; the subtle meaning of Cyril's gesture can be understood also in the light of the information in TAKÁCS 1995, pp. 50–53; finally see TAKÁCS 1992.

On the turbulent beginnings of Cyril's episcopate see SOCRATES VII 7, pp. 352–353, 21–8 Hansen; cf. WESSEL, pp. 102–103.

WATTS 2017, pp. 108–120, seems to underestimate the political strategy and power of Cyril, while also not grasping that the most moderate wing of Alexandrian Christians had never been (and would not be after the killing of Hypatia) on his side. As we shall see below (chapter "The Intimidation of Orestes"), Socrates Scholasticus (VII 14, 10–11, p. 360, 12–15 Hansen) underscores that Cyril was opposed by the "moderate wing" (οἱ σωφρονοῦντες) of the ecclesiastical "nation" (λαός) which, while being probably as numerous as the mass (πλῆθος) of Cyril's integralists, was in all likelihood more influential than them.

That, at the beginning of his episcopacy, Cyril was not as popular as later Church sources would have us believe, is also shown by the opposition encountered in the ecclesiastical world itself and partly also in the Egyptian monastic world; it is rightly emphasised, among others, by FREND, p. 16 ("He was utterly unscrupulous, overbearing, turbulent and greedy for power, ready to use the mob and the monks to do his bidding against his opponents") and by DZIELSKA 1995, p. 84 ("Church historians today express great respect for Cyril as theologian and dogmatist, but his contemporaries perceived him differently. The sources describe him as an impetuous, power-hungry man more relentless in pursuit of authority than his predecessor and uncle").

For an outline of the battle against the Origenist wing of Egyptian Christianity, undertaken by Theophilus, and the conflict with John Chrysostom, inaugurated by the patriarch uncle, see TAKÁCS 1995, pp. 54–56.

From the 5th century onwards, the anti-Chalcedonian Coptic Church would maintain the doctrine of Cyril, a doctrine close to Monophysiticism, but technically not Monophysite, referred to, according to a subtle distinction, as "miaphysite" (or Henophysite), as we have seen. In contrast with the formula of the Council of Chalcedon in 451, "two natures in one person", the Coptic Church professes the single nature of the incarnate Word, according to the Cyrillian doctrine of the incarnation: since to every nature there corresponds a person, in order for the Trinity not to become a Tetrade it is not possible to attribute to Christ more than a single nature.

During the schism orchestrated between 484 and 519 by Acacius, patriarch of Constantinople, the consolidation of Monophysitism in Egypt led the emperor Zeno to draw up the *Henotikon*, an attempt at compromise destined to fail. The Arab conquest definitively sanctioned the separation of the Coptic Church from Chalcedonian orthodoxy and from Constantinopolitan obedience; although with various vicissitudes, the Coptic Church prospered in the generally tolerant situation under Islam, whose legislation allowed the so-called religions of the Book (Christians, Jews and Zoroastrians) to freely profess their faith.

The political empathy with the papacy of Rome, which had grown over the centuries, would culminate in the 19th century, with the emergence of a Uniate branch of the Coptic Church. The proclamation of St Cyril as Doctor of the Church by Pope Leo XIII would occur in 1882: see below, part II, chapter "The Catholic Wing" and Appendix *ad loc*. During the 20th century the dialogue, made possible by the Vatican Council II and definitively inaugurated in 1973 by Paul VI, gave rise, under John Paul II, to the common declaration on Christological doctrine of February 12 1988, which at the same time anathemised the doctrines of Eutyches (that is pure Monophysitism) and of Nestorius (Duophysism).

On the evolution of the Coptic Church see MEINARDUS 1999a; DAVIS; PAPACONSTANTINOU; ZANETTI; further bibliography below, part III, chapter "An Age of Anxiety", Appendix *ad loc.*

On the relationship between theological-dogmatic elaboration, Church politics and Egyptian ethnic independence in the organisation of the nationalist Coptic Church see WIPSZYCKA 1992.

5 Good Use of Power

At that time, no one could imagine which fate the triumphal chariot of history, or of providence, was preparing in the province of Egypt, fertile soil for grain and intellect, where mathematics, poetry and the philosophy of the followers of Plotinus and Porphyry flourished. Nor could anyone imagine of what other adventurous speculations it would become the theatre, on which new and surprising chessboard the *pantotrophos* Alexandria would play her game.

Estuary of thought, the Egyptian outlet to Mediterranean civilisation and, in the 5th century, still a symbol, together with Athens, of ancient culture, Alexandria would shift the balance in the battle between the Christian Churches, wedged into the centre of the Islamic world. No one at that time would have been able to imagine it, not even the most acute minds who at the time taught at its famous Platonic university. Like Hypatia.

Yet she had an acute political intelligence and she combined dialectic talent in discussion with moderation in her judgement. Her intellectual tolerance made her impartial and, above all, her frankness before the powerful gave her a capacity for mediation, thanks to which she was listened to and loved by the various groups of citizens who disputed power in the polis. Even rulers asked her advice and "were the first to go and listen to her at her home."

As Suidas writes, drawning on Damascius, Hypatia was

> [...] eloquent and dialectic (διαλεκτική) in speaking, deliberate and with a strong sense of citizenship (*politike*, πολιτική) in her actions, so that the whole city sincerely admired her and venerated her. And the political chiefs who had come to administer the polis were the first to go and listen to her at her home, as continued to be the case also in Athens. Because, although Paganism had ended, the name of philosophy still seemed great and venerable to all those who held the most important positions in the cities.[34]

During the 4th and 5th centuries of the empire, complex relations bound the Roman governors to the autochthonous elites of the provincial territories. Handed down by birth, amongst the secular privileges of caste was a special "Hellenic" education with strong political connotations. Influential in the aristocracy, heiress to the intellectual dynasty belonging to the Museum school, Hypatia, the sources suggest to us, was above all mistress of the "Hellenic lifestyle". The *hellenike diagoge* (ἑλληνικὴ διαγωγή), by which the Pagan ruling class was inspired, brought together Hellenic religion, the classical ideal of education (*paideia*) and a commitment to public life that, despite the inevitable elitism, scrupulously respected the values of pluralism and of debate that were traced back to the Greek agora.

---

34 DAMASCIUS, *Vita Isidori* fr.*104, p. 79,12–18 Zintzen = fr. 43E, p. 130, 1–8 Athanassiadi = SUIDAS Y 166, IV, pp. 644, 31–645, 4 Adler (HARICH-SCHWARZBAUER 2011, p. 247).

5 Good Use of Power

For the representatives of the Constantinopolitan central government and in particular for Orestes, *praefectus augustalis* of Alexandria, Hypatia was, amongst other things, the expression of that urban aristocracy. For this reason, also, her words and her judgement influenced the internal policy of her city.

> You have always had power. May you have it for a long time, and may you put this power to good use.[35]

So we read in the letter of recommendation for two young friends, whose assets had been expropriated, which was addressed to her by the most devoted of her pupils: Synesius, an eclectic landowner who equally loved philosophy and hunting, for whom thoughts were like horses, hounds and a bow and the *hellenike diagoge* "the most fertile method and in general the most efficacious for cultivating the mind"[36].

---

35 SYNESIUS, *Ep.* 81, p. 207 Roques.
36 MARROU 1963, p. 157.

Appendix
Good Use of Power

The passage on the oratorical talent and political commitment of Hypatia, almost certainly taken from Damascius, can be read in DAMASCIUS, *Vita Isidori* fr. *102, *104, p. 77, 79 Zintzen = fr. 43E, p. 130, 1–8 Athanassiadi = SUIDAS Y 166, IV, pp. 644, 31–645, 4 Adler (HARICH-SCHWARZBAUER 2011, p. 247).

WATTS 2017, pp. 112–113, interprets Damascius' statement in a restrictive sense, situating the visits to Hypatia's house of the "political leaders and administrators of the polis" (that is of the Augustal prefect Orestes *in primis*), and in general of the city elite (ἥ τε ἄλλη πόλις), to the short period of time between the death under torture of Ammonius, *agent provocateur* of Cyril, and that of Hypatia herself as retaliation at the hands of the followers of Cyril (on this see below, chapter "The Intimidation of Orestes"). According to Watts, Orestes, in this specific moment marking the climax of his conflict with Cyril, turned to Hypatia to create a sort of crisis unit, a "coalition" with "the Alexandrian councilors and other members of the civic elite". Orestes and Hypatia met alone, and were later joined by "a religiously mixed group of Alexandrian elites" (p. 113). Again, according to Watts, Damascius was referring to this limited segment of time when he wrote that "the name of philosophy seemed most esteemed and worthy of honor to those who ran the affairs of the city" (*ibid.*). Such interpretation excludes the presence of patronage and/or esoteric meetings *idia* (ἰδίᾳ), "privately", in Hypatia's house as postulated by scholars (*in primis* Pierre Chuvin), in which the eminent *eteria* of her followers gathered (see below, part III, chapter "The Power of Hypatia"). Yet, it is precisely the discovery of such meetings that led Cyril to the "attack" of *phthonos* (φθόνος), "envy", that eventually led him to commission the killing of Hypatia (see below, chapter "Mortal Envy"). Moreover, it must be noted that the verbal tenses used by both Socrates and Damascius to witness to the habit of the city elite's members to frequent the house of Hypatia, whose wise prestige and venerable frankness were revered, express the idea of continuity and give a sense that Hypatia's role was established over time; see Damascius' statement, especially the use of ἀεὶ (*Vita Isidori* fr.*104, p. 79,14 Zintzen = fr. 43E p. 130, 4 Athanassiadi = SUIDAS IV, pp. 644, 31–645, 1 Adler = HARICH-SCHWARZBAUER 2011, p. 247): ἥ τε ἄλλη πόλις εἰκότως ἠσπάζετό τε καὶ προσεκύνει διαφερόντως, οἵ τε ἄρχοντες ἀεὶ προχειριζόμενοι τῆς πόλεως ἐφοίτων πρῶτοι πρὸς αὐτήν), as well as that of Socrates (SOCRATES SCHOLASTICUS VII 15, 2–4, p. 360, 24–28 Hansen [HARICH-SCHWARZBAUER 2011, p. 188]): Διὰ δὲ τὴν προσοῦσαν αὐτῇ ἐκ τῆς παιδεύσεως σεμνὴν παρρησίαν καὶ τοῖς ἄρχουσιν σωφρόνως εἰς πρόσωπον ἤρχετο, καὶ οὐκ ἦν τις αἰσχύνη ἐν μέσῳ ἀνδρῶν παρεῖναι αὐτήν. Πάντες γὰρ δι'ὑπερβάλλουσαν σωφροσύνην πλέον αὐτὴν ᾐδοῦντο καὶ κατεπλήττοντο. Κατὰ δὴ ταύτης τότε ὁ φθόνος ὡπλίσατο.

On the *hellenike diagoge* (ἑλληνικὴ διαγωγή) or "Greek lifestyle" that linked the religion of culture and the classical ideal of *paideia* to the commitment to manage the polis, see MARROU 1963, where we also read its definition, which paraphrases Synesius'

Dion, of the *hellenike diagoge* as the most fertile method and the most effective in general at cultivating the mind.

On the peculiar form of solidarity around these cultural values amongst late Roman and early Byzantine aristocracy see BROWN 1992, pp. 35–36.

Synesius' phrase on Hypatia's powers is taken from *Ep.* 81, p. 207 Roques (Engl. transl. p. 174 Fitzgerald). It is a letter of recommendation for two aristocrats, Nicaeus and Philolaus, youths and relatives, so that they might have their assets restored: "I would like them to have the support of all those who honour you, be they private citizens or magistrates." As summarised by CAMERON 2013, p. 80: "Synesius seems to have assumed that she had a pipeline to the imperial bureaucracy".

The equal love of Synesius for both philosophy and hunting is testified in particular by the well known *Ep.* 41, 121–123, p. 44 Roques (Engl. transl. *Ep.* 57, 121–123, p. 131 Fitzgerald); *Ep.* 105, 27–28 p. 236 Roques (Engl. transl. p. 198 Fitzgerald) and especially *ibid.*, 113–115 p. 240 Roques (Engl. transl. p. 201 Fitzgerald).

6 Treacherous Zeal

It was precisely from this local power based on clientelism, with its centuries-old, multiform and inextricable links between the provincial aristocracy and the administrators of the central government, from its reciprocal and direct influence in managing the affairs of the citizens, that the transformation of the ruling classes of the various regions of the empire derived. It was induced by the Church's striving for political legitimacy following the ascent of Christianity to State religion, permitted by the Edict of Toleration of the first Byzantine emperor, Constantine, and then imposed by Theodosius' "edict of intolerance". In the cities of the great Byzantine province it would from then on be for the bishop, and no longer the philosopher as in the past, to act as civic defender and counsellor of the representative of the State.

"The Christian bishop had to have the monopoly of *parrhesia!*"[37], has been written, proposing, precisely in the case of Hypatia, a historical syllogism all too evident: if, in the phase of transition from Paganism to Christianity, the role of the philosopher and the bishop overlap, what should the bishop do, other than eliminate the philosopher?

Phthonos personified rose up in arms against her[38],

denounced the Christian Socrates. In Greek, the word φθόνος indicates, from the origins of the language, a "maliciousness" that is expressed in "envy" of the excellence of others, whether it is a question of wealth or success or generic good fortune. There is a very ancient expression, belonging to classical Greek and used above all by the tragedians: the φθόνος θεῶν, "the envy of the gods", which dispenses misfortune, the retaliation that humans suffer when they are too fortunate. However, here the term is used in its more direct form, which was common in Late Greek: the feeling of malevolent rivalry of humans towards other humans.

Socrates Scholasticus alludes to its personification: the demon Phthonos in Hellenistic and Byzantine poetry incarnates a visceral jealousy, associated at times with amorous passion, and above all with that parallel destructive passion that is hatred. In our case, however, the sentiment was collective. The competitiveness of the most extremist Christians towards the Pagans, perceived by all the sources, constitutes that "jealous zeal" that will be the cause of the violent end not only of Hypatia, but also of the *hellenike diagoge* that she incarnates, the ancient "way of life" of the polis, hated with sullen resentment by the Christian zealots. It is not accidental that another name for the demon Phthonos is Zelos.

The fact that Hypatia frequently met with Orestes,

---

37 BROWN 1993, pp. 889–890; see BROWN 1992, p. 116.
38 SOCRATES VII 15, 4, p. 360, 28 Hansen (HARICH-SCHWARZBAUER 2011, p. 188).

the *praefectus augustalis* of Alexandria,

> made the people of the Church suspect that in effect it was Hypatia who would not allow Orestes to reconcile his differences with their bishop[39],

writes Socrates of Constantinople.

This idea emerged again two centuries later from a fourth and no less important source for our story, the chronicle of John of Nikiu, written a few years after the Arab conquest of Egypt and until the end of the 20th century neglected by those who researched the case of Hypatia, because it survived only in a late Ethiopic version.

---

39 *Id.*, p. 360, 28–361, 1 Hansen (HARICH-SCHWARZBAUER 2011, p. 188).

Appendix
Treacherous Zeal

In general, on the relations between the autochthonous provincial leaders and the administrators of the Roman government, see DESIDERI; NESSELRATH. On the interpretation of cultural, political and religious life in Alexandria at the time see HAAS 1997, pp. 302–316.

The phrase regarding the monopoly of *parrhesia* can be read in the Italian essay by BROWN, 1993, pp. 889–890, paralleled by BROWN 1992, p. 116: "It was essential to Cyril, as the newly installed patriarch, that he should have the monopoly of parrhésia (*sic*) in Alexandria". On *parrhesia* in the "holy man" see also FOWDEN 1982; COX; CRACCO RUGGINI 1979.

The *phthonos theon* (φθόνος θεῶν) appears for example in AESCHYLUS, *The Persians* 362 (significantly applied to Xerxes prior to the battle of Salamis) or in *Agamemnon* 947, when Agamemnon returns victorious from Troy and begs "may I not be struck from afar by any glance of the gods' jealous eye", which is actually precisely what will happen.

On Phthonos as the demon (*daimon*, δαίμων) of envy and jealousy see CALLIMACHUS, *Hymn to Apollo* 105 and 113 (on the role of Phthonos see WILLIAMS, pp. 3, 18, 40, 82, 85, 89); and above all, in the same fifth century and the same Egyptian environment, NONNUS, *Dionysiaca* 8, 34 ff. (NONNUS PANOPOLITANUS, pp. 121–124 Chuvin). Since the passage is very well-known, the analogy with Socrates Scholasticus might not be accidental. Socrates may have read the poem by Nonnus and the allusion to Phthonos personified in arms may be a more or less deliberate reminiscence. Amongst other things, Nonnus, who was based in Panopolis, certainly took sides in Alexandrian Christianity's struggles: according to his *Paraphrase of John* he was a follower, or at least an admirer of Cyril, as argued by LIVREA 1987; see also LIVREA 2000, p. 53 ("Cyril of Alexandria [...] from whom Nonnus takes not only the symbolic exegesis and a Christological orthodoxy that accentuates the divinity of the Saviour, but also some peculiar exegetical solutions" [my translation of Livrea]); on page 44 n. 8 Livrea calls Cyril "the doctrinal paradigm of Nonnus." On the other hand, in Nonnus himself, the reference to Phthonos found in the *Dionysiaca* – of which we do not know the precise date of composition, and which is in any case probably later, if only slightly, than the death of Hypatia – could be interpreted as a symmetrical and inverse, cryptic and ambiguous (like everything in this author's work) reference to the event of her assassination. Could Nonnus not perhaps openly pay homage to Cyril in the *Paraphrase* and cryptically describe his misdeeds in the *Dionysiaca*, just as Procopius exalts Justinian and Theodora in the *Wars* and in the *Buildings* to then accuse them in the *Anekdota*? This theory is however excluded, *per litteras*, by Enrico Livrea. Our hypothesis, however, seems to be supported by a recent contribution of FINCHER, who, on the basis of other elements, considers Nonnus' *Dionysiaca* to be among those sources favourable to Hypatia. Fincer focuses in particular on some episodes from book 41, which have

Beroes, Aphrodites and Harmonia as main characters. According to Fincher, the description of these Goddesses may recall that of Hypatia we read in Socrates and Suidas. His conclusion on the 'feminist' connotation of Nonnus' message seems to be influenced by clichés of gender studies on Hypatia, about which see below, chapt. "Miraculous Devotion. Chateaubriand, Péguy and the Flourishing of Feminist Literature", Appendix *ad loc.*

On the association between Phthonos and amorous passion, so that in at least one example of ancient ceramic painting the demon is portrayed as a winged boy, similar to Eros, beside Aphrodite, of whom he may be the son, see BERNARD 1991.

The female *pendant* of Phthonos is Nemesis, who is also associated with Aphrodites. The recent contribution of HILLMAN sheds light on the various and complex aspects of this character.

There is a subtle distinction in classical Greek between the terms *phthonos* (φθόνος) and *zelos* (ζῆλος), one destructive and the other constructive according to some, equivalent and respectively designated "envy" and "jealousy", according to others. But the two definitions blend when, in Late Antiquity, it is a question of the demon personified: see OPPIANUS, *Halieutica* 1, 499 ff., where the name of Zelos is given as "Jealous Rivalry" in the English translation by Mair (OPPIANUS Mair).

Alan Cameron casts some doubts on Cyril's jealousy: see CAMERON 2016c, pp. 200–203 (we will refer to the collection of essays as CAMERON 2016c; for his further suggestions and objections see also below, final chapter: "Aftershock: And What If…"; CAMERON 2016 is a revised and enlarged version of CAMERON 2013); cf. below, chapter "Mortal Envy" and Appendix *ad loc.*

7 The Bishop of Nikiu

John, Coptic bishop of Nikiu and rector of the bishops of Upper Egypt, reached the height of his ecclesiastical career in the 690s. In 696, he was nominated general administrator of the monasteries, but was later deposed following an accusation of abuse of power.

The discovery of the manuscript of his *Chronicle* in the Ethiopic version, during the British expedition to Abyssinia in 1867–1868, was a fundamental event without which it would have been impossible for the 20th-century scholars to reconstruct the history of the Arab conquest of Egypt.

Although the vicissitudes of the manuscript tradition make this source incomplete, and various parts have been mangled in the chain of translations that have handed it down to us – from the original to Arabic and then, in the 17th century, into Amharic, perhaps with further transmission, including one into Sahidic Coptic – the narrative of the authoritarian bishop, in its evident partiality and its ethnic-religious patriotism, is the only one to present the facts from the standpoint of the supporters of Cyril, most probably basing itself on more ancient sources, coming at least in part from the Coptic world, well-informed and close to the facts.

It is a point of view that would dominate Egyptian ecclesiastical opinion throughout the Byzantine age, diverging from that of the Constantinopolitan Church and paradoxically matching that of Catholic-Papist historiography, until the end of the 19th century. Since 'the enemy of my enemy is my friend', the Coptic Church, in contraposition to the great rival in Constantinople, would often come under the sway of the Catholic Church and part of it would, in the 20th century, reach doctrinal agreement with the Pope of Rome.

> At that time,

writes John of Nikiu,

> there appeared in Alexandria a woman philosopher, a Pagan by the name of Hypatia, who dedicated all her time to magic, the astrolabes and musical instruments, and she deceived many people with her satanic tricks. And the governor of the city honoured her exaggeratedly, because she had seduced him too with her magic. And so he stopped going to church, as was previously his habit. And not only that, but he won over to her side many believers. And he himself received the misbelievers at his residence[40].

The language of John of Nikiu may sound naïve in its rough partiality. However, we must read between the lines. In the alliance between the prefect Orestes and the philosopher Hypatia, if not secret in any case private, the Coptic bishop sees a vein of resistance, if not of Pagan reaction, against what has been called "the outrageous Chris-

---

[40] JOANNES DE NIKIU LXXXIV 87–88, pp. 100–101 Charles.

tianity of Cyril" (Rougé), against his armed proselytism. What is more, probably in his reading the bishop of Nikiu, from his own point of view, is right.

Appendix
The Bishop of Nikiu

The chronicle of John of Nikiu can be read in *Chronique de Jean, évêque de Nikiou, texte éthiopien* [...] (JOANNES DE NIKIU Zotenberg). On the personality and the biography of the author see above all JOANNES DE NIKIU Charles, which gives the English translation, amending and annotating Zotenberg's text in more than one place.

The fundamental importance of the discovery of John of Nikiu's Ethiopic manuscript was already mentioned by Alfred Butler (BUTLER 1978, pp. 6–7).

According to CARILE, p. 113, John of Nikiu relied upon John Malalas and John of Antioch. That John of Nikiu based his account on the life of Hypatia on previous sources is also supposed by WATTS 2006b, p. 340 and n. 37; see also WATTS 2010, pp. 203–205. On John of Nikiu's account of Hypatia and her assassination see WATTS 2017, pp. 131–134; on his partial dependence on Socrates Scholasticus and John of Antioch, as well as on other Egyptian sources, see p. 186, nn. 39–42.

The recovery of this source on the studies of Hypatia is owed to ROUGÉ 1990; see also CHUVIN–TARDIEU, pp. 60–61. The phrase quoted on "the outrageous Christianity of Cyril" comes from Rougé's work, while the presentation of Hypatia and her relationship with Orestes given in the *Chronicle* of John of Nikiu is indicated following Charles (JOANNES DE NIKIU LXXXIV, parr. 87–88, pp. 100–101 Charles).

On the level of resistance if not of Pagan reaction see also WATTS 2006b, p. 334, where it is supposed that in the months following the anti-Jewish pogrom "Orestes apparently tried to organize opposition to Cyril from among the civic elite", at the centre of whom "either in reality or in popular perception" stood Hypatia. This idea is now developed in WATTS 2017, pp. 112–114. As we have previously seen (see above "Good Use of Power", Appendix *ad loc.*), Watts believes that the meetings in Hypatia's house took place only in this very last period, and that only at this time did she act as 'civic consultant', thus excluding a pre-existing habit of the members of the government and city elite to gather in her abode in "private" (ἰδίᾳ) meetings. Such habitual meetings postulated by scholars (*in primis* Pierre Chuvin) have been described as something distinct from her "public" (δημοσίᾳ) lectures which she gave in an official city venue, yet just as habitual for Hypatia; see below, part III, chapter "The Power of Hypatia" and Appendix *ad loc.*

On the substantial reliability of the account of John of Nikiu, also regarding the image perceived and transmitted of Hypatia's philosophy by her contemporaries (a *philosophos*, φιλόσοφος, in the full sense of the word, inasmuch she was an astronomer and a musician, music being inseparable for the Platonists from the sciences of the stars), which the Coptic bishop renders negatively but which largely corresponds to the one given by Damascius, see the precise exegesis of the Ethiopic passage by Michel Tardieu in CHUVIN–TARDIEU, p. 67. As for the accusation of "magic" see below, part III, chapters "What Did Hypatia Teach?", "All Synesius' Mysteries", "Synesius, Hypatia and *Philosophia*", "Women who Philosophised", "The Power of Hypatia" and Appendices *ad loc.*

8 A Three-Handed Game

While their implicit common adherence to Paganism bound the Hellenic aristocracy to the representatives of the Roman government like a Freemasonry *ante litteram*, in the political game that in Alexandria saw these forces confront the new Christian ecclesiastical cadres, there was a third element at play: the Jewish component. Already a dominant lobby group prior to the appearance of that of the Christians, now a rival pressure group.

In effect, it was a three-handed power game between the ancient Pagan elite, close to the representatives of the imperial government; the Christian officials who wanted to replace it; and the rich and influential community of the Jews. The first act of Cyril's episcopacy would be an anti-Jewish pogrom, which would precede the more or less planned attack on the Pagan establishment, incarnated in Hypatia.

An entrenched antagonism opposed Christianity to the Jewish mother Church. Christianity was already a deviation from Judaism, a break-away sect in the early centuries, when it had grown "in the shadow of the synagogues". On the part of the Christians, theological hostility against the "deicidal" people was added to the preoccupation with proselytism. The bishops, from Cyril of Alexandria to Theodoret of Cyrus and Basil of Seleucia, preached against the Jews, who exercised over their flock a seduction "deliberate or not, but", as it has been observed, "unquestionable".[41] Anti-Jewish censorship, even more than the hostility towards Paganism, marked the first writings and acts of Cyril's episcopal career: for example, his first festal letter, dated 414, repeated, one after the other, all the scriptural accusations against the Jews.

In the provinces, the tradition of violence between Jews and non-Jews dated from the times of the first emperors. In his letters Synesius called the Jewish people "sworn enemies of the Hellenes", still recalling the revolt of the Jewish colonies of Egypt and the Pentapolis of 117, under Trajan, during which, according to Cassius Dio, two hundred and twenty thousand Gentiles were massacred. In the 5th century, street battles were the order of the day, like the riots of the Samaritans in Palestine. The anti-Jewish grudge was felt more deeply than ever in Alexandria, which had a Jewish colony of one hundred thousand souls.

In 414 the Jews, recounts Socrates Scholasticus, had convinced the prefect Orestes to have Hierax, an agitator operating on behalf of Cyril at the citizens' assembly in the theatre as well as master of grammar, arrested and tortured in public (John of Nikiu transformed him into "a learned and clever man, who had the healthy custom of admonishing the Pagans because he was entirely devoted to the illustrious patriarch and well versed in Christian doctrine"). According to Socrates, the Jews had subsequently carried out a nocturnal ambush on the Christian activists in the streets of Alexandria, "killing", he writes, we do not know how impartially, "a considerable number".

---

[41] See PATLAGEAN, pp. 977–978.

Whatever really happened, the patriarch immediately responded with the great pogrom that preluded the massacre of Hypatia, conducted against the Jewish synagogues by Cyril's militia, the *parabalani*.

> Some monks from the mountains of Nitria, whose spirit had been seething since the times of Theophilus, who had iniquitously militarised them [...] and they had from then onwards become zealots, decided in their fanaticism to fight in the name of Cyril[42],

continues Socrates. The new patriarch, who before being nominated had lived for some time amongst these monks in the desert, had absorbed them into the corps of the *parabalani*, essentially "nurse stretcher-bearers", clerics to all intents and purposes, as witnessed by the law that concerns them in the Theodosian Code, who constituted his private militia in Alexandria. Instigated by these agitators, the Christian population pillaged the homes of the Jews, who were even driven out of the city.

> The Jews, who since the time of Alexander of Macedon had lived in this city, were all forced to emigrate, stripped of their assets, and they scattered, some here, some there[43].

The patriarch's act of force was grave: it was not a spontaneous popular movement, but an abuse perpetrated by the Church, which once again, as at the time of the destruction of the Serapeum, used the monks as an instrument.

---

[42] SOCRATES VII 14, 1, p. 359, 23–26 Hansen (see HARICH-SCHWARZBAUER 2011, pp. 183–185).
[43] ID. VII 13, 16, p. 359, 7–9 Hansen.

Appendix
A Three-Handed Game

On the "three-handed game" in Alexandria see *in primis* CAMERON 2016c, p. 201: "There can be no question that Hypatia's death arose out of the anti-Jewish riots of 415 and the struggle for power between Cyril and Orestes"; CAMERON 2016b. On the relations between Pagans, Jews and Christians in the 5th century see SCHÄFER 1997; FELDMAN; CRACCO RUGGINI 1980.

On the Jewish community in the Alexandria of Late Antiquity, its topographical distribution and the tensions that opposed it to other ethnic groups see also KASHER

For the phrase on the "involuntary proselitism" of the Jews towards the adepts of Christianity see PATLAGEAN, pp. 977–978.

On religious violence in Late Antiquity see SHAW.

The first festal letter of Cyril (414) against the Jews can be read in CYRILLUS ALEXANDRINUS, pp. 142–186 Burns – Évieux – Arragon; see also WILKEN 1971.

The Jewish revolt of 117 is narrated in the *Roman History* by Cassius Dio 59, 32 (CASSIUS DIO VII, pp. 360–365 Cary – Foster).

The idyllic and certainly misleading description that John of Nikiu gives of Hierax can be read in JOANNES DE NIKIU LXXXIV par. 91, p. 101 Charles. About him see below: "Aftershock: And What If…", with bibliography.

For Socrates' account of the pogrom of 414 in Alexandria and its background, see V 13, 1–15, pp. 357, 19–359, 6 Hansen.

WATTS 2017, pp. 108–110, downplays the gravity of the 414 progrom described by sources such as Socrates Scholasticus and John of Nikiu: "While some contemporary Christian sources speak about this event leading to the complete expulsion of all Jews from Alexandria, such a thing was plainly impossible", he writes at p. 109; see p. 181, n. 13. However, as has already been highlighted by historians like Alan Cameron, Cyril's anti-Jewish pogrom is the key to understanding Hypatia's *affaire*. The trigger of the escalation of violence which preceded the assassination of Hypatia and the true reason for the split between Cyril and the Augustal prefect was undoubtedly the anti-Jewish campaign of the young bishop which followed his persecution against the Novatians.

On Cyril's sojourn in the desert of Nitria – Wadi el-Natrun, with its vast deposits of *natron* (νάτρον) – see *Synaxarium Alexandrinum*, p. 72 Forget; see also TAKÁCS 1995, pp. 54–55.

On the violence of the monks during the various stages of political affirmation of Monophysitism see FREND: in particular, pp. 142 and 154–155, on the assassination of the bishop Proterius who, like the Arian George, was lynched and subjected to the same torture as Hypatia; see also, with regard to the Late Antique perception of Hypatia's murder, WATTS 2006b; and the review of DZIELSKA 1995 by KAÇAR

On the "earthy Coptic reaction to all that is Hellenic" and the social aversion, even more than the ethnic-religious antipathy, of Egyptian monasticism in the 5th century for the Alexandrian ruling class of Greek origin, with specific reference to Hypatia's case, see AVERINCEV, p. 141.

The origin of the term *parabalaneus* (παραβαλανεύς) is linked to the Greek *balaneion* (βαλανεῖον), equivalent to the Latin *balneum*, "bath". In the classical era, the *balaneus* (βαλανεύς) was the attendant who worked in the public baths, and was therefore already a sort of nurse. In the acts of the Council of Chalcedon we find the term παραβαλανεύς, with the meaning "hospital attendant", used together with the term *monazon* (μονάζων), equivalent to *monachos* (μοναχός), "monk" (see SCHWARTZ, p. 179; see also GREGORY; PHILIPSBORN).

The erroneous spelling *parabolani* (παραβολᾶνοι) is due to a corruption linked to a *lectio facilior*, which nevertheless has been handed down through the centuries, particularly in Western writings, and also recently in lexica and valuable scholarly contributions, such as BOWERSOCK who, however, provides a different etymology on which grounds he bases his choice.

That the Alexandrian *parabalani* had the status of clergy is witnessed by the law that concerned them in *Codex Theodosianus* 16, 2, 42 (29 September 416), p. 850 Mommsen – Meyer: IDEM AA. MONAXIO P(RAEFECTO) P(RAETORI)O; see ROUGÉ 1987.

On the role of agitators played by the παραβαλανεῖς, and on the parallel, in this use of the monks, with Theophilus' action against the Serapeum, see ROUGÉ 1990, p. 491. "Die Schutztruppe des Bischofs" is the apt definition of HARICH-SCHWARZBAUER 2011, p. 209

Evelyne Patlagean summarises thus: "Cyril of Alexandria provoked the temporary exodus of the Jews from the city in 414, against the wishes of the *augustalis* and with the help of the monks. The latter actively opposed the Jews and the people followed them, as is shown by the attacks perpetrated by Barsauma's mobs throughout the East. The Jews reacted." (PATLAGEAN, p. 984).

9 The Intimidation of Orestes

> One who does not need the polis and is
> self-sufficient is either a beast or a god.
> ARISTOTLE

Cyril's *parabalani* came, as we have seen, from the second generation of monasticism in the Egyptian desert, from the ranks of those zealots who, as Socrates Scholasticus tells us, "had an incandescent spirit"[44] and who, as we read elsewhere, "had pushed ascetic impassivity to subversion". In fact, the entire monastic environment was "animated by a vindication of primacy", as argued by Patlagean, "and all the monks had, at that time, free access in the cities"[45]. Throughout the 5th century, during the Monophysite controversy, Cyrillian monks travelled around the East, disseminating terror everywhere they went to.

Suidas calls them,

> [...] abominable beings, true beasts[46].

The reference to the "bestial" coarseness of the monks, which we have already encountered in Eunapius, recurs frequently in Byzantine authors, not only as a factual judgement, but, perhaps, also as alluding to the passage from Aristotle's *Politics*, where he says that "one who does not need the polis and is self-sufficient is either a beast or a god"[47].

Having eliminated his Jewish adversaries in the pogrom of 414, even forcing them, according to Socrates Scholasticus, to temporarily leave the city, Cyril's punitive terrorist strategy turned to the *praefectus augustalis* in person, guilty of having sent to Constantinople a strongly worded letter of complaint against the attack by the bishop on the Jewish citizens – rich, well settled, influential, and moreover competitors of the Christian community, not only in religious matters, but also in the profitable monopoly of the maritime transport of grain[48].

Orestes, writes Socrates Scholasticus,

> [...] was very indignant about the events and had suffered greatly in seeing such an important city completely emptied of human beings[49].

---

44 SOCRATES VII 14, 1, p. 359, 23–24 Hansen; 15, 5, p. 361, 1–2 Hansen (HARICH-SCHWARZBAUER 2011, p. 188). See above "The Terrible Patriarch of Alexandria".
45 PATLAGEAN, p. 980 with n. 19.
46 DAMASCIUS, *Vita Isidori* fr. *104, p. 81,1 Zintzen = fr. 43E, p. 130, 18 Athanassiadi = SUIDAS Y 166, IV, p. 645, 13–14 Adler (HARICH-SCHWARZBAUER 2011, p. 247).
47 ARISTOTLE, *Pol.* 1253a 29.
48 See below "Aftershock: And What If...".
49 SOCRATES VII 13, 18, p. 359, 12–14 Hansen (cfr. HARICH-SCHWARZBAUER 2011, p. 183); see above "The Terrible Patriarch of Alexandria".

Cyril's direct intimidation against Orestes set off a chain reaction that probably became uncontrollable even for Orestes himself.

Orestes, in compliance with imperial legislation, was officially a Christian, as John of Nikiu also mentions, but "without renouncing what we today would call state secularism", as has been written[50]. He was actually bound, culturally if not also cultually, to the old establishment, and in any case understandably reluctant to endorse Cyril's policy of violence and his continual jurisdictional interference. In this he represented the position of the moderate elite of the city, which defected from Paganism to Christianity for reasons of *Realpolitik*, but was still anchored to the traditions of its social class and hostile to both the religious fundamentalism and the political maximalism of the Christian authority incarnated in the bishop.

The assault on Orestes' procession occurred in 415. Socrates says that the monks began insulting him, accusing him of being a "sacrificer" and a "Hellene". The prefect defended himself from the accusation of Paganism, saying that he had been baptised by Atticus, patriarch of Constantinople. It is this incautious mention of the rival throne of Constantinople that most likely incited the aggression of the Egyptians[51]. A stone, thrown it would seem by a certain Ammonius, hit Orestes as he sat in his carriage, wounding him on the head. The blood splashed onto the toga of the representative of the Roman government: this was more than could be allowed[52].

Ammonius is arrested and dies under torture. Two letters/dispatches reach Constantinople: Orestes' account and Cyril's counter-response, which allegedly contends, according to Socrates Scholasticus, that "Ammonius was tortured so that he would renounce Christ" and not because of his anti-government action[53]. Immediately after, Cyril organises a solemn funeral for the violent monk and pronounces a public eulogy, during which he not only attributes to him the title of martyr, but also changes his name from Ammonius to Thaumasius – "the admirable", as his gesture was admirable – thus openly offending the prefect.

By behaving in this manner, however, Cyril now had against him, warns Socrates, the more moderate wing (*hoi sophronountes*, οἱ σωφρονοῦντες) of the ecclesiastical population (*laos*, λαός) which was perhaps not more numerous, but was certainly more influential than the masses (*plethos*, πλῆθος)[54] of integralists driven to the streets by Cyril. Perhaps for this reason he was induced to ask Orestes for an audience. He went to him taking as a gift a copy of the Gospels – symbol of the religion of State, in contraposition to the Old Testament of the Jews, who were the real bone of contention – certain, as Socrates tells us, "that the respect for the new religion might induce

---

50 GIORELLO, pp. 101–104.
51 ROUGÉ 1990, pp. 492–493.
52 SOCRATES VII 14, 2–6, pp. 359, 26–360, 2 Hansen (cfr. HARICH-SCHWARZBAUER 2011, pp. 183–185).
53 ID. VII 14, 8–11, p. 360, 5–16 Hansen (cfr. HARICH-SCHWARZBAUER 2011, pp. 183–185).
54 ID. VII 14, 10–11, p. 360, 12–15 Hansen (cfr. HARICH-SCHWARZBAUER 2011, pp. 183–185).

the governor to set aside his ire." However, Orestes, continues Socrates, "was not to be appeased, and an implacable war continued between them"[55].

---

[55] *Id.* VII 13, 20–21, p. 359, 18–22 Hansen (cfr. Harich-Schwarzbauer 2011, pp. 183–185).

Appendix
The Intimidation of Orestes

For the first quotation of Socrates on the "incandescent spirit" of the *parabalani* (παραβαλανεῖς), see VII 14, 1, p. 359, 23–24 Hansen (cfr. HARICH-SCHWARZBAUER 2011, pp. 183–185); above, chapter "The Terrible Patriarch of Alexandria".

The quotation immediately following this and the subsequent one refer to PATLAGEAN, p. 980 with n. 19.

The definition of the Cyrillian monks as "beasts" (θηριώδεις ἄνθρωποι, ὡς ἀληθῶς σχέτλιοι) is in DAMASCIUS, *Vita Isidori* fr. *104, p. 81,1 Zintzen = fr. 43E, p. 130, 18 Athanassiadi = SUIDAS Y 166, IV, p. 645, 13–14 Adler (HARICH-SCHWARZBAUER 2011, p. 247).

The sentence from Aristotle's *Politics* 1253a 29 is taken from ARISTOTELES, p. 14 Aubonnet; the first to quote it in relation to Christian *anachoresis* (ἀναχώρησις, separation from the secular world) is Julian the Apostate.

In his first contribution on Hypatia LACOMBRADE 1954, pp. 23 and 25, already sees clearly that Hypatia's death is not only the result of a conflict of temporal interests, rather than an ideological duel, but also, in fact, collateral damage of a battle not just between Christians and Pagans, but also Christians and Jews. Seriously compromised by Cyril's violent policies, their interests were defended by official power, which thus attracted reprisals from the bishop and his militia first towards themselves and later towards Hypatia. See also LACOMBRADE 1972; for an authoritative summary of the dynamics of Hypatia's assassination and a useful, updated bibliographical compendium see LACOMBRADE 1994. It was for the protest sent to Constantinople against the anti-Jewish pogrom of Cyril's monks that Orestes was targeted by the violence of Ammonius and his men; they in turn, after the arrest and death of Ammonius under torture, perpetrated the lynching of Hypatia: see also below, part III, chapter "The Eminence of Hypatia." Let us recall CAMERON 2016c, p. 201, whose statement is reported above, chapter "A Three-Handed Game", Appendix *ad loc.*

A similar reconstruction of the facts and of the escalation that would lead to the assassination of Hypatia has recently been offered by SAFFREY, *s.v.* Hypatie d'Alexandrie: "Cyrille ne pouvant atteindre directement son adversaire, ses partisans dirigèrent leur hostilité sur un personnage de l'entourage du préfet, ce fut Hypatie […] sans doute à l'instigation du patriarche qui rétablit du coup son autorité." See also CHUVIN, pp. 91–94; HAAS 1997, pp. 313–316; WATTS 2006a, pp. 343–354.

Surprisingly, Watt's assessment (WATTS 2017, p. 111 ff.) differs significantly in the evaluation of Cyril's policy from that of the scholars who preceded him. The bishop, according to Watts, "did not intend for the incident to become violent" and "certainly neither planned nor sanctioned a physical attack on the prefect" like the one executed by Ammonius, who "acted on his own". According to Watts, the reaction to the arrest and death under torture of the perpetrator, as well as the solemn celebration of his burial, his proclamation as a martyr of the Church, the transformation of his name Ammonius into Thaumasius (namely "the admirable"), and the elevation of his gesture as present and future example for the conduct of the Christians of Alexandria, was not a calculated provocation, but rather "a gesture of profound appreciation to the Nitrian monks" (p. 112). Again in the concluding chapter (*Reconsidering a Legend*) Watts inexplicably insists on this by saying that "Cyril certainly did not want a conflict with Orestes"(p. 153), and even accuses Hypatia and Orestes of "forcing Cyril to unleash the [...] often incontrollable power of his ascetic and lay [?] supporters in the city" (pp. 153– 154).

On the mainly economic reasons for the anti-Jewish policies of Cyril, that is the battle for the monopoly of the shipping of grain to Constantinople, granted to the Jewish community (*Codex Theodosianus* 13, 5, 18 [18 February 390], p. 752 Mommsen–Meyer), but also to the Christian Church of Alexandria, see below: "Aftershock: And What If..."; TAKÁCS 1995, pp. 57–58.

The quotation from Socrates (VII 13, 18) on Orestes' indignation and suffering, following the pogrom, can be read on p. 359, 12–14 Hansen. The prefect's anger was augmented by the impossibility of acting against Cyril and his *parabalani*, clerics to all intents, in the courts, since on the basis of the Theodosian constitution of February 4 384 members of the clergy could only be judged by the ecclesiastical tribunal.

For the reference to Orestes' Christianity in the version of John of Nikiu, according to which it was Hypatia's magic that led him to stop going to mass "as was previously his habit", see above, chapter "The Bishop of Nikiu"; below, part III, chapter "Synesius, Hypatia and *Philosophia*".

The quotation on the defence of State secularism by the Christian Orestes is taken from GIORELLO, p. 104, a book that dedicates to Hypatia a brief chapter "Contro la scienza e la bellezza" [Against Science and Beauty], pp. 101–104.

The assault on Orestes' procession is in SOCRATES VII 14, 2–5, p. 359, 26–33 Hansen (see HARICH-SCHWARZBAUER 2011, pp. 183–185), where we read that the men from Cyril's militia "came in a group of around five hundred from the monasteries and reached the city, they lay in wait to surprise the prefect as he passed in his open chariot. Gathering around him, they began to call him "sacrificer" and "Hellene" and to shout many other insults. He then, realising that the instigator was Cyril, proclaimed that he was a Christian and had been baptised by the bishop Atticus. But the monks took no notice of what he was saying to them and one of them, by the name of Ammonius, hit Orestes on the head with a stone".

That it was the mention of the name of Atticus that cost the prefect this attack, provoking the animosity of the monks towards the throne of Constantinople, is convincingly argued by ROUGÉ 1990, pp. 492–493.

Ammonius is called "a brutal and vandalic monk" by CANFORA 2010, p. 93.

On the death under torture of Ammonius, the dispatches to Constantinople and the disinformation elements contained in Cyril's counter-response, as well as on the common opinion of the moderate wing of the Christian citizens, see SOCRATES VII 14, 8–11, p. 360, 5–16 Hansen, where we read that Orestes, "responding publicly to his provocation with a process in accordance with the laws, drove the torture to the point at which he died. Not long after this he made these facts known to the rulers. But Cyril sent to the emperor the opposite version [...]. In any case, those who had good sense, even if they were Christians, did not approve of Cyril's intrigues. They knew, in fact, that Ammonius had been punished for his recklessness *and he had not died under torture to force him to deny Christ*. However, Cyril himself strove that the event should be soon forgotten under silence".

A semantic contraposition between *demos* (δῆμος) and *ochlos* (ὄχλος), similar to that between *laos* (λαός) and *plethos* (πλῆθος; see on this point also Rougé 1990, pp. 493–494), is to be found, with analogous ideological connotations, in the Christian martyrological texts: see Ronchey 1990, pp. 147–158.

Socrates Scholasticus' reflection on the further distancing of the moderate wing of Alexandrian Christians (οἱ σωφρονοῦντες) from the conduct of Cyril is found in VII 14, 10–11, p. 360, 12–15 Hansen. It is not possible to discuss here the complex issue of the social composition (namely of the ratio between the moderate and the fundamentalist parties) of the Christian population of Alexandria (nor it is necessary, as it has already been done: see Delia). Yet it seems rash to evaluate Cyril's policy as Watts does (Watts 2017, pp. 108–120), without considering the poor popularity that it has had since the beginning, just as it seems rash to assume that the predominance of the "popular" Christian component, in which Watts sees "the supporters of Cyril", determined the escalation of violence, that "most Alexandrians" were in conflict with "Hypatia's world of educated governors and civic elites" (p. 114), and that Hypatia's murder was the product of social conflict and not, as ancient sources suggest (*in primis* the Constantinopolitan Socrates), of the precise political conduct of one single leader.

The account of Cyril's audience before the prefect can be read in Socrates VII 13, 19–20, p. 359, 15–20 Hansen (see Harich-Schwarzbauer 2011, p. 184).

10 Mortal Envy

"It was precisely the prestige that she rightly enjoyed amongst her fellow citizens that decided Hypatia's fate"[56], notes Diderot, faithful glosser of the Byzantine encyclopaedist Suidas. It is at this point that Suidas, whose source here is undoubtedly Hesychius, attributes to Cyril, and not to the Christians in general, the *pthonos* (φθόνος) that was the root cause of the drama and that we have already seen denounced by Socrates Scholasticus ("Phthonos personified rose up in arms against her")[57]. *Pthonos* here is not used in the sense of collective "jealous zeal", but in the precise and direct sense of personal "envy".

It was "the envy of her exceptional knowledge"[58] and for the exceptional favour in which Orestes held her, that possessed Cyril: the fatal rivalry of the bishop towards the philosopher, therefore; and certainly also the natural jealousy of the cleric for a woman of the world; two categories that throughout history have nurtured reciprocal great loves, or great hates.

One day, we read in Suidas (whose source is here Damascius),

> [...] it happened that the bishop of the opposing sect, Cyril, while he was passing before the residence of Hypatia, saw a great crowd at her doors, *both men and horses*[59], some who entered, some who were leaving, yet others who were standing around, waiting. Having asked what this crowd was doing, and why there was such a turmoil around this house, he heard that this was the day on which Hypatia had visitors, that this was her house. Having heard this, Cyril was bitten in his soul: for this reason, he soon organised her assassination, the most heinous of all assassinations[60].

We are in the "fourth year of Cyril's episcopacy, the tenth of the consulate of Honorius, the sixth of Theodosius II, in the month of March", in the year 415 AD. Socrates writes that when the attack took place the monks' rage had been increased, irony of fate, by the "period of fasting". We are, in this bloody Alexandrian spring, in the period of intense spiritual and liturgical preparation of the Christian Lent.

Monks and *parabalani* met under the command of Peter the Reader, who was a cleric, as his name reveals, and together they conceived, writes Socrates Scholasticus, "a secret plot". Suidas tells us, with Damascius, that

> [...] a multitude of enraged men suddenly attacked Hypatia one day as she, as usual, returned home from one of her public appearances[61].

---

[56] DIDEROT; see above "Once there was a Woman" and esp. below "The Glory of Her Own Sex and the Wonder of Ours".
[57] SOCRATES VII 15, 4, p. 360, 28 Hansen (HARICH-SCHWARZBAUER 2011, p. 188).
[58] HESYCHIUS = SUIDAS Y 166, IV, p. 644, 7 Adler (HARICH-SCHWARZBAUER 2011, p. 324).
[59] HOMER, *Il.* XXI 26.
[60] DAMASCIUS, *Vita Isidori* fr. *104, p. 79, 18–25 Zintzen = fr. 43E, p. 130, 9–17 Athanassiadi = SUIDAS Y 166, IV, p. 645, 4–12 Adler (HARICH-SCHWARZBAUER 2011, p. 247).
[61] *Ibid.*

Theon's daughter was pulled from her carriage and dragged, says Socrates, "to the church that takes its name from the Caesar emperor", that is the Caesareum, recently transformed into a Christian church. Here,

> [...] indifferent to the *vengeance by the gods and men*[62] these wretches massacred the philosopher,

denounces the Pagan Damascius, adding

> [...] and while she was still breathing, they put out her eyes[63].

And the Christian Socrates:

> They stripped her of her garments, they massacred her using sharp tiles (*ostraka*, ὄστρακα), and they tore her to shreds. Then they transported these remains to the place called Cinaron and there they fed her to the flames[64].

In the epitome that the Byzantine Photius gives of the *Church History* by another Christian author, Philostorgius, who openly sided with Arianism and was therefore hostile to Cyril, but also an ancient and privileged witness to the facts, we read:

> The woman was ripped to pieces by those who professed consubstantiality[65],

and that is, by the hand of the supporters of the theological doctrine, antithetical to the Arian doctrine, which had dominated in Alexandria from the time of Athanasius – the great enemy of Arius, who had been excommunicated by the Council of Nicaea in 325 at Athanasius' prompting – and continued with Theophilus and Cyril. For Philostorgius, therefore, the assassination was not the work of "an amorphous band of fanatics" but directly of that clergy, headed by Cyril, who in Alexandria, as has been written, "dominated both the Church and the streets"[66].

The fact that responsibility is certainly to be laid at the feet of Cyril is also indicated by a historian from the times of Justinian, the Antiochian John Malalas, who writes in his *Chronicle:*

---

[62] HOMER, *Il.* XVI 388 and *Od.* XXII 40.
[63] DAMASCIUS, *Vita Isidori* fr. *105, p. 81,3–6 Zintzen = fr. 43E, p. 130, 20–21 Athanassiadi = SUIDAS Y 579 s.v. ὑποσπαιρούσης, IV, p. 676, 1 Adler.
[64] SOCRATES VII 15, 5, p. 361, 4–6 Hansen (HARICH-SCHWARZBAUER 2011, p. 188).
[65] PHILOSTORGIUS 8, 9, p. 111, 3–8 Bidez = 8,9, pp. 366, 5–368, 2 Bleckmann-Stein (HARICH-SCHWARZBAUER 2011, p. 318).
[66] CANFORA 2010, p. 100.

> Having received licence from their bishop, the Alexandrians attacked and burned Hypatia, the famous philosopher, on a pyre of faggots[67].

According to Hesychius, quoted by Suidas:

> She was ripped apart by [Christian] Alexandrians, and parts of her mutilated body were scattered through the city, and she suffered this fate for envy (*phthonos*, φθόνος) of her extraordinary wisdom, but above all for hostility against her astronomic knowledge[68].

The Pagan Damascius calls the killing

> [...] an enormous stain, an abomination for their city[69].

Also for the Christian Socrates it was

> [...] no little infamy, this carried out by Cyril and by the Church of Alexandria, since assassinations and insurgences and similar things are wholly extraneous to the spirit of Christ[70].

The account given by John of Nikiu, clearly siding with Cyril in an almost confrontational manner, is quite different. The Coptic version shows that it considers the physical elimination of Hypatia not only an understandable retaliation for the killing of Ammonius, as clearly presented also by Socrates, but even a legitimate execution, a point of pride for the "faithful" who carried it out. While Peter is not only a *lector*, but also a magistrate and a perfect servant of Christ, the meeting between the executioners and the predestined victim, guilty of "mesmerising her students with magic" and exercising the "satanic" science of the celestial bodies, is not casual, nor did it occur in the clandestinity of a street attack, but rather at the house where Hypatia taught: symbolically it was from the cathedra, not from a carriage, that Hypatia was dragged[71].

---

[67] MALALAS XIV 12, p. 280, 68–70 Thurn; English transl. pp. 195–196 Jeffreys – Jeffreys – Scott (HARICH-SCHWARZBAUER 2011, p. 336).
[68] HESYCHIUS = SUIDAS Y 166, IV, p. 644, 5–8 Adler (HARICH-SCHWARZBAUER 2011, p. 324); see also PHILOSTORGIUS 8, 9a, 1–5, p. 368 Bleckmann-Stein.
[69] DAMASCIUS, *Vita Isidori* fr. *105, p. 81,7 Zintzen = fr. 43E, p. 130, 21–22 Athanassiadi = SUIDAS Y 166, IV, p. 645, 15–16 Adler (HARICH-SCHWARZBAUER 2011, p. 248).
[70] SOCRATES VII 15, 6, p. 361, 6–9 Hansen (HARICH-SCHWARZBAUER 2011, pp. 188–189).
[71] JOANNES DE NIKIU LXXXIV parr. 100–103, p. 102 Charles.

Appendix
Mortal Envy

The initial quotation is taken from DIDEROT, s.v. *Éclectisme*, see above, chapter "Once there was a Woman" and above all below, part II, chapter "The Glory of Her Sex and the Wonder of Ours".

An account of Cyril's fit of "envy" before Hypatia's home can be read in Suidas, who draws here from both Hesychius (HESYCHIUS= SUIDAS Y 166, IV, p. 644, 7 Adler = HARICH-SCHWARZBAUER 2011, p. 324), using, as Socrates, the word *phthonos* (φθόνος), and from Damascius (Damascius, *Vita Isidori* fr. *104, p. 79,24 Zintzen = fr. 43E, p. 130, 9–17 Athanassiadi = SUIDAS Y 166, IV, p. 645, 11 Adler (HARICH-SCHWARZBAUER 2011, p. 247), according to whom Cyril "was bitten in his soul" (δηχθῆναι τὴν ψυχήν).

Possibly following CAMERON 2016c, pp. 200–203 (cf. above, chapter "Treacherous Zeal", Appendix *ad loc.*), WATTS 2017 does not put too much weight on Cyril's φθόνος, which he mentions only once, almost incidentally, while referring to Hesychius' account found in Suidas ("A Pagan source tells us that Cyril soon grew jealous of the crowds who flocked to Hypatia's house and the influence she appeared to wield in the city", p. 113). Watts does not mention that the theme of φθόνος is found, as we have seen above (chapter "Treacherous Zeal" and Appendix *ad loc.*), in the main Christian narrative of Hypatia's murder, namely Socrates' *Ecclesiastical History* ("a personified Phthonos raised arms against her"), and opts out of discussing the other witnesses (among whom is Damascius, as we have just seen) to what has been considered, in the scholarship on Hypatia, a personal and possibly genuine misogynistic hostility of the bishop towards Hypatia.

On the fact that Suidas is the name of a person and denotes the author of the homonymous encyclopaedia of the 10th century, see above, chapter "Once there was a Woman", Appendix *ad loc.*

In describing the throng before the doors Damascius uses the words of Homer (*Iliad* XXI 26); and another Homeric formula (*Iliad* XVI 388 and *Odyssey* XXII 40) is used by Damascius later when he describes the monks' violence against Hypatia (both in italics in the text).

As Pierre Chuvin acutely noted, the term *othismos* (ὠθισμός), with which Damascius indicates the "throng" at the door to the private residence of Hypatia, awaiting her "appearance" (previously indicated by the technical term *proodos*, πρόοδος, which has a well attested ceremonial connotation), is linked to the flocking to await a solemn audience and a sacral appearance, such as, for example, that of Minos in the passages from Lucian of Samosata reported by CHUVIN–TARDIEU, pp. 61–62. This official and ceremonial character is confirmed by the description of the death, where Damascius uses the same term to denote the "official occasion" from which Hypatia is returning (προελθούση, to be connected to ποιουμένη τὰς προόδους) and John of Nikiu describes her as "seated on the cathedra" (see below). On the nature of the "private" (ἰδίᾳ) gatherings in Hypatia's house see below, part III, chapter "The Power of Hypatia" and Appendix *ad loc.*

According to Chuvin, the house was not situated in the centre of the city, where the philosopher went by carriage to hold her lessons in public, but "in the suburbs", that is a relatively distant residential area: CHUVIN–TARDIEU, p. 65. Hence – we can add – the delay in Cyril's discovery, not only of her address, but also of Hypatia's eminent role, and the suddenness of his attack of *phthonos*.

That the narrative of the sources on Cyril's attack of "envy" is not "a naïve fable" as in DZIELSKA 1995, p. 98, whose underestimation is later picked up by WATTS 2017, p. 113, is shown by both the precision and the agreement of the sources on this point, as also shown below, part III, chapter "The Power of Hypatia" and Appendix *ad loc.*

Socrates' later testimony (VII 15, 7) on the aggression of the monks sharpened by fasting can be read on p. 361 Hansen. In 415 Easter fell on April 11th and Holy Thursday on April 8th: therefore, the forty days of fasting had already begun at the end of February.

A different and unreliable dating of Hypatia's murder has recently been suggested by the astronomer Ari Belenkiy (BELENKIY 2010; BELENKIY 2016), according to whom Hypatia's murder was the result "of her involvement in the conflict between the Roman and Alexandrian Churches regarding the date of Easter in the year 417 and would have been committed therefore in March 416, after she had performed controversial astronomical observations that supported the Roman date over the Alexandrian one". According to Belenkiy, Hypatia became "a victim of a political cataclysm stemming from disagreement within the Roman empire on the date of Easter in AD 417, after she provided critical expertise in astronomy relating to the vernal equinox. Atmospheric refraction, a phenomenon unknown to Hypatia, could have led her to conclude that the equinox fell on 16 March, the date agreeable to the Roman Church, rather than on 21 March, the date championed by Alexandria. Her position could have threatened the Alexandrian Church's established authority in the matter of dating Easters for the whole of the Roman empire". Belenkiy argues that "this political threat led a Christian mob to kill her. As a corollary, this argument tips the scale in favour of year 416 for her date of death, rather than 415 as the majority hold". In addition, Belenkiy suggests that she died on 21 March and proposes instituting a memorial day for Hypatia on the day of the vernal equinox.

Belenkiy's bizarre theories do not find confirmation in any ancient sources. Moreover, considering Hypatia's personality and interests, it seems utterly improbable that she would have dealt with the calculation of the date of Easter or that she would have argued about such a topic with Christian ecclesiastical authorities.

Of Peter the Reader we know little, except that, according to Socrates, he held the position of *anagnostes* in the patriarchal church, the Caesareum: he was therefore a low-ranking ecclesiastical official (John of Nikiu calls him a "presbyter") and certainly not illiterate. His violent character and, above all, his impunity are emphasised by DIDEROT discussing BRUCKER's *Historia critica*.

On the location of the crime, the Caesareum in Alexandria, see MARTIN; HAAS 1997, pp. 280–295; MCKENZIE, pp. 77–78. It was the child emperor who had "the great church of Alexandria, which is still known as the church of Theodosius" built, as mentioned above (chapter "The Destruction of the Serapeum" and Appendix *ad loc.*), and as John Malalas informs us in his chronicle of the Justinian era: MALALAS XIV 11, pp. 279, 65–280, 67 Thorn; English translation p. 195 Jeffreys – Jeffreys – Scott.

The fragment from Damascius according to which Hypatia's eyes were put out when she "was still slightly breathing" is taken from SUIDAS, not under the item *Hypatia*, but further on, s.v. *hypospairouses* (ὑποσπαιρούσης), SUIDAS Y 579, IV, p. 676, 1 Adler: see DAMASCIUS, *Vita Isidori* fr. *105, p. 81,3–6 Zintzen = fr. 43E, p. 130, 20–21 Athanassiadi.

On the location of the Cinaron, or Kinaron, there is no certainty: see *in primis* HOCHE, n. 106.

The Photian summary of the *Church History* by Philostorgius can be read in PHILOSTORGIUS, p. 111, 3–8 Bidez. The passage in question is 8, 9, pp. 366, 5–368, 2 Bleckmann-Stein (HARICH-SCHWARZBAUER 2011, p. 318): "The heinous (*dyssebes*, δυσσεβής) [i.e., Philostorgius] says that under the reign of Theodosius the Younger the woman was massacred by the hand of those who professed consubstantiality."

Philostorgius' precise attribution of Hypatia's murder to the Alexandrian clergy is discussed in CANFORA 2010, p. 100 (from which the quotation has been taken). Canfora, in another of his writings on Hypatia, clearly summarises the events, which follow a universal political scheme: "The implicit instigation to act consisted of letting it be understood that Hypatia, with her influence over Orestes, constituted the only impediment to the reconciliation between the bishop and the prefect. From there, it was but a short step: to eliminate the obstacle. There was no lack, and Cyril well knew it, of fanatics ready to act, zealous interpreters of a will that desired nothing more than to be interpreted and put into practice" (CANFORA 2000, p. 196).

For the testimony on the death of Hypatia given by John Malalas see MALALAS XIV 12, p. 280, 68–70 Thurn; English translation pp. 195–196 Jeffreys – Jeffreys – Scott (HARICH-SCHWARZBAUER 2011, p. 336). On the value, here, of the Greek term *parrhesia* (παρρησία), similar to that certified in Justinian's *Novellae*, and on the importance of what Malalas testifies with that word see CANFORA 2010, p. 100; this is already the translation by PASCAL, p. 172. The exact meaning of the verb *authenteo* (αὐθεντέω) is clarified by Ludwig Dindorf, editor of Malalas in the *Corpus Bonnense* (MALALAS Dindorf), in the additions to the *Thesaurus Graecae Linguae* (II 2448 A): "Caedem propria manu perpetro", with other examples taken from Malalas.

The statements on the assassination by Hesychius of Miletus (the initial part of the item *Hypatia* is attributed to this source by Ada Adler, while others attribute the phrase in question to Damascius) can be read in SUIDAS Y 166, IV, p. 644, 5–8 (HARICH-SCHWARZBAUER 2011, p. 324); see also PHILOSTORGIUS 8, 9a, 1–5, p. 368 Bleckmann-Stein.

In disapproving the lynching, Damascius (in DAMASCIUS, *Vita Isidori* fr. *105, p. 81,7 Zintzen = fr. 43E, p. 130, 21–22 Athanassiadi = SUIDAS Y 166, IV, p. 645, 15 Adler [HARICH-

SCHWARZBAUER 2011, p. 248]) uses the ancient ritual terms *agos* (ἄγος, "stain") and *oneidos* (ὄνειδος, which we translate as "abomination").

Socrates uses the term *momos* (μῶμος), which in Greek also means, literally, "blame", "dishonour", "stain", and which we translate as "infamy": on this translation see lastly CANFORA 2010, p. 94.

Paradoxically, and unacceptably, WATTS 2017, pp. 114–117, exonerates the Alexandrian clergy from any responsibility. According to Watts, the murder of Hypatia was not wanted by the Christian bishop ("No source claims that Cyril ordered the attack on Hypatia", p. 117) nor by Peter the Reader, who guides the *parabalani* to her massacre: "It is unlikely that Peter and his band set out with the intention to kill Hypatia [...] Peter and his band of supporters probably set out to frighten Hypatia [...] Perhaps they intended to have a noisy demonstration outside of the walls of her townhouse. Maybe they were even angry enough that they wanted to burn her house down. It is hard to imagine, however, that they went out intending to kill" (p. 115). This interpretation does not seem to take into account the sources according to which, as we have seen, not only does the murder, in its bloody, precise, and ritualistic conception, appear all but accidental, but Cyril himself, and not just Peter the Reader, is unanimously charged (or, as in the case of John of Nikiu, accredited with) the murder of Hypatia. This should be no surprise. Hypatia's murder was political and Cyril was, at that time, the undisputed strategist of Alexandrian ecclesiastical policy. Nonetheless, according to Watts, the agreement of the sources only indicates that the bishop "was ultimately responsible for creating the climate that caused it". This is quite an interpretive leap. Socrates talks about an "infamy *enacted* by" Cyril, while Malalas (who, as we have seen, draws on a different ancient lost source) states that Peter and his followers had "been granted permission by their bishop" (MALALAS XIV 12, p. 280, 68–70 Thurn; English translation pp. 195–196 Jeffreys – Jeffreys – Scott [HARICH-SCHWARZBAUER 2011, p. 336]). It is also Cyril who, according to John of Nikiu, is accredited with the approval of that Christian "popular" wing which Watts identifies with the "supporters of Cyril" (p. 114).

The precise narrative design that both Pagan and Christian sources, in particular Socrates and Damascius, give to the dynamics of the murder seems to show precise ritualistic actions. As we will see later, part II, chapter "From Fielding to Gibbon Passing Through the Shadow of a Donkey", and above all part III, chapter "Hypatia's Sacrifice" and Appendix *ad loc.*, the death of Hypatia embodies the precise modalities of capital punishment, not those of an incidental lynching. Damascius describes Hypatia's killers as οἱ σφαγεῖς, "the slaughterers", "the sacrificers", while Christian authors such as Socrates and Philostorgius (8, 9, p. 111, 3–8 Bidez = 8, 9, pp. 366, 5–368, 2 Bleckmann-Stein [HARICH-SCHWARZBAUER 2011, p. 318]), use the verb διασπάω, "to tear asunder", a technical term to describe the ritual slaughtering of the victim, namely the punishment imposed on prostitutes and those guilty of witchcraft and magic.

It is possible that Hypatia was literally torn apart, if not dismembered in sacrificial fashion: eviscerated, with the heart pulled out (see again part III, chapter "Hypatia's Sacrifice" and Appendix *ad loc.*). Considering John of Nikiu's account (JOANNES DE

NIKIU LXXXIV, par. 102, p. 102 Charles), it is also possible that Hypatia's exemplary punishment described by the sources echoes the one imposed on the statue of Serapis at the moment of the destruction of the Serapeum under the oversight of Theophilus. As underscored by WATTS 2017, p. 116, "the statue was dismembered, the pieces dragged throughout the city, and the remains burned". In highlighting the analogy found in John's *Chronicle*, Watts refuses to make explicit what the chronicle suggests, namely that Hypatia's murder was not an accident, but a capital punishment devised from the beginning as ritual.

The interpretation of the passage of John of Nikiu that describes the place of the ambush in which Hypatia died does not seem to leave room for doubt: "And when they learnt the place where she was, they proceeded to her and found her seated on a (lofty) chair; and having made her descend they dragged her along till they brought her to the great church, named Caesareum"; so we read in JOANNES DE NIKIU LXXXIV par. 101, p. 102 Charles – unless there are problems arising not from the modern translation but from the successive manuscript versions, and the mention of "cathedra" derives in fact from a misunderstanding of the word *diphros*, "carriage"; see also CHUVIN–TARDIEU, p. 62. According to WATTS 2017, p. 183, n. 40, the term used by John of Nikiu could mean not only "the *thronos* used by teachers in their classrooms", but also "a litter". In any case, the image of Hypatia surprised by her killers "sitting on a lofty chair" in her own home and not in the public place in which she held her official lessons, an image which may simply have been imagined by John of Nikiu or one of his sources, is still quite consistent with what we feel can be inferred from her esoteric teaching: see below, part III, chapter "The Power of Hypatia" and Appendix *ad loc.*

11 The Cover-Up

Therefore, apart from the brief indications given by Philostorgius, in the ancient Christian accounts that have come down to us we have two versions of the facts. The first, the *Ecclesiastical History* by Socrates, contemporary to the events, probably provides the official version of the Church of Constantinople; the other, the *Chronicle* of John of Nikiu, written at a later date, but unquestionably taken from ancient sources close to Cyril, clearly reflects not only the thesis but also the ideology of the Egyptian Church, which from Cyrillianism developed in antithesis to the Constantinopolitan orthodoxy. In the conclusion to his account, the chronicler declares triumphantly:

> The entire people surrounded Cyril and acclaimed him the "new Theophilus", because he had rid the city of the last dregs of idolatry[72].

For the Alexandrians the year 415, that of Hypatia's death, was the year 5096 since the creation of the world, the twelfth indiction, and the eighth year of reign in the East of a child emperor. Theodosius II was cared for by his older sister Pulcheria, who held the title of Augusta and was to all intents and purposes the empress, although at the time she was only fifteen years old. Hostile to the Pagans, Pulcheria was so devoted to Christianity in general, and in particular to its Alexandrian version, as to be defined by one historian "a purpled nun"[73]. She was also eventually made a saint.

The assassination of Hypatia thus remained unpunished, and the magistrate in charge of the case covered it up.

Damascius writes:

> The ire of the emperor would have fallen most violently on them [the Christian clergy of Alexandria] if Aedesius [...],

an imperial official sent by Constantinople or more probably the duke of Thebaid, the highest military official in the region,

> had not been corrupt, so that he saved the butchers from their punishment[74].

Pulcheria's devotion prevailed over Orestes' indignation, who, in exchange for his silence, obtained from the State he represented certain measures, which were, in any case, insufficient to stem the intrusion of the bishops into civil government.

The *parabalani* were limited in number, and from then onwards they were nominated or at least controlled by the *praefectus augustalis*. They were also forbidden ac-

---

72 JOANNES DE NIKIU LXXXIV par. 103, p. 102 Charles.
73 BIGONI, pp. 397–437; 495–526; 681–710.
74 DAMASCIUS, *Vita Isidori* fr. *105, p. 81, 8–9 Zintzen = fr. 43E, p. 130, 22–23 Athanassiadi = SUIDAS Y 166, IV, p. 645, 16–17 Adler (HARICH-SCHWARZBAUER 2011, p. 248).

cess to public places[75], as we are informed by the report sent to the court of Constantinople by the citizens' council of Alexandria, whose answer is preserved in the Theodosian Code[76]. The bishop Cyril was therefore absolved on the juridical plane, but not on the political plane.

For him to serve his historical sentence we must wait not so much for the year 451, when Monophysitism, the heresy nurtured by his doctrines, would be condemned by the Council of Chalcedon, as much as for the judgement of future generations, for whom the fortunes of the doctrine of Cyril will always be inversely proportional to the fortunes of Hypatia.

---

75 *Codex Theodosianus* 16, 2, 42–43, p. 850 Mommsen–Meyer.
76 *Ibid.*, 12, 12, 15, pp. 729–730 Mommsen–Meyer.

Appendix
The Cover-Up

A synopsis of the facts of the court and the empire in the year of Hypatia's death is given in MURALT, pp. 25–26.

The definiton of Pulcheria is taken from BIGONI, pp. 397–437; 495–526; 681–710.

Pulcheria is still venerated as a saint by both the Catholic Church and the Orthodox Church. Her feast day is September 10th; on her personage see also DIEHL, pp. 29–34.

The testimony of Damascius on the corruption of Aedesius can be read in SUIDAS Y 166: DAMASCIUS, *Vita Isidori* fr. *105, p. 81,8 Zintzen = fr. 43E, p. 130, 22–23 Athanassiadi (HARICH-SCHWARZBAUER 2011, p. 247).

On Aedesius see TANNERY 1880, pp. 78–79, according to whom the name, altered by a textual error, in fact indicates Anthemius (a powerful minister of Theodosius II and previously the prefect of the East). The theory that he was in fact an emissary sent by the court of Constantinople is proposed by ZINTZEN in DAMASCIUS, p. 81 Zintzen. Nevertheless, as recently mentioned by ZUCKERMAN (cap. III: *Le comte Aidesios et les meurtriers d'Hypatia*), it was not the task of the Constantinopolitan authorities to commence legal proceedings, but that of the local authorities, in their twofold role of highest civil official, as the Augustal prefect, i.e. Orestes (although "visiblement dépassé par les événements"), and highest military rank, as the *dux Aegypti*. In addition to discussing the (not obvious) *constitutio textus* of Damascius' passage, Zuckermann presents the new and credible theory that the official charged with the inquiry and corrupted by Cyril was the same *comes* Aedesius officially found in the *praetorium* of Hermoupolis or of Antinoupolis in Thebaid and mentioned in a letter by Shenoute, the notorious hegumen of the White Monastery (historical ally, we add, of Cyril, who later accompanied him to the Council of Ephesus in 431). It had already been suggested that the high-ranking Egyptian official must have held the post of duke of Thebaid: see MARTINDALE, p. 11, s.v. *Aidesius* 5.

Inexplicably DZIELSKA 1995, p. 94, believes that after the events Orestes was removed from his post as prefect, or that he resigned; we have no evidence to support this. We read in *Codex Theodosianus* 16, 2, 42–43, p. 850 Mommsen–Meyer, the edict of 29 September 416, with which Theodosius ordered the reduction of the number of *parabalani* (παραβαλανεῖς) and forbade them from entering public places, and in particular the meetings of the city council and the courts: see ROUGÉ 1990, p. 501; ROUGÉ 1987, p. 346. That this measure alone shows that Cyril's guilt was taken for granted at the imperial court, at the time of the events, despite the cover-up that the bishop organised at local level by corrupting Aedesius, is rightly sustained by KLEIN, although BEERS, pp. 79–81, argues that the restrictive measures against the *parabalani* were merely fiscal in nature. At any rate, the fact that Cyril later managed to increase the number of *parabalani* from five hundred to six hundred and to take control of their nominations does not change – rather it confirms – the punitive nature of the ruling.

The other elements of the imperial response in the report sent to the court of Constantinople by the *boule* of Alexandria can be read in *Codex Theodosianus* 12, 12, 15 (5 October 416), pp. 729–730 Mommsen–Meyer.

Part II: **Betraying the Facts**

> What elation of heart and spirit! Where can we find a martyr
> with the same austere charm as Hypatia?
> ERNEST RENAN

> Wilt thou yet take all, Galilean? but these thou shalt not take,
> The laurel, the palms and the pæan, the breasts of the nymphs in the brake.
> ALGERNON CHARLES SWINBURNE

12 The Glory of Her Own Sex and the Wonder of Ours

"We would deserve the rightful reproofs of that part of humanity we most fear to disappoint, if we allowed the name of the famous and most unfortunate Hypatia to pass unmentioned," wrote Diderot in his entry *Éclectisme* in the *Encyclopédie*[77]. The parable of the assassination of Hypatia is presented there in terms that are absolutely correct, being taken with full understanding of Greek from the work of Suidas, the 10th century Byzantine encyclopaedist, whom the 18th century encyclopaedist seems to reflect.

Regarding Cyril of Alexandria, his opinion is clear. "At the time, the patriarchal throne of Alexandria was occupied by an imperious and violent man, [who] seethed with resentment at being outclassed" by Roman power. "Hypatia," continues Diderot placidly, "became his target: the patriarch could not forgive her the close bonds with the prefect, nor probably the respect that the establishment showed her." Consequently, Cyril, "driven by a malicious zeal for his religion, or rather the excruciating impulse to increase his authority in Alexandria," did not scruple to "encourage people with a natural propensity for revolt."

At this point, after envy, it was another of the great human passions that betrayed Hypatia: servility; in the person of

> [...] a certain Peter, reader at the church of Alexandria, undoubtedly one of those squalid servants that unfortunately always surround the powerful and wait impatiently to joyfully seize the opportunity to commit some major crime in order to gratify their superior.

Peter was a zealot, but in this case, the zeal that possessed him was above all to serve his patron, and that is what drove him to "incite a horde of miscreants" and set himself at their head. The mob of fanatical monks "awaited Hypatia on the threshold of her home, threw themselves on her as she was about to enter, seized her, dragged her to the church called Caesareum, stripped her, slit her throat, dismembered her and burnt her".

Although he clearly knows the Christian sources well, Diderot reports the versions of the two Pagan ones, Hesychius and Damascius. Nevertheless, this ex-pupil of the Jesuits does not disdain a jibe:

> Providence was so concentrated on shaping this woman that we could accuse it of being distracted when the time came to save her, if many experiences had not taught us to respect the profound inscrutability of its intents.

Apart from this sarcasm, minimal for an Enlightenment figure, Diderot's conscientiousness is undeniable, but only in the narration of the facts concerning the death of Hy-

---

77 DIDEROT.

patia. In the way of thinking of the French Enlightenment the inclusion of Neoplatonists within the ranks of Eclectic Philosophers does not come as a surprise. Yet, in this case, one could argue that this forced merging reveals a transference between the 18th century *philosophes* and the 'Alexandrian philosophers' of the 5th century – a century which appears to be absolved of any stereotype of decadence by Diderot, and in which he senses the upcoming of that new era of intellectual battles that would characterise the Byzantine empire. An empire in which precisely the presence of Christianity as the State religion would give rise to a subterranean crystallisation of heterodox and dissident philosophical thinking; which in turn was the root of the series of renaissances that marked the Byzantine millennium, and which would culminate in the Western European Renaissance. Now, 5th century Alexandria, as has been said, "was for the Roman world what 15th century Constantinople would be for Western Europe: the initiator of a new era"[78].

The vibrant entry *Éclectisme* in the *Encyclopédie* is a self-portrait of Diderot and his generation, and for this reason would be the object of an almost immediate offensive against the 'New Platonists', the Enlightenment thinkers. However, it also marks the daring metamorphosis in which the figure of Hypatia begins to stand out against the horizon of the Enlightment: the Platonic philosopher par excellence was honourably transformed into an Eclectic so that she would be better adapted to the role of patron of the Enlightenment. A role that the entry in the *Encyclopédie* inaugurated, making "Hypatia, the glory of her own sex and the wonder of ours", the first icon of secularism.

---

[78] Takács 1995, p. 48.

Appendix
Betraying the Facts

The first quotation in *exergo* is taken from RENAN ("Quels hommes qu'Ammonius, Plotin, Proclus, Isidore! Quelle élévation de cœur et d'esprit! Où trouver une martyre qui par son charme austère égale Hypatie?"); English transl. RENAN 2012, p. 28.

The second quotation in *exergo* is taken from SWINBURNE, *Hymn to Proserpine (After the Proclamation in Rome of the Christian Faith)*, vv. 23–24 (SWINBURNE, p. 78): "Wilt thou yet take all, Galilean? but these thou shalt not take, / The laurel, the palms and the pæan, the breasts of the nymphs in the brake; / Breasts more soft than a dove's, that tremble with tenderer breath; / And all the wings of the Loves, and all the joy before death; / All the feet of the hours that sound as a single lyre, / Dropped and deep in the flowers, with strings that flicker like fire. / More than these wilt thou give, things fairer than all these things? / Nay, for a little we live, and life hath mutable wings. / A little while and we die; shall life not thrive as it may? / For no man under the sky lives twice, outliving his day. / And grief is a grievous thing, and a man hath enough of his tears: / Why should he labour, and bring fresh grief to blacken his years? / Thou hast conquered, O pale Galilean; the world has grown grey from thy breath; / We have drunken of things Lethean, and fed on the fullness of death". The short poem, in whose *exergo* we find the phrase "Vicisti, Galilaee", is imagined to be uttered by the emperor Julian.

The Glory of Her Own Sex and the Wonder of Ours

The entry *Éclectisme*, as previously mentioned, is to be found in the fifth volume of *Encyclopédie* 1755 (see DIDEROT).

The definition of Eclecticism, attributed to the phase of ancient thinking that ranges from the death of Aristotle to the last Neoplatonists, can be found in the first modern history of philosophy, that of J. J. BRUCKER, *Historia critica philosophiae* (1742); however, Hypatia's philosophy was already classified as "Eclectic", for example, in the renowned and widely-read *Histoire ecclésiastique* by C. FLEURY (1722–1738), and would continue to be so in LIGIER, as found by GAJERI, p. 76, nn. 75 and 76.

For the identification of Enlightenment thinking with Eclecticism see DIDEROT: Eclecticism as "philosophie alexandrine" in the ancient world "finit à la mort d'Hypatie", but in fact it spread into modernity, coinciding not only with the "route tracée" of the "progrès des connoissances humaines", but with its infusion, from a strictly philosophical plane, into "all the dominions of human activity", according to the effective synthesis of GAJERI, p. 65; see now MERELLO, pp. 103–104.

The quotation, in which 5th-century Alexandria is compared to 15th-century Constantinople, is taken from TAKÁCS 1995, p. 48.

Two ponderous tomes were dedicated to refuting columns *a* and *b* of page 282 of the *Enciclopédie*, written by G. MALEVILLE, *Histoire critique de l'Éclectisme, ou de Nouveaux Platoniciens* (1766). As Voltaire wrote, just a little later: "Un homme, dont les intentions sont sans doute très bonnes, a fait imprimer deux volumes contre cet article de l'Encyclopédie. Encore une fois, mes amis, deux tomes contre deux pages, c'est trop. Je vous l'ai dit cent fois, vous multipliez trop les êtres sans nécessité. Deux lignes contre deux tomes, voilà ce qu'il faut. N'écrivez pas même ces deux lignes", VOLTAIRE 1772, p. 139 (= 1860, p. 586 = 2011, pp. 193–194).

In the *Préface* of the Cronk-Mervaud edition of the *Questions sur l'Encyclopédie* we can read that the entry on "Hipathie" was in effect written as a response to Maleville and his refutation of Cyril's involvement in Hypatia's murder. Such involvement had been confirmed by Diderot on the basis of ancient sources. In the *Préface* we can also read how Diderot came to know of Hypatia through the above mentioned *Histoire Ecclésiastique* by Fleury, which in Diderot's personal copy carries the note "Hyppatie" (Book 23, chapter 25). See MERELLO, p. 104, n. 3.

The first scholarly study dedicated to Hypatia dates from the previous century (17th): Johann Christoph KIESEWETTER, *Hipparchum Theonas, doctamque Hypatiam, in Mathesi celebres. Dissertatione Historico-Mathematica (...) exhibet (...)* (1689) (on which see below, chapter "A Very Beautiful and Well-educated Woman is Torn Asunder") followed by the review of FABRICIUS (1717) (on which see below, chapter "Refreshing Exceptions"), and then the dissertations of WERNSDORF (1747–1748) (on which see below, chapters "A Very Beautiful and Well-educated Woman is Torn Asunder" and "Refreshing Exceptions" with Appendix *ad loc.*) More robust is the thread of 19th-century studies, inaugurated by the essay by HOCHE and continued with ST. WOLF, *Hypatia die Philosophin von Alexandrien: ihr Leben, Wirken und Lebensende nach den Quelleschriften dargestellt* (1879); H. LIGIER, *De Hypatia philosopha et eclecticismi Alexandrini fine* (Thèse de Doctorat, Dijon, 1879); MEYER, *Hypatia von Alexandria: ein Beitrag zur Geschichte des Neuplatonismus* (1886).

13 The Excesses of Fanaticism

> Let us suppose that Madame Dacier was the most beautiful woman in Paris and that in the *querelle* between the ancients and the moderns the Carmelites insisted that the poem on Mary Magdalene, composed by one of them, was infinitely superior to Homer, and that it was an atrocious impiety to prefer the *Iliad* to the verses of a monk. Let us imagine that the archbishop of Paris had taken the part of the Carmelites against the governor of the city, partisan of the beautiful Madame Dacier, and had driven the Carmelites to massacre this comely lady in the church of Notre Dame and to drag her naked and bleeding to Place Maubert. Now, no one would have been able to deny that the archbishop of Paris had committed a terrible action, for which he should do penitence. This is precisely the story of Hypatia.

So writes Voltaire in his *Dictionnaire philosophique,* later integrated in the *Questions sur l'Encyclopédie*[79]. Gilles Ménage, one of the most important exponents of 'erudite libertinage' of the 17th century, had dedicated his *History of Women Philosophers* to Anne Dacier, the great Huguenot classicist, certainly not "the most beautiful woman in Paris". The work contained an entire chapter on Hypatia, introducing testimonies against Cyril that had emerged in the France of the absolute monarchy for the first time since the end of Byzantine autocracy. The complete collection of the ancient sources on Hypatia's assassination appeared a few decades later, in *Mulierum Graecarum, quae oratione prosa usae sunt, fragmenta et elogia,* the work of the Protestant Johann Christian Wolf[80].

Voltaire, who was writing not long after Wolf, added a final thrust against Cyril to his writing:

> I will simply note that Saint Cyril was a man, and a Party man, who perhaps allowed himself to be carried away by zeal. That when one strips beautiful women naked, it is not for the purpose of massacring them. That Saint Cyril has undoubtedly asked God to pardon him for this abominable action, and that I pray to the Father of Mercy to have pity on his soul[81].

Later, in the *Histoire de l'établissement du Christianisme,* he included the death of Hypatia amongst the "excesses of fanaticism"[82]. It would be thanks to the quotations by Voltaire that the personages of Hypatia's drama entered French 18th century narrative, animating the premonitory theatrical work *Hypatie* by Olympe de Gouges – destined to be attacked by the Jacobins for her Proto-Feminism, although with less tragic consequences than those met by her heroine – and they would appear *en travesti* in *Don Carlos* by Schiller, and even in the youthful work of Giacomo Leopardi[83] and in the verses of Vincenzo Monti.

---

[79] VOLTAIRE, s.v. *Hipathie,* in *Dictionnaire philosophique* = VOLTAIRE 1772, pp. 138–139 = 1860, pp. 585–586 = 2011, pp. 192–193.
[80] WOLF 1735, pp. 72–91.
[81] VOLTAIRE, s.v. *Hipathie,* in *Dictionnaire philosophique* = VOLTAIRE 1772, pp. 139–140 = 1860, p. 586 = 2011, p. 194.
[82] VOLTAIRE 1777 = 1876, pp. 613 = 2014, pp. 509–512.
[83] LEOPARDI, p. 207.

13 The Excesses of Fanaticism

The *Fanaticism* to which Monti dedicates the first poem (*Il Fanatismo*) of his polemical triad, which is completed by *La superstizione* [*Superstition*][84] and *Il pericolo* [*Danger*][85], is that which prevents the triumph of reason and encourages the Church to meddle in the State's affairs. As Monti writes in the introduction of the edition published in Venice in the euphoria of the "year 1797, the first of Italian Freedom", the brief poem is intended to review all "that was most barbarous in the ecclesiastical annals and in the immense history of fanaticism."

"To those hypocrites, who despairing that they could not accuse the poet of falseness, accuse him of a lack of delicacy in revealing interminable scandals, that have dishonoured the religion and made abhorrent the history of the most holy and the most blessed", the ex-seminarian and ex-*protégé* of Cardinal Scipione Borghese in the Rome of the artistic patronage of Pope Pius VI, now the cantor of the Cisalpine Republic and a follower of the Jacobin and Napoleonic ideals, answered that, "in good morality, the first of all the crimes is betraying the truth, just as the first of all social duties is to propagate it".

For Monti the "Roman harlot", the Church, and her "husbands" are immersed in a

[...] mar di vizj immenso, ove le vele	[...] immense sea of vice, where thought
Perde il pensiero,	Loses its sails,
Oh colpe, che ripieno	Oh sins, their pockets are
Han di Sodoma il sacco e di Babele!	Filled with Sodoma and Babel!

Christian fanaticism is "a terrible monster":

Più che d'incenso, d'uman sangue è grato   More than incense, he welcomes human blood...

In the climax of the poem, Monti invokes "the innocent shadow of Hypatia", sacrificial victim of that fanaticism caught at its origins, so that she could bear witness to the events through the "centuries past" to the present day. The "narration" of her "slaughter at the altar" must make its "hideous cry" resound from Africa to Asia, as far as the Western world, until she receives a response:

La voce alzate, o secoli caduti,	Raise your voices, o centuries past,
Gridi l'Africa all'Asia e l'innocente	Cry out Africa to Asia, and may
Ombra d'Ipazia il grido orrendo aiuti.	The hideous cry rescue
Gridi irata l'Aurora all'Occidente,	The innocent shadow of Hypatia.
Narri le stragi dall'altare uscite,	Let the Aurora cry out wrathfully to the Western
E l'Occaso risponda all'Oriente.	world,
	Telling the story of her slaughter at the altar,
	And may the West respond to the East.

---

[84] Monti 1797a.
[85] Id. 1797b.

Appendix
The Excesses of Fanaticism

The first two passages from Voltaire are taken from the same chapter in Fr. M. Arouet de VOLTAIRE, *Questions sur l'Encyclopédie, par des Amateurs* (VOLTAIRE 1772, pp. 138–139 = 2011, pp. 193–194), which takes up and integrates his entry *Hipathie* of the *Dictionnaire philosophique* (VOLTAIRE 1860, pp. 585–586). Criticisms against Cyril can be read in two of his earlier works: *Examen important de Milord Bolingbroke ou le tombeau du fanatisme* (VOLTAIRE 1736); and *Lettre XIV. À M. Covelle, citoyen de Genève, par M. Baudinet* (VOLTAIRE 1765).

Voltaire entitled chapter XXIV of his *Histoire de l'établissement du Christianisme* (1776) *Excès du fanatisme*. This work, destined perhaps to be printed under an English pseudonym (see chapter XII: "Notre roi Jacques", etc.), was found amongst his papers and published posthumously, in the first edition of the *Oeuvres complètes*, [Kehl]: Société littéraire typographique, 1784–1785, where it is assigned the date 1777, a year later than the effective date of composition indicated by Beuchot. It can be more easily read in VOLTAIRE 1777 = 1876, pp. 582–616 (where the events in Alexandria are mentioned on p. 613) = 2014, pp. 381–524: 509–512.

Voltaire had also described – with some poetic licence – the story of Hypatia in his *Examen du discours de l'empereur Julien contre la secte des Galiléens* (VOLTAIRE 1768) (see GAJERI, p. 67 and notes *ad loc.*), and above all in his treatise, published under a pseudonym, *De la paix perpétuelle* (VOLTAIRE 1770, p. 124 = 2016, p. 139), where he paraphrases Suidas, or better Diderot, making the story more piquant with a few imaginary details. "Il y avait alors dans Alexandrie une fille nommée Hypatie, qu'on regardait comme un prodige de la nature [...] Mais elle était de l'ancienne religion égyptienne [...] Saint Cyrille envoie [...] Pierre à la tête des moines et des autres factieux à la maison d'Hypatie; ils brisent les portes; ils la cherchent dans tous les recoins où elle peût être cachée; ne la trouvant point ils mettent le feu à la maison. Elle s'échappe; on la saisit, on la traîne dans l'église nommée la Césarée, on la dépouille nue: les charmes de son corps attendrissent quelques-uns de ces tigres; mais les autres, considérant qu'elle ne croit pas en Jésus-Christ, l'assomment à coups de pierres, la déchirent et traînent son corps par la ville". See the ironic comment of ASMUS 1907, p. 27.

A discussion of Voltaire's interventions, but especially of Hypatia's fortune in the 1720s, can be found in WATTS 2020b; see also below, chapts. "A Very Beautiful and Well-educated Woman is Torn Asunder" and "Refreshing Exceptions", Appendices *ad loc.*

In the first section of the *Questions sur l'Encyclopédie* (VOLTAIRE 1772), Voltaire is alluding to the quarrel between Madame Dacier and La Motte: the treatise *Des causes de la corruption du goust* with which Anne Dacier had defended the "purity" of Homer (see below) was from 1714. See FOURNEL.

The dedication of Gilles Ménage to "Anna Fabra Daceria, feminarum quot sunt, quot fuere, doctissima" is on pages 4–5 of MENAGIUS, *Historia mulierum philosopharum* (English translation: MENAGIUS Zedler). In the chapter on Hypatia (pp. 52–63) the versions of her death are compared for the first time, according preference to that of Socrates Scholasticus; the translation by Grotius of Palladas' epigram is also given, see below, chapter "Celestial Virgin".

At the time Anne Dacier, the daughter of the powerful and learned classicist Tanneguy Le Fèvre, had not yet published her translation of the *Iliad* or her *Traité de la corruption du goust* against Houdart de La Motte, and she had just converted from Calvinism to Catholicism, in those times of anti-Huguenot persecution, although prior to the revocation of the Edict of Nantes. The struggle relating to the last great heresy of the modern world, in which Anne Dacier was personally involved, leads us, and probably led Ménage and her other admirers and interlocutors, to that which had taken place in Alexandria many centuries earlier.

Information about the ancient sources on the women philosophers is gathered and ordered in WOLF 1735, where pages 72–91 are dedicated to Hypatia.

In the 17th century the figure of Hypatia had already emerged, for the first time in the modern era, in *Faramond où l'Histoire de France* by Gautier de Costes de LA CALPRENÈDE, a monumental novel left incomplete due to the death of the author (tomes I–VII) and completed by Pierre d'Ortigue de VAUMORIÈRE (tomes VIII–XII), who edited the definitive edition in twelve volumes (Paris: Sommaville et al., 1664–1670). Hypatia is fleetingly mentioned in chapter 3 of volume IX, by the empress Athenais Eudocia, who asks for news "of Alexandria, of the beautiful Hypatia and the continual disputes of Orestes with the learned and pious Cyril". "If God wills" she is told "this unfortunate maiden, after many misfortunes, will finally find happiness. But [...] I wish for this good without hoping for it [...] for a person who is dear to me and who I see threatened by a horrible death." See ASMUS 1907, p. 19; GAJERI, pp. 46–47.

An epigone of Hypatia's fortunes in French 18th-century literature is the *Eudoxie* of François-Thomas-Marie de Baculard d'ARNAUD (see ARNAUD, pp. 184–187 and notes *ad loc.*).

For the knowledge of the writings of Voltaire in Friedrich Schiller, the opinions on Hypatia that he expresses in the *Letters* and the use of the *dramatis personae* of the ancient tragedy in projects of poetic and theatrical works and in *Don Carlos* (1784), see ASMUS 1907, pp. 28–29, where is also mentioned, as a follower of Schiller in this vein, Kuno von der KETTENBURG, author of *Julian the Apostate* (1812), in which the name and the personality of Hypatia are attributed to the wife of Maximus of Ephesus, the master and great friend of the emperor who tried to restore Paganism to Byzantium.

For the drama *Hypatie* by Olympe de Gouges see BLANC, p. 32.

A fleeting note on Hypatia, which in any case testifies to the knowledge of the personage and her role by the young Giacomo Leopardi, who refers to Ménage, can be read in G. LEOPARDI, *Storia della astronomia dalla sua origine fino all'anno MDCCCXII* [*History of Astronomy from its Origins to 1811*] (written in 1813), p. 207 (passage taken from chapter III, *Storia dell'Astronomia dalla nascita di Ptolomeo sino a quella di Copernico*): "Theon was the father of the famous Hypatia, and he taught and trained her. She improved in sciences so much, especially in astronomy, that she was considered the most learned person of her time. She wrote various treatises in mathematics, which unfortunately have been lost. She was barbarously torn to pieces, as she was considered to stand in the way of reconciliation between St. Cyril and Orestes, the governor of the city; or, as Hesychius of Miletus argues, because of the envy her knowledge of astronomy raised against her. This opinion is supported by M. de la Lande, who quotes Bouillaud, who in turn quoted Suidas and the aforementioned Hesychius. Synesius of Cyrene, her pupil and later ordained bishop, called her 'mother, sister, teacher' in philosophy, and his 'benefactress'. Hypatia wrote an *Astronomikon Kanona*, according to Menagius and Fabricius, who understands Suidas' passage about Hypatia's writings like this: *Ypomnema eis Diophanton*, Commentary to Diophantus, and *Astronomikon Kanona*, Astronomical Canon. While Kuster interprets Suidas: *Ypomnema eis Diophantou astronomikon kanona*, Commentary to the Astronomical Canon of Diophantus. But Fabricius says that Diophantus was never considered an astronomer. Yet it should be noted that there was an astronomer Diophantus. Synesius, bishop of Ptolemais, not Cyrene, as Photius wrote, was a disciple of Hypatia's".

All three poems by Vincenzo MONTI were first published in 1797: *Il fanatismo* and *La superstizione* in Venice: *Il Fanatismo e La Superstizione. Poemetti due del cittadino Vincenzo Monti ferrarese* (MONTI 1797a), and *Il pericolo* in Genoa: *Il pericolo. Canto del cittadino Vincenzo Monti ferrarese* (MONTI 1797b). They would be published together in the subsequent edition of 1798; on this topic see BIGONI.

Probably in the same mood as Monti, if not directly influenced by him, a 19th-century painter, Vincenzo La Bella, chose for his fresco in the new building destined to be the headquarters of the University of Naples "the harrowing and magnificent scene of the death of Hypatia in a temple, under the clubs and the daggers of the Nazarene sectarians." See AGABITI, p. 13.

14 A Very Beautiful and Well-educated Woman is Torn Asunder

Far from the Vatican, the posthumous cause of Hypatia had already aroused great interest in the world of the reformed intellectuals; above all in Germany, where the first modern historian to advocate it was, in the mid 16th century, the leading proponent of the most intransigently Lutheran historiography: Matthias Flacius Illyricus, the head of the Centuriators of Magdeburg, the humanist who thanks to his *rabies theologica* was even deposed from his university chair in Jena[86].

In his *Centuriae* the "perverse zeal" of the followers of Cyril was denounced for the first time. On the basis of recent printed editions of the sources – the *editio princeps* of the epistolary of Synesius prepared by Marcus Musurus[87], that of Socrates Scholasticus edited by Robert Estienne[88], and that of Suidas edited by Demetrius Chalcondylas[89] – the assassination of Hypatia perpetrated by "the Alexandrian clergy" was condemned as a "most atrocious" example of ecclesiastical nefariousness.

A century and a half later, the first work entirely dedicated to the defence of Hypatia saw the light of day, anticipating France and Italy, in Britain, where, in 1720, the "Freethinker" John Toland dedicated an essay to her entitled *Hypatia; or the History of a most beautiful, most virtuous, most learned and every way accomplish'd Lady; who was torn to Pieces by the clergy of Alexandria to gratify the Pride, Emulation, and Cruelty of their Archbishop Cyril, commonly but undeservedly stil'd Saint Cyril*[90].

Toland, a Catholic from Ulster who converted first to Protestantism and later to a "heretical" philosophical Deist position, had fled to London in the last years of the 17th century after the public burning in Dublin of his first work *Christianity not Mysterious*.

After publishing his *Letters to Serena*, which were even more polemical regarding Christian "superstitions", and other increasingly critical writings against the dogmas and the ecclesiastical institutions, in 1705 he had dedicated to the history of the early Church and the polemic against its secular government a work with limited circulation, that would be published only after his death, *The primitive Constitution of the Christian Church*. Later Toland converted to a peculiar sort of materialistic pantheism and in the even more clandestine and scandalous *Pantheisticon* he composed a patchwork of extracts from ancient Pagan writers mockingly based on the Anglican liturgical service.

The work on Hypatia was published two years before his death, in his *Tetradymus*, when Toland's Neopaganism was self-evident, and this authentically eclectic philosopher and scientist, who in the meantime had become familiar with the writers of Ren-

---

86 FLACIUS, pp. 1068–1071.
87 MOUSOUROS 1499.
88 STEPHANUS 1544.
89 CHALCONDYLAS 1499.
90 TOLAND.

aissance Neoplatonic syncretism and had translated *Lo spaccio della bestia trionfante* [*The Expulsion of the Triumphant Beast*] by Giordano Bruno, had founded the Ancient Order of Druids.

For Toland, the assassins of "Hypatia [...] who will ever continue the glory of her own sex, and the disgrace of ours", had

> so brutal and savage a disposition, as, far from being struck with admiration at so much beauty, innocence and knowledge, to stain their barbarous hands with her blood and their impious souls with the indelible character of sacrilegious murderers[91].

It was "a Bishop, a Patriarch, nay a Saint, who was the contriver of so horrid a deed, and his Clergy the executioners of his implacable fury." In the third to last of the twenty-two chapters of his indictment, for which he gathers all the ancient witnesses, including Synesius and the "honest Socrates", Toland offers the reader a complete translation of the account of Hypatia's assassination as contained in the *Vita Isidori* by Damascius, "which I here give to you, reader, although it shou'd cost you the tribute of one tear more to her memory"[92].

In the penultimate chapter, he writes: "No, no, they were no Christians that kill'd Hypatia." While in the twenty-second chapter he emphasises: "How insufferable a burlesquing of God and Man is it to revere so ambitious, so turbulent, so perfidious and so cruel a man as a *Saint?*"[93]. He concludes:

> Tis no wonder then, that when the epithet *Saint*, which peculiarly belong'd to Piety and Innocence, was thus pompously bestow'd on Vice and Impiety, there shou'd prevail that deluge of Ignorance, Superstition, and Tyranny, which overwhelm'd almost the whole Christian World. All the Persecutions that insu'd, were so many forcible means, imploy'd to suppress any efforts that might be us'd for the restoring of Virtue and Learning. By that Antichristian spirit fell Hypatia, to whom the Clergy of her time could never forgive, that she was beautiful yet chaste; far more learned than themselves[94].

Toland's polemical essay was immediately contradicted in 1721, in a pamphlet written by Thomas Lewis, *The History of Hypatia, a Most Impudent School-Mistress of Alexandria, Murder'd and Torn to Pieces by the Populace, in Defence of Saint Cyril and the Alexandrian Clergy. From the Aspersions of Mr Toland*[95].

Lewis dwelt on the character of the "She Philosopher", as he calls her. "If the Learning of this Madam had been of the same size with her Modesty, she would scarce, in my opinion, have come recommended in such Pomp to Posterity".

---

91 *Id*,. p. 103
92 *Id*., p. 132.
93 *Id*., p. 135.
94 *Id*., p. 136.
95 Lewis.

While the testimonies of Suidas are unreliable as they are taken from "a rigid Heathen" like Damascius, who "therefore aggravated her History with the Blackest Circumstances", on the other hand, the Christian Socrates is accused of being a "Precise Puritan".

Even more revealing is yet another comment passed by Lewis, according to which the true harangue of Toland is not directed at the ancient Alexandrian Church, but at the conservative wing of the Anglican Church, and the true defendant is not Cyril, but his "modern successor", Henry Sacheverell, the implacable adversary of the Whig government and of its tolerance towards religious dissidents like Toland.

> The History of Hypatia, as he relates it, is a mere Lampoon, dress'd up with Malice, Prejudice and Ignorance, on purpose to blast the Reputation of the Venerable St. Cyril, a strenuous Assertor of Orthodoxy and Church Discipline, and of Dr. Sacheverell his faithful Successor in zeal, against the modern Novatians and the Arian Heresie.

As a result of his anti-government sermons, driven by religious fundamentalism, in 1710 Reverend Sacheverell was accused of slander, remanded and sent to trial. However, the sentence, decidedly mild for the times, which suspended him from preaching for three years, made Sacheverell the moral winner of the trial and humiliated the Whigs.

It was therefore an incident in the volcanic hotbed of religious politics in the Great Britain of Queen Anne that resuscitated the ghost of Hypatia, like Toland a "Freethinker", a martyr to freedom of thought and a Whig heroine, in juxtaposition to the fundamentalism of a bleakly Tory Cyril, behind whose mask hid the bellicose anti-deist preacher.

Appendix
A Very Beautiful and Well-educated Woman is Torn Asunder

The characterisation of Cyril and the comments of Flacius Illyricus on the assassination of Hypatia can be found in FLACIUS, pp. 1068–1071.

The first study on the scientific personality of "learned Hypatia" emerged once again from the Protestant environment, that is to say, in Johann Christoph Kiesewetter's dissertation (as already mentioned above, chapter "The Glory of Her own Sex and the Wonder of Ours", Appendix *ad loc.*). Kiesewetter was a student at the university of Jena, whose research was supervised by Johan Andreas Schmidt, the Lutheran theologian and abbot of Marienthal. This scholarly relationship led most of the scholars who worked on the reception of Hypatia to erroneously attribute Kiesewetter's work to Schmidt himself; the most recent scholar convinced of such is WATTS 2017, who mentions on p. 187, n.1, as "the first scholarly work of every sort devoted to her career", an elusive D.J.A. SCHMIDT, *De Ipparcho, duobus Theonibus doctaque Hypatia*, Jena 1689. Yet, as can be inferred from the frontispiece bearing the whole title, Schmidt was actually just the "advisor" for Kiesewetter's dissertation: *Rectore Magnificentissimo Serenissimo Principe Ac Domino Domino Joanne Wilhelmo Duce Sax. Iul. Cliv. ac Mont. & c. Hipparchum Theonas, doctamque Hypatiam in Mathesi celebres. Dissertatione Historico-Mathematica Praeside Magnifico Pro-Rectore Jo. Andrea Schmidio, P.P. Facult. Philosoph. Decano, Alumnorumque Ducalium Inspectore exhibet Ad D. Iulii MDCLXXXIX. Auctor Respondens M. Jo. Christoph. Kiesewetter Arnstad. Thur.*

The first printed edition of the *Epistulae* of Synesius, published in 1499 by Marcus Musurus in the Aldine *corpus* of Greek letter writers (MOUSOUROS), would be followed half a century later by the *Opuscula* edited by Adrien Turnèbe, Paris 1553 (TURNEBUS), and a few years later by the *editio princeps* of Socrates Scholasticus (1544) edited by Robert Estienne (STEPHANUS). In the same year as Musurus' Synesius (1499), the *editio princeps* of Suidas prepared by Demetrius CHALCONDYLAS saw the light of the day.

However, it would be with the Greek-Latin edition of Synesius' *Opera omnia*, published by Denys PETAU (1612) and above all the *Notitia historica* with the foreword by the same learned Jesuit (and with its continuation in the subsequent revised and augmented edition of 1633, *ibid.:* sumptibus Sebastiani Cramoisy), that the "magistra Hypatia", whose name opens the *Notitia,* would become known both to the intellectual community, attracting the attention of the great mathematician Pierre Fermat, who was interested in the hydroscope mentioned in Synesius' letters (on which see below, part III, chapter "What Did Hypatia Teach?" and Appendix *ad loc.*), and to the Catholic learned elite, also thanks to the mention of Caesar Baronius, on which see below, chapter "The Catholic Wing".

The essay can be read in TOLAND. Soon Toland's *Hypatia* (1753) would be published again in a new independent edition.

The designation "Freethinker" was coined at this time, and precisely for Toland, by the bishop George Berkeley: see DANIEL, pp. 164–180; SIMONUTTI, pp. 45–58 with bibliography.

The passages quoted from Toland's work can be found on pp. 103, 132, 135, 136.

According to GAJERI, pp. 56–57, in Toland the case of Hypatia is examined "in the light of the antagonism between the sexes" and in his work it is possible to see an original standpoint against discrimination against women and therefore the first "Feminist" reading of the case of Hypatia: unlike the "cataloguers" of *philosophae mulieres*, Toland's aim was "to celebrate in Hypatia the goal that every woman can attain if she is not excluded from education", so that the "vulgar prejudice" that discriminates against women in the field of culture repeats the gesture of the "barbarous hands" that did not admire Hypatia's "wisdom". WATTS 2017, p. 136, also underscores that "Toland's discussion", even when it shifts to other topics, "never entirely lets the matter of her gender drop" and constantly points out "how the example of Hypatia makes contemporary restrictions on intelligent women look ridiculous". It shall be noticed that, even if these Proto-Feminist elements are undoubtedly present, they fall within the paradigm of Toland's "free thinking" and should not, in our opinion, be put before the more immediate and urgent political value of his text nor overshadow the broader picture of his polemic against the early Church's secular government and his general criticism of ecclesiastical institutions.

WATTS returns extensively to Toland and the "proto-feminist" reading of Hypatia's case, which he sees prefigured in the 1720s, in his 2020 essay devoted to Hypatia's reception in the 18th century: see also below, chapt. "Refreshing Exceptions", Appendix.

Lewis' rebuttal of Toland's essay on Hypatia can be read in LEWIS.

On the dispute between the mathematician Whiston and Sacheverell, which prompted Toland to take up the affair of Hypatia, see WATTS 2020. On the proceedings against Henry Sacheverell see HOLMES 1973; HOLMES 1976; for a general framework of the political-religious situation of England in the late 17th and early 18th centuries see HOLMES 1986.

In defence of Cyril against Toland's accusations, and those of Arnold (below, chapter "Refreshing Exceptions"), see also the last of the four degree theses dedicated to Hypatia (Vitembergae 1747–1748) of which J. C. WERNSDORF was the supervisor (*Dissertationes Academicae de Hypatia philosopha Alexandrina I–IV*. Wittenberg: Schlomach, 1747–1748): J. C. WERNSDORF – A. L. Fr. DRECHSEL, *Dissertatio Academica IV. De Hypatia philosopha Alexandrina speciatim de Cyrillo episcopo in causa tumultus Alexandrini caedisque Hypatiae contra Gothofr. Arnoldum et Io. Tolandum defenso*. Together with the further three dissertations (see WERNSDORF I–III) this study constitutes, despite its strong ideological connotations, one of the first truly scientific contributions on the case of Hypatia.

15 From Fielding to Gibbon Passing Through the Shadow of a Donkey

As witnessed by the literary production of Anglo-German anticlericalism, Hypatia was known throughout the whole Anglican and Protestant 18th century: from the satirical novels of Henry Fielding, the author of *Tom Jones*, who imagined an improbable betrothal between the philosopher Hypatia and the emperor Julian the Apostate, lamenting the loss of the ring in the fire of the Cinaron[96], to the verses of the *Twelve Moral Letters* by Christoph Martin Wieland, the German Enlightenment thinker and later immortal author of *Die Geschichte der Abderiten* (1781, translated as *The Republic of Fools*, 1861), one of the bestsellers of the Century of Lights, which tells of a civil war that broke out in the flourishing city of Abdera, caused by the shadow of a donkey. In evoking the more ancient and deadly, but no less exemplary battle that took place in Alexandria, Wieland exalts Hypatia, comparing her "martyrdom for knowledge" to that of Socrates, as if they were "the alpha and the omega of Greekness", and he asks himself:

Wer stösst Hypatien, die Perle weiser Schönen,	Who drives Hypatia, a pearl amongst the beautiful and the sage,
Zu Menschen, die mit Wut dem Aberglauben frönen,	Amongst irate men and slaves to superstition,
Wo blind für ein Verdienst, das noch die Nachwelt preist,	Where, blind to her merits that the world still praises,
Auf eines Bischofs Wink der Pöbel sie zerreist?[97]	The masses tear her asunder at the nod of a bishop?

The rehabilitation of Hypatia by non-Catholic writers would result in a series of historiographical studies of Protestant positivism, where the "bonfire" of Hypatia – guilty, already in the opinion of John of Nikiu, of casting dark spells – would be classified as the first example of a witch hunt, and therefore the first Christian Church already assimilated to the Catholic Church of the Counter-Reformation, and Cyril seen in the guise of a real Roman inquisitor. Far from Rome, in the Anglican and Protestant world, as in the Byzantine world, Cyril's reputation was in tatters.

Prior to these developments, but already well underway in the afterlife of Hypatia, there is a milestone that marks the tipping point in her transformation into a universal icon of secular values: the judgment of Gibbon. Not even he, in *The History of the Decline and Fall of the Roman Empire*, has any regard for the good name of Cyril:

> [the daughter of Theon was] inhumanly butchered by the hands of Peter the Reader and a troop of savage and merciless fanatics: her flesh was scraped from her bones with sharp oyster shells, and her quivering limbs were delivered to the flames[98].

---

96 FIELDING.
97 WIELAND, *Vierter Brief*, p. 329.
98 GIBBON, II, p. 945 (first ed. IV, 1788, p. 549).

Gibbon has every reason in the world to say such things; yet his interpretation of the Greek word *ostraka* (ὄστρακα) is not right, as in this case it does not refer to shells, but to the shards of terracotta from pots or tiles, typical improvised weapon of the clerical militia who, under Roman rule, were forbidden to carry weapons, just like everyone else.

Thanks to the circulation of *The History of the Decline and Fall*, this version would become dominant, and its eccentricity would continue to torment the fans of Hypatia, until it became an almost stereotyped conversation piece, attributed in the 20th century by Evelyn Waugh, the English author who converted to Catholicism, to one of his frivolous characters: "I'll tell you an odd thing about Hypatia. I was brought up to believe she was murdered with oyster shells, weren't you? Forster says tiles"[99]. In fact, Edward Morgan Forster delights in desecrating a series of clichés on Hypatia in his *Alexandria. A History and a Guide*.

> The achievements of Hypatia, like her youthfulness, have been exaggerated; she was a middle-aged lady who taught mathematics at the Mouseion and though she was a philosopher too we have no record of her doctrines. [...] She is not a great figure[100].

Defining Cyril's monks as his "wild black army", which filled the streets "anxious to perform some crowning piety before they retired to their monasteries," Forster establishes that "they encountered Hypatia who was driving from a lecture (probably along the course of the present Rue Nebi Daniel)".

He tells his readers that:

> They dragged her from the carriage to the Caesareum, and there tore her to pieces with tiles.

Hypatia was probably skinned alive, the capital torture reserved in Antiquity for great heretics, or she may have been literally torn to pieces, according to the sentence for both those found guilty of witchcraft and magic and for prostitutes, or dismembered in a ritual manner, i.e., also eviscerated, according to the ancient custom of sacrifice; in which case her heart was also torn from her body.

Returning to Gibbon:

> The just progress of inquiry and punishment was stopped by seasonable gifts; but the murder of Hypatia has imprinted an indelible stain on the character and religion of Cyril of Alexandria.

Also John Bagnell Bury – the herald of Gibbon in the Victorian Age, the author of the fundamental *History of the Later Roman Empire* and master of William Butler Yeats – is "almost certain" of Cyril's guilt as the direct instigator of Hypatia's assassination, and

---

99 WAUGH.
100 FORSTER, p. 55.

in any case his craving to transform into a religious battle what at first was only a vulgar power struggle[101].

"After this, Alexandria was no longer troubled by philosophers", commented Bertrand Russell two centuries later, in his celebrated work with the pointed title *History of Western Philosophy and its connection with Political and Social Circumstances from the Earliest Times to the Present Day*, with regard to Saint Cyril:

> His chief claim to fame is the lynching of Hypatia, a distinguished lady who, in an age of bigotry, adhered to the Neoplatonic philosophy and devoted her talents to mathematics [...][102].

---

101 BURY, p. 210.
102 RUSSELL 1947, p. 387.

Appendix
From Fielding to Gibbon Passing Through the Shadow of a Donkey

Fielding's version of Hypatia is to be found in his *A Journey from this World to the Next* (1743) (FIELDING, chapt. XI, p. 44). The exhilarating parodic plot imagines Julian the Apostate talking of the adventures of his engagement "with one Hypathia" [sic] during his incarnation as "an avaricious Jew", one of the many punishments inflicted on him by Minos. GAJERI, p. 63, describes the novel as "a libertine satire against men of culture and their idols".

The exaltation of Hypatia and her juxtaposition with Socrates can be found in WIELAND, p. 329, in the context of a celebration of the "Athenian master of virtue" and in the re-evocation of his secular martyrdom, imposed by his "hateful city". In the parallels of destiny, the "reward" of Hypatia seems to be even more cruel than Socrates' hemlock and leads the severe ex-Pietist to legitimate doubts on the mysterious ways of God.

Wieland's definition of the two philosophers as a sort of "alpha and omega of Greekness" can be read in GAJERI, p. 72.

For the perception of Hypatia as the first victim of the witch hunts see SOLDAN – HEPPE, p. 82.

The passage from Gibbon is taken from chapter 47 of his *History of the Decline and Fall of the Roman Empire:* see GIBBON, II, p. 945 (first ed. IV, 1788, p. 549).

The term *ostraka* is also erroneously translated as "seashells" by the learned HOCHE, p. 462, following Gibbon. On the availability of terracotta tiles and their use as weapons in ancient cities see BARRY, pp. 63–65, who, however, only mentions the tactics of tile-barrage and tile-throwing in urban warfare.

The fragment of Mrs. Stitch's conversation is taken from WAUGH.

The disdainful attitude of the *connaisseurs* of Alexandria to the "commonplace" Hypatia can also be found between the lines of the last volume of the *Alexandria Quartet* by L. DURRELL, *Clea* (1960), in which we move from the "painted ecstasies of Cleopatra" to the "bigotry of Hypatia".

In the volume by E. M. FORSTER, *Alexandria. A History and a Guide* (1922), the story of Hypatia is to be found on page 55, preceded by that of the destruction of the Serapeum.

On the genuine sacrificial immolation of Hypatia witnessed and/or reported by the ancient sources, and on the possible theories concerning the development of the events and the studies on the question see below, part III, chapter "Hypatia's Sacrifice" and Appendix *ad loc.*

The conclusions and the correct political diagnosis of Bury can be read in BURY, I, p. 210.

Bertrand Russell's comments ("His chief claim to fame is the lynching of Hypatia, a distinguished lady who, in an age of bigotry, adhered to the Neoplatonic philosophy and devoted her talents to mathematics [...] After this Alexandria was no longer troubled by philosophers") are taken from RUSSELL 1947, p. 387.

16 The Catholic Wing

If we move on to the Catholic sphere of influence, we find from the start evident resistance to even mentioning the topic, and in any case to presenting it in its correct terms. Beginning during the Counter-Reformation, the *Annals* of that great puppeteer of refounded ecclesiastical historiography, Cardinal Caesar Baronius[103], while following Synesius in celebrating Hypatia's wisdom and calling her "the greatest philosophical mind of her time", counter Flacius Illyricus' deductions by attempting to subtly alter the accounts of Cyril's policies and insinuating doubt about the reliability of the sources – in particular Socrates Scholasticus – from which these accounts are taken.

If in the 19th century it was written that,

> Cyril must be considered fully justified for all crimes by every true believer because he was made a saint of the Church [...][104],

even at the start of the 20th century the Alexandrian events were dealt with by works with a confessional background like current events. The innocence or guilt of Cyril was a matter of heated debate. In an essay dating from 1901, Francis Schaefer, having sifted through the sources, made the accusation:

> If Orestes had accepted the offer of reconciliation, or at least seriously considered the altered attitude of Saint Cyril, that bloody crime might perhaps have been avoided [...][105].

The discrediting, introduced by Baronius, of the oldest Christian testimony on the events relating to Hypatia, Socrates Scholasticus, was handed down through this wing of historiography over the centuries, implicit and lingering like a rumour, up to the disconcerting entry on *Cyril of Alexandria* which even in the mid 20th century lived on in the *Catholic Encyclopaedia*: "It is not possible to impute to Cyril this assassination, despite the insinuations of Socrates, who is not impartial"[106].

If we examine the great scientific repertoires of 20th century Catholicism, from the *Ecclesiastic Dictionary* by the gallant Angelo Mercati – according to which Hypatia was "killed during a public riot" and the "guilt of Saint Cyril of Alexandria" was "never proven" – to the *Lexikon für Theologie und Kirche* and the monumental *Histoire de l'Église* by Fliche and Martin, a series of further silences or deliberate large-scale manipulations of the facts process like rosary beads before the wondering eyes of the reader[107].

---

103 BARONIUS, pp. 350–351; 379–380.
104 See RENSI, p. 9.
105 SCHAEFER 1902, p. 452.
106 JUGIE.
107 E.g., LIÉBAERT.

Yet, in their attempts to defend the ancient bishop, the 20th-century historians end up unwittingly accusing the attitude of the Church itself, revealing it to be in part similar to those past times.

It was not, after all, as we have seen, the Middle Ages or even the Counter-Reformation, but 19th-century Catholicism that raised Cyril to the status of Doctor of the Church. The title *Doctor Incarnationis* was conferred on him in 1882, almost one thousand five hundred years after his regrettable episcopacy, by Pope Leo XIII, "a pope obsessed by the new Paganism represented by Freemasonry", as has been said, "and by the fiercely anticlerical liberals who dominated in Rome at his time"[108].

In fact, between the 18th and 19th centuries, Hypatia had become a typical Freemasonic myth. A little after the initiative of Leo XIII, important essays would be dedicated to her, in Italy, by well-documented scholars such as Giulio Barni, Augusto Agabiti and Guido Bigoni, or Carlo Pascal, in whose *Figure e caratteri* [*Figures and Characters*] the icon of Hypatia is eloquently compared to those of the more recent heroes of Post-Risorgimento Masonic secularism like Giosuè Carducci and Giuseppe Garibaldi.

This thread of essays and studies would not however produce, for understandable reasons, an adequate literature, unlike the French, German and Anglo-Saxon worlds – apart from the libretto of *Hypatia* by Caetani, a theurgic-theosophical, somewhat Faustian opera which not by chance was very successful in Germany, but not in Italy[109]. The cult of Hypatia would remain underground, confined to transmission by word of mouth between the lodges; but no less potentially dangerous for all that, with all the judgements implied of the methods of governance of the Church and the legitimacy of its temporal power, in times when, following the Unification of Italy, the question of the Church State had become pressing and Risorgimento thought had allied with anticlerical ideas on the one hand and Masonic ideas on the other, to bring the issue – unsuccessfully – into question in the new Italian State.

In 1944 Pope Pius XII dedicated an appreciative encyclical to Cyril of Alexandria. Later, despite the apologies and the demands for pardon dispensed here and there between the end of the 20th and the beginning of the 21st centuries, and despite the seriousness and the almost terrorist nature of the ancient murder, deplored, as we have seen, by the rival Orthodox Church, the official position of the Church of Rome has never either asked for Hypatia's forgiveness nor questioned Cyril's actions, his sanctity, his probity. Right up to the celebrations that Pope Benedict XVI held on October 3rd 2007, praising "the great energy" of Cyril's ecclesiastical government, "without making any attempt", as has been observed, "to absolve him of that shadow that history has cast upon him"[110].

---

108 ECO 2010.
109 CAETANI.
110 ECO 2010.

Appendix
The Catholic Wing

Caesar Baronius illustrated Cyril's policies and the death of Hypatia in the fifth volume of the *Annales ecclesiastici* (1602), respectively on pp. 350–351 and 379–380, where he quotes almost verbatim, translating their words into Latin, both Synesius and Socrates Scholasticus, but he does all he can to discredit the reliability of the latter; see also BARONIUS, p. 24.

Baronius' text is the basis for the mention of Hypatia in MORÉRI 1674, which given its immense popularity, the large number of editions and the translations into various languages, made a decisive contribution to its dissemination.

That the source most troublesome for Catholic academics is Socrates, "a Christian with Novatianist sympathies", is promptly noted also by CANFORA 2010, p. 93. On the position of Socrates Scholasticus, see DZIELSKA 1995, p. 98: "From the context in which he speaks about the destructive feeling of jealousy of Hypatia's 'earthly' honors, it follows that he has Cyril and his party in mind even though he does not name the patriarch"; despite denying the direct responsibility of Cyril, the scholar admits "the existence of a cover-up campaign orchestrated to protect the perpetrators." (p. 100).

For the following quotation see the introduction of E. RENSI to AGABITI, p. 9.

The considerations of Father F. SCHAEFER are taken from his article *St. Cyril of Alexandria and the Murder of Hypatia* (SCHAEFER 1902, p. 452).

In some Catholic circles of the 1930s some less ideological studies were produced. See for example the article of the Polish LENKOWSKI, *Hypatia i jej epoka* (1930), a short excursus aimed at placing Hypatia within the cultural context of her time, understanding her teaching in relation to the school of Athens (pp. 476–477), analysing with neutrality the historico-political setting of her murder (p. 485 and following), and illustrating briefly the reception of her story in the Byzantine world up to Nicephorus Gregoras (p. 482). Another example is the dissertation discussed in Leuven by the Belgian Jesuit P. Henry (who later became a scholar of Plotinus), still unedited: *Étude sur Hypatie* (HENRY).

And yet, still in the mid-20th century J. LIÉBAERT, *Saint Cyrille d'Alexandrie et la culture antique*, was able to attribute the assassination of Hypatia to the spontaneous initiative of "un groupe de chrétiens fanatiques" and deny *certain late accounts* (that is, Suidas) which attribute the instigation to Cyril himself. For Liébart it is true that in Socrates Scholasticus, speaking of the case of Hypatia, the violence of Cyril's ecclesiastical policies is deplored, but "sans doute pensait-on aux incidents antérieurs, où Cyrille s'était montré très violent"; and in any case, "bien que l'évêque ne dût pas éprouver une grande sympathie pour la conseillère d'Oreste, rien absolument ne permet de supposer qu'il ait voulu sa mort".

The entry on Cyril in the *Enciclopedia Cattolica* was signed, moreover, by a historian of the Byzantine Church of the stature of Martin JUGIE, one of the leading although strongly contested 20th-century Byzantinists (see JUGIE). The entire passage reads as follows: "*Se bisogna credere a Socrate* gli inizi del suo [of Cyril] episcopato furono segnati da continue rivolte e violenze in cui restò compromesso indirettamente il vescovo stesso [...]. La causa principale di queste agitazioni fu la discordia con il prefetto Oreste. Nel 415 *durante una baruffa* la celebre Ipazia, versatissima nella filosofia neoplatonica, fu ammazzata da un parabolano [sic] a causa della sua presunta influenza presso il prefetto. Non si può imputare a Cirillo questo assassinio *nonostante le insinuazioni di Socrate, il quale non è imparziale.*" [*If we are to believe Socrates*, the beginning of (Cyril's) bishopric was marked by continuous riots and violence in which the bishop himself was involved (...). The conflict with the prefect Orestes was the main reason for these riots. In 415 *during a riot* the famous Hypatia, excellent in Neoplatonic philosophy, was murdered by a *parabolanus* (sic) because of her assumed influence on the prefect. We cannot ascribe this murder to Cyril *despite the insinuations of Socrates, who is not impartial*].

As glossed by CANFORA 2010, p. 95, n. 4, "riot" is the homemade version of the hypocritical formula adopted by the *Grand Dictionnaire* of Moréri s.v. *Hypatia* (MORÉRI 1674): "Elle fut tuée dans une sédition populaire". Doubts on the reliability of Socrates are also advanced by the more scientific *Dictionnaire de Théologie catholique* (AMANN), as already mentioned by CANFORA 2010, *ibid.*

In the *Lexikon für Theologie und Kirche* the item on Hypatia is signed by A. SPINDELER. The more recent edition of the same collection, at the item *Cyril of Alexandria* (VOGT), draws a pious veil over his ecclesiastical policies, as noted by CANFORA 2010, p. 96.

The *Lexikon für Theologie und Kirche*, in its intent to exonerate the bishop of Alexandria, appealed amongst others to the authority of a great philologist of Catholic formation, successor to Nietzsche in Basle and later to Wilamowitz in Berlin, a scholar of classical *paideia* and of its Christianisation in the great exponents of Christian Platonism of the fourth century, such as Gregory of Nyssa: Werner Jäger, who was also unexpectedly cautious in his evaluation or at least in declaring the guilt of Cyril. Jäger speaks of Hypatia and Cyril in the item *Hypatia*, in the third edition of an important theological collection, namely *Die Religion in Geschichte und Gegenwart* (JÄGER 1956), a work of the Protestant wing and yet decidedly craven on the subject, almost as much as the Catholic works.

In the *Histoire de l'Église* by Augustin FLICHE and Victor MARTIN, which also includes amongst its authors scholars of the rank of De Labriolle, G. Bardy, L. Bréhier, G. De Plinval (see FLICHE – MARTIN), Canfora unmasks, with "the freedom immanent in the philological method", a deliberate intent to "falsify not only the ancient texts but also the modern bibliography"; the misrepresentations of the French edition are further aggravated in the Italian edition (1961) of the same work (FLICHE – MARTIN – FRUTAZ): see CANFORA 2010, p. 97.

More recently, even an experienced scholar like ROUGÉ 1990, p. 500, although ruthlessly analysing the political dynamics of the event, remains firm in stating that Cyril did not order the death, but was only the indirect cause, because he had created tension in the city through his disagreements with Orestes; the position of Rougé is upheld, as already mentioned, by DZIELSKA 1995, pp. 97–98.

The observations on Popes Leo XIII and Benedict XVI which appear in inverted commas in the last paragraph of the chapter are taken from the article by ECO 2010.

The long "historical essay" by Guido Bigoni was printed five years after the initiative of Pope Leo XIII. The one by Carlo Pascal, *Ipazia e le ultime lotte pagane* (to whom we also owe, as already in the work by the older Freethinker Toland, a vibrant denunciation of the "superstitious antifemale tendency" behind the death of Hypatia, and in any case the correct identification of an element of misogyny in the *phthonos* [φθόνος] of the Christian bishop), would be included in PASCAL, pp. 143–196 where the portrait of Hypatia immediately precedes that of Carducci.

Similarly, the lecture on Hypatia by Giulio Barni, held in Geneva in 1868 (BARNI), stands alongside those on Bruno, Campanella, Vanini, Galilei and Huss. It is in Barni that the story of Hypatia becomes more explicitly an introduction to a consideration on the role of the Church in the civil State. "Quando una comunità religiosa s'impone ai poteri civili, sì da informare tutti gli atti della vita pubblica e da prescrivere norme e credenze, necessariamente vien meno ogni moto fervido di pensiero e si abbassa il livello intellettuale e quindi il livello morale." ["When a religious community imposes itself on the secular power, so as to shape every act in public life, and prescribe laws and beliefs, all lively impulse to thought fails, and intellectual and, therefore, moral standards are diminished."] (BARNI, pp. 175–176); on the text by Barni see the analysis by GAJERI, pp. 123–124.

The short volume by AGABITI, slim but dense with philosophical and literary references and therefore in some settings a genuine cult-text, is linked to a different branch of Masonic thinking, similar to occultism and close to the Theosophical movement (in fact Hypatia is explicitly compared to the famous occultist Olga Cavari, at the time president of the International Theosophical League), and emphasises more than any other the alleged theurgical component of Hypatia's teaching (on which see CHUVIN–TARDIEU, p. 67) and the priestly nature of her role. Although speaking of "sadism" with regard to her assassins, this is the first text to note the ritual relevance, the sacrificial value and the mythological resonances of her death by dismembering (on which see below, part III, chapter "Hypatia's Sacrifice" and Appendix *ad loc.*).

The *Hypatia* of Roffredo CAETANI, who wrote both the music and the libretto, was published in Mainz in 1925; the first performance, in German, was in 1926, at the Deutsches Nationaltheater in Weimar, as reported by GAJERI, pp. 127–129 and 131, n. 62. The libretto opens with a paraphrase of Synesius' Epistle 124, 1–2 (*To the Philosopher Hypatia*), p. 257 Roques (Engl. transl. p. 214 Fitzgerald), quoted below, part III, chapter "All Synesius' Mysteries": "Pur anco ne la nera cerchia de l'Averno / io mi ricorderò di te, diletta Hypatia" [Even in the doom circle of Avernus,/ Even there shall I remember you, beloved Hypatia].

The encyclical of Pius XII can be found in PIUS PP. XII, *Litt. enc.* Orientalis Ecclesiae de Sancto Cyrillo Patriarcha Alexandrino (1944). For the audience of October 3rd 2007 of Pope Benedict see BENEDICTUS XVI.

The most recent and updated "Masonic" contribution on Hypatia is Neri, *In cerca di Ipazia* (2016). To the same cultural environment belongs the theatrical play by Gómez de Liaño, *Hipatia, Bruno, Villamediana: tres tragedias del espiritu* (2008).

17 Refreshing Exceptions

To our relief there are exceptions to this general conspiracy of silence of the Church of Rome which has lasted for more than a millenium. However, they are exclusively to be found in the modernist wing of Catholicism, in French and of Gallican lineage. In his *Histoire ancienne de l'Église* Louis Duchesne, friend and disciple of Alfred Loisy, later a follower of the doctrines and study methods of the Belgian Bollandists, does not mince words in supporting the credibility of Socrates Scholasticus' account, which "agrees only too well with what other documents, and the most reliable ones, tell us of the character and the behaviour" of the one he calls "the terrible bishop"[111].

Of the "illustrious Hypatia", on the other hand, he exalts "the extraordinary literary faculties" and emphasises the universal "esteem for her way of life and her intelligence". Although "she was still a Pagan and directed the Neoplatonic school", she was respected by the Christians: "It was not only Orestes: she was also honoured by the bishop Synesius." The actions of the *parabalani*, "fanatics led by one of the lectors of Cyril, by name Peter", who killed her "using potsherds, then chopping up the body and burning it", is defined by the Abbé Duchesne as "an orgy of cannibalism"[112].

The anti-Cyrillian positions of Modernism, which are to be found also in more recent contributions from Francophone ecclesiastical historians, were already put forward between the 17th and the 18th centuries. In the France of absolute monarchy, where aversion to the interference of the Roman Church in matters of the State had led to an ideological re-evaluation and a scholarly rediscovery of the Byzantine world, in which for eleven centuries the Church had been systematically ousted from secular power, Henri de Valois, the ex-pupil of the Jesuits, later the *protégé* of Cardinal Mazarin and finally official biographer of Louis XIV, also gives the testimony of Suidas in the commentary on his edition of Socrates Scholasticus and affirms beyond doubt that "the author of Hypatia's murder was Cyril"[113].

A less open but similar condemnation of Cyril appeared in reformed Germany at the end of the 17th century in the *Unparteiische Kirchen-und Ketzerhistorie* by the Lutheran Pietist Gottfried Arnold, an "impartial", or rather "non-confessional" history of the Churches and the heretics. His work may be regarded as a counter-history of Christianity in which "the advent of the Anti-Christ" is made to coincide with the decision of Constantine to "unify the two things most contrasting, the divine government and that of the devil", that is Church and State, "as if Christ and Belial could become good friends"[114].

At the start of the 18th century the events relating to Hypatia were mentioned in the *Bibliotheca Graeca* by the Protestant Fabricius, whose position on the policies of Cyril is

---

111 DUCHESNE, vol. III, p. 301 and n. 1.
112 *Ibid.*
113 VALESIUS in CANFORA 2010, p. 99.
114 ARNOLD, part I, book V, chapt. III, par. 11, pp. 245–246.

even more veiled, but who in any case emphasises the "stubborn arrogance" of the patriarch of Alexandria[115].

It may perhaps seem surprising that in his *Mémoires pour servir à l'histoire ecclésiastique des six premiers siècles* Louis-Sébastien Le Nain de Tillemont, Jansenist and therefore usually a rather more severe judge than others, was prudent and justificatory towards Alexandrian Christianity. In fact, he wrote that the massacre of Hypatia not only "appeared odious to the Christian souls", but also "it was a great grievance for their bishop", who must be exonerated "of that which enemies of our religion say". In Tillemont's *Mémoires* the responsibility is completely attributed to Peter the Reader, on the basis of the presumed testimony of a letter written by Isidore of Pelusium. Although without accrediting it, the writer also mentions the spurious and shameless account of a belated conversion of Hypatia, corroborated by the notorious forged Latin letter in which the philosopher, on the occasion of the Council of Ephesus (that is fifteen years after her death), was said to have presented the Christian, although Dyophysite, Nestorian doctrine to Cyril[116].

But Jansenists like Tillemont defend, evidently, the Church's right to control politics. The proof lies in the fact that it was another of them, Claude-Pierre Goujet, who soon after openly celebrated Cyril's efforts, in direct contrast with the article by Diderot in the *Encyclopédie*, with his *Dissertation sur Hypacie, où l'on justifie Saint Cyrille d'Alexandrie sur la mort de cette Sçavante*, contained in *Continuation des Mémoires de littérature et d'histoire* by the Oratorian Pierre-Nicolas Desmolets[117].

---

115 FABRICIUS, vol. VIII, pp. 219–221, and vol. IX, pp. 718–719.
116 TILLEMONT, t. XIV, pp. 274–276; 276–278; on the false letter from Hypatia to Cyril, see also p. 606.
117 GOUJET.

Appendix
Refreshing Exceptions

The modernist *parrhesia* of Louis Duchesne can be appreciated in his *Histoire ancienne de l'Église* (DUCHESNE, vol. III, p. 301) ("Amongst the persons most admired by the prefect Orestes was the illustrious Hypatia, a woman of great literary abilities, esteemed for her way of life and for her talent. She was still a Pagan and directed the Neoplatonic school; Orestes was not the only Christian to respect her, she was also honoured by the bishop Synesius. The court of Cyril considered her the instigator of all the evil projects of the prefect and responsible for the hostility of Orestes towards the bishop. One day, some fanatics, led by one of Cyril's readers, by the name of Peter, ambushed her in the street, pulled her from her carriage, and dragged her to the Caesareum and there they stripped off her clothes and killed her with blows from roof tiles, then cutting the corpse into pieces and burning it in an orgy of cannibalism") and note 1 ("Les histoires ci-dessus nous sont racontées par Socrate. Elles représentent les bruits accrédités à Constantinople et comportent ainsi une certaine dose d'exagération. Toutefois l'impression qui s'en dégage ne saurait être négligée, car elle ne concorde que trop avec ce que d'autres documents, et des moins discutables, nous apprennent sur le caractère et les procédés du terrible archevêque").

In the edition of Valesius (Henri de Valois) of the ecclesiastical historians, the tome that includes Socrates' text dates from 1668; in 1673 the one containing Philostorgius would appear. As reported by CANFORA 2010, p. 99, in the passage that speaks of the "shame that fell on Cyril", Valesius notes: "Certe Damascius in vita Isidori philosophi quam ego duplo auctiorem editurus sum [...] caedis Hypatiae auctorem facit Cyrillum"; he then translates in a magnificent Latin the entire page of Damascius "et caetera quae leguntur apud Suidam" without raising any doubts on the reliability of the reconstruction by the Byzantine encyclopaedist. "We should always be grateful," concludes Canfora, "for the 'Gallican' independence shown by some French Catholic culture."

It must be said that Valois' work almost immediately raised an ecclesiastical dispute in France: the Jansenist Louis Ellies du Pin would soon severely criticise the testimony of Damascius in the *Vita Cyrilli Alexandrini* published in his renowned *Bibliothèque*: DUPIN, vol. IV, p. 41.

The standpoint of Gottfried Arnold on Cyril can be read in ARNOLD, part I, book V, chapt. III, par. 11, pp. 245–246. On the German theologian and historian, loved by Max Weber and Ernst Bloch, see *Allgemeine Deutsche Biographie*, vol. 1, p. 587; BLAUFUß – NIEWÖHNER.

Also in the field of the Reformation culture the perspective of the orientalist and librarian of Frederick I of Prussia, Mathurin Veyssière de La Croze, is interesting. In his *Histoire du Christianisme des Indes* (1724), he interpreted the battle of Cyril against the Nestorian Church as "the start of the corruption of Christianity" and issued against the bishop of Alexandria a judgement without appeal ("on auroit de quoi le regarder avec horreur"): see GAJERI, pp. 49–50, with bibliography in the notes.

An attempt to redeem Cyril from Arnold's accusations would come shortly afterwards from the ideologically biased, although well-documented, dissertation of WERNSDORF – DRECHSEL, see above, chapter "A Very Beautiful and Well-educated Woman is Torn Asunder" and Appendix *ad loc.*

Johann Albert Fabricius' prudent comments on Cyril can be read in *Bibliotheca Graeca* (FABRICIUS, vol. VIII [1717], pp. 219–221, and vol. IX [1719], pp. 718–719).

Still greater prudence had been adopted a little earlier, in the Anglican setting, by the Canon of Windsor, William Cave, in his *Scriptorum Ecclesiasticorum Historia Literaria* (CAVE, p. 251).

The information on Hypatia, which exonerates Cyril from "ce qu'on dit les ennemis de notre religion" and lingers on the pseudo-epigraphic letter by Isidore of Pelusium to Peter the Reader ("un homme qui avoit besoin de remèdes forts pour guérir les plaies de son âme. Ainsi il merite qu'on le croie auteur du massacre d'Hypatie"), as well as the information on the Latin letter to Cyril (which however the author, following Ménage, considers to be "une fiction de quelques Nestoriens") are to be found in TILLEMONT, vol. XIV, pp. 274–276 (*Article III: Hypacie philosophe payenne est massacrée l'an de Jésus-Christ 415*). There follows *Article IV: Des parabolans d'Alexandrie* (pp. 276–278); on the false letter from Hypatia to Cyril, see also p. 606.

The dissertation of C.-P. Goujet, dated June 27th 1727, appeared soon after and was then published in tome V (Paris 1749) of the *Continuation des Mémoires de littérature et d'histoire* by his friend of the Congregation of the Oratory of Jesus and Mary Immaculate P.-N. Desmolets. The text by Goujet, signed "M. G." (= Monsieur Goujet) can be found in GOUJET, pp. 138–187, and is followed on pp. 187–191 by an answering letter signed by a certain "Mademoiselle B."; on the content of the latter, which also links to the work by Ménage, see GAJERI, p. 62, who however in the previous pages erroneously attributes the text of the *Dissertation* to Desmolets rather than to Goujet, in the wake of a widely documented misunderstanding in scholarly literature. I owe the correct reference to the courtesy and patience of Luciano Canfora, whom I wish to thank.

While focusing on Hypatia's fortune in the 1720s and on Mademoiselle B.'s letter (WATTS 2020, pp. 204–205) Edward Watts fails to interpret the initials "M.G.". The schola sees in Mademoiselle B.'s short text a reading of Hypatia closer to historical reality, turning thus away from Toland's reading, which was anchored to an idea of Hypatia as a symbol of martyrdom, in the wake of Socrates Scholasticus and then Voltaire and Gibbon, and foreshadowing a proto-feminist reading consistent with current research trends. See also above, chapts. "The Excesses of Fanaticism" and "A Very Beautiful and Well-educated Woman is Torn Asunder", Appendices *ad loc.*

Both Cave and Desmolets would be calmly criticised in the entry *Hypatie* in the monumental *Nouvelle Biographie Générale*, directed by a German Protestant man of science, Jean-Chrétien-Ferdinand Hœfer (see AUBÉ), where after a balanced description of the accounts in the sources of the "lynching" of Hypatia he wrote the following remark: "Il est difficile de croire que saint Cyrille ne trempa pas les mains dans cette sanglante tragédie [...] La dissertation de l'abbé Goujet, qui a essayé de le disculper (dans la *Continuation des Mémoires de Littérature et d'Histoire* du P. Desmolets, tom. V, première partie), ne nous paraît pas très concluante. D'autre part, c'est raisonner d'une étrange manière que de prétendre avec Cave (*Hist. Littér.*, p. 251) que Damascius, qui le premier a chargé saint Cyrille de cette accusation, ne mérite point d'être cru, étant un ennemi de la réligion chrétienne, et que le caractère bien connu de saint Cyrille suffit à le laver d'une pareille tâche" (Aubé, coll. 712–713).

18 Uncontrolled Effects on the Poets

The positions, widely varied and misleading, taken by the Catholic historians produced uncontrolled effects on the poets. The marchioness Diodata Saluzzo Roero, less scholarly but no more attractive than Madame Dacier, member of the Academy of Sciences of Turin and also of the Accademia dell'Arcadia under the name of Glaucilla Erotria, who to the magnificence of her aristocratic birth "added the greater splendour of a soul adorned with every virtue", as her friend Enrichetta Dionigi Orfei said[118], in the long poem, entitled *Ipazia, ossia delle filosofie* [Hypatia, or on Philosophies], invented a Christian Hypatia, perhaps autobiographical, struggling throughout the twenty cantos of the work with her faith, the quarrels of her academic *entourage* and a promise of marriage from none other than the Neoplatonic Isidore, the protagonist of the *Vita* by Damascius, although presumably at that time an infant.

Mentr'ei seguia, la vergin tra l'oscuro	As he chased the virgin, into the hands of the black
Volgo precipitando: Io son cristiana,	Mob she stumbled: I am a Christian,
Gridò, cristiana, né celarlo curo	She cried, and do not deny it!
Nulla può sul mio cor possanza umana;	Human puissance has no hold over my heart;
Nulla! Saria delitto or l'occultarlo,	None! To hide it now would be a crime,
E delitto appressar l'ara profana.	And a crime to approach the profane Altar.
Ahi lo sdegno del padre! e chi frenarlo	O the disdain of my father! And who can
Potrìa? ... l'allòr perduto! ... il perder quelli	Contrast it? ... The crown of laurels is lost!... lost are
Sì fidi amici! ... lassa, di chi parlo?	Such trusted friends! ... but of whom do I speak?
Pèra il mio nome, il volgo empia m'appelli![119]	May my name perish, let the rabble call me impious!

Trembling at the thought of her father's disdain, the heroine is aided by none other than Cyril, who

Udì 'l gran fatto, venne: Io t'apparecchio	Hearing of the dire events, he came: I readied
Tetto umil d'alga, o de la vincitrice	For you a humble roof of moss, o triumph and mirror
Virtù d'Iddìo (sclamò) trionfo e specchio.	(He proclaimed) of the vanquishing virtue of God.
Seguimi, vieni, vergine felice![120]	Follow me, come, o happy virgin!

We would have had a happy ending if it had not been for the "godless Altiphon, the unrequited lover of furious passion", according to the author. Hypatia is presented, dying, as a Christian martyr:

Languida rosa sul reciso stelo	Languid rose, her stem severed,
Nel sangue immersa la vergin giacea	In a pool of blood the virgin lay,
Avvolta a mezzo nel suo bianco velo	Wrapped in her white veil,

---

118 DIONIGI ORFEI.
119 SALUZZO ROERO, II, p. 55.
120 SALUZZO ROERO, II, p. 64.

Soavissimamente sorridea	Smiling most sweetly,
Condonatrice de l'altrui delitto	Forgiving the crime of others,
Mentre il gran segno redentor stringea[121].	As she clutched the great sign of redemption.

In an oil painting by Ferdinando Cavalieri (1834–35), currently held at the entrance of the Biblioteca Angelica in Rome, next door to the headquarters of the Arcadia, it is still possible to see Glaucilla Erotria holding a half-closed book, in which the name of Hypatia is mentioned: perhaps her own *opus magnum*. In addition to being a rather reactionary patriot ("the moral purpose of the work" was intended to show "how baleful are the effects of the discordant opinions of the Parties"), Diodata Saluzzo corresponded with Monti, Parini, Manzoni, Madame de Staël, and above all she was a reader of Tillemont, whose information on Hypatia her poem was intended, as she explains, "to grasp". The Jansenist version is therefore partly responsible for her total historical misunderstanding.

Contemporary critics of the poem used rather strong terms to describe it: a fundamentally mistaken historical interpretation. Among these critics was Niccolò Tommaseo, who, despite being Catholic, took a stance against Cyril, that we will find again, as just mentioned, in the moderate wing of Catholicism, which did not overlook the political essence, already underscored by Socrates Scholasticus and the ecclesiastical historians of the seventeenth and eighteenth centuries, of the patriarchal policy of Cyril of Alexandria: "It is certain that Saint Cyril [...], during his patriarchate, endeavored too much to extend the temporal power of the clergy; [...] persecuting forty thousand Jews (who, despite killing some Christians [...], did not deserve such a general and lucrative vendetta) and canonising Ammonius the Monk, who with a crowd of five hundred assaulted the chariot of the Roman prefect, are definitely not great examples either of tolerance (although such word may be equivocal) or of meekness nor charity"[122].

A precedent to the work of Diodata Saluzzo is the poem *Atenaide* by the learned Barnabite Francesco Maria Franceschinis, in which we also find a Hypatia converted to Christianity and fated to a martyrdom similar to that of Saint Catherine of Alexandria, which is considered factual. Professor of mathematics at the Universities of Bologna and Padua, polygraph, friend of Vincenzo Monti, philo-Napoleonic during the 1810s, pro-Austrian and reactionary during the years of the Restoration, the unscrupulous Franceschinis partly anticipated the account of Hypatia of Diodata Saluzzo. On a superficial level, he presented Cyril as if through rose-tinted glasses and Hypatia attracted to the Christian persuasion by Athenais, the young protagonist, portrayed as a restless traveller, philosopher *in pectore*, future Christian, bride-to-be of the *basileus* Theodosius and future *basilissa* of Constantinople. Yet, under the surface, the poem bears also another meaning, an undertext which shines through here and there and which witnesses to a more historically accurate and better documented version of the facts, more layered and politically articulated than the later version of Diodata.

---

121 EAD., II, pp. 183–184.
122 TOMMASEO 1828, p. 147.

The *Athenais* does not simply provide, disguised among the arabesques of rhyme and meter, a more realistic depiction of the figures and the situations that led to Hypatia's muder, but presents a version of the story which, with the proper precautions, depicts Cyril as fully accountable for it. In the final edition of 1837 a calm Orestes "enemy of all contention" provides such a version to Synesius "the good"[123]:

Giunto era intanto alla cittade, tratto	In the meantime the good Synesius
Dall'udito d'Ippazia fatto atroce,	had come to the city,
Il buon Sinnesio, che un dì s'era fatto	After having heard the atrocious thing
Un di lor che pendean dalla sua voce.	that happened to Hypatia,
	He who once was among those
	Who hung on her every word.
E, per tutto saper l'orribil fatto,	In order to know about the horrible deed,
D'Oreste in casa se n'andò veloce,	He swiftly went to the house of Orestes,
Che molto riverìa, come nemico	Whom he much respected,
D'ogni briga, e comun d'Ippazia amico.	as enemy of all contention,
	And common Friend of Hypatia.
Questi, accoltolo in casa, la dolente	After having welcomed him into his house,
Tutta narrògli istoria; e in guisa il fece,	He (i.e. Orestes) narrated to him the whole sorrowful story,
	and he did it in such a way,
Che Sinnesio aggravato di ciò sente	That Synesius considered Cyril,
Cirillo, cui non val scusa né prece;	Unworthy of excuse nor prayer,
	accountable for it;
E in bei modi rammentagli che mente	And well he reminded him
Spesso il pubblico grido, e ch'egli vece	That the public cry often lies,
	And that he has to stay
Dee sostener d'indagator disciolto	An investigator of the truth,
Da tutti affetti, e solo al ver rivolto.	unbound from affection.

We may recognise a sort of disguised signature of the author in this last definition – 'investigator of the truth' –, which opposes the "lie screamed in public". In the earlier version (dating to between 1822 and 1823), the culpability of Cyril is already cautiously uttered by two "bad guys": firstly by a sorceress, and secondly by an insidious Pagan called Giulio, who does not simply invoke the truth of the facts (later disavowed by the author, in bad or in good faith), but also the "clerical tradition of violence and struggle against the civil power initiated by Cyril's uncle Theophilus and continued by Cyril himself"[124].

Giulio allor, che in nequizia non men vale	Giulio then, not less iniquitous than her,
Di lei, come mal grado sia condutto,	While being led against his will declares
Contro i chierci declama, e chi li regge,	Against the clergymen and those who
Esclamando: gran Dio! Qual seguon legge!	Support them: great God! What a law they follow!

---

[123] FRANCESCHINIS, XIV, 1–2 (ed. 1837).
[124] BADINI CONFALONIERI 2014, p. 34.

Sempre a tumulti e a vïolenze istiga,
Per onor del suo Cristo, la plebaglia
Col suo clero Cirillo; ed aver briga
Con chi governa par ch'onor gli caglia.
E molto è che di tal gente castiga
Il Ciel d'Egitto: e ricordar ne vaglia
Per tutti un sol: Tëofilo, che audace
Sento nomar perturbator di pace.
Di sangue a questi, e più d'ardir congiunto,
Cirillo in guerra è sempre col Signore
Che per Cesare impera.

Through his clergy, he always instigates
The mob to turmoil and violence,
For the honor of his Christ; and it seems
Like it brought him honor to be in strife
with whoever was in charge.
And the sky of Egypt has been castigating
Such people for a long time, and I
want to mention only one of them:
Theophilus, whom I hear of having been an
Audacious disturber of peace.
Linked to him by blood and by daring,
Cyril is always at war with the lord
Who rules in the name of Caesar[125].

---

[125] FRANCESCHINIS, XIII, 58–60 (ed. 1822–23); see BADINI CONFALONIERI 2014, pp. 33–35.

Appendix
Uncontrolled Effects on the Poets

The statement on Diodata Saluzzo Roero is taken from the review of her poem *Ipazia ovvero delle filosofie* [*Hypatia, or on Philosophies*] (1827) written in the same year for the "Giornale Arcadico" by her friend Enrichetta Dionigi Orfei, *Del poema d'Ipazia, ossia delle Filosofie, mandato alla luce dalla Marchesa Diodata Saluzzo Roero*; see also the *Biografia di Diodata Saluzzo, scritta da se medesima*, published *ibidem*.

The invention of a Christian Hypatia is based on the purported letter in defence of Nestorius that Hypatia herself had allegedly sent to Cyril manifesting the desire to be baptised. An evident forgery, which can be read, in Latin, in *PG* 77, col. 389–390 and *PG* 84, col. 848. This letter was first printed by Lupus, and would be later mentioned, with reasonable scepticism, by authors such as Tillemont in his *Mémoires*, which probably represented the source of Diodata's knowledge on the subject. The explicit demonstration of the inauthenticity of the letter can be found in Hoche, p. 452.

The quotations in verse are drawn from Saluzzo Roero, vol. II, pp. 55, 64, 183–184.

On Diodata and her literary production see Tissoni; on the genesis and the sources of the poem see Berardo, and, more recently, the valuable contribution by Badini Confalonieri 2014, in which the reader will be able to find a detailed summary of the work, Diodata's biography, and an attentive overview of her *entourage* and political and cultural influences; see also Badini Confalonieri 1983.

The union between Hypatia and the Neoplatonic Isidore, although quite improbable, is not merely the fruit of Diodata's imagination; rather, it comes from a misunderstanding, probably dating from as early as Hesychius and reported by Suidas at the start of his article (Suidas, Y 166, IV, p. 644, 2–3 Adler [Harich-Schwarzbauer 2011, p. 324]), where Hypatia is said to be the "wife" of Isidore: see above, part I, chapter "Elegant Insolence".

Niccolò Tommaseo's review, which appeared in the 1828 issue of "Antologia" and was signed K.X.Y. (Tommaseo 1828), would be republished by the author (signed with his real name) in the *Dizionario estetico*, which came out in the same year as Diodata's death (1840), where the item *Ipazia* (Tommaseo 1840, pp. 354–357) is a shortened and partially modified re-publication of the February 1828 review; see Badini Confalonieri 2014, pp. 18–19 and n. 14, whence the above mentioned passage on Cyril is taken. That version of the passage appears in the "Antologia" (p. 147) but not in the *Dizionario*.

On the *Atenaide* by Francesco Maria Franceschinis see Badini Confalonieri 2014, who for the first time investigates the figure of this multi-faceted yet little studied ecclesiastical figure and his poem (reported for the first time in connection with the reception of the figure of Hypatia in Ronchey 2010, p. 238) and contextualises him in the cultural and political milieu of his time. He also provides an accurate list of his works and transcribes and analyses several key passages of the above mentioned poem.

On the close connection between the Pagan martyrdom of Hypatia and the genesis of the hagiographical legend of Saint Catherine of Alexandria see below, chapter "Celestial Virgin" and Appendix *ad loc.;* cf. also part III, chapter "Hypatia's Sacrifice".

The passages of Franceschinis' poem are taken from the version provided by BADINI CONFALONIERI 2014, pp. 33–35, and include the editor's corrections to the text.

19 New Faces For Old Foes

On the death of Hypatia, as with other episodes from the early centuries of Christianity, Catholic historiography has, as we have seen, contrasted with the Protestant, Anglican, and Jansenist versions, not to mention the Enlightenment and secular ones. And this has also produced quite bizarre effects on the literati.

Another invaluable case of doctrinal dispute applied to literature is, in the mid 19th century, the novel *Hypatia: Or, New Foes with an Old Face* by the Anglican Charles Kingsley. His prose has been called "a condensate of sadistic eroticism" and its author "a perverse cleric"[126].

> On, up the nave, fresh shreds of her dress strewing the holy pavement – up the chancel steps themselves – up to the altar – right underneath the great still Christ: and there even those hell-hounds paused.
> She shook herself free from her tormentors, and springing back, rose for one moment to her full height, naked, snow-white against the dusky mass around – shame and indignation in those wide clear eyes, but not a stain of fear[127].

This is the pale, slim Hypatia of Charles William Mitchell, the pre-Raphaelite painter inspired by Kingsley's *feuilleton*, which had appeared two years earlier: she was portrayed naked before the altar of a paleo-Christian church, her long blonde hair spread to cover the pubic area, a thin breastbone and perfectly round breasts, her hand proudly raised to advocate her doctrine, against a background of gloomy mosaics.

But apart from the Victorian coloratura, we must consider that Reverend Kingsley was not at all an erotic sadist nor a perverse cleric. He had very different and preeminent interests: a follower of Carlyle, a supporter of Social Reform, he was above all the main literary defender of the Christian Socialist movement, of which he was one of the founders, against the contemporary Oxford Movement. His *New Foes with an Old Face* in fact owes less to the canons of aestheticism in the manner of Pierre Louÿs, with whom he has been, not unreasonably, compared[128], but rather much more to the continuance of the heresiological controversy onto which historiography has projected the figure of Hypatia. The "New Foes with an Old Face" are the protagonists of a new and feared Catholic revanchism hybridised with Anglicanism, which in the eyes of English public opinion could lead to the resurfacing, in mid-19th century England, of the intellectual and political issues, interests, and powers which the Reformation and the Schism of Henry VIII had disposed of three centuries before.

Just like the pamphlet by Toland, we could call Kingsley's work a religious ideological puppet theatre, a *Puppenspiel*. In the middle of the Anglican 19th century, under the Alexandrian drapery, we can recognise the targets of the Oxford Movement, of its Trac-

---

126 RIST, p. 215.
127 KINGSLEY.
128 MARROU 1963, p. 142.

tarianism – the "heretical" intention to refound Anglicanism finding a *via media* between Romanism and Protestantism in the early Patristic period – and its principal exponent: Cardinal John Henry Newman, who hides behind the mask of Cyril and who uncoincidentally admitted Cyril's guilt from a historical and political perspective but defended his sanctity from a theological one: "Cyril, I know, is a saint; but it does not follow that he was a saint in the year 412. I am speaking historically [...] I don't think Cyril himself would like his historical acts to be taken as the measure of his inward sanctity; and it is not honest to distort history for the sake of some gratuitous theory. Theologically, he is great; in this respect Catholics of all succeeding times have been his debtors [...] We may hold St. Cyril to be a great servant of God without considering ourselves obliged to defend certain passages of his ecclesiastical career"[129].

---

[129] NEWMAN, vol. II, pp. 341–342.

Appendix
New Faces For Old Foes

Even though Protestant historiography has in general been in opposition to Catholic historiography on the subject of Hypatia, it must be observed that on the Anglican side the official positions on the case of Hypatia often were and still are no less reticent and misleading than those of the traditional Catholic wing. While in the *Historia literaria* by William Cave, already mentioned (see above, chapter "Refreshing Exceptions", and Appendix *ad loc.*), the "exemplary probity" of Cyril is celebrated, as pointed out by CANFORA 2010, p. 102, in the 20th century the widely distributed and frequently revised *Oxford Dictionary of the Christian Church* by the Reverend Frank Leslie Cross (inspirer in 1941 of the Theological Literature Association and for many years the theological advisor of the Anglican Bishop of Bradford) not only states that "Cyril's responsibility was never proved" (CROSS, s.v. *Hypatia*, p. 813) or even that there was nothing "personal" since Hypatia's assassination "was certainly the work of his supporters" (CROSS, s.v. *Cyril, St.*, p. 443), but the brutal campaign of Theophilus' successor "against the Neoplatonics and Jews" and "against the imperial prefect Orestes" is praised for its "impartial vigour" (*ibidem*).

Kingsley's novel's first edition, after its initial serialised publication in "Fraser's Magazine" in 1852, is C. KINGSLEY, *Hypatia, or New Foes with an Old Face*, London 1853. Its most accessible edition is published by Everyman's Library, London-New York 1968.

The opinion on the author and his prose is from RIST, p. 215. On the personality of Kingsley see in particular KLAVER and UFFELMAN 1979. On Kingsley's interest in Hypatia and on his novel see specifically UFFELMAN, 1986; LAMIRANDE, pp. 477–480; and most of all the recent, valuable article by SERTOLI, which also includes a detailed bibliography; in precedence, amongst other studies, cf. HARTLEY, chapt. 5; BALDWIN, chapt. 7; SCHUBERT. And see the synthesis offered by John THORP in his address *In Search of Hypatia*, presented at the Canadian Philosophical Association in 2004 and recently published online: "Charles Kingsley's novel exalts Protestant rationality against Catholic superstition; he injects an erotic subplot by having Hypatia fall in love with Orestes, the Roman prefect of Egypt; he resolves the awkwardness attendant on having a Pagan heroine by having her convert to Christianity – though not the Catholic brand – in the last days of her life".

On the stigmatisation of the figure of Hypatia and on the polemics against the elitism of the Platonic schools of Alexandria, juxtaposed to the "democratic" message of the Gospel, in the novel of the Christian Socialist Kingsley, see the statements found in his letters and his Edinburgh conferences of 1854 in SERTOLI, pp. 39–40 and nn.

The comparison with Pierre Louÿs is owed to MARROU 1963, p. 142.

On the close connection between the novel and the political situation of its time (in particular the "Catholic question", which emerged in England between the Catholic Emancipation Act of 1829 and the reintroduction in 1850 of the Roman Catholic hierarchy, with the papal nomination of the first Roman Catholic Archbishop of Westminster since the time of Henry VIII) see SERTOLI, pp. 42–43 (with bibliography at n. 14). On the 'duel' between Kingsley and Cardinal Newman, who would publish the novel *Callista: A Tale of the Third Century* (1856) as a response to his opponent's *Hypatia*, and on their open conflict, see SERTOLI, pp. 43–44 (with bibliography at n. 15). On the Oxford Movement's reuse of the theology of the early Fathers of the Church see *ibidem*, pp. 44–45 and n. 16.

The quote by cardinal Newman is taken from NEWMAN, vol. II, p. 341; the full text is available in BADINI CONFALONIERI 2014, pp. 11–12, n. 2.

Kingsley's book, which would become a best-seller in the Victorian era and would be translated into multiple languages, inspired two theatrical plays. The first, authored by the famous American actress Elisabeth Bowers, went on stage in Philadelphia in 1859, with the author herself in the role of Hypatia (BOWERS, *The Black Agathe: or Old Foes with New Faces*). The second (and more famous) one, by the rich amateur Glencairn Stuart Ogilvie, was a luxurious theatrical blockbuster. Its stage design was created by Alma Tadema and it had its debut at the Haymarket in London in 1893, starring Julia Neilson as the protagonist (OGILVIE, *Hypatia: A Play in Four Acts [and in Prose and Verse]. Founded on Charles Kingsley's Novel*). The success of this play was due more to the high quality of its scenography than to the quality of the script, which nonetheless showed an anti-Cyrillian *verve* significantly more prominent than that of its complex and considered literary model. On both 'toga plays' see the detailed article by TORCUTTI and its rich documentation and bibliography.

20 *Kulturkampf.* Hypatia à la Bismarck

In the modern era, as a German historian wrote, both clericalism and *Kulturkampf*, the "clash of civilisations" that opposed the Catholic Church and the Germanic world from the mid-19th century onwards, immediately following the Vatican Council I, "made the case of Hypatia a battleground"[130].

The novel by Fritz Mauthner, *Hypatia. Roman aus Altertum* (1892), offers a grass-roots account of such a phenomenon. This Austro-Hungarian Jew, a socialite and regular visitor of the intelligentsia of Freiburg, which included Martin Buber, and of Berlin salons, where he came in contact with intellectuals like Lou-Andréas Salome, Elsa Lasker-Schüler, Herman Hesse, Theodor Fontane, and Theodor Mommsen, wrote a monumental history of Atheism, and was one of the very few who looked at Hypatia in the German world. In his novel he describes her with rather grotesque traits which give a nod to Expressionism. White cheeks, the temples vascularised by light blue veins, big teeth, a big nose, "dead" and marble-like eyes like those of a statue or a vampire, Hypatia marries, in this novel, the "schwartzlockige halbbeduine Synesios von Kirene", the young Synesius, "with curly black hair and half-Bedouin".

What matters the most, though, is that just as Kingsley's *Hypatia* had running through her veins the political and ecclesiastical debate of the Oxford Movement England and, in general, the "Catholic question", which emerged towards the end of the 1820s with the Catholic Emancipation Act and ended in 1850 with the first pontifical nomination of a Catholic Archbishop of Westminster since the Anglican schism of the first half of the sixteenth century, the same was true of Mauthner's Hypatia with regard to the political situation and the cultural environment of the Germanic world. Here the Catholic Church had reacquired power after the failure of Bismarck's *Kulturkampf*, which had culminated twenty years earlier with the expulsion of Jesuits from Germany, the rupture with the Vatican in 1872, and the "Laws of May" in 1873–74.

As someone wrote, in Mauthner's novel "re-presenting the story of Hypatia, while in France and Italy antichristian and anticlerical positions were strengthening, was equivalent to a deliberate reprise of the *Kulturkampf*, which had ended officially only five years earlier, and to calling into question, from a cultural and not political or parliamentary perspective, its outcomes in Germany"[131]. The conflict between Hypatia and Cyril represented by Mauthner clearly echoes the ancient yet always relevant strife between Church and State, between the idea of a secular State and that of theocratic rule. In Mauthner's work, the erosion of secular power by the Church and already detected by Socrates Scholasticus[132], is, in the words of Bismarck, a "power struggle as old as the human race". It is not about "the clash between faith and agnosticism",

---

130 Praechter 1916, col. 248.
131 De Pol, p. 91.
132 Socrates VII 13, 9, p. 358, 13–14 Hansen; VII 7, 4, p. 353, 2–6 Hansen.

Bismarck argued, but about "the defense of the State; we need to set the limits of the power of priests and of that of the ruler: such limits must be drawn".[133]

---

[133] BISMARCK.

Appendix
Kulturkampf. Hypatia *à la Bismarck*

The initial quotation is taken from the article *Hypatia* by PRAECHTER 1916, col. 248.

The first scientific study on Fritz Mauthner's novel (MAUTHNER, *Hypatia. Roman aus dem Altertum*, 1892) is that of DE POL. De Pol offers not just an intellectual biography of the author and an accurate analysis of his thought within the cultural context of Bismarck's empire, but also an exegesis of his work on Hypatia, which sheds light on the complexity and the coherence of its political message, and stands against the previous reductive judgments, like that of GAJERI, pp. 114–116, who defines Mauthner's work as a "parodic novel". According to De Pol, Mauthner's *Hypatia* should be considered an ideological and metahistorical "novel of ideas", centred around the contrast between "a secular account of the State which enables the existence of a multicultural and multiethnic society, in which Christians, Jews, and followers of Pagan cults can coexist, versus the vision of a Church that takes over and conditions society": DE POL, p. 100. The deliberate "modernisation" of the historical event by which Mauthner's work is inspired is evident in the frequent and blatant lexical anachronisms that permeate his prose, such as the use of "Sacred Roman Empire" ("das heilige römische Reich") to indicate the Roman-Byzantine empire of the fifth century: DE POL, pp. 94–100.

On the author, beside the excellent DE POL, see RUPRECHTER. On the theory of language as "monster without substance" ("wesenloses Unding"), described in previous work, see ESCHENBACHER quoted in DE POL, p. 83, n. 5.

On his history of Atheism (*Der Atheismus und seine Geschichte im Abendlande*, I-IV, 1920–23) see DE POL, p. 83 and n. 6.

The quotations on Hypatia are taken from MAUTHNER, pp. 72 e 80.

On Kingsley's *Hypatia* and its systematic references to the political and ecclesiastical debate in England see above, chapter "New Faces For Old Foes" and Appendix *ad loc.*

The quotation is taken from DE POL, p. 91.

According to Socrates Scholasticus, Cyril aimed to "erode" and "influence the power of the State" beyond every limit ever conceded by the ancient world "to the priestly sphere": SOCRATES SCHOLASTICUS VII 13, 9, p. 358, 13–14 Hansen; see also VII 7, 4, p. 353, 2–6 Hansen; cf. below, part III, chapter "The Power of Hypatia" and Appendix *ad loc.*

The final quotation is taken from Bismarck's speech at the High Chamber, which can be found in Otto Von Bismarck, *Über Königtum und Priestertum (10 March 1873)*, in *Fürst Bismarcks gesammelte Reden*, Globus, Berlin, s.d., vol. II, pp. 7–8.

More information on Hypatia's fortune in 19th-century literature – for example the theatrical work of BEER, – as well as on many other literary works of the previous centuries can be found in the item by ASMUS 1907; see also SCHUBERT; and GAJERI, pp. 111–116, with bibliography in the notes *ad loc.*

Among the modernising works so far quoted there is also the edifying and still felicitious short volume dedicated to Hypatia by Elbert Hubbard, the eclectic American activist famous for his *A Message to Garcia* (HUBBARD). The short volume is the tenth of his series *Little Journeys to the Homes of Great Teachers*. Hubbard's book is somewhat similar to *The Martyrdom of Hypatia or The Death of the Classical World: A Lecture*, a speech delivered by Mangasar Magurditch *Mangasarian* at the Majestic Theatre of Chicago on May *1915*, first published by the Independent Religious Society. It can be found in MANGASARIAN.

21 Celestial Virgin

Yet, in truth, the great popularity of Hypatia in poetry and literature is due to the dramatic contrast between her sex and her involvement in two male things: philosophy and a violent death, so much so that she became a martyr, though not a Christian one.

In the *Palatine Anthology* there is an epigram, attributed to Palladas, probably a funerary inscription for her tomb or her cenotaph, whose past translations, starting from the Latin one by Grotius, have seized on debatable Christian allusions and only rarely noted by contrast the undeniable and secret astrological resonance:

> Whenever I look upon you I pay reverence
> To you and your wise learning,
> And I look upon the heavenly House of the Virgin.
> For your deeds are inscribed in the heavens,
> Revered Hypatia, you who are yourself the perfection
> of reasoning,
> The immaculate star of philosophy[134].

The assumption into heaven or, as the ancients called it, the 'catasterism' of Hypatia, that is to say her probable though arcane and unfathomable identification with the astral Virgin, are perfectly compatible with the Pagan mentality and even more appropriate since Hypatia is not only a great aristocrat like Berenice, whose tresses celebrated by Callimachus transmuted into a constellation, but also a Neoplatonic philosopher, an astronomer, an observer and a connoisseur of the heavens.

While it would be hard to interpret the epigram of the *Palatine Anthology* as a Christian celebration, or to share the abstruse but stubbornly pleaded conjecture that, with the expression 'house of the Virgin', the author refers to an ecclesiastical building dedicated to the Mother of God, therefore celebrating not our Hypatia but a namesake and anonymous Christian benefactress, or even, as recently suggested, a nun, it is however true that in both the forms the memory of Hypatia was honoured with – that of philosopher and that of celestial figure – her story was transfused, in the later imagination, into another effectively Christian event: that of the phantom Saint Catherine of Alexandria, the virgin and aristocratic philosopher martyred in the Egyptian metropolis at the beginning of the 4th century, according to a belated Byzantine hagiographical legend. As famous as Hypatia for her knowledge and eloquence and for the daring manner in which she spoke to the powerful, Catherine is said to have been martyred by Maximinus Daia, one of the adversaries of Constantine during the tetrarchy.

The story or *Passio* of this martyr, which would later inspire Joan of Arc, appears in hagiographical texts after the death of Hypatia, not before the 6th century; yet it was only in the 9th century that she appeared in the devotions of the holy men of the Mount

---

[134] *AP* IX 400.

Sinai monastery built by Justinian. Although the complex was firstly dedicated to the Transfiguration of Christ, it later took the name of Saint Catherine of Sinai. The elusive saint then became a celebrity both in the Byzantine world and, above all, in the West, probably more due to the iconographic diffusion than to the literary circulation of her *Lives*.

Scholars who have worked on the exiguous number of Byzantine *Passiones* that mention her suspect that the Christian saint was loaned the traits of the 'lay saint' – and lay virgin and martyr – massacred not by the Roman emperor Maximinus, pretender to the legitimate sceptre of Constantine, but by the "Pharaoh of Egyptian Monophysitism", Cyril, the usurper of the lawful State power stemming from the central government of Constantinople, the capital that Constantine would found[135].

That the martyrdom of Saint Catherine of Alexandria and even her historical existence were false was argued in the 18th century by the Maurine scholar Jean-Pierre Déforis, and indeed her name day was abolished by the Breviary of Paris. Although poor Dom Déforis died on the guillotine in 1794, the scepticism of both lay and ecclesiastical scholars survived, motivated also by the absence of traces of a veneration of her tomb in the pilgrimage routes of the Early Middle Ages to Sinai, despite the legend about her body and her head being miraculously carried there by two angels, straight after her martyrdom. Uncertainties about her were such and so many as to induce the Catholic Church, in 1969, to exclude the saint from the liturgical calendar; she would only be reinstated in 2002. Nevertheless, the identification of Saint Catherine of Alexandria with Hypatia, or rather the theory that the story of the Christian martyr was from the beginning a transposition of the Pagan martyr, dates from the Victorian 19th century and is owed to the adventurous intuition of Anna Jameson, an Irish writer, a historical Proto-Feminist and pioneer of women's studies, who, with the encouragement of Charles Eastlake, the discoverer of the *Flagellation* by Piero della Francesca, meticulously evaluated ancient sacred art. In her *Sacred and Legendary Art* she was explicit:

> But it is a curious fact connected with the history of Saint Catherine, that the real martyr, the only one of whom there is any certain record, was not a Christian, but a Heathen; and that her oppressors were not Pagan tyrants, but Christian fanatics.
>
> Hypatia of Alexandria, daughter of Theon, a celebrated mathematician, had applied herself from childhood to the study of philosophy and science, and with such success, that, while still a young woman, she was invited by the magistrates to preside over one of the principal schools in the city. She, like Saint Catherine, was particularly addicted to the study of Plato, whom she preferred to Aristotle. She was profoundly versed in the works of Euclid and Apollonius of Perga; and composed a treatise on Conic Sections and other scientific works. She was remarkable, also, for her beauty, her contempt for feminine vanities, and the unblemished purity of her conduct. As, however, she resolutely refused to declare herself a Christian and was on terms of friendship with Orestes, the Pagan [sic] governor of Alexandria, she was marked out by the Christian populace as an object of vengeance. One day, as she was proceeding to lecture in her school, a party of

---

135 See BRONZINI.

these wretched fanatics dragged her out of her chariot into a neighbouring church, and murdered her there with circumstances of revolting barbarity[136].

The transfer Hypatia/Catherine of Alexandria would rebound amongst the pages of the *Encyclopaedia Britannica* and it would spread from there to the common opinion of cultured lay classes. In the wake of the early scepticism of Dom Déforis and its followers, Catholic and not, it would also contaminate the ecclesiastical lexicons. It would become the focus of mystical syncretism, with an esoteric, astrological background, of the early 20th century.

However, in a poem written in 1937, the devoutly Catholic Paul Claudel rebelled against this version. He wrote in magnificent rhyme:

Reste le corps !	May the body rest!
Un ange alors	An angel
Est venu le ramasser.	Has come to take it.
Un ange en or	An angel dressed in gold
A pris le corps,	Has taken the body.
L'autre la tête coupée !	Another has taken the severed head!
Que le païen	Let the Pagan
Garde son bien,	Conserve his hoard,
George Sand et Hypatie!	George Sand and Hypatia!
Toi, Vérité,	You, Truth,
On t'a portée	Were brought
Sur la cime du Sinaï!	To the peak of the Sinai!
Sur cette assise,	Sitting here,
Là où Moïse	Where Moses
Regarda Dieu face à face,	Looked into the face of God,
C'est là, précise,	It was there
Que t'on a mise,	That you were placed,
Sagesse pleine de grâce![137]	o gracious wisdom!

---

[136] JAMESON; see JAMESON – HURLL, vol. II, p. 467.
[137] CLAUDEL, vol. II, p. 354.

Appendix
Celestial Virgin

The epigram from PALLADAS can be found in the *Palatine Anthology: AP* IX 400 (*Anthologia Palatina*, vol. VIII, p. 25 Waltz). See also HARICH-SCHWARZBAUER 2011, p. 304. On the dating of Palladas see CAMERON 2016a.

The Latin translation of Grotius (H. van Groot) is reported in a footnote to the *editio princeps* of PHILOSTORGIUS and reproduced in Ménage: see above, chapter "The Excesses of Fanaticism", Appendix *ad loc.*

The attribution to Palladas was debated for (in reality inconsistent) chronological reasons; or, otherwise, was maintained, but it was then supposed that the Hypatia, to whom the epigram was dedicated, was not the daughter of Theon: see MEYER, p. 52; LUCK, who wants to see in it a Christian celebration, contested by IRMSCHER; see also BOWRA; CAMERON 1965, and CAMERON 1993, pp. 323–325, who even identifies the Hypatia in the epigram with "a nun author of religious songs, of whom the poem describes the image portrayed beside that of the Theotokos in a church beside the convent", provocatively extremising the erroneous Christian interpretation of the poem already proposed by LUCK, and repeated by DZIELSKA 1995, pp. 22–23. The (false) problem is repeatedly taken up also by BERETTA 1993, pp. 89–90, 139–140, 187–233, 250–251; see also HARICH-SCHWARZBAUER 2011, pp. 302–312.

Already allayed by IRMSCHER, the error has now been thoroughly dealt with by LIVREA 1997, who confirms the epigram by Palladas to have been written "as an epigraph on Hypatia's tomb or cenotaph, which would probably have been placed in a Pagan temple or, better, in an educational institution (for example of Platonic stamp) in Alexandria" and in which "the portrayal perhaps in mosaic of the celestial face that welcomes Hypatia as a hypostasis of the Virgin would be very little different from contemporary Christian mosaics".

For an interpretation – perhaps an overinterpretation – of the epigram's content in the light of Palladas' poetic context, and of the debate on the 'fair political practice' that inflamed the Hellenic milieu between the end of the 4th and the beginning of the 5th century, see BERETTA 2012.

The catasterism of Hypatia, alluded to by the epigram, is compared by LIVREA 1997 to that of the Cynic Diogenes, although the Cynic look (*ibidem*, p. 100) of Hypatia, presented by Damascius, may cast some doubts: see below, part III, chapter "Hypatia in All Her States of Being".

GAJERI, pp. 29–30 and nn. 140–144, interprets what she considers the *syngeneia* (συγγένεια) established by Palladas with the astral Virgin as an allusion to the traditional virtues associated by astrology with those born under this sign. Her translation of the epigram is inspired by this reading, where the word *logoi* (λόγοι) would seem to be seen not only and not merely as Hypatia's "discourses", "thoughts" or in general "knowledge", but also her esoteric prophecies.

On Saint Catherine of Alexandria see in general BALBONI – BRONZINI – BRANDI; BARDY 1949.

For the late martyrological texts that tell the story of the fictitious saint, their criticisms and in general the argumentation on the lack of historical basis for this figure see BRONZINI, a vast and comprehensive study of all the historical material on the subject, to which we refer readers also for the comprehensive bibliography of the previous editions of the *Passiones* (*PG*, Viteat, Varnhagen etc.) and the studies of ecclesiastical scholarship relating to them, amongst which we will only mention DELEHAYE; see also BADINI CONFALONIERI 2014, p. 13 and n. 4.

With regard to the iconographic diffusion of Saint Catherine of Alexandria there is, amongst others, the well-known painting by Caravaggio held in Madrid; or the unacknowledged painting, attributed to Barna da Siena, now preserved at the Museum of Fine Arts of Boston, spotted in 1858 by Otto Mündler in the Roman house of that Anna Jameson, to whom, as we shall see below, we owe the identification of St. Catherine with Hypatia, (*The Travel Diaries of Otto Mündler*, "Walpole Society" 51, 1985. p. 234). However, the most glorious pictorial homage to the saint is that realised between 1427 and 1430 in Rome by Masolino (and partially by Masaccio) in the frescoes of the chapel of Saint Catherine in Saint Clement's Basilica, where there are also precise allusions to the historical events of Byzantium, particularly significant on the 15th-century international chessboard and particularly noted by the party who commissioned the work, the Humanist Cardinal Branda Castiglioni, linked to the Council of Constance and later delegated to the Byzantine question by Pope Martin V.

Many collections, also ecclesiastical, describe a suspension of Saint Catherine between 1969 and 2002 "from the Roman Martyrology", which never really took place: Saint Catherine of Alexandria has always been present there as she is now. In 1969, however, due to a lack of "scientific proof" of the sources, her memory was officially removed from the liturgical calendar of the Catholic Church through the *Motu Proprio* of February 14th 1969, under Pope Paul VI; see MEINARDUS 1999b, p. 44 and n. 16. She was restored to the liturgical calendar in the *editio typica tertia* of the MISSALE ROMANUM (2002), with her saint's day on November 25th. See also BADINI CONFALONIERI 2014, p. 14 and n. 8.

The *Sacred and Legendary Art* (1874) by Anna JAMESON, who for the first time, following in Charles Eastlake's footsteps, matched the information of the *Acta Sanctorum* and the hagiographical collections like the *Legenda Aurea* with the interpretation of Christian art, remained incomplete; the last part was completed and published by Lady Eastlake with the title *The History of Our Lord in Art* (JAMESON-EASTLAKE). The normative edition of the work is the posthumous one, curated and annotated by Estelle M. Hurll (1904), where the passage quoted is to be found (JAMESON – HURLL, vol. II, p. 467).

The identification proposed by Anna Jameson is taken up and extended by the item *Hypatia* in the 1881 edition of the XII volume of the *Encyclopaedia Britannica* (p. 598); see also KUNST, p. 180 and n. 2; ASMUS 1907, p. 18. It was recently made popular by the famous novel about Hypatia by Andrée FERRETTI, *Renaissance en Paganie* (1987), which ends with and culminates in the identification of Hypatia with Saint Catherine. An extensive study of this novel is found in CACCHIOLI.

According to THORP's synthesis: "The Bollandists – the rigorous Jesuit society which looks into the historicity of saints – began to suspect about a hundred years ago that the legend of Saint Catherine was simply without historical foundation. Their doubts led to the dropping of Saint Catherine from the Roman Catholic calendar of feast days in 1969. But they also suspected – and this suspicion is now widely shared – that the story of Saint Catherine was merely a Christian reworking of the story of Hypatia, Hypatia who had maintained a high if blurry reputation in the minds of the Alexandrian populace. So, colleagues, I leave you with a little puzzle for the theory of reference: Saint Catherine does not exist; she is really Hypatia".

Amongst the recent positions on the genesis of the Christian legend of Saint Catherine of Alexandria from the Pagan martyrdom of Hypatia see first of all BRONZINI, p. 296 and the footnote, in which the author also mentions the opinion of previous scholars. See also MEINARDUS 1999b, pp. 46–47; GAJERI, pp. 43–44; BERETTA 1993, pp. 232–233, where the opinions of A. GUIDUCCI and L. MURARO are also cited; DEAKIN 2007, pp. 135–136; DZIELSKA 1995, pp. 21–22.

The overlapping of Hypatia and Catherine has at times generated confusion and, paradoxically, lent grist to the mill of the purported conversion of Hypatia to Christianity: see for example RICHARDSON, p. 173; but also MEINARDUS 1999b and others.

Finally, see the interesting information on the dedication to "Saint Hypatia Catherine" of a church near Laodicea on the Lycus in Asia Minor, provided by MYRSILIDES and repeated in SPETZIERIS.

Claudel's *Sainte Catherine d'Alexandrie* (1937) can be read in CLAUDEL, vol. II, p. 354.

22 Miraculous Devotion. Chateaubriand, Péguy and the Flourishing of Feminist Literature

It may seem surprising that an equally fervent Catholic author, an expert in martyrdoms moreover, such as Chateaubriand, should not share the intolerance for the Pagan 'ancient George Sand' showed by Claudel, but rather exalted her for being "the expiator of the blood of the martyrs shed by the Hellenes"; and without betraying the temptation to validate in any way her compatibility with the ideals of Christianity, let alone a belated adherence to its *génie*.

The fact is, that once again current events influenced the consideration of past events. In the *Génie du christianisme*, where we firstly find mentioned Hypatia's assassination, Chateaubriand is disturbed by the violent events of the French Revolution[138]; in particular, by the affinity between the death of Hypatia and that of an astronomer, his contemporary, Jean Sylvain Bailly.

In his *Histoire de l'astronomie moderne*, Bailly dealt with the Alexandrian teacher and drew a parallel between antiquity and modernity: "She was massacred and torn apart by the inhabitants of Alexandria, who were jealous of her glory. The invidious modernists mangle reputation, but at least they spare life"[139]. An idea that history would promptly contradict. Mayor of Paris during the Revolution, but an exponent of the moderate wing and considered responsible for the massacre in the Champs de Mars of 1791, Bailly would be guillotined two years later before a howling mob.

As in Toland, in Kingsley and in Mauthner, also in Chateaubriand the interest in Hypatia's tragic story is therefore bound to the identification of its actors with characters from the present; and to the idea of a continuation, in the historical mechanism, of a recurrent model: the antagonism between the moderate intellectual, destined to assume a difficult position when s/he enters the political fray, and the extremist mass stirred by demagogy.

Chateaubriand returns to the topic in the *Third Discourse on the Fall of the Roman Empire*. Here it is the uprisings of 1830 that weigh on the opinion of the now-aged author. Defining Hypatia "a celestial creature who lived in the company of the stars, who equalled them in beauty and who had taken from them the most sublime influences", he concludes the narration of her life and death, taken, it would seem, first hand from the ancient sources (Damascius' *Life of Isidore* in the edition by Fabricius, Socrates Scholasticus in Valois' edition) with an interesting consideration:

> *Le combat des idées anciennes contre les idées nouvelles à cette époque offre un spectacle que rend plus instructif celui auquel nous assistons. Ce n'était plus, comme au temps de Julien, un mouvement rétrograde, c'était, au contraire, une course sur la pente du siècle; mais de vieilles mœurs, de vieux souvenirs, de vieilles habitudes, de vieux préjugés disputaient pied à pied le terrain: en abandonnant*

---

138 CHATEAUBRIAND 1828, p. 552.
139 BAILLY, vol. I, p. 207.

le culte des aïeux, on croyait trahir les foyers, les tombeaux, l'honneur, la patrie. La violence, exercée en opposition avec l'esprit de la loi, rendait le conflit plus opiniâtre; on reprochait aux chrétiens d'oublier dans la fortune les préceptes de charité qu'ils recommandaient dans le malheur.[140]

In this period, the contrast between ancient and modern ideas offers a spectacle that makes more instructive the scenario we are witnessing now. It was no longer, as in the times of Julian, a question of a retrograde movement; it was on the contrary a long race along the slippery slope of the century. Nonetheless, some of the old customs, memories, habits and prejudices contended for ground inch by inch against the new: in abandoning the cult of the ancestors, many believed that they were betraying the household hearths, the tombs, the honour and the homeland. The violence, exercised in contrast with the spirit of the law, made the conflict more obstinate; the Christians were accused of forgetting in their fortune the precepts of charity that they recommended in adversity.

In fact, what made the 'pure' men of letters of the 19th century love Hypatia was certainly not her presumed conversion to Christianity, but on the contrary her devotion to Platonism and Hellenism under siege from cultural barbarities inside, and ethnic assaults outside the empire.

In this completely secular predilection for Hypatia, the modern poets built a bridge with the Alexandrians that straddled the rest of literature. In the notes of Renée Vivien, "Hypatia comes on the scene in a long, fluttering, white gown, with Ionic draping, inspired and glorious, as beautiful as an ancient goddess" and "she preached the ideal when all around her was impoverished and dilapidated. She knows that her words fall like pearls into the sea, lost in the abyss"[141].

Yet, to have been not so much a philosopher as a martyr, though secular, subtracts Hypatia from the presumed exemplary status that her story assumes in the variegated flourishing of Feminist literature grown up around her since the 19th century, without escaping the sarcasm of Henry James, who at the end of *The Bostonians* suggests an exhilarating parallel between the lessons of Hypatia and the fanciful rally planned by the suffragette Verena Tarrent[142]. The flourishing of Feminist literature, after the authentically activist phase witnessed in writings such as the Fabian-socialist *Hypatia* by Dora Russell, who uses the name of the "University lecturer denounced by Church dignitaries and torn to pieces by Christians" as the title of a properly political pamphlet on the condition of women[143], became unruly and slightly suffocating at the end of the 20th century. On the contrary, the death and the historiographical transfiguration of Hypatia are not an exception, but rather a confirmation of the inflexibility of the roles, in the traditional and implicitly masculine viewpoint that determines them. And which at a popular level is quietly perpetuated in the Christian metamorphosis of her martyrdom, that of Catherine of Alexandria.

As Charles Péguy wrote in his *Cahiers:*

---

[140] CHATEAUBRIAND 1832, pp. 51–52.
[141] VIVIEN, p. 57.
[142] JAMES, p. 448.
[143] RUSSELL 1925, p. iii.

> *Ce que nous aimons, ce que nous honorons c'est ce miracle de fidélité [...] qu'une âme fut si parfaitement accordée à l'âme platonicienne et à sa filiale, l'âme plotinienne, et généralement à l'âme héllenique, à l'âme de sa race, à l'âme de son maître, à l'âme de son père, d'un accord si profond, si intérieur, atteignant si profondement aux sources mêmes, aux racines, que dans un anéantissement peut-être total, quand tout un monde se désaccordait, pour toute la vie temporelle du monde et peut-être pour l'eternité, seule elle soit demeurée accordée jusque dans la mort.*[144]
>
> That which we love and that which we honour is this miracle of fidelity [...] that a soul should be so perfectly in harmony with the Platonic soul, and with its descendant, the Plotinian soul, and in general with the Hellenic soul, with the soul of her race, with the soul of her master, with the soul of her father, in such a profound agreement, so intimate, reaching so deeply into the sources themselves and into the roots, that perhaps in total annihilation, when the entire world fell into discord, for all the temporal life of the world, and perhaps for eternity, she alone would remain in harmony, until death.

This reactionary Socialist, according to whom Hypatia died only in the 20th century, killed in her essence by the "stupidity of modern times", while the "rough and dirty monks who came from Thebaid like a nocturnal pack of emaciated dogs had assassinated only her body", can identify in her every true intellectual and therefore, to paraphrase Flaubert, also himself: "Hypatie c'est moi!"

---

[144] PÉGUY, pp. 1110–1111.

Appendix

Miraculous Devotion. Chateaubriand, Péguy and the Flourishing of Feminist Literature

That in Chateaubriand the anti-Cyrillian position, which was also contrary to the 'revolutionary' Christianity of the origins, was born from the reality of his era, that is, from the disapproval of the revolutionary massacres, is argued by GAJERI, pp. 89–92. According to the different opinion of MERELLO, p. 105, Hypatia's death was implicitly laid, in Chateubriand, on "antichristian thought".

Yet, the amazement for the position of Chateaubriand regarding Hypatia is in fact unfounded and purely superficial, since originally his *Martyrs* were conceived to celebrate Paganism.

The mention of the assassination of Hypatia as an example of barbarity can be read in CHATEAUBRIAND 1828, p. 552 (Engl. transl.: p. 133 White).

The fatal phrase of Bailly can be read in BAILLY, vol. I, p. 207: "Hésychius raconte qu'elle fut massacrée et déchirée par les habitants d'Alexandrie, jaloux de sa gloire. Les envieux modernes épargnent au moins la vie, en déchirant la réputation".

The precise parallelism between Bailly and Hypatia is established by Chateaubriand in the same page of the *Génie du christianisme:* "Ce savant est mort victime des principes que nous avons entrepris de combattre. [...] Il ne se doutait guère qu'il serait lui-même une preuve lamentable de la fausseté de son assertion, et qu'il renouvellerait l'histoire d'Hypatia!" ["That philosopher fell a victim to the principles which we have undertaken to refute. [...] Little did he suspect that he would himself afford a lamentable proof of the fallacy of his assertion, and that in his own person the tragic story of Hypatia would be repeated!"].

The interesting opinion on Paganism in the 5th century by Chateaubriand in the *Troisième discours sur la chûte de l'Empire Romain* can be read in CHATEAUBRIAND 1832, pp. 51–52.

His portrait of Hypatia comes immediately before this: "Le sang chrétien que répandirent les mains philosophiques d'Hellade fut trop expié plusieurs années après par celui d'Hypatia. Fille de Théon le géomètre, d'un génie supérieur à son père, elle étoit née, avoit été nourrie et élevée à Alexandrie. Savante en astronomie, au dessus des convenances de son sexe, elle fréquentoit les écoles et enseignoit elle-même la doctrine d'Aristote et de Platon: on l'appeloit le Philosophe. Les magistrats lui rendoient des honneurs; on voyoit tous les jours à sa porte une foule de gens à pied et à cheval qui s'empressoient de la voir et de l'entendre. [...] L'évêque d'Alexandrie, Cyrille, devint jaloux de la gloire d'Hypatia. La populace chrétienne, ayant à sa tête un lecteur nommé Pierre, se jeta sur la fille de Théon, lorsqu'elle rentrait un jour dans la maison de son père: ces forcenés la traînèrent à l'église Cesarium, la mirent toute nue, et la déchiquetèrent avec des coquilles tranchantes; ils brûlèrent ensuite sur la place Cinaron les membres de la créature céleste qui vivoit dans la société des astres qu'elle égaloit en beauté, et dont elle avoît ressenti les influences les plus sublimes".

In the German world, almost one century later, the position of Chateaubriand appears to be echoed in the essay by Johannes Scherr, where Hypatia is celebrated with empathy and characterised as "swimming against the tide" ("gegen den Strom zu schwimmen") but Cyril is exonerated by the author, who lays all the blame at the feet of the fanaticism of the mob and actualises the ancient event in the light of an anti-revolutionary polemic in which the death of Hypatia is (rightly) compared to that of a well-known victim of the French Revolution, Princess Lamballe: SCHERR; see GAJERI, p. 111.

The undeniably grandiose project on Hypatia of Renée Vivien, where the visionary representation of the Platonic philosopher in austere Neoclassical Art Nouveau garb is united with a reading of her character that is both decadent and Proto-Feminist, can be read in VIVIEN. The quotation is taken from p. 57: "Une conférence d'Hypathie... Description de la salle, où sont assemblés les Grecs efféminés, l'entrée d'Hypathie, comme une statue de Pallas Athénée, dans sa longue robe blanche flottante, draperie ionique, inspirée et glorieuse. Belle comme une déesse antique. La conférence inspirée par Platon, toute en vers... Mais, pour cela, il faut que j'étudie et que je comprenne Platon, il faut que je sache le grec". And a few lines further on: "Elle prêche l'Idéal, lorsque tout autour d'elle est déchu et dépravé, elle parle à une race dégénérée, elle sait que ses paroles tombent comme des perles dans la mer, perdues au fond de l'abîme".

On Hypatia as a martyr and on the features of the martyrological genre traceable in the most ancient narrations of her case see below, part III, chapters "Hypatia's Sacrifice" and "The Martyrdom of Hypatia", with Appendices *ad loc.*

On the Proto-Feminist versions of Hypatia by Olympe de Gouges and Anna Jameson see above, chapters "The Excesses of Fanaticism" and "Celestial Virgin".

On the mention of Hypatia in Henry James see GAJERI, p. 143. The page with Verena Tarrant's renunciation of the long-awaited, crowded meeting, for love of Basil Ransom, can be read in JAMES, p. 448: "If he had observed her, it might have seemed to him that she hoped to find the fierce expiation she sought for in exposure to the thousands she had disappointed and deceived, in offering herself to be trampled to death and torn to pieces. She might have suggested to him [...] the sacrificial figure of Hypatia, whirled through the furious mob of Alexandria".

Dora Russell, the second wife of Bertrand Russell, wrote her *Hypatia* as a Feminist response to Anthony Ludovici's *Lysistrata, or Woman's Future and Future Woman* (1925). Russell's pamphlet does not deal directly with Hypatia, but as is explicitly written in the brief preface, it was written *in the name* of Hypatia: "Hypatia was a University lecturer denounced by Church dignitaries and torn to pieces by Christians. Such will probably be the fate of this book: therefore it bears her name. What I have written here I believe, and shall not retract or change for similar episcopal denunciations": RUSSELL 1925, p. iii.

A symbol of Feminist literature on the case of Hypatia in America is the journal "Hypatia: A Journal of Feminist Philosophy", published since 1986 at the Indiana University, not to be confused with the journal with a similar name published in Athens from 1984 onwards, "Hypatia: Feminist Studies", which in the first issue, on pages 3–11, under the title *Hypatia, the Alexandrian Philosopher*, hosted the English summary of the slim informative work by Voula Lambropoulou which had already appeared in modern Greek (Υπατία, ἡ Ἀλεξανδρινὴ φιλόσοφος), with a summary in French ("Hypatia, philosophe alexandrine"): see LAMBROPOULOU. In the American journal, where Hypatia is proclaimed "foresister", over the years, there have been rather eccentric contributions on her life and work. One example is *A Christian Martyr in Reverse: Hypatia 370–415 A.D.: A Vivid Portrait of the Life and Death of Hypatia as Seen through the Eyes of a Feminist Poet and Novelist* by Ursule MOLINARO, who makes Hypatia a symbol not only of Feminism, but also of sexual liberation and represents her not only married to an open and tolerant Isidore, but also surrounded by a harem of young lovers and linked by an *amitié amoureuse* to the prefect Orestes. The long poem was published in the journal in 1989, precisely ten years after the inclusion of Hypatia in the last installation, at the San Francisco Museum of Modern Art (1979), of the *Dinner Party*, a work by the Feminist artist Judy Chicago, which marked in that year the beginning of the great visibility of Hypatia in American Post-Feminism.

Amongst the most pompous but not therefore more reliable Anglo-Saxon publications on this thread of women's studies, see OSER, where it is erroneously stated (p. 27) that "Hypatia carried out her philosophical and rhetorical studies in Athens", and that "the majority of her mathematical works were destroyed together with the Ptolemaic libraries of Alexandria, when the Serapeum was ransacked by the mob and only fragments of her work remain", as well as that "a portion of her original treatise on the *Astronomical Canon* by Diophantus was found in the 15th century in the Vatican library: it is probable that it was taken there after the fall of Constantinople" [*sic*]. Equally unreliable on this topic, MILES; certainly not reliable, but more interesting, VARE – PTACEK, pp. 24–26; disarming DONOVAN. A work well documented yet tainted by gender prejudice ("We must consider Hypatia's gender as cause for her murder") is MINARDI.

In the Germanic field, beside the already quoted and more serious work by HARICH-SCHWARZBAUER 2002, see e.g. ENGELS; and of course the various works dedicated to Hypatia and self-published by MAEGER 1995; MAEGER 1999; MAEGER 2002. A vanguard of this *lignée* in the Germanic world is ADAM.

Even French culture was not immune from the Feminist reading of the case of Hypatia. Despite the fact that it had noble ancestors in Olympe de Gouges and in Renée Vivien, in the 1980s this thread precipitated into a version such as that of Michel Clévenot: "On ne sait pas très bien pourquoi autour de toi un jour ils s'assemblèrent. Fanatisme, obscurantisme… Sexisme aussi, assurément" (CLÉVENOT, p. 147).

The first passage from Charles Péguy is taken from *De la situation fait au parti intellectuel dans le monde moderne* (PÉGUY, pp. 1110–1111). The second passage is from *Les Suppliants parallèles* (PÉGUY, pp. 933–935).

On the context of the evocation of Hypatia in the *Cahiers* in question (in *Les Suppliants parallèles* the analysis of the petition to the Tsar by the workers of Petersburg during the uprisings of 1905, in relation to the "Great Meeting" of the Socialist Party in favour of the Russian Revolution, organised at the end of the same year at the Trianon; in the *Onzième cahier* the polemic over the philosophy of progress and the destructive effects of the freedom of the moderns) and on their role in the Socialist debate of the time see GAJERI, pp. 133–137.

23 Superfluous Heroisms

Before Péguy, the 'purity' of Hypatia could not but strike the heart of a lover of both the Hellenic race and its mysticism like Maurice Barrès[145], who, by his own quirk, calls her 'Athénée' instead of using her own name, underscoring thus her symbolic incarnation as last priestess of Hellenism, and challenging posterity to recognise, concealed in the name, the identity of a heroine who is all too well-known to the 19th century and even entered the dialogues of Bouvard and Pécuchet via Flaubert's irony[146].

To avoid uselessly distracting his readers from his poignantly reactionary objective – to show the superior elegance of the conservation of the past opposed to the barbarity of the new, which pressed forward together with the threatening power grab of the masses and the regrettable march of Socialism – Barrès pre-dates the symbolic death of Athénée/Hypatia to the time of Theophilus, simultaneous with the destruction of the Serapeum, with the twofold advantage of presenting his heroine, with some chronological congruity, as a young maiden, and giving the *grand guignol* of her assassination a theatrically worthy scenario:

> With the triple crown of its crumbling galleries and the hundred broken steps, the Serapeum dominated the splendour, the luxury and all the fanaticisms of the city. On its fissured walls flowered wild capers. Yet it looked like the tomb of Hellas. The images of ancient glories and more than seven hundred thousand volumes filled it. These noble reliquaries lived on in the piety of an august virgin, Athénée, personification of our disheveled sensitivity that withdraws into its ivory tower.

The *Superfluous Heroisms* by Barrès, later included in *Sous l'oeil des barbares* [*Under Barbarian Eyes*], are set in that Alexandria "capital of philosophies and religions, of the Gnosis and the syncretisms" that Louis Ménard had already evoked in *Rêveries d'un païen mystique*. In *La Légende de Saint Hilarion*, with deliberate anachronism, he turned the hermit saint into a pupil of the "ingenious allegories" and the "serious parables" of Hypatia's lessons. He had called her "an austere virgin and a Pagan saint", whose "radiant serenity dissipated the storms of the soul; the distraught souls were calmed when contemplating her calm beauty, listening to her austere words". Hypatia was a "calm, azure lake that reflected the sky"[147].

Barrès, on the other hand, describes her immobile in her white peplos at night, "in ecstasy on the towers of the Serapeum". Not in her private residence, thus, but within the colossal and decadent symbol of Paganism: "[…] in a great hall clad in splendid mosaics and decorated with human thoughts", the "virgin initiated into the secrets and protected by the gods" transmitted "like a young sovereign, from her glances and her harmonious and calm gestures" the arcane traditions, and with them "the dignity of thought and the courage of memory", to a restricted circle of elite spirits – "Romans

---

145 Barrès 1885.
146 Flaubert, p. 329.
147 Ménard 18862, pp. 56, 58–59, 66.

and Greeks, also with some elegant female admirer of eloquence" – who felt, like Barrès, exiled from their own century:

> She had received the teachings, and every week she gathered the Hellenes. She supported in those spirits, exiled from their century and from their homeland, the dignity of thinking and the courage of remembering. Also those who were not able to understand loved her.

When in the distance, in a cloud of dust, she sees the gang of monks approaching – "the Hermits!" – as an "immense galloping herd", the "granddaughter of Plato and of Homer" realises she has no escape, that she is destined to become a martyr. She glances at the gardens of the Serapeum, "at the sterility, the ruin of the workrooms", and "a gloomy sadness pervades her like a premonition." She wants to see no more. "From those people who bask in their bestiality she raises her gaze, to the sky, to the divine Helios, surrounded by the immense ether where the most noble souls revolve to the rhythm of the stars."

Before the assembly of her acolytes,

> she raises her hand, and in a low and laboured voice, while the distant bells of Mithra and those of the Christians call their faithful, as the howling mob gathers and only the evening whispers in the cool air, "I swear," she says "I swear that I will always love the noble phrases and high thoughts, and that I would rather renounce life than my independence." And in a calm, almost divine voice, "Swear all of you, brothers!" "Athénée, on what do you want us to swear?" "On me," she answered "I am Hellas."

Appendix
Superfluous Heroisms

The *Héroïsmes superflus* of Barrès appeared in the journal "Tâches d'Encre" in February 1885 and were re-published three years later in *Sous l'oeil des barbares*, Paris 1888. The author was probably influenced by two articles that appeared in 1876, signed by a friend of Renan (who was also interested in Hypatia: see RENAN), Henri Blaze de Bury. Here we find, according to Maurice Davanture, "[…] le modèle d'Athénée dans les *Héroïsmes superflus*. Barrés at-il lu cet article?".

In his *Examen* of the *Culte du moi* (BARRÈS 1892, p. 27, as underscored in MERELLO, p. 109), Barrès openly declared that he identified with Athénée/Hypatia, who was exiled in her own century and lived secluded in her Serapaeum like in an ivory tower, and projected on her what he defines as "the deep layers" of his personality ("la description sincère des couches profondes de ma sensibilité").

The *Rêveries d'un païen mystique* by Louis Ménard, which appeared in Paris in 1876, had had a considerable influence on Ménard's contemporaries. Plotinus' Orientalising Greek thought "turning to the wisdom of the Persians and the Indians" and his followers' thinking met with the philosophical, religious, mystic and esoteric curiosity that the young Barrès shared at the time with his friends Charles Vignier, Jean Moréas, Laurent Tailhade and above all Stanislas de Guaita; curiosity fed, apart from Ménard's text, by impassioned readings of erudite books from late Alexandrian Paganism, for which see FRANDON, p. 47.

The quotations from the *Légende de Saint Hilarion* can be read in MÉNARD 1886^2, pp. 56, 58–59, 66.

The personage of Hypatia is present in many threads of French 19th-century literature with a Masonic stamp and anti-ecclesiastical orientation: for example, a biography entitled *Vie d'Hypatie, femme célèbre, professeur de philosophie dans le deuxième siècle* [sic] *à l'école d'Alexandrie*, decidedly accusatory against Cyril, was published by LASTEYRIE in an appendix to the "translation" of the *Sentences de Sextius, philosophe pythagoricien* (1843).

At the beginning of the 20th century, with the intensification of the clash between the conservative-clerical wing and the secular government of Clemenceau, who fostered a radical separation between Church and State and issued sanctions to expropriate ecclesiastical properties, there was a direct political actualisation in France of the story of Hypatia. Such actualisation resembled that of Kingsley's England and Mauthner's Prussia. An example of this can be found in the drastically anti-Cyrillian stance taken by Maurice Barthélemy (BARTHÉLEMY, pp. 17–18). In his play *Hypatie*, published one year after Barthélemy's work and rediscovered by MERELLO, pp. 110–113, Frédéric Sauvage would respond to Barthélemy's stance with a hesitant and torn Cyril, secretly attracted by Hypatia and completely at the mercy of the fanatical Peter the Reader (SAUVAGE). The clerical Paul Barlatier, in turn, would respond to the work of Sauvage, which mitigated the guilt of Cyril while still denouncing the violence of the Christian

Church, with his *Hypatie. Drame antique en deux parties et en vers*, an even more mediocre play, which was nonetheless staged in grand style in Marseille in 1907 (BARLATIER); on this see MERELLO, pp. 114–116 and nn.

Hypatia is mentioned by Pécuchet, together with Giordano Bruno, in the amusing debate with the curate on the excesses of fanaticism, which can be read in FLAUBERT, p. 329: "Des gouttes d'eau tombèrent. Le curé déploya son parapluie; et Pécuchet, quand il fut dessous, osa prétendre que les catholiques avaient fait plus de martyrs chez les juifs, les musulmans, les protestants, et les libres penseurs que tous les Romains autrefois. L'ecclésiastique se récria: 'Mais on compte dix persécutions depuis Néron jusqu'au césar Galère!' 'Eh bien, et les massacres des Albigeois! et la Saint-Barthélemy! et la Révocation de l'édit de Nantes!' 'Excès déplorables sans doute mais vous n'allez pas comparer ces gens-là à saint Étienne, saint Laurent, Cyprien, Polycarpe, une foule de missionnaires.' 'Pardon! je vous rappellerai Hypatie, Jérôme de Prague, Jean Huss, Bruno, Vanini, Anne Du Bourg!'".

24 The Forces of the Universe

Even before Barrès, the Parnassian Leconte de Lisle, a militant intellectual, whose positions were originally antithetical to those of Barrès, had fallen for that lonely devotion to lost and losing ideals. A follower of Fourier, a committed and activist Republican Socialist, the defeat of the revolutionary hopes caused him a syndrome of anarchic isolation similar to that of Barrès after the uprisings of 1848. However, from the verses of the two immortal poems that he dedicated to Hypatia on the eve of this fatal date, the cult of Hypatia as a libertarian heroine, streaked with Neopagan mysticism and Parnassian decadence, was transmitted not only to Barrès and to Péguy, but also to Gautier and all the subsequent French men of letters, even to Proust.

"Last chaste ray of the Gods' heavens", Hypatia received "the breath of Plato and the body of Aphrodites" according to Leconte de Lisle, who managed to suppose not that Hypatia converted to Christianity, but rather that the followers of Cyril turned to Paganism – completely the opposite of Diodata Saluzzo, but with no less arbitrariness:

Et la terre écoutait, de ton rêve charmée,	And the Earth listened, enchanted by your dream
Chanter l'abeille attique entre tes lèvres d'or […]	To the song of the Attic bee from your lips of gold […]
Le grave enseignement des vertus éternelles	The severe teaching of the eternal virtues
S'épanchait de ta lèvre au fond des coeurs charmés;	From your lips spread to the depths of the spellbound hearts;
Et les Galiléens qui te rêvaient des ailes	And the Galileans who dreamed you winged
Oubliaient leur Dieu mort pour tes Dieux bien aimés[148].	Forgot their dead God for your beloved Gods.

In addition to this first poem by Leconte de Lisle, *Hypatie*, repeatedly reworked, there is a second poem in dramatic form, *Hypatie et Cyril*, which describes these 'Gods' of Neoplatonism in a debate between her and the bishop:

Tels que les ont vus de sublimes esprits	Just as the sublime spirits saw them
Dans l'espace étoilé n'ayant point de demeures,	In the starry space without any abode,
Forces de l'Univers, Vertus intérieures,	Forces of the Universe, inner Virtues,
De la Terre et du Ciel concours harmonieux	Harmonious meeting between the Earth and the Heavens
Qui charme la pensée et l'oreille et les yeux[149].	That enchants the mind and the hearkening and the vision.

---

[148] LECONTE DE LISLE, pp. 64–65.
[149] Ibid., p. 284.

Appendix
The Forces of the Universe

The two works in verse by LECONTE DE LISLE, the first, *Hypatie*, from 1847, later re-elaborated in 1874, and the second, *Hypatie et Cyrille*, from 1857, can be found in LECONTE DE LISLE, pp. 63–66 and 273–287.

As GAJERI writes on p. 98: "The poem and the 'dramatic action' of Leconte de Lisle constitute an almost total rewriting of the 'legend' of Hypatia. From a symbol of 'reason' for the Enlightenment thinkers, the philosopher has become an allegory of the 'soul' and of 'beauty' in the Romantic cult of 'eternal Greece'"; see also MERELLO, pp. 105–108.

Leconte de Lisle's poems would inspire Théophile Gautier to praise the "belle Hypatie, cette sainte païenne qui souffrit le martyre pour les anciens dieux": GAUTIER, p. 93.

See MERELLO, pp. 108–109 and notes 14–16, for further shorter references on Hypatia in French works of the second half of the 19th century, such as the anticlerical reference in Louis Delâtre in his 1858 essay *L'Egypte*, the philo-Catholic comment by Joséphin Péladan in his 1883 *Femmes honnêtes*, or the never completed project of an "ardent and sublime" theatrical Hypatia authored by the symbolist poet Ephraïm Mikhaël referenced in Catulle Mendès' *Art du théâtre* of 1897.

25 A Name, a Mantra

From the 19th century onwards, the name of Hypatia was given to celestial bodies and entities. Hypatia, or 238 Hypatia, is a main-belt asteroid, with an inclination of 12°, discovered in 1884 by the Russian astronomer Viktor Knorre. The lunar crater Hypatia, or Hypatia I, splits into a satellite crater Hypatia II, not far from the point where Apollo 11 landed on the moon. About seventy kilometres to the north of Hypatia, there is a system of rilles called Rimae Hypatia. It runs for about one hundred and eighty kilometres along the northwestern bank of the Sinus Asperitatis, an inlet of the Mare Tranquillitatis at a latitude of 0.4° South and longitude 22.4° East.

In the firmament of human memory, also, there are "black holes, the invisible stars with prodigious force of attraction", as Mario Luzi writes in his *Libro di Ipazia* [*Hypatia's Book*]. The author describes Hypatia as a "minimal star, contracted in itself, lost in the black holes of outer space, kernel of matter packed with time, lost in our inner firmament"[150].

The word *hypate* (ὑπάτη), etymologically linked to an idea of dominant acuity, is a feminine superlative derived from the preposition ὑπέρ, which can be associated with the masculine ὕπατος. In Late and Byzantine Greek it denotes, substantivised, the "supreme" position of consul (ὑπάτεια), but the feminine noun ὑπάτη, in Greek, also denotes – and this is how we want to interpret Theon's choice – the highest note in the chord in terms of its position on the kithara.

For Luzi, who was not aware of this, the name of Theon's daughter was "a mantra name", releasing "a stream, message, warning or reserve of unexpressed force". "Why Alexandria? Why Hypatia?" he asks last, among the great poets, and with temporal and spatial arbitrariness, aware that as a poet he is not really interested "in those persons glimpsed between the phrases of recapitulation of a philologist", nor really "attracted to recognising them". The story "does not end because it happened". No poet speaks but in the first person present tense; but as a modern thinker Luzi does not fear poetry's unfaithfulness, rather, he celebrates it:

Questo timore d'infedeltà... a che cosa,
diciamo al preciso struggimento
Dell'attimo come fu vissuto – o come ci parve.
Eppure quale realtà è più reale in sé
Che nella sua trasformazione in altro?

This fear of unfaithfulness... to what,
let's say to the precise yearning
For the moment as it was lived – or as we believed it to be.
Yet what reality is more real in itself
Than in its transformation into something else?

---

[150] Luzi 1978.

Appendix
A Name, a Mantra

Mario Luzi's words are taken from his *Libro di Ipazia* (Luzi 1978), which includes two theatrical pieces previously published separately: Luzi 1972 and Luzi 1977. See Pozzi 2014a.

The meaning of the word *hypate* in Greek music is not only to be found in technical texts, but also in Plato: see *Republic* 443d, on the three interior faculties, the rational, the spirited and the appetitive, which the righteous man accords as the three notes of the harmony, in which the highest note of the chord ('highest' in terms of its position on the *kithara*), the *hypate*, has the lowest tone.

In the Italian literature of the second half of the 20th century the name of Hypatia appears – increasingly indecipherable and deliberately devoid of any content – to designate one of the imaginary cities in Italo Calvino, *Le città invisibili* (1972) [*Invisible Cities*, 2009], for which see Gajeri, pp. 147–149. Later, another imaginary "Hipazia" would appear in Italian works such as the comics *Favola di Venezia* by Hugo Pratt (1976, 2009[2]), where the figure of Hypatia was inspired by the Venetian singer Patty Pravo, or Umberto Eco's *Baudolino* (2000); on the latter see Lovascio, pp. 178–181.

Fictionalised versions of Hypatia's story can be found, between the end of the 20th century and the start of our century, also in other examples of popular narrative, of a not directly Feminist lineage, but nevertheless no less chimeric or more scientifically based. We will mention here classics such as Andres; Ferretti; Zitelmann; Marcel, the latter being an epistolary novel composed of fabricated letters written by Hypatia, Synesius, Euoptius, Palladas and a Bollandist; Ehret. On the literary reemergence of Hypatia in 20th century French literature see Thulard. The curious appraisal of the stories of Hypatia and Synesius, conducted by Lamirande, pp. 467–489, is dedicated to the narratives of Andrée Ferretti and Jean Marcel, in addition to those of Kingsley.

Among the 20th century fictional contributions on the topic, two Hellenic texts should be mentioned: the brief narrative (16 pages) on the death of Hypatia by two francophone writers of Alexandria: Patrice Giorgiadès – Radamès Lackany, *Une Martyre païenne: la mort d'Hypatie* (1982); and the more interesting and even less known theatrical piece *Hypatia* by the Greek poet, writer, and translator Theophilos D. Phrangopoulos (1923–1998).

Two interesting versions of the case of Hypatia, seen respectively through the eyes of Hindus and Muslims, can be read in Ramakrishnan, and in Ziedan. In the latter, the historical figure of Hypatia, her teaching and her fate, narrated in the tale's "ninth parchment", is also evoked by the very name of the protagonist, a monk, physician and poet from southern Egypt, who baptises himself Hypa in honour of her. In this remarkable, controversial best selling novel, winner of the Arabic Booker Prize in 2009, the portrayal of St. Cyril of Alexandria as a rabble-rousing fanatic and in general the subtle presentation of the struggle between Christians and Pagans allude to the present day clash between lay thought and religious fanaticism in the Islamic world and has aroused a heated debate in Egypt; see LA SPISA.

Amongst the most recent and dismaying retellings see DE ANGELIS, *I giardini di Ipazia* (1982); BARRIOLE, *Hypatie, la lionne de l'apocalypse* (1987); CHOTJEWITZ, *Der Fall Hypatia. Eine Verfolgung* (2002); PEDRAZA, *La perra de Alexandría* (2003); STOPPA, *Ipazia e la rete d'oro* (2004); MENZIO, *Senza fine* (theatrical work, 2005); TRENT, *Remembering Hypatia: A Novel of Ancient Egypt* (2005); D'OSORIO, *Hypathia, arpenteur de l'absolu* (2005); BOUYOUCAS, *Hypatie ou la mémoire des hommes* (theatrical work created in 1999) (2005); KRAMER, *Holy Murder. The Death of Hypatia of Alexandria* (2006); SWEET, *The Story of the Death of Hypatia* (2007); MARCIANO-JACOB, *Hypatia – Un phare dans la nuit* (2008); COLAVITO – PETTA, *Ipazia. Vita e sogni di una scienziata del IV secolo* (2009); LONGFELLOW, *Flow Down like Silver. Hypatia of Alexandria* (2009, on which see SALVATORE); GALI, *Hypatia y la eternidad* (2009); VAQUERIZO, *La última noche de Hipatia* (2009); GARCÍA, *El jardin de Hipatia* (2009); CALVO POYATO, *El sueño de Hipatia* (2009); MONETI CODIGNOLA, *Ipazia muore* (2010; the 1st edition under the pseudonym C. Contini was entitled *Ipazia e la notte*); VINCENZI, *Il sogno di Ipazia* (theatrical work, 2010); PECOUT – GREINER, *Hypathie* (2010); FOURIKIS, *Hypatia's Feud* (2011); URSELLI, *Ipazia. La nota più alta* (2012). The habit of daydreaming about Hypatia and the literary expedient of "translating" the accounts of her lessons by her contemporary and pupil Synesius have inspired many more explicitly fictionalised narratives after Amenábar's *Agora*.

Alejandro Amenábar's 2009 movie *Agora* gave rise to a series of publications on Hypatia in the Spanish-speaking world, which are aimed at a broad public and cannot be entirely considered scholarly; yet they should not be deemed as fictional either: see e.g. TERUEL 2011 and TERUEL 2012. Before Amenábar's movie, Spain, the only European country that was not impacted by the Enlightenment, almost completely lacked any literature on Hypatia: on this phenomenon see POZZI 2014b. The few, recent exceptions are: FERNANDEZ, *La muerte de Hipatia* (1985); TRABAL SVALUTO – FERRO – RIVERA GARRETAS, *Auctoridad cientifica autoridad feminina: Hipatia* (1998); GONZÁLEZ SUÁRES, *Hipatia* (415? D. de C.) (2002); MARTINEZ MAZA, *Hipatia: la estremecedora historia de la ùltima gran filosofa de la Antiguëdad y la fascinante ciudad de Alejandrìa* (2009); GONZÁLEZ SUÁRES, *Hipatia: otra hija del Nilo* (2012). On the representation of Hypatia according to Amenábar see HERNÁNDEZ DE LA FUENTE; LÓPEZ MARTÍNEZ; and the penetrating short essay by VIGANÒ.

Part III: **Interpreting the Facts**

> What can there be in common between the people and philosophy?
> — Synesius

> We only have time to philosophise, not for doing harm.
> — Synesius

26 May the Witnesses Return to the Court

"History is not the master of anything that concerns us" wrote the Italian poet Eugenio Montale. Poetry, however, is aesthetics, ethics, pedagogy. Poetry in the name of beauty ignores the truth; yet not even history reconstructs it, insinuate the poets. Poetry unites, history separates, distinguishes. Poetry issues a judgment. History brings a prosecution, calls its witnesses one by one, and even the most reticent witness is, in the end, discovered – though their address be remote, changed, untraceable – by the diligent court of the historians. Who, however sometimes do not judge, suspending judgment until they have tested their witnesses' credibility.

Setting out the facts. In the first part we have outlined the essential threads of the historical and political events that led to Hypatia's murder. *Betraying the facts.* In the second section we have described the historical-literary destiny of Hypatia, her afterlife in modernity, which brings with it misrepresentation or falsification, or at any rate a frenzied, even exhilarating, confusion, in which each period and each ideology that develops within it transforms the ancient homicide. This produced, time after time, a Hypatia disguised according to the period's concerns, transformed into the symbol of an idea or even just into the banner of a current political movement. Such an operation, it would seem, appeared more interesting to some than conducting a genuine inquiry into the truth of the ancient facts.

This is to some extent normal: according to the Italian philosopher Benedetto Croce, "all history is contemporary history", and every era, in explaining the past, twists it to serve its own interests reading it in the light of its own political dialectic[151]. Yet there is something singular in the posthumous fortunes of Hypatia and in the variety of the garments that the history of ideologies has her wear: in that "vibration of an atom of ashes of the beautiful body of Hypatia", as has been written, for every rekindling of "a great ideal"[152].

The interest in Hypatia from the 17th century onwards almost became a litmus test for the political-cultural militancies in the various phases of modernity, revealing the aims and unveiling the methods of their propaganda. Yet in this way, paradoxically, the incessant distortion to which Hypatia seems to have been condemned by the moderns throws a retrospective light on the less evident animosity, on the partiality and tendentiousness of the ancient historians.

Precisely the ideological distortion, expressed in the variety of the masks that Hypatia slowly takes on in the modern era, helps us to evaluate the apparent objectivity of the ancient accounts. And it forces us to seek a historical method suitable for re-reading those early accounts and understanding their motivations. Thus leading us to *interpreting the facts.*

---

151 CROCE, p. 19 Sprigge.
152 AGABITI, p. 102.

The assassination of Hypatia traumatised the entire world of culture and all the upper classes of the Eastern Roman empire, which was by then to all intents and purposes the Byzantine empire. From Damascius on, secular historiography has reflected on the murder of Hypatia, making it the symbol of hatred towards culture by a politically populist and demagogical dogmatism, the event-symbol of intolerance and fanatical violence which the sectarian mentality can be capable of when a religion, or a pervasive ideology, becomes the ideology of the State and inaugurates its bond with State power.

For its part, Christian ecclesiastical historiography, in addition to trying to defend the behaviour of Cyril, its leader and a saint, used the icon of Hypatia for its own internal struggles. In some cases the more advanced fringes of the confessions not aligned with the Catholic Church made it an anti-Papist battle-cry. In the Anglican literary manipulation of the story of Hypatia, a direct participation in the heresiological campaign inaugurated by Byzantine witnesses prevails: in the case of Toland, the polemic on Deism, which opposed the Tories and the Whigs in Queen Anne's Great Britain; in the case of Kingsley, wrapped in the poetic intervention, pre-Raphaelite and 'decorative', veined with sadism, the scuffle of Victorian England on the positions of Cardinal Newman. Only recently, only occasionally, and in any case almost never without omissions or sophisms, the Modernist wing of Catholicism has used Hypatia's case to advance, under the form of an investigation into the ancient Church, its own profound criticisms of the traditionalist wing of the contemporary Church.

By raising the case of Hypatia, the innovative modern Christian currents pointed the finger at the practices of the temporal power of the Church from its very beginning, starting from the original political and dogmatic divergences between the Constantinopolitan Church and the Egyptian Church, which according to the most ancient sources seem to determine the actions of Cyril, and his impunity.

If we want to tell the "true story" of Hypatia we need to reconstruct the journey of this twofold ideological path and re-examine the interpretations of the ancient sources, considering them testimonies of a process of distortion and transformation of the facts that is already underway; evaluating their reliability, their judgement and prejudices, and also future developments that they may trigger.

Let us then allow our witnesses back in the courtroom. They will not be summoned based on their age, because this order would be compromised by the fact that some of the sources have come down to us through summaries or quotations of a later date. It is better to proceed by arguments, ordering the original testimonies by orientation, trying to schematically classify their versions and variations.

Appendix
Interpreting the Facts

The first sentence from Synesius is in *Epistle* 105, 104 (*To his brother Euoptius*), p. 239 Roques (Engl. transl. p. 200 Fitzgerald) and is inspired almost literally by a passage from Plotinus: see DZIELSKA 1995, p. 60 e n. 81. See also *Epistle* 143, 13–15 (*To Herculian*), p. 285 Roques (Engl. transl. p. 237 Fitzgerald), in which Synesius quotes the letter from ps.-Lysis to Hipparchus (which can be consulted in THESLEFF, p. 114): "To explain philosophy to the masses serves only to arouse in humans disdain for the divine".

The second sentence from Synesius is in *Epistle* 148, 66–67 (*To Olympius*), p. 295 Roques (Engl. transl. p. 245 Fitzgerald).

May the Witnesses Return to the Court

According to Lapatz's well-known phrase, in a certain sense "le jour de sa mort fut proprement son *dies natalis*" [the day of her death was Hypatia's *dies natalis*]: LAPATZ, p. 340.

Benedetto Croce's idea according to which "all history is contemporary history" is fully developed in B. CROCE, *La storia come pensiero e come azione* [*History as Thought and as Action*] (Bari 1938), translated into English as B. CROCE, *History as the Story of Liberty*, by S. Sprigge (New York 1941) (CROCE): "The practical requirements which underlie every historical judgment give to all history the character of 'contemporary history' because, however remote in time events there recounted may seem to be, the history in reality refers to present needs and present situations wherein those events vibrate.") ["Il bisogno pratico, che è nel fondo di ogni storico, conferisce a ogni storia il carattere di 'storia contemporanea', perché, per remoti e remotissimi che sembrino cronologicamente i fatti che vi entrano, essa è, in realtà, storia sempre riferita al bisogno e alla situazione presente, nella quale quei fatti propagano le loro vibrazioni".] The most recent edited translation, based on that of Sprigge, with a foreword by Claes G. Ryn, is Carmel, IN: Liberty Fund, 2000.

The quotation is taken from AGABITI, p. 102: "Quando ad un grande ideale sobbalza il nostro cuore [...] vibra un atomo di cenere del bel corpo soave d'Ipazia".

The first study entirely dedicated to Hypatia's fortune and her image's reception in historical literature and historiography is that of ASMUS 1907, followed by SCHUBERT; the most recent, that of GAJERI; see also LACOMBRADE 1994, coll. 966–967; LACOMBRADE 1972, pp. 5–7; CHUVIN–TARDIEU, pp. 59–60. On Hypatia's image perceived by 19th-century historiography see above all HOCHE; WOLF 1879; LIGIER; MEYER; see also PRAECHTER 1916. For a recent excursus on Hypatia's *Nachleben* in contemporary times (with a mention of the eponymous font, lectures by astrophysicist Fran Bagenal and, of course, the film *Agora*, about which see above, chapt. "A Name, a Mantra", Appendix *ad loc.*) see SCHEIDEGGER LAEMMLE, pp. 209–237.

As THORP summarised: "Hypatia is the perfect hero. [...] Already in Late Antiquity she was a heroine of the Pagans because she was butchered by the Christians, or a heroine to the Arians because she was butchered by the Orthodox, or a heroine to the tolerant Constantinopolitan Christians because she was butchered by the intolerant Alexandrian ones. In more recent centuries she has been the heroine of Anticlericalism – the victim of the hierarchy –, of Protestantism – the victim of Catholic extremism –, of Hellenising Romanticism – the victim of Western civilisation's move away from the Glory that was Greece –, of Positivism – the victim of the subjugation of science to religion –, and, most recently, of Feminism – the victim of advancing Christian misogyny. A busy lady".

The contemporary or almost contemporary authors of Hypatia's story whose testimonies are handed down by epitomes from the Byzantine era (Photios and Suidas) are, we recall, Philostorgius, Hesychius and Damascius: see above, part I, chapter "Once there was a Woman" and Appendix *ad loc.*

27 The DNA of the Ancient Tradition

Originally, two versions of Hypatia's assassination coexisted, one Pagan and one Christian, both transmitted in twofold variants, one more moderate, the other more radical.

In the three centuries that lie between the events and the development, after the Arab conquest, of the strictly Byzantine historical tradition, one of the Christian narratives was lost to the West and only the oriental tradition remained. The *Chronicle* of John of Nikiu, who relied on an earlier version, according to which the murder of Hypatia was actually considered a moment of glory for Cyril, survives only in a late Ethiopic version. It is unlikely that the West was able to draw directly from this source. Yet, the pro-Cyril movement, only testified by the bishop of Nikiu's written testimony, but most likely widely available in the Coptic Church of the Middle Ages, would always be the version *de facto* adopted by the non-Modernist Catholic historiography.

The more moderate Christian version, yet mostly unwelcome, as we have seen, to the Western ecclesiastical opinion that dominated until the Counter-Reformation, is that of Socrates Scholasticus. Generally objective, his treatment of the case in point in his *History* probably conforms to the standpoint of the central Byzantine Church: not decidedly accusatory, like the Pagan sources, but certainly not favourable to the bishop of Alexandria. Socrates emphasises Cyril's tendency to "avidly erode the power of those who exercised it on behalf of the emperor".

According to Socrates, Cyril "inaugurated an episcopate even more similar, with respect to that of Theophilus, to a principality", and "starting with him, the Alexandrian episcopacy began to interfere in State power beyond the limits accorded the ecclesiastical sphere"[153]. At the court of Constantinople, Socrates was a lawyer (*scholastikos*, σχολαστικός); but he was certainly not Cyril's advocate.

Finally, both the Pagan narratives were handed down through Suidas, that of Hesychius and that of Damascius. The lineage that would lead to Diderot, Voltaire and Gibbon and, through the Masonic literature of the 18th and 19th centuries and its cult of Hypatia, to the purely secular 20th historians who, like Bertrand Russell, revealed themselves to be judgmental and accusatory towards Cyril, multiplied from there.

Linked to one of the variants of the Pagan version, that of Damascius, and in fact connected to it from the genesis of the manuscript tradition, is that of a Christian heresy inverse and symmetrical to Monophysitism: Arianism, the most important amongst the doctrines simmering in the dogmatic magma from which the monolith of Christian theology would emerge. According to the Arians, Christ was only a man, the Son was not of the same substance as the Father, which scattered the cards of the Trinity and made defining the nature of Christ problematic.

As a Pagan Damascius was hostile to Cyril, as was Philostorgius, because he shared the Arians' ancient hatred of Alexandria, homeland to Athanasius, the great enemy of Arius. Thus, also the mention of Hypatia's fate in his *Church History*, the attribution of

---

[153] SOCRATES VII 13, 9, p. 358, 13–14 Hansen; VII 7, 4, p. 353, 2–6 Hansen.

the lynching to the "party of consubstantiality" (*to homoousion*, τὸ ὁμοούσιον)[154], is evidently influenced by doctrinal rancour, by the wish to harm the adversaries. Philostorgius' text is preserved in extensive fragments by Photius' *Bibliotheca*, and we should note that some of the expressions present in Photius' *epitome* correspond exactly to those used by Suidas in handing down Damascius: perhaps, thus the Arian and the Pagan sources, both of which undermine Cyril's image, drew from the same tradition.

The *Chronicle* of John Malalas, dating from the time of Justinian, close to the court clerics, but above all to the Church of Antioch, habitually hostile to that of Alexandria, seems to rely on another traditional Byzantine thread. The version offered by Malalas identifies Cyril, as Socrates does, as the direct instigator of the murder and the moral culprit. However, he probably draws on his own sources, agreeing with Socrates on the bishop's guilt, but aware of details lacking in Socrates and in Suidas-Damascius: for example the bundles of dried wood (*phrygana*, φρύγανα), piled into a pyre[155], on which Hypatia was burned, "the first witch" immolated by the Christian Church.

However, the most widespread version in Byzantium was still that of Socrates: an orthodox Christian, more cautious in the terms used than the Pagan and Christian-Arian versions, slightly different from that on which Malalas drew, but equally anti-Cyrillian. The same alignment would emerge from the later Byzantine testimonies, which however would slowly add useful elements taken from Pagan sources.

During iconoclasm, a concise yet significant mention of the murder is found in Theophanes' *Chronicle*[156]; in the 9th century the accusatory position against Cyril was brought back to life, as we have seen, by Photius, who recovered Damascius and Philostorgius' opinions (along with Socrates Scholasticus); in the 10th century, Suidas, as mentioned, recovered at least Damascius and Hesychius; in the 14th century, Nicephorus Callistus Xanthopoulos[157] relied directly on Socrates and his anti-Cyrillian position. In the eyes of the Byzantinist, accustomed to detect the political allusiveness of historians and, more broadly, the ideological purpose of textual retrieval and reuse, the condemnation of Cyril's policies in the Byzantine ecclesiastical sources is evident. And it derives from the 5th and 6th century information, from their influence and their manuscript tradition, which appears to be more ramified than is generally thought. Now, the fact that this information was so scrupulously and widely handed down perhaps finds its own explanation.

---

154 Philostorgius 8, 9, p. 111, 3–8 Bidez = 8, 9, pp. 366, 5–368, 2 Bleckmann-Stein (Harich-Schwarzbauer 2011, p. 318).
155 Malalas XIV 12, p. 280, 68–70 Thurn; English translation pp. 195–196 Jeffreys – Jeffreys – Scott (Harich-Schwarzbauer 2011, p. 336). For a possible identification of Malalas' (ultimate) source with the 5th century historian Priscus of Panion see Carolla, pp. 142–143 and 149.
156 Theophanes, *Chronographia* I, p. 82, 16 de Boor, *ad annum* 415.
157 Xanthopoulos XIV 15 and 16, *PG* 146, coll. 1105–1107.

Appendix
The DNA of the Ancient Tradition

The quotations of Socrates on the jurisdictional interference of Cyril are taken respectively from VII 13, p. 358 Hansen, and VII 7, p. 353 Hansen.

On the meaning of the term *scholastikos* in the 5th century see above, part I, chapter "Once there was a Woman", Appendix *ad loc.*

The story of Hypatia reverberated in the West following the *Historia tripartita*, so called because it was based on the Latin translation of the narratives of Socrates, Sozomen and Theodoret, re-elaborated by Epiphanius, erroneously attributed to Cassiodorus and generally close to the testimonies of the three Greek sources. On the Greek *Historia tripartita* by Theodorus the Lector, see now Émerance DELACENSERIE's and Bernard POUDERON's contributions. On the Latin *Historia tripartita*, see COLOMBI. It would be later that Western ecclesiastical historiography would increasingly tend to justify Cyril's actions: see above, part. II, chapter "The Catholic Wing".

The testimony of the *Historia tripartita* can be read in CASSIODORUS – EPIPHANIUS, pp. 643–644 Jacob – Hanslik; see also HARICH-SCHWARZBAUER 2011, pp. 222–223.

Philostorgius' comment can be read on p. 111 Bidez (PHILOSTORGIUS 8, 9, p. 111, 3–8 Bidez = 8,9, pp. 366, 5–368, 2 Bleckmann-Stein [HARICH-SCHWARZBAUER 2011, p. 318]. See above, part I, chapter "Mortal Envy").

On the Arians' ancient hatred against Alexandria, home to Athanasius, the great enemy of Arius and the victor of the Council of Nicaea (325), see above, part I, chapter "Mortal Envy"; below, chapter "An Age of Anxiety" and Appendix *ad loc.*; see also RIST, p. 222, and the capable synthesis by CANFORA 2000: "It was certainly Philostorgius [and not Photius] who wrote 'the supporters of consubstantiality', meaning to refer, in a disdainful tone, to the 'orthodox' Athanasians, the winners and undisputed 'masters' of orthodoxy. As we know, Athanasius, in Alexandria, was, as a firm advocate of 'consubstantiality', a symbolic character: to say, therefore, with reference to the assassination committed in Alexandria by the followers of Cyril, that it was committed by 'supporters' of 'consubstantiality' was particularly cutting."

See the critical note in PHILOSTORGIUS 8, 9, p. 111, 1–8 Bidez = 8,9, pp. 366, 1–368, 2 Bleckmann-Stein (HARICH-SCHWARZBAUER 2011, p. 318), for the partial overlap of the wordings of the Arian source and the Pagan one (μαθήματα, καὶ μάλιστα, ἀστροθεάμονα, διασπασθῆναι), which are unusually similar, and for the consequent theory that the former made use of the latter in formulating the accusations against Cyril.

John Malalas' testimony is in MALALAS XIV 12, p. 280, 68–70 Thurn; English translation pp. 195–196 Jeffreys – Jeffreys – Scott (HARICH-SCHWARZBAUER 2011, p. 336).

That Malalas based his account on his own sources, and that we are therefore "in the presence of a vast and ramified tradition that agrees on the main point, that is the responsibility of Cyril, but which draws on different accounts […]", is argued by CANFORA 2010, p. 101. The tradition might have started with a passage from the lost history of Priscus of Panion, see CAROLLA, pp. 142–143 and 149, where the text is labelled as Priscus' fr. *dubium* 52* bis.

The laconic comments of the Iconoclast Theophanes can be read in THEOPHANES, p. 82, 16 de Boor, *ad annum* 415: "In this year certain men (*tines*, τινες) inflicted a violent death on Hypatia the philosopher, daughter of the philosopher Theon."

The information from Xanthopoulos can be read in MIGNE, *PG* 146, book XIV, chapter 15 (*De dissensione Cyrilli contra praefectum Oresten: et ut lapide Orestes in fronte ictus sit, et de zelo Nitriensium monachorum* [About Cyrillus' conflict against Orestes: and how Orestes was hit on the forehead by a stone and about the zeal of the monks from Nitria]) and above all 16 (*De philosopha Hypatia ut a clero Cyrilli sit necata* [About the philosopher Hypatia how she was killed by Cyrillus' clergy]). On the responsibility attributed to Cyril, see at col. 1105 the definition of the killers of Hypatia as τινες [...] ἔνθερμον Κυρίλλῳ τρέφοντες ἔρωτα, and in coll. 1105–1107: "This fact caused considerable blame for Cyril and his Church, because assassinations and insurgencies [...] and similar actions are totally extraneous to the spirit of Christ." The almost literal dependence on Socrates' account is evident, for which see also GENTZ – WINKELMANN.

Unexpectedly, WATTS 2017 assumes that "the role of Cyril in creating the conditions [*sic*] that led to her murder is increasingly downplayed" by Byzantine authors, with the one exception of Xanthopoulos (pp. 130 and 185–186, n. 34). Quite the opposite. The re-emergence, during the Byzantine era, of the memory of the ancient murder, and the resurfacing in collections, like Photius' and Suidas' (and, possibly, the *Excerpta Constantiniana*), of passages taken from the ancient texts (Damascius, Hesychius, Philostorgius, and Socrates) that openly unmask the guilt of Cyril, witness the opposite of the reverential awe towards the "eventual legacy of Cyril, a bishop who was canonised and came to represent one of the touchstones of Orthodoxy in Byzantium", described by Watts (*ibidem*). Moreover, this last statement on Cyril is questionable as well, if we consider the role of the nationalist Coptic Church, which Cyrillian Miaphysitic heterodoxy would always be a banner of, in Egyptian separatism from the Church of Constantinople, and the support lent to the West in the political-ecclesiastical battle between Rome and Constantinople: see above, part I, chapter "The Terrible Patriarch of Alexandria" and "The Bishop of Nikiu"; esp. below, "An Age of Anxiety" and Appendix *ad loc*.

28 Church and State

Was Cyril guilty of Hypatia's death? Of course. For many of the ancient and modern historians, who raised such a question, another promptly follows: was it inevitable for Christianity to be compromised by the most harsh methods of politics, the contagion of violence and fanaticism? And yet another: was the jurisdictional dispute and the need of the Church to interfere in State government inevitable?

Throughout the Byzantine millennium, sources dealing with Hypatia, also in the ecclesiastical realm, give a clear answer to those questions: they say no. Rather, we can add that they speak of Hypatia to show that not only were these things avoidable, but that they should have been avoided. At the time when the Byzantines emitted a negative sentence against Cyril, these sources reflected the point of view of an empire, where for eleven centuries the dominating principle was that the State, although pervaded by an otherwordly ideology, was secular and that the clerics were excluded from secular power and had no political prerogatives. In Byzantium the Church's interference in political affairs, in the few cases in which it was attempted, was stigmatised and repressed, in antithesis to what was happening in the papacy of Rome, the kingdom of the "fatal gift of Constantine", as Kingsley said, that is to say of the temporal power of the Catholic Church which followed the alleged Donation of Constantine.

Therefore, quite naturally, the latter maintained its defence of Cyril to the bitter end, even flying in the face of common sense, curiously showing itself to be close to the position of John of Nikiu, out of all the ancient ecclesiastical sources, and therefore to the position of the Coptic Church. It even persevered in this defence throughout the Modern Era, involving in the code of silence, or the open misrepresentation of the facts, not only the great ideologists of the Counter-Reformation, who dictated the canons for the rewriting of the official history of the Church, like Caesar Baronius, but also the more moderate and enlightened interpreters of the early Christian centuries, like the Jansenist Tillemont.

While this falsification, in the name of the "raison d'Etat" of the Church State, is deplorable, we can only find highly oversimplified, and therefore in its own way misleading, although with greater discretion, the position of the Damascius-Gibbon thread, in which the judgement, or prejudice, or ultimately the meaning given to the story of Hypatia is a simple condemnation of the Church. Christianity, an all-encompassing doctrine and therefore potentially totalitarian, overlaps the polis and opposes the tolerance of the secular sage, the philosopher. The bishop's substitution of himself for the philosopher, to recall the syllogism above (if in moving from Paganism to Christianity the role of the philosopher and the bishop overlap, what is the bishop to do, if not eliminate the philosopher?), leads, according to the last Pagans and the first Enlightenment thinkers, to a deterioration in the life of the polis, to a progressive degeneration in politics up to contemporary times.

Yet in the Byzantine empire, where the Church would be ousted from secular power, the ancient Greco-Roman art of government would continue to live in that great Polis, Constantinople, which would incorporate the ancient *poleis* (πόλεις), continuing, in the alliance between Greek philosophical reflection and Roman juridical-administrative tradition, to be a crucible of theories and a theatre of political experimentation, up to the last of the Platonic thinkers, like George Gemistus Plethon, who would significantly influence our Renaissance. In Byzantium, the philosopher and the bishop would live side by side: they are often identified as the same person, as in the case of the patriarch Photius, who, in fact, recovered the dossier on Hypatia to re-open the debate on Cyril and therefore also on the limits of Church interference in the State.

Thus, we arrive at the crux of the matter and at a crucial turn in our trial. Does the importance attributed to Hypatia's fate in Late Antique historiography, and through its direct influence in Byzantine historiography, and later, by various means and with further inspirations and suggestions, in modern Western historiography, not perhaps derive not so much from her existence or the essence of her character as from the stature of Cyril?

Of this event, political in a strict sense, and at the same time political-ecclesiastical, and symbolic not so much of the relationship of the intellectual with (ecclesiastical) power as of the relationship of the ecclesiastical with (State) power, Hypatia may be the false protagonist.

However, if we were to conclude this first trial and open the second, the trial of the policies of the bishop of Alexandria, this would become a maxi-trial: the defendants in the dock would be the entire ruling class and Platonism itself, the first to be involved in the great Arian controversy and in the Nestorian and Monophysite controversy, which also were at the roots of the various judgements and prejudices concerning this story.

Appendix
Church and State

Curiously, and erroneously, DZIELSKA 1995 believes that only Damascius laments Cyril's responsibility (p. 18) and she presents as a legend, derived in Gibbon from the *Vita Isidori*, the mention of the "envy" (*phthonos*, φθόνος) of the young Christian bishop towards the philosopher (p. 4); on the contrary, as we have seen, they were both also blamed by other ancient sources (directly by Philostorgius, with some diplomacy by Socrates Scholasticus), except for John of Nikiu. Our opinion is also shared by CHUVIN–TARDIEU, p. 60, according to whom John of Nikiu "est le seul qui prenne fait et cause pour le patriarche".

WATTS 2017 as well, as we have previously seen (see above, part I, chapter "The Intimidation of Orestes", Appendix *ad loc.*), ignores or underestimates in several ways the condemnation of Cyril found in almost the totality of the ancient sources, thus harbouring in his own historical judgement a surprisingly forgiving position towards the unscrupulous bishop.

BERETTA 1993 correctly writes: "Cyril and his supporters tried to hide the true nature [of the conflict] and to present the question in the terms of a religious struggle, bringing once again to the fore the spectre of the conflict between Paganism and Christianity"; however, the salient nature of the clash between Cyril and Orestes was that of a jurisdictional conflict, see KLEIN; ROUGÉ 1990; LACOMBRADE 1954, p. 23; LACOMBRADE 1972, pp. 14–15; and even the testimony of Socrates (VII 7) quoted above, chapter "The DNA of the Ancient Traditions", according to which under Cyril "the Alexandrian episcopacy began to interfere excessively in State power beyond the limits accorded the ecclesiastical sphere." See also HAAS 1997, pp. 302–316.

For the fortune of Cyril in the medieval Western Church see esp. HARING.

The close dependency of the first great heresies on the contemporary Platonic speculation is well-known. If it is true that the Christian speculation of the 4th and 5th centuries is drenched in Platonism, Monophysitism is even more so. Perhaps the most evident vestige of Alexandrian Platonism in fact belongs to Christianity, which from Clement and Origen in the 3rd century through the Fathers of the 4th came to produce in Cyril the fruits – heretical, or considered so by posterity – of that form of Monophysitism better identified as Miaphysitism and now accepted by the Church of Rome; see above, part I, chapter "The Terrible Patriarch of Alexandria" and Appendix *ad loc.*

29 An Age of Anxiety

The 5th century was marked by both Christological disputes and Barbarian invasions. While the ethnic crisis triggered by the pressure of the new populations on the frontiers of the Mediterranean empire exacerbated the social storm, in the cities the internecine war between the sects of early Christianity intertwined with and had already come to dominate the ongoing battle against Paganism.

The competition between Antioch and Alexandria ran transverse to the passage from Paganism to Christianity. The Platonism of the Syrian and the Alexandrian schools, the two opposing poles of Hellenistic speculation, had belligerently battled each other for cultural power for centuries. A hostility that would not die out, but would rather be accentuated in the Christian version of their philosophy: at first, the theology of the new Church was of entirely Platonic ancestry. In fact, we could say that the philosophy of Christianity was created from one or more ribs of Platonism.

Following the Trinitarian disputes of the 4th century, in which the Arian heresy was overcome, and the Alexandrian Creed was declared the winner at the Council of Nicaea of 325, to be perfected in 381 by the first Council of Constantinople with the definitive formulation of the Niceno-Constantinopolitan Creed – which since the schism of 1054 still divides the Orthodox and Catholic Churches on the question of the *Filioque* –, the relationship between the divine and human nature of the God-Word incarnate opposed the philosophical schools of the East in a new and wider contest, in which philosophy, or theology, were more explicitly transformed into politics. And the 'people of the Church' became means through which this happened.

Never before as in this period of migration of races and of powers had the theories of the intellectuals been capable of mobilising the masses. Never before had such abstract propositions brought the multitudes into the streets, rioting for a single word, however dense with meaning, as would happen in Constantinople when the Syrian Nestorius, the adversary of the Alexandrian Cyril, would change the name of Mary from *Theotokos* (Θεοτόκος, i.e. Mother of God) to *Christotokos* (Χριστοτόκος, i.e. Mother of Christ).

With the same belligerency shown during the tumults of 415, for another twenty years Cyril would support the anti-Nestorian Christological doctrine, which radically denied the human nature of Christ, which would later be called Monophysitism and which seems to have been associated everywhere with a wave of violence, perhaps because everywhere, it would seem, the *parabalani* accompanied the bishop.

The controversy with Nestorius began in 430. In the following year there was the Council of Ephesus, where the Alexandrians, guided by the turbulent ascetic Shenoute, would attain victory in the initial session by intimidating the members of the Council. A similar situation occurred once again eighteen years later, when Cyril's successor, Dioscorus, opposed the new patriarch of Constantinople, Flavian. The two Councils of Ephesus, that of 431, with the street demonstrations that marked the assizes, and that of 449, not surprisingly called the 'robber synod' (*Latrocinium*), stamped a negative brand on the political strategies and the Christological doctrines of the bishops of Alexandria. Justice would be meted out to both of them in 451 by the canons of the Council of Chalcedon.

At the start of the century, in the case of Hypatia, ecclesiastical opinion and a precise imperial mandate – the Theodosian constitution of February 4th 384, which sanctioned the impunity of the clerics in the civil courts – had protected the bishop of Alexandria, before events took a turn for the worse. At that time, the Alexandrian clergy was not in the least associated with heresy but rather quite the opposite: Athanasius, the champion of Nicene orthodoxy against Arianism, came from Alexandria; the august Pulcheria, the regent for her younger brother Theodosius, was the personal advocate of Alexandrian Christianity and of Cyril, and she would later be proclaimed a saint, like Cyril. The Roman prefect Orestes spoke directly with the most authoritative representative of the Church.

The Council of Chalcedon was to change the situation by condemning Monophysitism, although not directly Cyril's "Miaphysite" doctrine. This was perhaps only because Cyril had died ten years earlier. Yet, the position of the official Byzantine historians on the case of Hypatia cannot be explained unless we consider the fate of the doctrine, which Cyril had initiated a few years after the lynching of 415. The great weight of the controversy on the nature of Christ in the later interpretation of the event is confirmed (if confirmation were necessary) by the bizarre Latin forgery that purports to be a letter from Hypatia to Cyril, in which the philosopher, no less than fifteen years after her death, sets out the doctrine of the bishop's great enemy, Nestorius[158].

While the Orthodox Byzantine Church for more than one reason made the problematic bishop of Alexandria a saint, the Coptic Monophysite Church, repudiating as heretical the canons of Chalcedon, would do much more. They would make Cyril of Alexandria their father and master, they would call him "Judge of the entire Ecumene" and "Cyril the Pharaoh"[159], they would be faithful to his definition of the single nature of the God-Word incarnate as to a banner and wholly supported, as we have seen in John of Nikiu, the acts of violence of 415.

Also for this reason, the figure of Cyril, although it is still linked to Orthodoxy and is therefore present in the theological tradition and the work of the catenists, would in fact be a very controversial figure or at least an embarrassment for the official Byzantine Church, as it freed itself of the more extreme factions that were, curiously, at the same time more compromised by Platonism.

Even the *Dictionnaire d'histoire et de géographie ecclésiastiques*, founded by the vehemently anti-Modernist future cardinal Baudrillart, admitted:

> The Monophysites considered him the Doctor *par excellence*, the unquestioned master who was to be followed in all things and at all times. The Nestorians could not find sufficient anathemas for him. Between these two groups of heretics, the position of the Church was at times difficult.

---

158 PRAECHTER 1916, col. 245; GAJERI, pp. 41–42.
159 MASPÉRO, *passim* and p. 83 n.

Adding:

> It was impossible to forget that the bishop of Alexandria had been charged by Pope Celestine to proceed with the deposition and excommunication of Nestorius, and that in the name of the Pope he had chaired the Council of Ephesus[160].

The anti-Monophysite hatred of the dominant Byzantine culture was after all also an anti-Egyptian grudge. The sentence of 451 caused in fact the extinction of Hellenism in Egypt, since the eclipse of Greek and the adoption of Coptic in the liturgy followed the sanction of the Council. Nominally overcome in the middle of the 5th century, the heterodox secessions of the Nestorian and Monophysite strains would live on through the centuries in the area of the empire, proliferating with different customs and names from Armenia to Tibet, throughout the Middle Ages and beyond.

While it might be a platitude to directly link the influence of these movements to the scarce or non-existent resistance offered by Egypt to the Arab invasions in the 7th century, it is in any case evident that the doctrinal separatism was the symptom of a widespread cultural and political dissent towards Byzantium and its formula for coexistence between State and Church, reserving the political initiative to the central Constantinopolitan government and denying it to the politicised ecclesiastical hierarchies such as those in the province of Egypt.

The Nestorian Church and the Monophysite Church would settle in the Islamised territories. Their contacts and conflicts, with each other and with the Constantinopolitan culture, would mark the second Byzantine iconoclasm of the first half of the 9th century and the immediately subsequent period of transition of the Abbasid Caliphate, during which Photius lived and was the patriarch of Constantinople, on the eve of the Byzantine encyclopaedism of the 10th century, the most typical exponent of which is Suidas himself. This may, perhaps, be the reason for the survival and revival of the ancient sources, even in their verbatim versions, where the Christian and Pagan perspectives converge to accuse Cyril.

---

160 BARDY 1956, col. 1176.

Appendix
An Age of Anxiety

The now proverbial expression that gives the chapter its title is taken from DODDS.

On the rivalry between schools see WATTS 2006a and, more recently, WATTS 2017, pp. 31–35, where the author describes briefly but accurately the roots and the context of the Alexandrian teaching of Hypatia among the Neoplatonic Pagan schools and their scholastic filiations; see also *ibidem*, pp. 41–44, and WATTS 2011.

On Christian Platonism, and on the birth of Christian theology from a rib of Pagan Platonism, and therefore on the ample tolerance exercised by the Church towards philosophical Paganism, see below, chapter "Dramatis Personae" and Appendix *ad loc.*

The Council of Constantinople of 381, called by Theodosius I, was dominated by the three greatest brains of early Christian theology, the three Cappadocian Fathers Basil the Great, Gregory of Nyssa and Gregory of Nazianzus. Following the anathemisation of Arius at the Council of Nicaea in 325, dominated by the Alexandrian Athanasius, and the rekindling of Arianism in Constantinople during the episcopal mandate of Eusebius of Nicomedia, who managed to have Athanasius sent into exile and to substitute the bishops of Nicaean obedience with Arian bishops in various Eastern sees, the new Council of 381, which was the second Ecumenical Council and the first Constantinopolitan, once again condemned Arianism (together with Macedonianism and Apollinarism) and confirmed the Nicene Creed, however developing it with the introduction, in its formula, of the Holy Spirit's consubstantiality, τὸ ἐκ τοῦ Πατρὸς ἐκπορευόμενον, "qui ex Patre procedit", thus affirming both the divinity of the Son, against the Arians, and that of the Holy Spirit, against the Macedonians or Pneumatomachi (see DENZINGER – SCHÖNMETZER, n° 125 e n° 150).

Thus armoured, the Niceno-Constantinopolitan Creed would resolve once and for all the Christological dispute and would be unassailable for centuries until the schism of 1054, when precisely the carefully calibrated formula produced by the thinkers of the Councils of Nicaea and Constantinople was questioned by the Church of Rome, which, for reasons less genuinely dogmatic than political, included in the expression "ex Patre" (from the Father) of the Niceno-Constantinopolitan Creed the addition "Filioque" (and from the Son), which contradicted the Trinitarian doctrine definitively fixed by the Fathers of the second Ecumenical Council. The dispute has not yet been resolved and the question of the *Filioque* divides the Catholic Church from the Orthodox Church, which has remained faithful for almost two thousand years to the Niceno-Constantinopolitan Creed.

Within the massive scholarship on the council of Chalcedon, its controversies and their consequences, see, along with FREND, the recent contribution by BLAUDEAU. For a general orientation and a historical framework of the two Ephesian Councils and the Council of Chalcedon see CROSS, s.v. *Ephesus, Council of (431)*, p. 550; *Latrocinium*, p. 957; *Chalcedon, Council of (AD 451)*, p. 315; *Chalcedon, the Definition of, ibid.*

Initially, Cyril was protected in his "armed proselytism" in Alexandria by the Theodosian constitution of February 4th 384, according to which the members of the clergy could only be tried by the ecclesiastical tribunal.

In general for the ecclesiastical vicissitudes of Christian Africa in the 5th century see Duchesne, vol. I, pp. 287–518; on the religious controversies and their social repercussions, see also Gouillard.

On the false letter from Hypatia to Cyril, see Praechter 1916, col. 245, with bibliographical indications, and Gajeri, pp. 41–42, who gives the Latin text in full; see also above, part II, chapter "Refreshing Exceptions" and Appendix *ad loc.*

For the Cyrillian definition of "one nature of the incarnate God-Logos" (μία φύσις τοῦ θεοῦ λόγου σεσαρκωμένου) and for the other elements of his doctrine see amongst the most recent scholarly studies Gebremedhin (bibliography on pp. 112–119).

For the definition of Cyril in the Coptic Church as "Pharaoh" and "Judge of the Ecumene" (κριτὴς τῆς οἰκουμένης) see Maspéro, *passim* and p. 83 n.; see also the classic work of Kopallik; Vona with further bibliography.

That Cyril of Alexandria, despite the immense prestige he retained even after his death, "was neither an educated man nor a philosopher", but rather a cleric "entirely absorbed by the problems of his Church" and that although he was above all concerned with his position in the government of the State, "he did not leave a doctrine on the relations between temporal power and spiritual power", but rather "he never even considered the problem", is admitted even by the ardently pro-Cyrillian Liébaert, pp. 5, 6–7, 14, 21.

The works of Cyril would be used and commented on by authors of the 11th and 12th centuries such as Nicetas of Heraclea, John Zonaras, Eustratius of Nicaea among others, and in the 15th century translated into Latin by George of Trebizond. On Cyril's fortunes with these and other ecclesiastical writers and in particular already in the 6th, 7th, 9th and 10th centuries with the catenists, that is the authors of that particular and crucial genre of dogmatic literature that are the *Catenae*, it is useful to consult Reuss.

The item *Cyrille d'Alexandrie* in *Dictionnaire d'histoire et de géographie ecclésiastiques* is written by Gustave Bardy, like that on Saint Catherine of Alexandria; the quoted phrases can be read in Bardy 1956, col. 1176.

On the extinction of Hellenism in Egypt, the structuring of the nationalist Coptic Church and Cyril's role within it see Frend, pp. 34, 59, etc.; Meinardus 1999a, pp. 43 ff.; Bagnall; Cannuyer – Hawkes; Elli; Roncaglia. On the ecclesiastical culture of the Islamised territories in the 9th century and the challenges of the new Christian apologetic literature in the language of the Qur'an, the "lingua franca" of the caliphate, see Griffith. On the Monophysite kingdoms in the Middle-Byzantine age see Frend, pp. 296–314.

30 Hypatia in All Her States of Being

It is from this twofold perspective that, already in the Byzantine era, the posthumous transfiguration of the figure of Hypatia takes shape. If we re-examine one by one the traits lent to her character by a source writing just one century after her death, namely Damascius, it seems difficult not to consider them, if not imaginary, at least strained.

The episode of the *aischrourgia* (αἰσχρουργία), the scandalous gesture of Hypatia when, according to the fragment of the *Life of Isidore* by Damascius, reported in the article by Suidas, in order to reject the courtship of her pupil she waved a menstrual cloth in his face, thus clamorously breaking one of the most deeply-rooted taboos in the ancient world regarding the female figure, has been compared, for its blatancy, to the *kynogamia* (κυνογαμία), the shameless "dog coupling" of the aristocratic Cynic philosopher Hipparchia, i.e., her public copulation with her well-known companion in the sect, Crates.

This and other less openly provocative, but at the time transgressive aspects of Hypatia's behaviour, such as "appearing without a shadow of modesty in the male audiences" or the "total freedom of speech" (*parrhesia*, παρρησία), certainly have a basis of truth. However, the context, the details and the emphasis with which they are proposed seem intended to overlay her physionomy of philosopher with a Stoic-Cynic connotation[161]. Conventional, stereotypical, and improbable, given the facts.

At the end of the Philostorgius' account we do not find the female noun (ἡ γυνή, 'the woman') to designate the victim, but the neutral (*to gynaion*, τὸ γύναιον), diminutive and pejorative, to be understood – although in Late Greek – as 'the poor', or better, 'the elderly' woman[162].

Hypatia, in 415, may still have been fertile, but she could not have been considered young. Forster was right in defining her an elegant middle-aged lady. As was Proust before him, when, at the end of the second volume of his *Recherche*, he compared Hypatia to the beautiful and by then mature Odette, writing about her, implicitly quoting Leconte de Lisle:

> Majestic, smiling, kind, as she advanced along the avenue of the *Bois*, she saw like Hypatia, beneath the slow tread of her feet, worlds revolving[163].

That Hypatia was a mature beauty is suggested by all the sources and emphasised by Suidas. On the basis of his account the majority of the scholars have fixed her date of birth around 370: a woman of forty-five at that time was *palaia*, old. This is confirmed by Malalas, the historian of the Justinianic period, close to Socrates' position, but aware of other sources:

---

161 CHUVIN–TARDIEU, pp. 59–68.
162 PHILOSTORGIUS 8, 9, p. 111, 7 Bidez = p. 368 Bleckmann-Stein (HARICH-SCHWARZBAUER 2011, p. 318).
163 PROUST, p. 57.

> Having received authorisation from their bishop, the Alexandrians attacked and burned on a pyre of brushwood Hypatia, the famous philosopher, despite the fact that she had an excellent reputation and was an elderly [*palaia*, παλαιά] woman[164].

The same should be said for the physical appearance of the victim, for Suidas "extraordinarily seductive and beautiful" (σφόδρα καλή τε οὖσα καὶ εὐειδής). While in the "purity" and "perfection" attributed to her by Palladas we should read an astral allusion, the haughty attractiveness that 5th-century Pagans attributed to Hypatia, her unquestionable, charismatic beauty, must have had less to do with the Romantic imagination of the 19th-century historians and much more, on the contrary, with the superiority of caste, the ascetic composure and the gifts of aristocratic reserve, which combined with the natural sense of social duty and political commitment marked the upper classes of antiquity.

The meaning of the adverb *demosia* (δημοσίᾳ), which Suidas uses in reference to Hypatia's teaching, deriving it from Damascius, has been discussed at length. Some translate it as "officially", meaning that Hypatia held lessons, like her father, at the Museum, or in any case had been assigned a chair subsidised by the State, or by the municipal treasury of Alexandria. Knowing the Byzantine *usus*, this technical meaning of the term does not appear necessary, and to others it seemed more correct to believe that it meant "publicly", in a "public" place, or even "popular" (δημοσίᾳ from the root of *demos*, δῆμος, "people"), if not "in the public road". Moreover, as we have seen, this is how some of the ancient interpreters understood the rest of the passage. They were wrong.

We can exclude that at that time a representative of Greek intellectual aristocracy in Alexandria would walk through the streets preaching Plato: stones flew, even against the Augustal prefect, even into his carriage. Hypatia's means of transport must have been tightly closed when she moved from the place where she held her official lessons to her personal residence, so envied by the Christian bishop[165].

It has been suggested that Damascius, a representative of the Athenian wing of Platonism and a rival of the Alexandrian, tends to maliciously belittle the figure of such a revered teacher, and appears concerned to separate the teachings of the philosopher from her illustrious Platonic background, in order to bring her closer to those which were customary, in Pagan circles, to the Cynics. For his part Suidas, using this scrap of Pagan tradition, might aim to subtly discredit Cyril by accrediting an image of Hypatia as close as possible to Christianity, that is, to the "popular" type of preaching that from the Cynic street philosophers would be transmitted to the Christian saints.

---

164 MALALAS XIV 12, p. 280, 68–70 Thurn; English translation pp. 195–196 Jeffreys – Jeffreys – Scott (HARICH-SCHWARZBAUER 2011, p. 336).
165 See also CHUVIN–TARDIEU, pp. 63–65.

According to Damascius, Hypatia, in divulging her philosophy to people, wore the *tribon* (τρίβων)¹⁶⁶, not a simple cloak, as some translators state, seeing in the information only an emphasis on her austerity, but a garment which marked a specific philosophical status. On the one hand, the more widespread meaning of *tribon* in Late Antiquity is κατ' ἐξοχήν that of the livery of the Cynic: the rough cape typical of the street philosopher. The same term is applied by the sources, legendary or not, to the garment worn by Hipparchia. We might therefore consider Damascius' mention as a further proof of his tendency to make Hypatia's behaviour fit this pattern. On the other hand, textual parallels show that the term *tribon* was used already in the 4th century to designate either a "formal professorial garment", comparable to the modern academic gown, or an official, ceremonial and even ritual garment which fell to the feet, as has been suggested (Chuvin). Both of these two meanings are preferable to the one indicating the uniform of the Cynic preacher. It is unlikely that a Platonic teacher of high rank would appear in public wearing a short rough cloak on bare skin¹⁶⁷.

However, we must say, in the confessional persecution of Pagan Hellenism, the model best tolerated by the Church was that of the Cynic preacher, the last to disappear from the Christianised world, fading into that of the Holy Man. The image of Hypatia conveyed by Suidas through Damascius, accrediting to his victim a teaching close to the "popular" preaching of the Cynic philosopher and later of the Christian saint, is already, in effect, a hagiographical image, consistent with that of "public" saint or "civic consultant" with which the cities of the Christianised empire were soon to be crowded. A popular image, far from the type of elitist teaching, very probably initiatory, practised in the Platonic school of Alexandria.

Here what was meant by *philosophia* was not merely the presentation "of Plato, Aristotle or some other of the philosophers to anyone who wanted to listen", according to the words of Damascius/Suidas, but the prerogative of a few, that was also an access code to an elite within an elite. One zealous pupil of Hypatia, Synesius, asked in one of his letters: "Whatever can the people and philosophy have in common?"¹⁶⁸ Or we should write, the people and the *philosophia* that linked Hypatia to Synesius and to only a few others.

---

166 DAMASCIUS, *Vita Isidori* fr. *102, p. 77, 5 Zintzen = fr. 43A, p. 128, 4–5 Athanassiadi = SUIDAS Y 166, IV, p. 644, 15–16 Adler (HARICH-SCHWARZBAUER 2011, p. 246).
167 See below, Appendix *ad loc.*
168 *Ep.* 105, 104, p. 239 Roques.

Appendix
Hypatia in All Her States of Being

A solid scepticism regarding the "Cynic" traits overlaid by Damascius on Hypatia's physionomy was shown by scholars from the early 20th century, and the tendentiousness of the expressions is pointed out first of all by PRAECHTER 1916, col. 243; his arguments were taken up and developed by DZIELSKA 1995, pp. 55–58. On the Stoic-Cynic connotation of Hypatia's figure see also RIST, pp. 220–221.

CAMERON – LONG state, in our opinion rightly, that Damascius, the last exponent of the Platonic academy of Athens, wanted to compare Hypatia to the "vulgar" model of the Cynic preacher in order to retaliate against the disdainful opinion of the Alexandrian Platonists regarding the Athenian school, as testified by Synesius in *Ep.* 136 (Engl. transl. pp. 228–229 Fitzgerald): see CAMERON – LONG, pp. 27–28, 56–57, 63 ff.

On the other hand, other scholars – *in primis* LACOMBRADE 1995 – have considered real Hypatia's *penchant* for the ways of Cynic preaching, "in a period in which", as Enrico Livrea writes (*per litteras*), "the *kynikos bios* (κυνικὸς βίος) seems to live again above all on the Christian side, of which the philosopher would have created a Pagan counterpart" (see LIVREA 1995, pp. 131–132); and they conclude, like ÉVRARD, p. 71, "that Hypatia's method of teaching was in effect similar to Stoic-Cynic preaching, for which the Christians did indeed show a certain indulgence".

The definitive word on the topic was formulated by CHUVIN–TARDIEU, pp. 59–68, in which it is rejected out of hand that Hypatia was really "une prêcheuse de carrefour" ["a wandering preacher"] (p. 62) and it is instead emphasised with regard to her *semnotes* (σεμνότης) – her 'honourability', the 'respectability' that marked all her behaviour, including her "honourable freedom of speech" (*semne parrhesia*, σεμνὴ παρρησία), on which the ancient sources insisted so much, from Socrates to Palladas – how it placed her "aux antipodes du cynisme" ["the antithesis of Cynism"] (p. 65); see also below in this chapter.

In particular, on the *aischrourgia* (αἰσχρουργία) and on the *gynaikeia rhake* (γυναικεῖα ῥάκη) see LACOMBRADE 1995, who while crediting as real the influence of the Cynic model in Hypatia's teachings, as it was the only style of Pagan thinking tolerated in Theodosian Egypt, takes care to purify it of the more despicable anecdotal elements; and above all LIVREA 1995, who, as we have seen, corrects the text of the "impressive chronicle" of Damascius, more than once discussed by editors and scholars, confirming both the undeniable Cynic overtones and the affinity with the version traditionally attributed to Hipparchia, and giving, moreover, precious Neoplatonic parallels to what we read "in Hypatia's provocative disdain for the physiology of the sex and in the search for a didactic *sophronismos* (σωφρονισμός)".

On this last point see also CHUVIN–TARDIEU, p. 66, where Pierre Chuvin interprets the gesture in the light of the "obsession de pureté physique qui règne chez les païens tardifs, Proclos et sa hantise des tâches, Héraïscos à qui la présence d'une femme ayant ses règles suffisait à donner mal à la tête", but reassesses it, trusting excessively however in Damascius, without considering the possibility of contrivances, or even a precise interest, given the rivalry of the schools, in exaggerating the more trivial aspects similar to the Cynic anecdote, as CAMERON – LONG suggest.

On the *kynogamia* (κυνογαμία) of Hipparchia and Crates of Thebes, handed down amongst others by Diogenes Laërtius and by Suidas, see the clear analysis of DOYSON, p. 135. The comparison with Hypatia's *aischrourgia* is in SHANZER, pp. 62–63; the author also proposes an interesting, but not conclusive parallel with the passage from PLOTINUS, *Enneads* V, 8, 2 Henry – Schwyzer (Engl. transl. by A. H. Armstrong: "What then is the beauty in these [the beautiful beings imitated by the arts]? Certainly not *their blood and menstrual fluid* […] there is nothing unless sheer ugliness or a bare recipient, as it were the mere Matter of beauty"), in the light of which Hypatia's gesture could be interpreted, in her opinion.

BERETTA 1993, pp. 199 ff., decidedly over-interprets when seeing in the episode an allusion to the duties of the Alexandrian *kerykainai* (κερυκαῖναι, "town criers"), who gathered the menstrual cloths and took them to the sea, and interprets Hypatia's gesture as a Proto-Feminist example of liberation of women from the "blame" of the matter, if not even a provocative assertion of the female right to priesthood (*ibidem*, p. 201). See also LEONARD, pp. 171–192.

The correct interpretation of Hypatia's gesture – which removes the Cynic overtones introduced by Damascius – is, as we have seen, that of DZIELSKA 1995, pp. 50–52: "Hypatia's revolting act was intended to make the student understand the deeper meaning of Eros and to 'turn' him in that direction" (see above, part I, chapter "Elegant Insolence", Appendix *ad loc.*).

Sensible, although marginal, are the observations of DEAKIN 2007, pp. 62–63, who reads the episode as a proclamation of chastity: in the ancient world "there was no really effective contraception, and so, since both pregnancy and lactation inhibit ovulation, menstruation was actually a rare event. A woman who menstruated regularly would thus (infertility aside) be a celibate woman and her monthly periods the insignia of a forsworn lifestyle."

Hypatia's date of birth can be deduced, as we have seen, from the vague indication given by Hesychius and reported in SUIDAS Y 166, IV, p. 644, 3 Adler (HARICH-SCHWARZBAUER 2011, p. 324), who places her *floruit* in the reign of Arcadius (395–408), cross-referencing it with the biographical data in our possession on her father Theon (for which see above, part I, chapter "Once there was a Woman", Appendix *ad loc.*). We are also assisted in reconstructing it by the dates of the eclipses of the sun and the moon that Hypatia's father personally observed: see below, chapter "Synesius, Hypatia and *Philosophia*", Appendix *ad loc.* The combination has led the majority of scholars to fix an approximate date around 370, like HOCHE; RIST; PRAECHTER 1916 etc. However, there has been a recent resurgence of the theory – advanced by the 19th-century scholars who studied Synesius and by WOLF 1879, p. 12, and welcomed by LACOMBRADE 1951, p. 39 – that the date was even earlier: see DZIELSKA 1995, pp. 67–68, according to whom Hypatia was born around 355; PENELLA tends towards 355 to 368, followed by BERETTA 1993, p. 34 and n. 40; see also HARICH-SCHWARZBAUER 2011, p. 339. WATTS 2017, pp. 21

et al., cf. p. 161, n. 2, follows Dzielska 1995 and Penella, who base their incorrect, in our opinion, evaluation on Malalas, according to whom Hypatia was *palaia*, παλαιά, old, at the time of her death (Malalas XIV 12, p. 280, 68–70 Thurn; English translation pp. 195–196 Jeffreys – Jeffreys – Scott [Harich-Schwarzbauer 2011, p. 336]). In the end, it is this statement (again, in our opinion, incorrectly interpreted) that leads the mathematicians Benedetto – Isola – Russo, pp. 30–32, to backdate Hypatia's birth to 335. If we were to accept their datings, Hypatia at the moment of her utmost prestige and her consequent assassination would have been sixty years old; she would therefore, for the ancient parameters, have been a *very* old woman. Yet it is a well known fact that the perception of female age was significantly different than ours. It appears more probable that, as most scholars have hypothesised, Hypatia was born around 370 and that at the moment of her death in 415 she was forty five, and was consequently considered old according to the parameters of her time.

For the opinion of Forster see above, part II, chapter "From Fielding to Gibbon Passing through the Shadow of a Donkey".

The comparison between Odette and Hypatia is in Proust, p. 57; the image of the worlds rolling under her feet derives from a verse of the *Hypatie* by Leconte de Lisle (see above, part II, chapter "The Forces of the Universe" and Appendix *ad loc.*): "Elle seule survit, immuable, éternelle; / La mors peut disperser les univers tremblants. / Mais la Beauté flamboie, et tout renaît en elle, / *Et les mondes encore roulent sous ses pieds blancs*".

That, in any case, in 415 Hypatia was to be considered an elderly woman is confirmed, apart from the explicit declaration of Malalas, also by the terms used by Philostorgius: as we have seen, at the end of his account (Philostorgius 8, 9, p. 111, 7 Bidez = p. 368 Bleckmann-Stein [Harich-Schwarzbauer 2011, p. 318]), we find, to designate the victim, not the feminine noun τὴν γυνήν (the woman), but the neutral τὸ γύναιον, diminutive and pejorative, which is to be translated 'the poor' or better 'the old' woman (διασπασθῆναι τὸ γύναιον ὑπὸ τῶν τὸ ὁμοούσιον πρεσβευόντων).

On the Museum of Alexandria, founded eight centuries earlier by Ptolemy I Soter, and on its library see Erskine.

Amongst others, Ammianus Marcellinus, *Res gestae* XXII 16, testifies that the teaching at the ancient school of the Museum of Alexandria had continued also after the destruction under Aurelian. That Theon taught at the Museum is implied by Suidas (who calls Theon ὁ ἐκ τοῦ Μουσείου). The majority of scholars consider this to be its last chair: see above all Lacombrade 1972, p. 10. On the places and methods of Platonic teaching in 5th century Alexandria see Chuvin, pp. 366–367.

That Hypatia taught in public at least from 393 is testified by the letters of Synesius and in particular by *Ep.* 137 (Engl. transl. pp. 229–231 Fitzgerald). According to some scholars this letter was written in the same year, yet it is much more probable that it was written several years after Synesius' sojourn in Alexandria: see Synesius, tom. III, p. 398, n. 1 Roques (who dates the epistle to 398).

On the 'public' teaching of Hypatia see Évrard, according to whom Hypatia did not teach with an official position, but on her own initiative, and the expression *demosia* is to be understood as "in a public place", or "on the public road"; an opinion taken up by GOULET–CAZÉ, pp. 245–46, and, more recently, by WATTS 2006a, pp. 194–195 and WATTS 2017, pp. 63–65 e p. 173, n. 6, who has contested the idea that Hypatia's was a "publicly funded profession", following VINZENT, pp. 63–69, and highlighting the discrepancy between the use of Damascius of *demosia* as an adverb (δημοσίᾳ) (DAMASCIUS, *Vita Isidori* fr. *102, p. 77, 6 Zintzen = fr. 43A, p. 128, 6 Athanassiadi = SUIDAS Y 166, IV, p. 644, 17 Adler = HARICH-SCHWARZBAUER 2011, p. 246) and the technical denomination *demosia* (δημόσια, adj.) *sitesis* (σίτησις, "public salary") attested in DAMASCIUS, *Vita Isidori* fr. *124, p. 107, 4–5 Zintzen = fr. 56, p. 156, 17–18 Athanassiadi = SUIDAS Αι 79, II, p. 161, 33 Adler. On the other hand LACOMBRADE 1951, p. 44, considers Hypatia to be the holder of a genuine "public chair", municipal if not State, in any case not connected to the Museum. See also LACOMBRADE 1994, col. 958; MEYER; HOCHE, p. 442; RIST, pp. 220–21; MARROU 1963, p. 148. A recent and basic commentary on Damascius' passage can be read in HARICH-SCHWARZBAUER 2011, pp. 258–259.

The definitive word on Hypatia's teaching was pronounced by CHUVIN–TARDIEU, pp. 63–65, in which the public and official nature of the role was confirmed, with all probability "au frais (ou: à l'initiative, ou: au service) de l'Etat", supporting this interpretation with convincing parallels and emphasising, as we have seen, that Hypatia taught lessons linked to her public chair in the city centre, travelling there solemnly in a carriage, while she held her private lessons (*idia*, ἰδίᾳ) for her esoteric circle in her private residence, situated some distance from the city centre (*ibidem*, p. 65).

Incidentally, Hypatia's public outings were far from being 'promenades', since they are described using the technical-ceremonial term *proodos* (πρόοδος), and must be considered genuine "official appearances", of a presumably solemn nature; and the image of a "Hypatie comme une prêcheuse de carrefours" or also "comme une promeneuse bavardant librement avec les officiels qu'elle rencontrait 'en passant' dans la ville", although asserted (because it was suggested by Damascius) by scholars such as Lacombrade, is to be excluded. See CHUVIN–TARDIEU, esp. pp. 62 e 65; see above, part I, chapter "Mortal Envy" and Appendix *ad loc.*

On Hypatia wearing the *tribon* (τρίβων) see DZIELSKA 1995, p. 66, and CHUVIN-TARDIEU, pp. 62–63, who show a series of textual parallels in which the term does not mean the livery of the Cynic but is on the contrary used in an academic sense as "une tenue professionelle distinctive, l'équivalent de ce qu'était chez nous la toge professorale." In Chuvin's reading, Damascius does therefore not intend to belittle Hypatia's teaching, giving it a 'Cynic' connotation, but on the contrary suggests the image "du célèbre professeur se rendant en grande tenue à ses cours".

On one hand, it is difficult to ignore the fact that the *tribon*, in ancient times the cloak of the Spartans and the "philosophical cloak" *tout court*, common to the philosophers of the various schools, including the Stoics, in Late Antiquity was seen as the authentic livery of the Cynics: see the oration VIII of Julian the Apostate *Eis tous apaideutos kynas* (Εἰς τοὺς ἀπαιδεύτους κύνας), in JULIANUS APOSTATA, p. 1 Rochefort, *Contre les cyniques ignorants*, 18, 1–17, in which he identifies the three *gnorismata* (γνωρίσματα) or "identification marks" of the Cynic livery – the rough cloak (the *tribon*), the knapsack of the beggar and the stick. See also Ps.-Crates 33, 2, in HERCHER

On the other hand, it is interesting for the Byzantinist to read the reference of CHUVIN–TARDIEU, p. 63, to the definition of the *tribonophoros* (τριβωνοφόρος), that is the "wearer of a *tribon*", in the Byzantine lexica (the *Etymologicum Magnum* and Suidas himself) as "he who wears a garment that has a motif like small *gamma.*" This appears to confirm Chuvin's idea that in the Proto-Byzantine era, and possibly already in Late Antiquity, the term *tribon* did not mean, or no longer meant, a short rough cloak, but an official, ceremonial, and even ritual – we may believe – garment, which fell to the feet, such as those mentioned in the *De magistratibus* by John Lydus (quoted by Chuvin).

On the relations of the Church with the last Cynic preachers see LABRIOLLE, pp. 83–87; LIZZI TESTA.

On the saint as a "civic consultant" see BROWN 1971; SEIBER.

On the social background and the peculiar link of caste that united Hypatia's pupils, see, in addition to DZIELSKA 1995, pp. 27 ff., also what is written, as a useful summary, by THORP: "We know the names of some of them: Herculianus, Olympius, Ision, Hesychius, Euoptius (Synesius' brother), Alexander, Theotecnus, Athanasius, Theodosius, Gaius, Auxentius. It is significant that many of these young men were well-born, and well off. They were to become high-ranking civil servants or ecclesiastics or otherwise important in various parts of the empire. Athanasius became a famous sophist; Theodosius became a famous grammarian. They hailed from many different parts of the empire: certainly from the Cyrenaica, from Syria, from Alexandria (of course), from the Thebaid and from Constantinople, and doubtless from other places as well. The bonds of friendship they established seem to have been enduring ones; and Synesius' letters imply that they visited one another in their various cities after their student days were over. These were the *jeunesse dorée* of the Eastern empire; part of the unforgettable richness of their student days, of course, will have derived from who *they* were".

The rhetorical question of Synesius (δήμῳ γὰρ δὴ καὶ φιλοσοφίᾳ τί πρὸς ἄλληλα;) is taken from *Ep.* 105, 104, p. 239 Roques (Engl. transl. p. 200 Fitzgerald); on his Plotinian ascendance see above, chapter "May the Witness Return to Court", in Appendix, commenting on the same quotation in *exergo* of part III.

31 What Did Hypatia Teach?

> Isidore was very different from Hypatia, not only inasmuch as a man is different from a woman, but as far as a real philosopher can be different from a woman skilled in geometry.[169]

Damascius, the biographer of Isidore, his master of mysteries, is a well-informed witness from the Pagan milieu and also member of the Platonic confraternity. The statements made in the *Life of Isidore* may not be sufficient to convince us that Hypatia's teaching was limited to scientific initiation, which, however, the Platonists considered the presupposition of all philosophy. It may also be that the leaders of the Athenian current of Neoplatonism, to which Damascius belonged and which was opposed to the Alexandrian one, nurtured hostility for the members of the latter, underrating and misunderstanding them. However, it is the work of Theon and Hypatia itself, or at least what is preserved of it via the direct or indirect tradition, which suggests that father and daughter, in their official lessons (δημοσίᾳ), did not impart theoretical Platonism, but rather its technical-mathematical, geometric and astronomic basics.

According to Suidas, Hypatia wrote commentaries on classical works, but with a strong scientific connotation: not on Plato or the Neoplatonics, but on the *Conics* by Apollonius of Perga and the *Arithmetica* by Diophantus. Hypatia's name is also associated with a work called by the sources *Astronomical Canon* (Ἀστρονομικὸς κανών), probably a commentary on the *Handy Tables* (Πρόχειροι κανόνες) by Ptolemy, and we owe to her the "revision" (*paragnosis*) of the third book of the *Almagest* by Ptolemy, that is in reality, according to a recent hypothesis, the edition of its text as part of Theon's commentary. In the title handed down by the principal witness of the manuscript tradition we read: "Edition revised by my daughter, the philosopher Hypatia"[170].

If we look closely at these pages, we can see that Hypatia must really have been, as Damascius writes, "versed in geometry". However, while the testimony of the title confirms her unquestionable activity as a scientist and a scholar, it is arbitrary and imaginative to deduce the existence of her astronomical observations as anticipating the modern scientific revolution. Just as it is risky to see an original work in the *Astronomical Canon* mentioned by the sources.

The only inventions by Hypatia which we can be certain of are the machines that she had her pupils build: a flat astrolabe, considered by scientists today quite banal, a hydroscope, which would attract the attention of the great mathematician Pierre Fermat, and an aerometer, if we go by what Synesius tells us.[171] All the rest is inference, or conjecture.

---

[169] Damascius, *Vita Isidori* fr. *164, p. 218 Zintzen = Photius, *Bibl.*, vol. VI, p. 38, 13–15 Henry = fr. 106A, p. 253 Athanassiadi (Harich-Schwarzbauer 2011, p. 248).
[170] Ἐκδόσεως παραγνωσθείσης τῇ φιλοσόφῳ θυγατρί μου Ὑπατίᾳ: see Rome 1943, p. 807, 4–5.
[171] Synesius, *Ep.* 15, p. 26 Roques (hydroscope) and *De dono*, par. 4, pp. 179–180 Lamoureux – Aujoulat.

Still, it must be said that the presumed "mystery" of Hypatia's works, the hypothesis that her other writings may have been lost, has been an additional element of fascination for scholars. Historians of the sciences have suggested "the possibility that they still exist in more or less mutilated form or under a false name"[172]. While this conjecture was already presented at the end of the 19th century, in recent times the speculations about "a Hypatian system"[173] as the precursor of the Copernican system have multiplied, or in any case about possible and fundamental scientific intuitions contained in further works by Hypatia that have not been handed down to the modern era due to her assassination and were destroyed because of the "ecclesiastical persecution" of her thinking and her school.

These conjectures come from the writings of mathematicians and historians of science, who seem to have retrospectively projected onto the political-ecclesiastical scenario of the 5th century the repressive methods of the Catholic Church of the Counter-Reformation, thus adding to the fantasy of the literary afterlife of Hypatia a further mask, that of a Galilean scientist condemned by the Church of the Inquisition.

While on the one hand it could be that the assassination of the head of the school was followed by the ransacking of its books, in reality the hypothesis conflicts with both the events reported by the contemporary sources, and with the framework into which they fit, which is that of an individual persecution, and that of the fundamental defence of the memory of Hypatia shared by the entire Orthodox Christian tradition. And in any case, the meticulous way in which the Byzantine millennium dedicated itself to conserving the works of the thinkers of Late Antiquity makes it very difficult to imagine the total shipwreck of a *corpus* of works, and even more of the scientific advances of an entire school.

On a more strictly philosophical plane, from the doctrines of Alexandrian thinkers of the time it has generally been deduced, very hypothetically, that Hypatia "professed a Neoplatonism of a primitive type" [174], which "defined itself carefully between opposition to the oriental inclination of Neoplatonism on the one hand, but also to its Athenian physiognomy: the former was opposed in the name of a certain rationalism, the latter in the name of a certain neutrality towards Christianity".[175] As proof of all this, the Christian Neoplatonism of Origen is called on as a direct witness, inasmuch as he was a pupil of Ammonius, of the Middle Platonic and not Plotinian tradition of Alexandria. Reference has also been made to the doctrine of Hierocles, to whom Christian pupils are attributed, as they were to Hypatia herself and later to Aeneas of Gaza and John Philoponus. This, however, does not leave room to hypothesise – another legend, which has recently flourished once again – Hypatia's inclination towards Nestorian Christianity.

---

172 TANNERY 1896.
173 FERRETTI, p. 37.
174 ÉVRARD, p. 69.
175 GARZYA, p. 32.

According to Edward Watts[176], Hypatia's "distinctive brand of philosophical teaching" combined the "mathematical rigor characteristic of the teaching of the fourth century mathematicians like Pappus and Theon with the philosophical system of the Neoplatonists Plotinus and Porphyry" and was different from the "Iamblichan trend", namely that mix of Neopythagoreanism and "innovative philosophical approaches of the Alexandrian-trained philosopher Plotinus and ritualistic elements inspired by the third-century Chaldean oracles"[177], which, according to Watts, was embodied in Alexandria in the teaching of Antoninus (who nonetheless ἐπεδείκνυτο [...] οὐδὲν θεουργόν, as stated in Eunapius' account)[178], and Olympus, who, as described in Damascius' *Vita Isidori*, taught in the Serapeum "the rules of divine worship, the ancient traditions, and the happiness that accompanied them"[179].

Watts' idea according to which Hypatia's philosophy was, contrary to the intransigent Paganism of Iamblichus and of the followers of Antoninus and Olympus, a neutral philosophy that did not have Pagan elements, is not convincing. The statement according to which "Christian students of Hypatia could then practise Platonic philosophy in a way that was philosophically sound and not radically inconsistent with Christian theology" is correct, and this helps us understand her "broad appeal to both Pagan and Christian students in the 380s and early 390s"[180]. But this is not enough to prove that her Platonic school was confessionally neutral.

To tolerate does not mean to accredit, let alone to believe. It is necessary to distinguish between tolerance – of popular beliefs, amongst which the pupils of Hypatia officially converted to Christianity would include the principal dogmas of their religion, and in general of the plurality of cults, according to the consolidated Pagan tradition that had seen also Julian the Apostate concede a corner to Christ in the restored Hellenic Pantheon – and intellectual consent; between the ancient Platonic art of the "noble lie", practised by the learned in the name of usefulness for the simple souls of the *superstitiones*, both Christian and Pagan (or Jewish, or Egyptian, or Zoroastrian), and doctrinal ambiguity, incoherence or interference in the vision of the world.

After all, if the teaching imparted by Hypatia's school had been really this side of the threshold of the problems with which metaphysics and therefore religion interfere, why would there be so much malevolence (φθόνος) from the Christians for Hypatia's "astronomical knowledge", as Damascius writes?

It is definitely possible that Hypatia's philosophical teaching was rooted "firmly within the Plotinian and Porphyrian interpretative traditions but outside that of Iam-

---

[176] WATTS 2017, p. 37.
[177] ID., p. 32.
[178] EUNAPIUS VI 10, 7, p. 37, 16–17 Giangrande.
[179] WATTS 2017, pp. 55 and 58–59; DAMASCIUS, *Vita Isidori* fr. *97, p. 73, 7–8 Zintzen = fr. 42F, p. 126, 3–6 Athanassiadi, who translates: "He used to gather together those around him and teach them the rules of divine worship, the ancient traditions and the happiness which attends on them – that great and wonderful happiness sent by the gods to those who faithfully observe them."
[180] WATTS 2017, pp. 56, 57, 49.

blichus"[181]. Nonetheless, excluding any ritual and theurgical element from the practices of the circle of Hypatia's closest followers, namely those who had access to the most esoteric dimension of her teaching, is underestimating her deep affiliation to Hellenism and the allusions to "magic, astrolabes, and musical instruments" provided by the only (and consequently crucial) Christian-Coptic source, namely the *Chronicle* of John of Nikiu, as well as the precise account of our major source on the school of Hypatia: namely Synesius, who employs, in his epistles, the technical terminology of mystery rites,[182] and in his *De insomniis* uses openly the term *teletai* (τελεταί)[183].

---

[181] ID., p. 43.
[182] SYNESIUS, *Ep.* 137, 5–9 (*To Herculian*), p. 276 Roques.
[183] ID., *De insomniis*, p. 281 Lamoureux – Aujoulat.

Appendix
What Did Hypatia Teach?

Damascius' quote on the difference between Isidore and Hypatia is taken from DAMASCIUS, *Vita Isidori* fr. *164, p. 218 Zintzen = PHOTIUS, *Bibl.*, vol. VI, p. 38, 13–15 Henry = fr. 106A, p. 253 Athanassiadi (HARICH-SCHWARZBAUER 2011, p. 248).

On scientific initiation as presupposition of all philosophy and "the messy border between mathematics and philosophy" in Neoplatonic schools see WATTS 2017, pp. 31–35; on this matter see also O' MEARA; see also below, chapter "Synesius, Hypatia, and *Philosophia*", Appendix *ad loc.*

The most recent, most accurate and most reliable assessment of the scientific personality of Hypatia, her mathematical attainments and what we can reconstruct of them is in DEAKIN 2007, pp. 87–113 (presentation of the works attributed to Hypatia by the sources and their evaluation) and 189–196 (notes); pp. 115–133 (mathematical considerations) and 196–202 (notes). See also LACOMBRADE 2001, pp. 404–409.

An attempt at contextualising Hypatia's and Theon's personalities within Late Ancient philosophy of science can be found in BERNARD 2010.

Hypatia's contribution as editor of the annotated *Almagest* (and not the revisor of her father's commentary, as previously thought) is argued in CAMERON 1990; see also CAMERON 2016c, pp. 190–194, which refutes and rectifies the theories formulated by ROME 1943, pp. cxvii–cxxi; by Anne Tihon in MOGENET – TIHON, I, p. 221; and by KNORR, pp. 756 ff. Finally, see the conclusions of DEAKIN 2007, pp. 91–94 and his notes on pp. 189–190. A fleeting mention of Hypatia's scholarly commitment is in HERRIN, p. 25.

Theon's *inscriptio* (Ἐκδόσεως παραγνοσθείσης τῇ φιλοσόφῳ θυγατρί μου Ὑπατίᾳ) can be read in ROME 1943, p. 807, 4–5; see DEAKIN 2007, pp. 91 and 109 (in which it is considered "the action of a proud father: suppressing his own work in favour of a manifest improvement by his daughter").

Paradoxically, the more creative asserters of Hypatia's intelligence and the innovative nature of her scientific thinking have avoided consulting and reading the manuscript text (codex Laurentianus Plut. 28.18); see for example BERETTA 1993, p. 47, who complains that "her" only surviving work was written in Greek and calls for a translation "into a modern language" in order to be able to judge "whether the astronomical observations for which Hypatia was praised by Philostorgius concerned the delicate questions on which the modern scientific revolution is based."

On the other works of Hypatia, and in particular on the interpretation of the passage in Suidas (taken from Hesychius of Miletus) in which there is a mention of the *Astronomical Canon*, see TANNERY 1880, p. 199; DEAKIN 2007, pp. 95–101 and notes on pp. 190–192.

As noted also by CAMERON 2016c, pp. 193–195, and by KNORR, the two principal scholars who have tried to extract and isolate Hypatia's work within the exegetical tradition incorporated in the texts that according to the sources she is believed to have commented on, her contributions seem to be elementary and essentially pedagogical: "The more extravagant expectations are dashed", and the content is "what we might today call a school edition, designed for the use of students rather than professional mathematicians", according to CAMERON 2016c, p. 194. KNORR even considers that the results show that Hypatia had "an essentially trivial mind."

See *contra* KRISCHER, who from a passage in *Ep.* 4 by Synesius sees possible innovative elements in the speculations of Theon and Hypatia, which return a century later in the work of John Philoponus.

WATTS 2017, pp. 29–31, provides a rather questionable assessment of what he calls Hypatia's "projects", namely her few witnessed or alleged works, and in particular of her first "editorial project", namely the above mentioned *paragnosis* of the third book of the *Almagest*, whose text, according to the *inscriptio* handed down to us by the main witness of the manuscript tradition, Hypatia reconstructed, as we have seen, so as to enable her father to write a commentary on it. According to Alan Cameron, this work by Hypatia was probably a sort of proto-critical edition, produced through the collation of multiple manuscripts. Yet the *inscriptio* does not seem enough to conclude, like Watts does, that Hypatia also reconstructed the text of the following ten books (4–13) of the *Almagest*. This idea, which is first cautiously presented by Watts as a hypothesis, is later presented as a fact ("Hypatia's edition of Books 3–13 of the *Almagest* was no simple project [...] Her work brought readers closer to truth. This meant that Hypatia and her contemporaries would have understood her edition to be a quite significant scholarly contribution", p. 31). Let us recall that nowhere, in the data provided by the manuscript tradition as well as by the secondary sources, is there support for the hypothesis that Hypatia extended her "project" on the *Almagest* beyond the point indicated in the above mentioned *inscriptio*, just like there is no support for the theory that the *Astronomikos Kanon* was an original work, or that the commentaries on Diophantus' *Arithmetica* and on Apollonius' *Conics*, which were merely mentioned in Suidas and did not survive the erasure of time, were scientifically significant works and not just basic handbooks.

The most accurate formulation of the improbable hypothesis that the *Astronomikos Kanon* was an original work by Hypatia, in which the philosopher would make "accessible to men and women of her time" a "new scientific acquisition" deriving from "the ingenious intuition of combining the studies and the methods set out in Apollonius' *Conics* and the studies and methods of Diophantus' *Algebra*" can be read in BERETTA 1993, pp. 51–55; an intuition with which Hypatia would have anticipated by more than one thousand years even Descartes, and which would however not reach the modern era simply because of her assassination, which would have determined "the dispersion of the school that she headed".

Synesius speaks of the machines Hypatia designed in *Ep.* 15, p. 26 Roques (hydroscope) and in *De dono* (to Paeonius), par. 4, pp. 179–180 Lamoureux – Aujoulat; see LACOMBRADE 1951, pp. 42–43. Their reconstruction and appraisal is to be found in DEAKIN 2007, pp. 102–105. On the hydroscope see also DEAKIN – HUNTER According to NEUGEBAUER, p. 873, the astrolabe (or whatever that was), which some scholars assume Synesius had made by a silversmith on the instructions of Hypatia and is declaimed in the *Discourse on Gifts* – and taken seriously a few years earlier by scholars such as VOGT–SCHRAMM – was "a totally useless instrument".

On the probable divinatory use of both instruments by Synesius, and in particular on hydromancy, see DZIELSKA 1995, pp. 78–79 and 142, with nn. 67 and 68.

The *Observation de Monsieur de Fermat sur Synesius*, originally published in the French translation of the treatise *Della misura delle acque correnti* [*On the Measurement of Running Water*] by the Benedictine monk Benedetto CASTELLI (pp. 84–87), can be read in TANNERY – HENRY, I, *Appendix*, p. 362.

The theory of a survival of important works by Hypatia preserved anonymously or under a false name was already advanced by TANNERY 1896 and seems to be accepted in DZIELSKA 1995, p. 72. However, it is excluded by DEAKIN 2007, who considers possible, although there is no proof, only the theory of Wilbur Knorr. The latter, on the basis of stylistic features, suggests that Hypatia contributed also to the edition of Archimedes' *Measurement of a Circle*, handed down to us mainly in Latin version, and, in some form, to an anonymous treatise *On the Isoperimetric Figures*, as well as to a brief geometric work, the *De Curvis Superficibus:* see KNORR, chapter 11.

In 19th-century America, Hypatia's popularity amongst scientists was reawakened by the versatile and popular chemist and physiologist J.W. Draper, who described her with fervidly neo-Enlightenment accents in his *History of the Intellectual Development of Europe* (DRAPER, pp. 238–244).

The lost works of Hypatia, abusively appropriated by the masculine culture, are sought – and even found – in the embarrassing chapter *Hypatia of Alexandria* in WAITHE, pp. 176–192. A "Hypatian System" (as the precursor of the Copernican one) is mentioned, although in a non-scientific setting, by a book admired and widely distributed: FERRETTI, p. 37 (on which see also also below, chapter "The Martyrdom of Hypatia", Appendix *ad loc.*).

For the recent speculations on Hypatia by misinformed and misinforming mathematicians and historians of science see for example WHITFIELD, in which the analysis is reduced to the simplistic and bizarre idea that Damascius was "anxious to exploit the scandal of Hypatia's death", and therefore blamed the Christians and the bishop Cyril; a version that would become official after the incorporation of the account by Damascius "in the Byzantine lexicon-encyclopedia known as the *Suda*". See also OSER, p. 27; OGILVIE; L. GRINSTEIN–CAMPBELL; and the interventions of RICHESON, WAERDEN, JACOBACCI and PERL, quoted in DZIELSKA 1995, p. 25 and nn. *ad loc.*

Much more accurate and reliable, as we have seen, is DEAKIN 2007, a useful book in which the eminent Australian mathematician, who had already authored contributions of various kinds on the subject (see in particular DEAKIN 1994; DEAKIN 1995), summarises and also comments on the specific contributions of Cameron, Knorr and other scholars who have tried to untangle the works of Hypatia from the complex manuscript tradition of the mathematical and astronomical texts she glossed; almost a *unicum* in the thread of contributions on Hypatia expressed by the mathematicians, to be added to the brief article of SCHREK, and to what can be read about Hypatia in KLINE.

On Antoninus and Olympus see above, part I, chapter "The Destruction of the Serapeum" and Appendix *ad loc*; WATTS 2017, pp. 55 and 58–59. On Olympus' teaching see *Vita Isidori* fr. *95, 97 and fr. *E48, 92, pp. 71,15, 73, 5–8 and 68–70, 16–2, 69–71, 5–2 Zintzen = fr. 42F and 42B, pp. 126, 1–6 and 124, 1–4 Athanassiadi.

The idea of a "primitive Platonism" professed by Hypatia is expressed by ÉVRARD, p. 69; see LACOMBRADE 1951, pp. 49–50.

The "rationalism" and the "neutrality towards Christianity" of the Platonic school of Alexandria, contrasted with both "oriental-style" Neoplatonism and Athenian Neoplatonism, are suggested by GARZYA, p. 32.

On the Platonic tradition (διαδοχή) which linked Hypatia's teaching to that of Plotinus, according to Socrates Scholasticus (SOCRATES VII 15, 1, p. 360 Hansen), discordant interpretations are given by the ancients themselves, amongst whom the school of Athens dominates in terms of prestige, while that of Alexandria is belittled. In effect, when Socrates Scholasticus speaks for Hypatia of "succession in the Platonic school brought back to life by Plotinus," he seems to imply that in her teaching she was the direct heir to the interpretation of Platonism given by Plotinus: but this is denied both by Hierocles (*De providentia*, preserved in Photius), a pupil, like Syrianus, of Plutarch of Athens (for Hierocles the *diadoche* or legitimate succession of the Platonic Academy began with Ammonius Saccas and through Origen, Plotinus, Porphyry and Iamblichus arrived at Plutarch of Athens), and later by the *Theologia platonica* by Proclus (a disciple of Syrianus, therefore 'great-nephew' of Plutarch of Athens): see RIST, pp. 217–219. We are, here, in the more 'magical' wing of Platonism, and according to FOWDEN 1982, it was precisely the wish to "show that the only true heirs to Plato and Plotinus were the adherents of Iamblichean theurgy" which led, in the *diadoche* of the Athenians, to the "most complete omission of the Alexandrian Neoplatonics, from Hypatia to Synesius onwards."

The parallel with the doctrines of Origen and Hierocles is suggested by RIST, pp. 218 ff.; see also HADOT.

That Hypatia might have been "affiliated to a Christian belief" is quite arbitrarily suggested by DZIELSKA 1995, pp. 20–22, who for this purpose misinterprets both the words of Damascius, and those of Philostorgius, and even validates the false letter from Hypatia to Cyril in defence of Nestorius (for which see above, part II, chapter "Refreshing Exceptions", and part III, chapter "An Age of Anxiety"), and with disconcerting overturning of logic considers the formation of the (spurious) legend of Saint Catherine of Alexandria proof "of Hypatia's association with Christianity."

The quotations from Watts are taken from WATTS 2017, respectively from pp. 37, 32, 55, 56, 57, 49. It is highly probable that, as Watts writes, Hypatia's teaching was "a sort of retro-Neoplatonism based on the ideas of Plotinus and Porphyry that emphasised contemplation over ritual" (p. 50). Yet it is dangerous to rely on the fact that "her surviving editorial work betrays no Iamblichan influence" (p. 45): how could it? Or on the statement, found in Socrates Scholasticus, according to which Hypatia "inherited" (διαδέξασθαι) the teaching of the Platonic school of Plotinus, a statement that Watts overinterprets as follows: "He says, in essence, that Hypatia was a Plotinian Platonist and not an

Iamblichan Platonist, a Themistian Aristotelian, or any other breed of philosopher" (p. 45). In reality Socrates says much less than this. It is equally dangerous to rely on what Watts calls the "reading list" of her students, that is, we believe, on Synesius', who was, it is true, a reader of Porphyrius, but was also well acquainted with the Chaldaean Oracles (as it appears in his *De Insomniis*, see on this the recent TOULOUSE and TANASEANU-DÖBLER 2012; see also BREGMAN, pp. 29–36; 63; 83): below, chapter "Synesius, Hypatia and *Philosophia*".

That the version professed by Hypatia, given the assured use of the Chaldean Oracles attested by Synesius in the treatise *On Dreams* and the *Hymns*, was on the contrary a Neoplatonism similar to that of Iamblichus is suggested in CAMERON – LONG, pp. 50–51; see also CAMERON 2016c, pp. 195–197 and CAMERON 2016, n. 60 p. 329 (cautiously); *e contra* WATTS 2006a, pp. 192–193. Below, "Aftershock: And What If...".

On the reading and the use of the *chaldaika logia* (χαλδαϊκὰ λόγια) and its implications, both philosophical and ritual, see in any case FOWDEN 1986, pp. 179–182; ATHANASSIADI; also LEWY – TARDIEU; SHAW 1985; TARDIEU.

References to a "confessional neutrality" of the school of Alexandria are to be ambiguously found in GARZYA, p. 32 (as we have seen above), and also in MARROU 1963, p. 151; BREGMAN, p. 38; see also PRAECHTER 1920; a different position in CAMERON 2016c, pp. 195–197 (see below the final chapter: "Aftershock: And What If...", n. 11).

John Thorp states that the enormous universal success of Hypatia's teaching was linked to her ability to reconcile the "schizophrenia" of the times in a "secret" Platonic initiation imparted to her pupils, giving them a theological key capable not – please note – of conciliating, but of ethically/practically leaping over the dilemma represented by the Christian dogmas, which were unacceptable to the Pagan intellectuals as we can see in Synesius' letter to his brother Euoptius (*Ep.* 105, 79–108, pp. 238–239 Roques; English transl. p. 200 Fitzgerald; see below, chapter "Synesius, Hypatia and *Philosophia*", Appendix *ad loc.*); see THORP: "She helped her students with the great tensions of the age by applying to certain Christian teachings the typical Platonic doctrine of the noble lie – as she would also have done with many Pagan teachings [...] Consider again Hypatia's students. In one way or another they were all schizophrenic. As Hellenes they will all or most have had a Greek classical education, with the whole view of the world that that entailed. But they were living in a society – and were set to become important players in a society – in which Christianity was clearly gaining ground; indeed it had recently become pretty much obligatory. They cannot have been immune to these tensions. And Hypatia was able to resolve them, or seemed able to do so. She offered them a way of reconciling their Pagan culture with the requirement to be Christian by pointing to a common philosophical truth behind them both. [...] Many of the doctrines of Christianity are 'noble lies' which it is good for the populace to believe; the truth, however, is attained by philosophy. Must this not have been the secret teaching of Hypatia, the balm for the worried souls of her students, and the ultimate source of their undying loyalty to her? Hypatia had found the way to make being Christian acceptable to a philosopher, by the utterly Platonic device of the noble lie".

The last quotation from Watts is taken from WATTS 2017, p. 43.

A theurgical imprint in the teachings of Hypatia is regarded as unquestionable by CHUVIN–TARDIEU, p. 67.

DZIELSKA 1995, pp. 63–64, resolutely denies the use of theurgical practices in Hypatia's circle, and even suggests that alongside the sacred Pagan hymns, Christian texts were recited there.

On the circle of Hypatia see DZIELSKA 1991, an article later taken up in DZIELSKA 1995, pp. 27–65.

The clear affiliation of Hypatia to Pagan Hellenism is rightly and without hesitation affirmed by LACOMBRADE 2001, p. 421, on the basis of the analysis of Synesius' *Ep.* 105: "Ce témoignage indirect mais tangible confirme l'appartenance d'Hypatie à l'hellénisme païen." See also RONCHEY 1994.

John of Nikiu's account, probably based on older and well informed Coptic sources, presents the figure of Hypatia as a "woman philosopher, a Pagan" who "dedicated all of her time to magic, the astrolabes, and the musical instruments, and deceived many people with her Satanic tricks". On this see below, chapter "The Power of Hypatia" and Appendix *ad loc.*

A properly mystery terminology is found in SYNESIUS, *Ep.* 137, 5–9 (*To Herculian*), p. 276 Roques (Engl. transl. pp. 229–230 Fitzgerald). The term *teletai* (τελεταί), a technical term of mystery cults, occurs in SYNESIUS, *De insomniis,* p. 281 Lamoureux – Aujoulat; see also below, chapter "Synesius, Hypatia and *Philosophia*" and Appendix *ad loc.*

32 All Synesius' Mysteries

> How wondrous a poem was our voyage! It was granted to you and me to experience things of which mere recital would not have been sufficient to convince us: we have seen with our own eyes, we have heard she who presides over the mysteries and the orgies of philosophy[184].

Thus wrote Synesius, probably from Cyrenaica in 398, after his first Alexandrian sojourn, in a letter to a companion of studies who had remained at Hypatia's school.

Very few people had the opportunity to read Hypatia's writings, assuming that she ever systematically composed any, yet many, since the Byzantine era, from Psellus to Metochites, and then Renaissance and modern scholars from Politian to Erasmus and Wilamowitz, have admired those of her pupil Synesius. Descendant of an ancient family of landowners in a region of modern-day Libya, Cyrenaica, who boasted, like many provincial aristocratic dynasties of the time, nothing less than a semi-divine genealogy, Platonist, polygraph, politician, later a Christian bishop, Synesius represented the maximum level of vitality, tolerance and at the same time political dexterity of the educated aristocracy of Late Antiquity. Trained at Hypatia's school, unlike his teacher he has left for posterity a long literary trail.

In the great epistolary, almost an autobiography, which links him to his Pagan and Christian environment, Synesius is a key witness in our inquiry, not only because he was an intimate of Hypatia, but also because he stands, at least officially, in a position equidistant between the protagonists of the conflict of which she was a victim. A Hellene in essence, even if he probably followed the new religion of the empire even from birth, and later on was baptised and married to a Christian with the good offices of the infamous uncle of Cyril, the patriarch Theophilus, the destroyer of the Serapeum, Synesius wanted to be initiated, as he informs us, "in all the mysteries". Christianity, like the cult of Ammon or Mithra or Isis, was one of those which, from the pragmatic, tolerant (or opportunistic) standpoint of the upper classes, safeguarded the heritage of both the soul and social life, not to mention property and inherited wealth, and therefore had to appear in the baggage of a well-educated and aristocratic intellectual of Late Antiquity.

The election of Synesius as bishop of Ptolemais, originally due to his political activism in the Pentapolis, was solemnised by the verdict of history. Yet it may be considered, by his own admission, accidental. It occurred notwithstanding the second canon of the Council of Nicaea, which precluded neophytes. Moreover, the authorities were obliged to accept that he would not leave his wife, as a Christian prelate, and even more so a bishop, should be forced to do.

Above all, the bishop of Ptolemais never repudiated the Hellenic wisdom or the philosophical sciences, he never believed in the "dogmas" (δόγμασιν), seen as "popu-

---

[184] SYNESIUS, *Ep.* 137, 5–9 (*To Herculian*), p. 276 Roques; see *ibidem*, 58–62, p. 277 Roques.

lar" beliefs of Christianity. In fact, he was openly sceptical about the resurrection of the body, as we read in one of his letters:

> As far as the resurrection is concerned, of which much has been said, I am far from conforming to the opinions of the populace[185].

Synesius' first journey to Egypt was in any case much earlier than the facts which we are now speaking of. It dates to 393, a year after the 'edict of intolerance' issued by Theodosius and the destruction of the Serapeum. Paganism was persecuted, Platonism was not only unpopular in the new classes promoted and manipulated by the Christian authorities, but fragmented in competing *sectae*. "Nowadays it is Egypt that keeps alive the seeds of knowledge", writes Synesius in another letter, "and it receives them from Hypatia"[186].

Hypatia is "the most venerated philosopher beloved by God"[187]. The other pupils of the school of Alexandria are "the blessed ranks that listen to the wonderful voice"[188] of her who will always be "adored teacher"[189], "benefactress"[190], "mother, sister, teacher"[191], "the being and the name that are dearest to me in the entire world"[192], as well as "judge of all matters,"[193] "blessed lady"[194] with the "most divine soul"[195]. Years later, in the eighty-first letter, Synesius would write to her: "Believe me, I think of you as the only good thing no one can take away from me, along with virtue"[196].

Teacher and pupil were of the same age as at the time of their first meeting they both were twenty-three years old. Strangely twinned by destiny, they would die in different places almost at the same time. Synesius did not see the assassination of Hypatia, but shortly before it, paraphrasing the Homeric *Nostoi*, he sent her a couplet that has all the strength of an epitaph:

---

185 SYNESIUS, *Ep.* 105, 85–90 (*To his brother Euoptius*), p. 239 Roques.
186 ID., *Ep.* 136, 16–17, p. 275 Roques.
187 ID., *Ep.* 5, 306 (*To his brother Euoptius*), p. 18 Roques (τὴν σεβασμιωτάτην καὶ θεοφιλεστάτην φιλόσοφον).
188 ID., *Ep.* 5, 307–38 (*To his brother Euoptius*), p. 18 Roques (τὸν εὐδαίμονα χορὸν τὸν ἀπολαύοντα τῆς θεσπεσίας αὐδῆς).
189 ID., *De dono* (*To Peonius*), par. 4, p. 180 Lamoureux – Aujoulat (σεβασμιωτάτη διδάσκαλος).
190 ID., *Ep.* 16, 3 (*To the philosopher Hypatia*), p. 26 Roques (εὐεργετική).
191 ID., *Ep.* 16, 2 (*To the philosopher Hypatia*), p. 26 Roques (μῆτερ καὶ ἀδελφὴ καὶ διδάσκαλε); see *Hymn* 2, vv. 101–103, p. 63 Lacombrade.
192 ID., *Ep.* 16, 3–4 (*To the philosopher Hypatia*), p. 26 Roques (ἅπαν ὅ τι τίμιον καὶ πρᾶγμα καὶ ὄνομα).
193 ID., *Ep.* 154, 91–92, p. 304 Roques (ὑπὲρ δὴ τούτων ἁπάντων σε κρίνουσαν).
194 ID., *Ep.* 10, 2 (*To the philosopher Hypatia*), p. 22 Roques (δέσποινα μακαρία).
195 ID., *Ep.* 10, 13 (*To the philosopher Hypatia*), p. 22 Roques (τῆς θειοτάτης σου ψυχῆς).
196 ID., *Ep.* 81, 15–16 (*To the philosopher Hypatia*), p. 207 Roques.

> Even though the dead shall be forgotten in Hades,
> Even there shall I remember the beloved Hypatia[197].

In the last letter, he is lying in a bed, after the death of his young children. "Synesius should have lived only until he had not known the evils of life," he would write. And he would send her these words: "If you take any interest in what happens to me, good; if not, it doesn't matter to me either."

---

[197] ID., *Ep.* 124, 1–2 p. 257 Roques. See also the paraphrase by CAETANI.

Appendix
All Synesius' Mysteries

The first quotation from Synesius is taken from *Ep.* 137, 5–9 (*To Herculian*), p. 276 Roques; on the need to acquire religious knowledge from all the sources (ἀπανταχόθεν) see *ibidem*, 58–62, p. 277 Roques (Engl. transl. p. 231 Fitzgerald).

On the Byzantine fortunes of Synesius, who includes amongst his admirers all the authors who mentioned Hypatia, from Photius to Psellus, from Gregoras to Metochites, see below, chapter "Women Who Philosophised" and Appendix *ad loc.*

On the consecration of Synesius as bishop of Ptolemais, although the date is controversial, see LACOMBRADE 1951, pp. 210–212; BARNES; and above all LIEBESCHÜTZ. See Synesius' words in *Ep.* 5, 296–297 (*To his brother Euoptius*), p. 18 Roques.

On Synesius' lack of enthusiasm for his ecclesiastical office, which annoyed him because it took him away from his studies and his family, see *Ep.* 105 (*To his brother Euoptius*), pp. 235–241 Roques (Engl. transl. pp. 196–202 Fitzgerald), and *Ep.* 96 (*To Olympius*), pp. 219–220 Roques (Engl. transl. p. 184 Fitzgerald). According to some interpretations his being away from his studies and his family was the cause of his early death.

Of a sort of divided personality, or at least the intersection of Synesius' personality with "two apparently irreconcilable sociological-cultural orders", speaks, with specific reference to his relationship with Hypatia and dealing with her assassination, AVERINCEV, p. 325. We cannot exclude the possibility that Synesius was a Christian from birth, although on the basis of the first of his *Hymns* it is more likely that he received baptism during his adulthood. There are no traces of a conversion in the fashion of Augustine, despite the fact that much scholarship seems to cling to this idea (see in particular SCHMITT; see also CONAN, who gives a substantially affirmative answer). At the same time, other scholars have completely ruled out the possibility of a conversion of this kind (TANASEANU-DÖBLER 2008, pp. 155–286). ROQUES 1982 suggests a "trajectoire en ligne brisée", from a Christianity known from infancy to a mature and conscious Christianity, passing through a period of "cultural Paganism"; this hypothesis is, in our opinion, implausible. WATTS, 2017, pp. 48–49, after pointing out that "there is now a growing consensus that Synesius was always a Christian", analyses briefly his hymns and concludes that although they contain what he calls "Christian markers", they are ultimately "Platonic variations on a Porphyrian idea of a single divine principle with three aspects present in the same reality" (thus following BREGMAN, pp. 81–83). According to Watts "we miss the point if we try to use Synesius' *Hymns* to trace his confessional development or mark the moment of his supposed conversion to Christianity". In effect, the lasting adherence of Synesius to Hellenic philosophy and Pagan truths, his disdain for Christian dogmas and in particular his proclaimed scepticism on the resurrection of the flesh (in addition to the creation of the soul and the end of the world), ultimately the fact that he accepted only the Christian aspects compatible with his own philosophical, Pagan and Platonic theology, rejecting both the principle of the "religion of one

Book" and the idea of redemption through Christ, are directly admitted by him in the well-known *professio in-fidei* in *Ep.* 105, 85–90 (*To his brother Euoptius*), p. 239 Roques. This is perfectly understood by his principal interpreters such as Lacombrade or BREGMAN, pp. 178–184.

However incomprehensible the ways of grace, we cannot therefore consider Synesius, at least in the writings from the Alexandrian period, a Christian thinker. As an impartial Byzantinist such as Alexander Vasilev has written, "despite all the circumstances of his life, he always felt more Pagan than Christian": VASILEV, I, p. 121.

The chronology of Synesius' journeys to Egypt and his periods of study at Hypatia's school have recently been questioned by DZIELSKA 1995, pp. 28–29, on the basis of the reconstructions of Cameron and of Roques, quoted *ibidem*, p. 126, n. 5; a general agreement remains, however, on the date of 393 for his first journey to Alexandria.

On the supremacy of Hypatia's school with respect to other Platonic schools, and in particular to the Athenian Platonic teaching, see SYNESIUS, *Ep.* 136, 16–17, p. 275 Roques (Engl. transl. p. 229 Fitzgerald); see above, part I, chapter "Once there was a Woman", Appendix *ad loc.*

The subsequent quotations are taken from SYNESIUS, *Ep.* 5, 306 (*To his brother Euoptius*), p. 18 Roques ("the most venerated philosopher beloved by God", τὴν σεβασμιωτάτην καὶ θεοφιλεστάτην φιλόσοφον); ID., *Ep.* 5, 307–38 (*To his brother Euoptius*), p. 18 Roques ("the blessed ranks that listen to the wonderful voice", τὸν εὐδαίμονα χορὸν τὸν ἀπολαύοντα τῆς θεσπεσίας αὐδῆς); ID., *De dono* (*To Peonius*), par. 4, p. 180 Lamoureux – Aujoulat ("adored teacher", σεβασμιωτάτη διδάσκαλος); ID., *Ep.* 16, 3 (*To the philosopher Hypatia*), p. 26 Roques ("benefactress", εὐεργετική); ID., *Ep.* 16, 2 (*To the philosopher Hypatia*), p. 26 Roques ("mother, sister, teacher", μῆτερ καὶ ἀδελφὴ καὶ διδάσκαλε); ID., *Ep.* 16, 3–4 (*To the philosopher Hypatia*), p. 26 Roques ("the creature and the name that are the dearest to me in the entire world", ἅπαν ὅ τι τίμιον καὶ πρᾶγμα καὶ ὄνομα). For the supremacy of her judgement cf. ID., *Ep.* 154, 91–92, p. 304 Roques. And then: ID., *Ep.* 10, 2 (*To the philosopher Hypatia*), p. 22 Roques ("blessed lady", δέσποινα μακαρία); ID., *Ep.* 10, 13 (*To the philosopher Hypatia*), p. 22 Roques ("most divine soul", τῆς θειοτάτης σου ψυχῆς); ID., *Ep.* 81, 15–16 (*To the philosopher Hypatia*), p. 207 Roques.

In particular, the apostrophe to Hypatia as "mother, sister, teacher" (μῆτερ καὶ ἀδελφὴ καὶ διδάσκαλε), in *Ep.* 16, 2, certainly has a priestly value: the formula can be compared, in Synesius' works, to the similar formula in *Hymn* 2, vv. 101–103 (SYNESIUS, p. 63 Lacombrade), in which the epithets "mother, daughter and sister" are attributed to the *Hagia Pnoia* (ἁγίαν Πνοιάν), see below, chapter "The Power of Hypatia" and Appendix *ad loc.*

Watts' description of the relationship between Hypatia and Synesius (WATTS 2017, pp. 66–74), which he draws from an analysis of the epistles of the latter, deliberately aims to downplay the "sacral" dimensions of the master-apprentice relationship, describing them as mere *clichés*. Watts, possibly in an attempt to correct the excesses of the literary transfiguration that throughout the centuries has coloured with romantic shades their fellowship (see above part II), downplays the authenticity of the relationship between Hypatia and Synesius. Unfortunately, though, Watts goes to the opposite extreme. He almost exclusively underscores the elements that are most conventional and rhetorical, as well as most prosaically utilitarian, of the small corpus of epistles addressed to Hypatia by Synesius. For instance, the tenth letter, which has moved generations of learned readers, is described as "a performance piece [...] designed to impress a later audience" (p. 68) as well as "an artful but gentle chastisment of Hypatia" (p. 69), and letter 16 is considered "a miniature masterpiece of literary passive-aggressiveness" (p. 69).

The remaining quotations are taken from *Ep.* 124, 1–2 (*To the philosopher Hypatia*), p. 257 Roques: Εἰ δὲ θανόντων περ καταλήθοντ᾽ εἰν Ἀίδαο, αὐτὰρ ἐγὼ κἀκεῖ τῆς φίλης Ὑπατίας μεμνήσομαι, which paraphrases *Nostoi*, fr. 6 Allen. See also *Ep.* 123, with n. 3, p. 378 Roques.

An accurate (German) reading of many passages mentioned can be found in VOGT 1985.

The age of twenty-three years is inferred from Synesius' date of birth, which, like that of Hypatia inferred by Hesychius (see above, part III, chapter "Hypatia in All Her States of Being" and Appendix *ad loc.*), was around 370; on the contrary, if we were to accept the date of birth for Hypatia proposed by PENELLA and DZIELSKA 1995, pp. 67–68, and accepted by WATTS 2017, pp. 21 et al., cf. p. 161, n. 2, the difference in age between the pair would be around fifteen years.

Generally, the date of Synesius' death is placed around 413, precisely because he did not know of that of Hypatia: see LACOMBRADE 1951; BREGMAN; GARZYA p. 13.

33 Synesius, Hypatia and *Philosophia*

The Alexandrian connection between Hypatia and Synesius, which lasted perhaps two years, has been attributed "more subterranean activities" in the field of Platonism[198]. Even though Synesius is not to be identified in the homonymous "scholar of nature" (ἀνὴρ φυσικός), the inventor of a strange type of alembic and the author of a contemporary work on alchemy, which carries the dedication "to a priest of the Great Serapeum" in one of Synesius' manuscripts, yet twice in his epistles Synesius repeats that "geometry is a sacred thing". Elsewhere he speaks of the virtues of the tetractys (*tetraktys*, τετρακτύς), the symbol of Neoplatonic/Neopythagorean numerology, which also inspired a "sacred" and youthful pact of study between four of Hypatia's pupils[199].

In his letter 154 to Hypatia, Synesius mentions "inviolable doctrines" (*abebela dogmata*, ἀβέβηλα δόγματα):

> Those who are not inexpert in gathering the traits of the divine also under a vile aspect, like that of the Athenian artists who in their statues portrayed Aphrodite, the Caryatids and similar beauties embraced by Silenus and Satyrs, will not fail to note that in my book I reveal a number of *inviolable doctrines* that remain hidden to the profane thanks to the capacity for dissimulation and the great nonchalance with which they are instilled in the discourse, in order to show that it is naturally saturated[200].

Also in his *Dion*, dedicated to Hypatia, Synesius mentions *ta abebela* (τά ἀβέβηλα):

> Although he who possess a very rich language is more suited to conceal *inviolable doctrines*, as he can lead his interlocutors wherever he wants, it is inevitable that even such a man, without a proper initiation into the circle of knowledge and the Mysteries of the Muses, will fall short.[201]

The treatise *On Dreams* "was composed", writes Synesius, "in just one night, or rather the last part of the night that brought me the dream that urged me to write it, and in some moments, two or three, it seemed to me that I was almost a third person, the listener of myself"[202]. In addition to Porphyry, Synesius quotes abundantly the *logia* (λόγια), the *Chaldean Oracles:*

> Do not tilt toward the world Black Light
> Beneath which lies the infidel, treacherous Abyss,
> Dark all round, vomiting Filth,
> Full of Images, void of Intellect[203].

---

[198] Lacombrade 1951, p. 64.
[199] SYNESIUS, *Eps.* 93 and 131; on the *tetraktys* (τετρακτύς) *Eps.* 140 and 143.
[200] ID., *Ep.* 154 (*To the philosopher Hypatia*), p. 304 Roques.
[201] ID., *Dion* 5, p. 154 Lamoureux – Aujoulat.
[202] ID., *Ep.* 154 (*To the philosopher Hypatia*), 91–95, pp. 304–305 Roques.
[203] ID., *De Insomniis*, p. 282 Lamoureux – Aujoulat = fr. 163 des Places.

A few years after the destruction of the Serapeum, the *Chaldean Oracles* figured in the list of forbidden books whose possession exposed the owner to accusations of magic and led to the terrible sanctions that had followed the Edict of Constantine and preceded that of Theodosius: the law of Constantius "against sorcerers and seers"[204]. If, as has been written, "in turbulent times mathematics can be a dangerous science", in those times the union of Neoplatonism and Pagan rituals – even when they were not performed in the ostentatious fashion of the radical Iamblichaen wing of Platonism – could cost one one's life.

Throughout Antiquity it is difficult to separate the "positive" scientific interests from the sphere of the irrational. Astronomy was a field inseparable from that of astrology. Theon, the father of Hypatia, last lecturer officially known at the Museum of Alexandria, a personage of very high prestige not only amongst his contemporaries, but throughout the Byzantine millennium, had published, according to Suidas, a study on the birth of Syrius, another "on the presages, on the observation of the birds and the cries of the ravens"[205]. Other works, according to John Malalas, who, as we have seen, draws on one otherwise undiscovered vein of ancient sources, concerned the writings "of Hermes Trismegistus and of Orpheus", and in the Hermetic and Orphean tradition, in addition to the Neoplatonic, he had composed religious hymns celebrating the stars[206].

Hypatia, as her contemporary Philostorgius wrote, "became much better" than her father "above all in the art of observing the stars"[207]. That she had dispensed to her most chosen students "an esoteric doctrine on the margins of the official programmes", that "the technical-astronomical teaching of Hypatia was nothing more than a deceptive façade behind which an esoteric revelation was dispensed, the truly original one", appears evident, amongst others, also to the principal biographer of Synesius[208].

But astronomy was, in fact, more than a façade. One of the "secrets" of Pagan esotericism was precisely the identification of the Gods of the polytheist Olympus with celestial bodies and constellations: here lies their reducibility to mathematical formulas. The universal language of mathematics and astronomy had made it possible from early times to globalise what the ancients (and later modern esotericism) call the Tradition: the circulation of the same doctrines and ancestral wisdom, and the same astral figures (numerical, "divine"), from the nucleus of the mythical Chaldean wisdom both to the West – to Asia Minor, to Greece and perhaps even further west – and to the East, even to India, where the ancient mythology and epic poetry break up and recom-

---

204 *Codex Theodosianus* 9, 16, 5 (25 January 357), p. 461 Mommsen – Meyer: IMP. CONSTANTIVS A. AD POPVLVM.
205 SUIDAS Θ 205, II, p. 702, 10–16 Adler
206 MALALAS XIII 36, p. 265, 38–40 Thurn (English translation p. 186 Jeffreys – Jeffreys – Scott).
207 PHILOSTORGIUS 8, 9, p. 111 Bidez = 8,9, p. 366, 1–5 Bleckmann-Stein (HARICH-SCHWARZBAUER 2011, p. 318).
208 LACOMBRADE 2001, pp. 408–409 e 419–421; see SYNESIUS, *Hymns*, pp. 49 ssg. Lacombrade.

pose, as in a giant kaleidoscope, divine and semi-divine personages, similar to those of the Greek myths.

These often surprising consonances and affinities, at times considered by the ancient mystics and by the moderns, particularly of confessional extraction, "miraculous" and the fruit of a transcendent "revelation", come in fact from ordinary observations of the starry skies and the possibility of communication and circulation of the results through the quantitative language, invariable and indifferent to the linguistic diversities, offered precisely by mathematics and astronomy.

In *De Dono* by Synesius we read:

> Astronomy is in itself a more than worthy science, but it may serve perhaps to reach something higher, it may be the last stage, I believe, towards the mysteries of theology, a stage suited to them, since the perfect body of the heavens has matter below it and its motion has been compared by the highest philosophers to the activity of the intellect. This science proceeds in its demonstrations in an incontrovertible manner and makes use of geometry and arithmetic, which I do not consider improper to call canon of truth[209].

As the persecution of Valens against the *mathematici* proves, the technical nature of the teaching of Theon and Hypatia not only does not exclude, but rather validates the interest in the sphere of esotericism and in those rituals, which were practiced in one way or another not only by the schools of pythagoreanising Iamblichans, but by almost all the Neoplatonists.

These initiatory teachings of Platonism would remain attached, more or less clandestinely, to the entire thread of Byzantine thinking, from Arethas to Psellus and Italus, Choniates, and especially the Palaeologan circle of Theodore Metochites (where the study of Synesius is well attested), and were not incompatible with the highest levels of Christian initiation. Later they were transmitted, always with Platonic philosophy, through the school of George Gemistus Plethon at Mystras and the last Byzantine thinkers transplanted them to Italy, to the Renaissance and the Italian and European Platonic academies, where Marsilius Ficinus would be the first to be interested in the works of Synesius. These Western academies followed the principles and the initiatory rituals of Platonism, but excluded women.

The 19th-century imagination, which saw the figure of Hypatia silhouetted against the setting of the empire in the masculine garments of the rationalist philosopher, a sort of Alexandrian Mademoiselle de Maupin, therefore fell into another trap, because Hypatia wore robes more akin to those of a priestess. The devotion and the exalted veneration that Synesius expressed in his epistolary, even more singular if destined for a peer, can only be explained by a "sacred" bond, as Synesius himself calls it, but in the strict sense, i.e., a sacerdotal bond.

---

[209] SYNESIUS, *De dono*, par. 4, pp. 179–180 Lamoureux – Aujoulat.

Appendix
Synesius, Hypatia and **Philosophia**

For an account of the "subterranean activities" of the Platonism of Synesius and Hypatia, see LACOMBRADE 1951, p. 64.

The dialogue on alchemy πρὸς Διόσκορον, ascribed to Synesius of Cyrene at the end of the 19th century by BERTHELOT – RUELLE, vol. II, pp. 56–69 (for information about the manuscript which witnesses it see: vol. I, p. 199), is now no longer attributed to him. Already LACOMBRADE 1951, pp. 64–71, argued against the identification of Synesius with the *aner physikos* (ἀνὴρ φυσικός) in question. See now CAMERON-LONG, pp. 52–54, but above all MARTELLI 2011, pp. 117–118. For a brief introduction to Synesius as alchemist see MARTELLI 2016, pp. 676–678. The fact that Synesius made, as previously mentioned, innovative astronomical equipment on Hypatia's instructions (see above, chapter "What Did Hypatia Teach?" and Appendix *ad loc.*), in particular the instrument "which led to the resolution of the problem of projecting a sphere on a plane" (GARZYA), and that would be given as a gift to the eminent Constantinopolitan citizen Peonius, the addressee of *De dono*, led some modern scholars to believe that Synesius was possibly the inventor of the new alembic.

On the sacrality of geometry, see Synesius in *Eps.* 93 and 131 (Engl. transl. pp. 178–179, 221–223 Fitzgerald); on the *tetraktys* (τετρακτύς) see *Eps.* 140 and esp. 143 (Engl. transl. pp. 233–235, 237–239 Fitzgerald); for the allusions to the initiatory secret see *Eps.* 143 and 154 (Engl. transl. pp. 250–254 Fitzgerald); on the latter see HARICH-SCHWARZBAUER 2011, pp. 96–128; TANASEANU-DÖBLER 2008, pp. 229–252.

On the "tetrad" formed by Synesius, Herculian, Olympius and Isidore of Pelusium, all Hypatia's pupils, see *Ep.* 143 (*To Herculian*), pp. 285–287 Roques (Engl. transl. pp. 237–239 Fitzgerald).

The two phrases on the *inviolable doctrines* that remain hidden to the profane are in SYNESIUS, *Ep.* 154 (*To the philosopher Hypatia*), p. 304 Roques (Engl. transl. pp. 250–254 Fitzgerald), and in SYNESIUS, *Dion* 5, p. 154 Lamoureux – Aujoulat.

Dion is probably Synesius' major work. As has been written (LACOMBRADE 1951, p. 39), "while amongst the masters of the past Dion certainly represented for Synesius the sage par excellence, in the present Hypatia", to whom the work is dedicated, "incarnates for him the tangible form of the ideal."

The declarations on *Dion* and on the treatise *On Dreams* come from *Ep.* 154, 91–95, pp. 304–305 Roques (Engl. transl. p. 253 Fitzgerald), with which Synesius, before publishing the two works, sent them to Hypatia. "Concerning all of this I shall await your decision. If you decree that I ought to publish my book, I will dedicate it to orators and philosophers together. The first it will please, and to the others it will be useful, provided of course that it is not rejected by you, who are really able to pass judgment." (*Ep.* 154, 91–95, p. 253 Fitzgerald).

The quotation from the *Chaldean Oracles*, taken from Synesius' *De Insomniis*, p. 282 Lamoureux – Aujoulat, corresponds to fr. 163 of the DES PLACES edition (ORACULA CHAL-

DAICA, p. 106 des Places), with the exception of the variant ἄπιστος (*apistos*) instead of the reading ἄμορφος (*amorphos*) attested by Damascius and accepted by des Places (who discusses the issue at n. 2, p. 106). Synesius' relationship with Chaldean *logia* – and in general, though more questionably, with demonological and apocalyptical Greek-Egyptian literature and with Hermetism – has been widely analysed by many scholars of his works, starting with Wilamowitz, and directly linked to the Alexandrian teaching of Hypatia by FOWDEN 1986; CAMERON – LONG et al.

WATTS 2017, p. 45, underscores that a familiarity with the *Chaldaen Oracles* in Synesius, and therefore probably in Hypatia's school, does not entail an association with the "Iamblichan trend", but rather an "approach to Chaldean texts in a Porphyrian manner". As we have seen above (chapter "What Did Hypatia Teach?", Appendix *ad loc.*), this is confirmed also by the majority of modern scholars of Synesius, see *in primis* TOULOUSE.

For a general overview on the readings of the Neoplatonic circles see GOULET–CAZÉ, pp. 259–273; on the interest in the occult of the Alexandrian mathematicians of the time, see also FOWDEN 1986, pp. 177–186; HAAS 1997, pp. 221–222; below, chapter "The Eminence of Hypatia" and Appendix *ad loc.*, on the activities within the last Platonic *hetaireia* of Byzantium, that of Gemistus Plethon in Mystras, known to us thanks to the (malicious) testimonies of George of Trebizond.

Although, as Watts underlines (WATTS 2017, p. 32), Hypatia's teaching was clearly different from the "Iamblichan trend", as it connected instead "with the philosophical system of the Neoplatonists Plotinus and Porphyry" (*ibidem*, p. 37), and was consequently far from the theurgical imprint which may have characterised some of the later Platonic Byzantine circles such as the school of Mystras (see also below, chapter "The Eminence of Hypatia" and Appendix *ad loc.*), what we read in the epistles and in the works of Synesius nonetheless confirms, as we have seen above (chapter "What Did Hypatia Teach?" and Appendix *ad loc.*), the presence of ritualistic elements (which Watts rules out categorically) in the practices performed within the innermost circle of Hypatia's school. In particular, in the *De insomniis* Synesius uses the technical term *teletai* (τελεταί): cf. SYNESIUS, *De insomniis*, p. 281 Lamoureux – Aujoulat; cf. also above, chapter "What Did Hypatia Teach?" and Appendix *ad loc.*

The law of Constantius against sorcerers and seers (357) is to be found in the *Codex Theodosianus* 9, 16, 5 (25 January 357), p. 461 Mommsen – Meyer: IMP. CONSTANTIVS A. AD POPVLVM. On the persecutions of Valens against the *mathematici* see PIGANIOL.

The following quotation is taken from RIST, p. 216: "Mathematics might in turbulent times be a dangerous science".

On geometry and arithmetic as "canon of truth" and their overlap in the philosophical Neoplatonic teaching and in the school of Hypatia, see above, chapter "What Did Hypatia Teach?" and Appendix *ad loc.*, where we cited Watts' useful summary (WATTS 2017, pp. 31–35, who, however, draws a distinction between mathematics and philosophy which appears too rigid and anachronistic).

The prestige of Theon is still alive today: on his scientific personality and his eminence as a mathematician see HOPPE, pp. 425–426; beside DEAKIN 2007, pp. 107–108.

In the Byzantium of the 10th century Theon would be celebrated by Leo the Mathematician, alongside Proclus, as one of the greatest "wise men" of ancient times; also later his name would recur frequently in astronomical and astrological texts: see DZIELSKA 1995, pp. 76 and 141–142, nn. 56–58.

The ancient sources about Theon's works are SUIDAS Θ 205, II, p. 702, 10–16 Adler, and MALALAS XIII 36, p. 265, 38–40 Thurn, according to whom he also wrote "commentaries on books by Hermes Trismegistus and Orpheus" (see above, part I, chapter "Once there was a Woman" and Appendix *ad loc.*). And it is, once again, Suidas who informs us that Theon observed the solar eclipse of June 15th 364 and the lunar eclipse of the following November 26th.

For the comments by Theon on Ptolemy, see ROME 1936, pp. lxxxii–lxxxvi; MOGENET – TIHON; TIHON; see above, chapter "What Did Hypatia Teach?" and Appendix *ad loc.*

Still uncertain is the attribution to Theon of an astrological poem found in a corpus of Hermetic writings and included in the *Anthologia graeca* (see FOWDEN 1986, p. 178, note), like that of a commentary on the *Phaenomena* by Aratus (MAAS, pp. 146–151) and other poems – or rather religious hymns – attributed to him by the manuscripts.

Watts' interpretation (WATTS 2017, pp. 34–35) of the intellectual personality of Theon, according to which he was a direct follower of Pappus and a pure mathematician, is questionable. It is certain now that Theon, like Hypatia, was a mathematician and an astronomer. Yet ancient sources attribute to him "esoteric little pieces" (see DZIELSKA 1995, pp. 69, 74–77 and bibliography *ad. loc.*) that reveal his magical and divinatory interests. It is no coincidence that the Byzantine tradition would describe Theon as a "philosopher" (from SOCRATES VII, 15, p. 360, 20 Hansen, to SUIDAS Θ 205, II, p. 702, 10–16 Adler; Π 265, IV, p. 26, 4 Adler). Watts contends that "Theon may have disputed" this description "as inaccurate" (p. 34). He seems here to be tampering with the data in order to substantiate his reconstruction of Hypatia's teaching and education which, as we have seen above (chapter "What Did Hypatia Teach?" with Appendix *ad loc.*), is highly speculative and to an extent questionable. Overinterpreting the account of Damascius on Hypatia handed down by Suidas ("Since she was by nature more gifted than her father, [Hypatia] did not stop at the kind of technical and mathematical teachings of his, but fully dedicated herself to philosophy"), Watts aims to show that the development of Hypatia's *Bildung* represented a distancing from Theon's purely mathematical approach to intellectual inquiry, and eventually led her to an autonomous and original conversion to philosophy which "allowed her to push beyond the intellectual limits of her mathematician father" (p. 35). It must be noted that Damascius' account is contradicted by Philostorgius ("Hypatia became much better than her teacher, especially in astronomy, and ended up being herself the teacher of many in the mathematical siences"), and, while it is undoubtable that Hypatia did go beyond the intellectual interests of her father, this does not mean that she progressed from "pure" mathematics to philosophy, simply because Theon was far from being what in any time could be considered a "pure" mathematician.

The observation of PHILOSTORGIUS (8, 9) is found on p. 111, 1–3 Bidez = 8,9, p. 366, 2–3 Bleckmann-Stein (HARICH-SCHWARZBAUER 2011, p. 318). The words of Photius in these lines present literal coincidences with the previously cited text of Suidas: see above, chapter "The DNA of the Ancient Tradition" and Appendix *ad loc.*; on the motives that led the 5th-century historian to such a characterisation of the philosopher Hypatia, see PHILOSTORGIUS, pp. cix–cx Bidez.

The theory of Hypatia's esoteric teaching is corroborated by LACOMBRADE 1951, pp. 49 ff., from whom the quotation is taken; LACOMBRADE 2001, pp. 408–409 (on the "mysteries" and the oath of silence taken by the students), and above all 419–421, where Lacombrade regards as referring to Hypatia's teaching the mention, in *Ep.* 105, of those anti-Christian *dogmata*, which Synesius declares he has not conceived on his own, but learned "by scientific demonstration" (τὰ δι' ἐπιστήμης εἰς ἀπόδειξιν ἐλθόντα δόγματα, pp. 238–239 Roques): from whom, comments Lacombrade, if not from his mother-sister-mistress Hypatia? See also CHUVIN, pp. 366–367; CHUVIN–TARDIEU, pp. 65 and 67.

On the initiatory nature of the bond between Synesius and the philosopher see also BREGMAN, p. 28.

That astrology and divination were also studied at the school of mathematics in Alexandria at that time is suggested by KLINE, p. 198, among others.

The passage from Synesius on astronomy comes from the *De dono*, par. 4, pp. 179–180 Lamoureux – Aujoulat.

Curiously (and erroneously) DZIELSKA 1995, p. 60, believes that the initiatory circle that met at Hypatia's home excluded women ("Their circle, of course, excluded women"), basing this opinion on two passages from Synesius' letters (*Eps.* 146 and 132; Engl. transl. pp. 240–242 and 223–224 Fitzgerald) in which Herculianus declares his misogyny.

On female Platonic and Neoplatonic philosophers in Antiquity and Late Antiquity see below, chapter "Women Who Philosophised" and Appendix *ad loc.* The fact that female Platonic initiation was still possible in the late Byzantine times is testified, for instance, by the example of Cleopa Malatesta, who "climbed to the highest levels of initiation" in Mystras, as stated in her funeral oration written by the head of the school, Gemistus himself, which can be read in LAMPROS, vol. IV, pp. 161–175. It is probable that the wise Byzantine women mentioned by Michael Psellus and by Nicephorus Gregoras (see below, chapter "Women Who Philosophised" and Appendix *ad loc.*) are to be considered adepts of the Platonic teachings jealously preserved underground throughout the millennium of the Eastern Christian empire, and not incompatible with the highest levels of Christian initiation: see below, chapter "The Eminence of Hypatia" and Appendix *ad loc.*

The singularity of the expressions of devotional esteem addressed to Hypatia by her peer Synesius in the letters is noted for example in ROUGÉ 1990, p. 495.

That Hypatia was the "high priestess" of Alexandrian Neoplatonism is directly affirmed also by BREGMAN, p. 20.

34 Women Who Philosophised

It may seem surprising that history numbers so few female "philosophers" in the true sense of the word. This circumstance has been attributed to the incapacity of the female psychology to adapt itself to speculative rigour; a 19th-century opinion that can be confuted and which in any case never appears in either Antiquity, nor in Late Antiquity or the Byzantine era.

A comprehensive treatise *On the Women Who Philosophised* is attributed to Apollonius the Stoic, as we learn from the *Bibliotheca* of Photius[210]. Philochorus of Athens also wrote about female Pythagoreans, as Suidas tells us[211]. Life and customs of the women philosophers were derided by Juvenal and narrated by Diogenes Laertius – our source on Hipparchia, and others – and by Athenaeus.

As we have seen, in the 17th century Gilles Ménage discovered "on his own" the existence of sixty-five female philosophers and wrote his *Historia mulierum philosopharum*, with an entire chapter on Hypatia, dedicating it to Anne Dacier, the Huguenot philologist who would be compared ironically to Hypatia by Voltaire. In the following century, Johann Christian Wolf published a catalogue of them, with the fragments of the related ancient works.

Platonists or Neoplatonists like the Roman Arria and Gemina, the latter a pupil and patron of Plotinus in Rome, or Lasthenia of Mantinea; Cynics like Hipparchia; Epicureans like Teophila; Stoics like Portia; Pythagoreans like Themistoklea, Theano, Myia, Arignote, Damo, Sara, Tymicha, Abrotelia, Echecratia; and then the Dialecticians, Cyrenaics, Megareans, Aristotelians, "those of uncertain sect" yet noble, such as Julia Domna, the wife of Septimius Severus, Fabia Aconia Paulina, the wife of Praetextatus, and Aelia Eudocia, the wife of Theodosius II, or like the Byzantine Kassia and Anna Komnene: the list of the *philosophae mulieres* could continue for centuries, to the "wise Eudocia", the wife of Constantine Palaeologus celebrated by Nicephorus Gregoras, or Irene, of the highest Palatine position of *panhypersebasta* (πανυπερσεβάστη), daughter of the Great Logothete Theodore Metochites, philosopher of the 14th century under the last Palaeologan dynasty.

However, the "philosophy" practised by the many female personalities of Antiquity and Late Antiquity had become – particularly amongst the last Platonists, as it would later amongst the Christians – mainly knowledge of the divine. From the legendary Diotima of Mantinea to figures contemporary with Hypatia such as Pandrosion of Alexandria, the unnamed wife of Maximus of Ephesus, Asclepigenia of Athens, and Sosipatra of Ephesus, mentioned by Philostratus and Eunapius, or Aedesia, Damiana, Theodora, of whom Damascius speaks, a succession only of women, often gifted with psychic faculties, had become the depositary of that oral tradition of the "secrets" of Platonism that Synesius mentions in *Dion* when referring to the relationship be-

---

210 Cf. PHOTIUS, *Bibl.*, vol. II, p. 127, 13–17 Henry.
211 Cf. SUIDAS Φ 441, IV, p. 736, 19–20 Adler (Συναγωγή ἡρωΐδων ἤτοι Πυθαγορείων γυναικῶν).

tween Socrates and Aspasia, perhaps with an autobiographical nuance. The superiority of the female in the supra-rational sphere is a heritage of the spirituality of Late Antiquity also received by the Qabalah and throughout the Middle Ages.

The Byzantine model of female philosopher is both Pythagorean and Platonic and while in Psellus "the Egyptian" (ἡ αἰγυπτία), that is Hypatia, is associated with the great Pythagorean leader Theano[212], the Eudocia of Nicephorus Gregoras is called "new Theano and second Hypatia"[213]. It is not by chance, after all, that the greatest number of women philosophers is to be met in the most irrationalist *secta*, where the monopoly of the sacerdotal function was openly female. Yet in many of the cases reported by the modern cataloguers, with their sometimes naïve rationalism, esoteric wisdom is associated, as the reverse of the coin, to a strictly technical "exoteric" competence.

Hypatia is one of these cases: on the one hand, undoubtedly a mathematician, on the other, more obscure but no less credible, a sacerdotal figure. Certainly not unusual in the field of knowledge in which the perfection of numbers has often represented a mysticism in itself, her quality of inspired observer of the cosmos and "initiator of the mysteries and the orgies of *philosophia*"[214] is widely testified and compatible with the gender, the caste, the political role, the condition of last illustrious heir to the intellectual dynasty of a centre of power such as the Alexandrian school.

---

[212] PSELLUS, *Funeral Oration for his Mother*, p. 59f. Sathas.
[213] GREGORAS VIII 3, 2–3, I p. 294 Schopen.
[214] SYNESIUS, *Ep.* 137, 5–9 (*To Herculian*), p. 276 Roques.

Appendix
Women Who Philosophised

As is written by CHUVIN–TARDIEU, p. 59, Hypatia owes her uniqueness to the fact that she was "saluée avec tendresse et respect par son disciple chrétien Synésios comme aucune femme sans doute ne le fut dans l'Antiquité".

It should be the task of women's history, the field of studies in which most recently and most frequently the character of Hypatia has attracted attention and gathered writings and research, especially from the Post-Feminist school, to deal with the exact status of Hypatia as a female "philosopher", belonging to the category of women (*domnae, dominae*) in which the ancient tradition suggests we include her, and to deduce her role from the information handed down by the sources on other ancient female philosophers. Unfortunately – with few exceptions such as HARICH-SCHWARZBAUER 2002; cf. also RONCHEY 1995 – almost all the studies that have appeared in this field have drawn historical information about Hypatia's life and violent death, political role, and social condition, as well as her philosophical or priestly activities, from no more than fervent but specious reconstructions or imaginative *rêveries* relying, more often than on the actual examination of the sources, on arbitrary preconception. Even more often such literature has been based on misconceptions at the service of discussions and fashions of the present – Feminism, New Age neo-Spiritualism, the counter-history of science – rather than the effective understanding of the past. For this type of literature on Hypatia see for example, ALIC; McALISTER, pp. 164–65. For a wider bibliographical review of the Post-Feminist fortunes of Hypatia see below, chapter "The Martyrdom of Hypatia", Appendix *ad loc.*

For the observations on female "philosophy" in Late Antiquity and the accounts of the authors who mention it see *Women in Philosophy*, in BLACKBURN; see also, with some caution, the brief contribution of WYDER; and CRACCO RUGGINI 1988, p. 275; POMEROY; LUCCHESI.

The mention of a comprehensive treatise on women philosophers by Apollonius the Stoic is found in PHOTIUS, *Bibl.*, vol. II, p. 127, 13–17 Henry. That of a Συναγωγή ἡρωίδων ἤτοι Πυθαγορείων γυναικῶν by Philochorus of Athens is found in SUIDAS Φ 441, IV, p. 736, 19–20 Adler and mentioned by MÉNAGE, p. 81.

On the work of Ménage and that of Wolf see above, part II, chapter "The Excesses of Fanaticism" and Appendix *ad loc.*

That the accentuation of the public dimension and the social weight of women in Late Antiquity, testified by honorary inscriptions, clearly marked the evolution in the Late Roman empire of the female priestly power into a form of directly and concretely political power, is confirmed in particular by BROWN 2012, pp. 273–288. On the charismatic role of the female figure, its ideal attributes and political-social implications in the Late Roman empire, see CRACCO RUGGINI 1988, pp. 255–256 *et al.*; CRACCO RUGGINI 1989.

For the esoteric and often theurgic *diadoche* (διαδοχή) handed down by women, see MARINUS, *Vita Procli* (MARINUS, p. 33, 8–13 Saffrey – Segonds): Proclus received his initiation into the Chaldean rites from Asclepigenia, Plutarch's daughter. CAMERON – LONG, p. 51, suggest, as we have seen, a *diadoche* Sosipatra-Hypatia: see above, chapter "What Did Hypatia Teach?", Appendix *ad loc.*

WATTS 2017, pp. 100–101, too, in clarifying how "the theurgic virtues that Asclepigenia helped Proclus to develop" represented for his successors "the absolute pinnacle of Proclus's philosophical accomplishment", explicitly states that "her gender enabled her to do the sort of esoteric theurgical teaching that male counterparts like Syrianus [i.e., Proclus' main teacher] sometimes avoided". Nonetheless, as in the case of Sosipatra (see above, part I, chapter "Elegant Insolence", Appendix *ad loc.*), Watts underestimates the shared elements between Asclepigenia and Hypatia which emerge from the narrative of the sources.

A clear though too drastic negation of all theurgical influence in the teaching of Hypatia can be read, as we have seen, in DZIELSKA 1995, pp. 63–64 (see above, chapter "What Did Hypatia Teach?", Appendix *ad loc.*).

The mainly oral character of the feminine transmission of knowledge is often downplayed or forgotten. Despite knowing and displaying extensively the main historical and biographical data provided by the sources, WATTS 2017 does not simply avoid dwelling on the unwritten character of the teaching handed down by "Hypatia's sisters", the depositaries and teachers of those "secrets" of Platonism that Synesius mentions in his *Dion*, but is even surprised by the fact that Pandrosion "left no significant imprint on the historical record" (p. 94) and that "no texts by Pandrosion currently survive" (pp. 96–97); the same happens with Sosipatra, Asclepigenia, and the wife of Maximus of Ephesus.

On the affinities and differences between Sosipatra and Hypatia see above, part I, chapter "Elegant Insolence" and Appendix *ad loc.*; as we have seen, WATTS 2017, pp. 97–100, fails to notice those features of Sosipatra that can help us understand Hypatia better.

On the occurrence, in Synesius' *Dion*, of the *exemplum* of Socrates and Aspasia, and the probability of an allusion to Hypatia, see AZEVEDO.

The association of Theano and Hypatia is in the *Funeral Oration for his Mother* by Michael PSELLUS (pp. 59 f. Sathas), where the author admits that he teaches, despite his ecclesiastical investiture, the profane sciences and mentions, after Homer, Menander, Archilochus, Orpheus, Musaeus, "the works of the Sibyls [that is probably the Sibylline Books (*Libri Sibyllini*)] and of Sappho the poetess, and of Theano and of the Egyptian female philosopher" (καὶ ὁπόσα καὶ τὸ θῆλυ ἦσαν Σιβύλλαι τε καὶ Σαπφὼ ἡ μουσοποιός, Θεανώ τε καὶ ἡ Αἰγυπτία σοφή); a more recent edition is provided by Ugo CRISCUOLO (see PSELLUS, p. 151 and n. [1873–4, pp. 325–326] Criscuolo), on whose text is based the English translation by WALKER.

That the *Aigyptia sophe* (Αἰγυπτία σοφή) is Hypatia was suggested for the first time by KRUMBACHER, vol. I, p. 504.

It is therefore with Michael Psellus that Hypatia enters in full in the ranks of the womanly *exempla* of Antiquity, and this "new canon" (Gajeri) is also applied by Nicephorus Gregoras in his encomium for Eudocia Palaeologina, in GREGORAS VIII 3, 2–3, I p. 294 Schopen. On Eudocia, second wife of the despot Constantine Palaeologus, and the *panhypersebasta* (πανυπερσεβάστη) Irene, daughter of Theodore Metochites, see below, chapter "The Eminence of Hypatia" and Appendix *ad loc.*

The definition of Hypatia as "initiator of the mysteries and the orgies of *philosophia*" is in SYNESIUS, *Ep.* 137, 5–9 (*To Herculian*), p. 276 Roques (Engl. transl. p. 229 Fitzgerald); cf. above, chapter "All Synesius' Mysteries", with Appendix *ad loc.*

35 The Power of Hypatia

"You have always had power". This is therefore the *dynasteia* (δυναστεία), the "power", that Synesius attributed to Hypatia in his eighty-first epistle. This is her "affinity with knowledge" (φιλοσοφία).[215] This is what the epithets of "mother", "sister" and "mistress" (μῆτερ καὶ ἀδελφὴ καὶ διδάσκαλε)[216] used by the pupil allude to: the traditional appellatives of members of the inner circles of Platonic schools and of those female "protectors" of the mystical-religious fellowships, that frequently, at the end of the Roman empire and throughout the Byzantine empire, mingled sacred and secular functions.

This is what it is, and why it so hurts the pride and the ambitions of Cyril, to see the amassing of carriages before the house of Hypatia, as mentioned by Suidas: it is a question of the "private sessions" (ἰδίᾳ) in which the teacher gathers her circle, her *hetaireia* (ἑταιρεία), as Synesius calls it, of initiated. Lessons in counterpoint to the "public" ones (δημοσίᾳ) – but certainly not "peripatetic" like those of a street philosopher – held, as were those of her father, in a public place, although no longer at the Museum, probably subsidised by the State or by the municipal treasury of Alexandria.

Private sessions, those at Hypatia's home, which led, as has been written, to a "revelation" and at which "the elite of her disciples" were present[217]: in addition to Synesius, the exponents of the dominant class, which also ruled the city, according to the Hellenic tradition that linked the aristocratic condition to the initiatory privilege, the prerogative of the ancient Tradition.

For this apprenticeship is also a "lifestyle, a constant, religious and disciplined search for the truth"[218] and as such is independent of individual positions taken after the election of Christianity as State religion. A part of this class, predominant by birth, wealth, and position in the public administration, had formally converted to the new religion. However, they remained tacitly and discreetly bound to the ancient "Hellenic" *religio* through a bond that was at the same time social, political and philosophical.

The observation was frustrating for Cyril, who was designated as the only legitimate religious head in the city by the Theodosian decrees, and who was the political strategist of the winning confession, and the aspiring arbiter of the doctrinal controversies. He who aimed to "erode" and "influence the power of the State" beyond every limit ever conceded by the ancient world "to the priestly sphere", as Socrates Scholasticus wrote[219]; and who, in almost three years of episcopacy, had not yet realised that

---

215 SYNESIUS, *Ep.* 81, p. 207 Roques.
216 ID., *Ep.* 16, 2–3, p. 26 Roques.
217 ID., *Hymns*, p. 50 Lacombrade.
218 BREGMAN, p. 28.
219 SOCRATES VII 13, 9, p. 358, 13–14 Hansen; VII 7, 4, p. 353, 2–6 Hansen.

this limit was presided over by a sort of Pagan Freemasonry, moreover led by a woman.

A "sorceress", who with her elitist practices and her haughty charisma seemed to irresistibly attract – as John of Nikiu explains[220] – everybody who was anybody in the city, including the Augustal prefect. A busybody Egyptian woman, like the one mentioned by the bishop of Alexandria in his homilies, where the derogatory mention ("the Egyptian woman has been silenced") can be seen as a reference to Hypatia, using in fact the same name (ἡ αἰγυπτία) which for the Byzantines would, over the centuries, designate par excellence the female philosopher whom Cyril silenced for ever.

---

[220] JOANNES DE NIKIU LXXXIV par. 88, p. 101 Charles.

Appendix
The Power of Hypatia

The epithets μῆτερ καὶ ἀδελφὴ καὶ διδάσκαλε bestowed on Hypatia by Synesius (*Ep.* 16, 2–3 p. 26 Roques) are traditional in Platonic schools, yet they still have a salient character here. According to WATTS 2017, pp. 69–70, who, as we have seen, downplays excessively the "sacral" dimension of the relationship between Hypatia and Synesius (*ibidem*, pp. 66–74; cf. above, chapter "All Synesius' Mysteries", Appendix *ad loc.*), the use of such terms in the passage is traditional and therefore irrelevant. Yet, as we have seen, the invocation to Hypatia is reminiscent of an analogous formula in another work of Synesius, *Hymn* 2, vv. 101–103, p. 63 Lacombrade, where the epithets of "mother, daughter, and sister" refer to the divine Generating Will of Neoplatonists: see above, chapter "All Synesius' Mysteries", Appendix *ad loc.*

Regarding the "private sessions" (ἰδίᾳ) that were held at the residence of Hypatia, see CHUVIN, pp. 366–367: "Hypatie donne sans doute des séances privées (hidia [*sic*]), en cénacles, et peut-être chez elle, auxquelles assistaient Synésios et ses condisciples", and CHUVIN–TARDIEU, p. 65.

That during these meetings Hypatia offered an esoteric 'revelation' to a close circle is recognised by LACOMBRADE 1951, p. 50, who sees in Synesius' output an unquestionable imprint of the "revelation of the thinking of those venerated masters that Hypatia revealed to the elite of her disciples"; see also RONCHEY 1994.

"Arrête, lyre audacieuse, / arrête, ne révèle pas les mystères aux foules / des non initiés./ Allons, chante les choses d'en bas / et que celles d'en haut demeurent voilées de silence": thus runs Lacombrade's translation of the ninth hymn of Synesius (*Hymn* 9, 71–75, pp. 102–103 Lacombrade). Synesius' statement here, as well as in other passages, matches the mysterious and initiatory-esoteric character of the "private sessions" (ἰδίᾳ) at the residence of Hypatia, which were open exclusively to the circle of her closest pupils. The scrupulousness in not divulging the mysteries to the non-initiated is frequently found in Synesius' works (see for example *Ep.* 37). WATTS 2017, p. 48, admits that, according to Synesius, the union with the divine through philosophy is accessible only to a restricted group of initiates, but still believes that Synesius describes such union as something that can be achieved "through mysteries without rites". According to Watts, this is a formula that, by proclaiming the absence of rituals, provides a "clear indication [...] that this was not a Iamblichan union arising from theurgy but more of a Plotinian and Porphyrian union achieved through contemplation". Nonetheless, Watts bases this assumption on a form of the text of the hymn which is not that of the critical edition of Synesius by Lacombrade, where at the verses 72–73 we read μηδὲ φαῖνε δήμοις τελετὰς ἀνοργιάστοις, and the adjective ἀνοργιάστοις clearly patterns with δήμοις ("Do not reveal the mysteries to the crowds of non-initiates"). Following BREGMAN, pp. 32–33 (who relies on the nineteenth century edition by Migne and on Terzaghi's edition, produced between 1939 and 1944, and avoids any reference to Lacombrade's edition, which appeared four years before the publication of his study), Watts reads, in our opinion tendentiously, ἀνοργιάστους, which patterns with τελετὰς. This reading, which is apparently worse than that of Lacombrade and which Garzya rejected in his 1989 edition in favour of Lacombrade's, allows Watts to obtain a text saying "mysteries without rites", which appears to be absent from both this hymn and from the rest of Synesius' production. Such reading appears to us at least forced.

On the nature of the teaching imparted by Hypatia during these sessions see also BREGMAN, p. 19: "Synesius seems to have experienced at Hypatia's school an authentic conversion to philosophy [...] As shown in his letters to Hypatia and to others, he was part throughout his life of a circle of Alexandrian initiates, with whom he shared the mysteries of philosophy".

The quotation, according to which the affiliation involved not only a philosophical-religious initiation, but a genuine 'lifestyle' – the famous *hellenike diagoge* (ἑλληνικὴ διαγωγή) – can be read *ibidem*, p. 28.

Curiously DZIELSKA 1995, pp. 57–58, although inferring the existence of two teachings of Hypatia, one public and 'exoteric' (generic "lessons in history of philosophy starting with Plato and Aristotle" in addition to oral comments "on the works of famous mathematicians and astronomers, *ibidem* p. 57) and the other private and esoteric (imparted to a "closed circle of the initiated"), attributes to the first teaching, rather than to the second, that "coming and going of persons and carriages" before her residence, which struck Cyril so markedly. Instead, we would believe it is the opposite: persons and carriages were there for the meetings of the *hetaireia* (ἑταιρεία) (for the meaning see Synesius, *Ep.* 10 [*To Hypatia*], p. 22, 1–2 Roques, Engl. transl. pp. 95–96 Fitzgerald; see GAJERI, p. 24) of which Hypatia is the leader. This sort of Proto-Masonry comprising those who attended her "private" lessons (ἰδίᾳ) – held at her residence, unlike the "public" ones, held as the name suggests in a public place (δημοσίᾳ) – was not intended merely for young pupils such as Synesius and his correspondents, but also for those "public officials" and members of the elite of the city (DZIELSKA 1995, p. 58) whose familiarity with Hypatia, finally revealed in the light of initiatory fellowship, sparked the *phthonos* of Cyril. Dzielska, on the other hand, considers the latter consumers of her "public" and "exoteric" lessons. Yet, if this were so, we could not explain the reaction of Cyril, nor the subsequent development of the events.

Not even the expert Pierre Chuvin fully understands, in our opinion, when he links the gathering before the residence of Hypatia, which gives rise to the irrational *phthonos* of Cyril, not to the esoteric sessions mentioned above, but to some generic "audiences" granted to her *clientes* (this is what the verb *prosagoreuein*, προσαγορεύειν, used by Damascius/Suidas means: the technical sense of *prosagoreusis*, προσαγόρευσις, inasmuch as it is "the greeting of the client to the patron" is highlighted also by HAAS 1997, pp. 311–312): see CHUVIN-TARDIEU, p. 65, where three types of activity of Hypatia are distinguished: (1) public teaching, open to all, in a place in the centre of the city; (2) formal audiences reserved for the *clientes*, also open to a large public, but held at her residence; (3) esoteric teaching, imparted to a close circle of disciples, also held, most probably, at her residence. According to Chuvin, the gathering seen by Cyril would have been linked to the same type of ceremonial visit to which Suidas/Damascius alluded earlier in his account, with regard to the city administrators who "went first to her home": see above, part I, chapter "Good Use of Power".

Nevertheless, knowing the nature of the Platonic *hetaireiai* and of their Byzantine offshoots, it appears inevitable that during their meetings they would also deal with political topics and that positions would be taken regarding city affairs, according to the dictates of public commitment innate in the *hellenike diagoge* of which Hypatia "serious and with a sense of citizenship" (*politike*, πολιτική, as we can read in Damascius, *Vita Isidori* fr. *104, p. 79,13 Zintzen = fr. 43E, p. 130, 6–8 Athanassiadi = Suidas Y 166, IV, p. 645, 2–4 Adler [Harich-Schwarzbauer 2011, p. 247]) was an exemplary exponent, according to Synesius' testimony. If, as Watts 2017 underscores, Hypatia provided to the members of the "city's political establishment" (p. 61) a "set of principles according to which all Alexandrians could better organize their lives and their city" (p. 62) and "a contemplative path to union with the divine without explicitly specifying the [...] character of that highest divine power" (p. 56); if, in other words, confessional belonging was transcended in the name of the common philosophical creed, then it must be the case that the esoteric meetings, aimed at the most advanced and mature members of Hypatia's Platonic circle, focused on topics in which philosophy and (especially religious) policy could not be separated. In such meetings, local aristocracy must have met with the notables and officials sent from Constantinople to determine strategies and alliances.

In our opinion, therefore, the gathering that Cyril noted at the entrance to Hypatia's residence should be referred to her esoteric circle, which together with the older aristocracy of the city also included (as shown by Dzielska 1995) the city fathers and political administrators who came from outside Alexandria. What Cyril suddenly noted, and what provoked his attack of *phthonos*, was the existence of a vast and arcane alliance amongst the Hellenes, led by Hypatia, influential in the political decisions of the elite and of the leading administrators.

That Cyril, in three years, had not realised the effects of the long-standing underground Pagan solidarity is implied by Chuvin, p. 367, according to whom the private nature of the meetings "explique que Cyrille, en poste depuis 412, ne se soit rendu compte qu'en 414 ou 415 de la popularité d'Hypatie".

Quite conjectural, as the scholar himself admits, is the theory of Rougé 1990, pp. 486–487 with n. 13, according to which Cyril himself attended Hypatia's school. Although it is right to emphasise the interconnected and permeable nature of the Alexandrian intellectual setting, the fact that Theophilus, Cyril's uncle, was the marriage mediator for Synesius is not sufficient to make the conjecture plausible.

The quotations of Socrates (on Cyril's tendency to "avidly erode the power of those who exercised it on behalf of the emperor" and on the fact that he "inaugurated an episcopate even more similar, with respect to that of Theophilus, to a principality", and that "starting with him, the Alexandrian episcopacy began to interfere in State power beyond the limits accorded the ecclesiastical sphere") are taken respectively from VII 13, p. 358 Hansen, and VII 7, p. 353 Hansen.

We recall the words of John of Nikiu LXXXIV par. 88, p. 101 Charles: "[...] And the governor of the city honored her exceedingly; for she had beguiled him through her magic. And he ceased attending church as had been his custom. And he not only did this, but he drew many believers to her, and he himself received the unbelievers at his house". Our only interpretive hesitation concerns the place where the "enchantments" took place: should we really believe that they took place, according to John of Nikiu, at the home of Orestes ("and he himself received the unbelievers at his house")? or is it a misunderstanding ("her" and not "his") which has been insinuated somewhere into the chain of translations of the original text?

On the passage from Cyril's *Easter Homilies*, in which the mention of the Egyptian woman could be read as an allusion to Hypatia (σεσίγηται ἡ Αἰγυπτία, "the Egyptian has been silenced"), see BERETTA 1993, p. 278, n. 135.

On the designation of Hypatia as *Aigyptia sophe* (Αἰγυπτία σοφή) par excellence in Byzantine literature, and in particular in Michael Psellus, the 11th century scholar of the Chaldean Oracles and the more secret currents of Platonism, see above, chapter "Women Who Philosophised".

36 Dramatis Personae

The Late Antique Christian Church was not, generally speaking, at all ignorant of this tacit, subterranean survival of the ancient Pagan *religio* amongst the upper classes and the intellectual elites. Rather, it was systematically tolerated. Members of those castes, such as Synesius, could often belong to the Christian clergy without repudiating either Hellenic wisdom or sciences. Theirs was a philosophical Paganism that did not believe in the "popular" dogmas of Christianity, just as it had never trusted the popular beliefs of polytheism, the fables, the legends destined for simpler spirits. In turn, on the other hand, the popular cults and superstitions of Paganism survived in the popular Christian devotions, in which the Mother of God was substituted for the ancient Greek, Latin and oriental female divinities, and the veneration of a plurality of gods, semi-gods and heroes were substituted, sometimes with surprising parallelisms, by the cults of saints.

Rather, at first "what marginalized, or at least kept away, the men of letters of the old aristocracy from Christianity for a certain period, was not so much Paganism as the religion of culture, the classical ideal of *paideia*"[221], as has been written, the *hellenike diagoge* (ἑλληνικὴ διαγωγή) or "Greek life" that Synesius' *Dion* presents as "the most fertile and in general the most efficacious method for cultivating minds".

It is the history of philosophy that shows us how artificial the opposition between Pagan and Christian Platonism was. The need for conciliation between Christian culture and classical *paideia*, to which Paganism was connected by innumerable bonds, had long been felt and encouraged. The best brains of the Christian *intelligentsia* had already worked on this assimilation. The ancient Church organised its persecution against ritual Paganism, but towards intellectual Paganism it maintained since the 4th century a shrewd neutrality. It was the common heritage, in the literary, philosophical, political language of the autochthonous ruling classes, whose collaboration it could not renounce.

Cyril's activism aimed at the direct participation of the Christian bishops in the management of the imperial State, in theory and in practice, as we have seen; and this appeared unacceptable to the political mentality of the Byzantine period. However, his activity did not aim at an ideological discussion with the Pagan intellectuals: only at cultic supremacy in the city and at control of the social disputes. The problem was the masses, not the elite, already partly accustomed to educated Christianity and in any case co-opted into its political version, as the example of Synesius shows.

Hence, the bipolar disorder of Cyril's policies. The persecution, though brutal, of ethnic Jews, who represented competition, and the destruction of the temples make sense and, after all, conform to the imperial will. The physical elimination of Hypatia does not. The initiative of striking, through her, an establishment so discreet in its remaining Pagan, as well as tolerant and willing in its inclusive vocation to welcome

---

[221] MARROU 1963, p. 157.

Christ into its pantheon and Christianised Platonism into its theology was, as the ancient sources tell us, irrational.

An outburst of anger and of intolerance, inspired by the demon – Phthonos – of personal envy that erupts together with the revelation of the secret intellectual 'second profession' of Hypatia. In Cyril's eyes, Hypatia's 'private sessions' (ἰδίᾳ) explain, once he discovers them, the unattainable admiration and the political regard that the Alexandrian ruling class pays to her, the imperturbable and composed lay priestess, and not to him, the vehement and unruly Christian bishop, nor to the obstinate demand for power to which his demagogical manoeuvres and theological tactics tend.

The irrational burst of envy is disguised as a programmatic act of confessional struggle, or as an application – hypothetical and summary – of the imperial sanctions of Constantine and Theodosius "against soothsayers and magicians". Hypatia suddenly becomes – as the Coptic vulgate of John of Nikiu states – a magician and a witch.

Some intellectual stances close to the modern Church have also tried to justify Cyril's actions, stating that Hypatia was not a philosopher, but a priestess of the sect opposed to Christianity. They forget, however, the history of their own Church and the fact that in the 5th century the struggles of Christianity were not (or were no longer) against Paganism, except where it was practised in the popular form of sacrifices to the gods in the temples. And they were certainly not directed against philosophical Paganism, which was Hypatia's field, because, as Damascius writes, "even though Paganism was ended, yet the name of *philosophia* still seemed great and venerable"[222] in the cities of the Christianised empire. And those who followed it were not sentenced to death by any type of decree, constitution, or law.

Nor would it ever be so throughout the Byzantine millennium, in which ecclesiastical history, not by accident more similar to that of the European Church of the Renaissance than to that of the Middle Ages or the Counter-Reformation, saw many more Nicholas of Cusa than Giordano Bruno.

---

222 DAMASCIUS, *Vita Isidori* fr. *104, p. 79, 16–17 Zintzen = fr. 43E, p. 130, 6–8 Athanassiadi = SUIDAS Y 166, IV, p. 645, 2–4 Adler (HARICH-SCHWARZBAUER 2011, p. 247).

Appendix
Dramatis Personae

On the "passation des pouvoirs" in Alexandria at the end of the 4th and the beginning of the 5th centuries, see ROUGÉ 1990, p. 489. On this article, to this day the most analytical – although not ideologically impartial – assessment of Cyril's policies, see in particular pp. 487–490 and 502–503.

On the tolerance of philosophical Paganism by the Late Antique and Byzantine Christian Church, which opposed Pagan cults but concentrated more on the doctrinal controversies present in its own midst than on the discreet doctrines of the "Hellenes", see MARROU 1963; LACOMBRADE 2001, pp. 412–416, who emphasises the forbearance of the Alexandrian Church authorities – Theophilus above all, "but for a certain time also Cyril" – towards Hypatia's teaching. That Cyril's policy, at the start of his episcopacy, was no different from that of the other contemporary Christian leaders, and did not foresee a militant struggle against Paganism, nor against the philosophical elite, is rightly pointed out also by ROUGÉ 1990, pp. 502–503 ("Quant au paganisme intellectuel, c'est avec d'autres armes que la force que Cyrille essaya de lutter contre lui: la controverse [...] Je me demande, d'ailleurs, dans quelles mesures l'affaire d'Hypatie pouvait lui permettre une propagande active du côté de l'intelligentsia païenne?"). Nonetheless, the scholar scales down to an unacceptable extent the responsibility of the bishop in the assassination of Hypatia (see above, part II, chapter "The Catholic Wing", Appendix *ad loc.*).

For the quotation on the *hellenike diagoge* (ἑλληνικὴ διαγωγή), taken from MARROU 1963, p. 157, see above, part I, chapter "Good Use of Power" and Appendix *ad loc.*

On the work of integration of classical *paideia* and Christianity, already undertaken by Clement and Origen and developed in the 4th century by the previously mentioned Cappadocian fathers Basil the Great, Gregory of Nyssa and Gregory of Nazianzus, protagonists of the First Council of Constantinople, the mid-20th century produced a vast amount of literature, now classic: from JÄGER 1961 to DANIÉLOU; from MARROU 1956 to CHADWICK.

Amongst the recent positions of the Catholic writers who have spoken on the polemic regarding the death of Hypatia raised by the film *Agora* directed and co-written by Alejandro Amenábar, see for example that of S. MIESEL, *Agora-phobia: The True Story of Hypatia* (2010); S. D. GREYDANUS, *Agora: An Atheist Sets the Record Straight* (2010); R. CAMMILLERI, *Ipazia la "martire" usata come clava contro i cristiani in barba alla storia* (2010).

For the imperial sanctions of Constant and Theodosius against soothsayers and magicians in the *Codex Theodosianus*, see above, chapter "Synesius, Hypatia and *Philosophia*", and below, chapter "Hypatia's Sacrifice", Appendices *ad loc.*

The well-known phrase on the lasting grandeur of the "name of the *philosophia*" even after the end of Paganism can be read in DAMASCIUS, *Vita Isidori* fr. *104, p. 79, 16 Zintzen = fr. 43E, p. 130, 6–8 Athanassiadi= SUIDAS Y 166, IV, p. 645, 2–4 Adler (HARICH-

SCHWARZBAUER 2011, p. 247). According to WATTS 2017, p. 113, in writing that "the name of philosophy seemed most esteemed and worthy of honor to those who ran the affairs of the city", Damascius is referring exclusively to the moment when Orestes, at the height of his conflict with Cyril, turned to Hypatia to put together a sort of coalition with "the Alexandrian councilors and other members of the civic elite". As we have seen above, Watts situates the visits to Hypatia's house of the political leaders (including the Augustal prefect Orestes) who came to administer the polis, and of the city elite (ἥ τε ἄλλη πόλις) more generally, in the segment of time that runs from the death under torture of Ammonius to that of Hypatia herself. Such interpretation is, in our view, questionable: see above, part I, chapt. "Good Use of Power" and Appendix *ad loc.*

37 Hypatia's Sacrifice

One day when Hypatia was, as usual, returning home from one of her public appearances, a horde of enraged men attacked her. These wretches, heedless of the *vengeance of the gods and men*, massacred the philosopher. And while she was still breathing, they put out her eyes. It was a terrible stain, an abomination for their city. And the ire of the emperor would have fallen violently on them, had Aedesius not been corrupt, thus saving the butchers from their punishment[223].

This is what the Pagan Damascius wrote.

And those zealots, those beings with incandescent spirit, led by a certain Peter the Reader, conceived a plan and ambushed the woman when she was returning home. They pulled her from her carriage and dragged her into the church that takes its name from the Emperor Caesar. And here they stripped off her garments, they killed her using shards of pot, they cut her to ribbons. And they carried those remains to the place called Cinaron, where they burned them. And it was no minor infamy this carried out by Cyril and the Church of Alexandria. Because assassinations and insurgencies and similar actions are totally extraneous to the spirit of Christ[224].

This is what the Christian Socrates writes.

The woman was torn to shreds by those who professed consubstantiality[225]

of the human and the divine.
Thus writes the Arian Philostorgius.

A multitude of believers in God rose under the guidance of Peter the Reader – a man who on Jesus Christ professed exemplary dogmas from any point of view – and they began seeking the Pagan woman who had bewitched the people of the city and the prefect with her enchantments. And when they came to know the place where she was to be found, they marched to punish her and they found her sitting on a high chair. And after pulling her from her cathedra they dragged her to the great church called Caesareum. Note that this occurred in the days of fasting. And every one of them began to tear off her clothes, and they had her dragged [behind a wagon] through the city, until she died. Then they took her body to a place called Cinaron and there they burned it. And the entire [Christian] population surrounded the patriarch Cyril and acclaimed him "New Theophilus", because he had freed the city from the last residues of idolatry[226].

This is the account given by the Coptic bishop John of Nikiu.

---

223 DAMASCIUS, *Vita Isidori* fr. *104, *105, pp. 79,25–81,10 Zintzen = fr. 43E, p. 130, 17–22 Athanassiadi = SUIDAS Y 166, IV, p. 645, 12–17 Adler (HARICH-SCHWARZBAUER 2011, pp. 247–248).
224 SOCRATES VII 15, 5–6, p. 361, 1–9 Hansen (HARICH-SCHWARZBAUER 2011, pp. 188–189).
225 PHILOSTORGIUS 8, 9, p. 111, 3–8 Bidez = 8,9, pp. 366, 5–368, 2 Bleckmann-Stein (HARICH-SCHWARZBAUER 2011, p. 318).
226 JOANNES DE NIKIU LXXXIV parr. 102–103, p. 102 Charles.

Re-reading these first testimonies on the death of Hypatia, we may notice that already the ancient sources described it in terms of a genuine sacrifice. While Damascius calls her assassins οἱ σφαγεῖς, "the butchers", "the immolators", Socrates and Philostorgius use the verb *diaspao* (διασπάω), "to tear to pieces", a technical term commonly used to indicate the ritual dismembering of the victim. It is possible, as we have seen, that Hypatia was literally torn to pieces, as both Socrates (μεληδὸν διασπάσαντες) and, above all, Suidas, in the passage ascribable to Hesychius (καὶ τὸ σῶμα [...] διεσπάρη)²²⁷ seem to indicate; if not also "dismembered" in the sacrificial manner; and that then she was also eviscerated, with her heart torn from her body. It may appear more likely to modern mentality, perhaps wrongly, that with the shards of pottery they had available the Christian monks skinned her alive, reproducing the capital punishment reserved in ancient times for the great heretics, like Mani, the heresiarch par excellence, and that the use of the technical-sacrificial verb *diaspao* should not be taken literally, but as a clarification, and a denouncement, of her quality as a victim.

While the Pagan sources use sacrificial terms, in the Christian versions we find those of martyrdom. John of Nikiu, who is more indulgent with the persecutors, regarding the "arrest" of Hypatia uses the verb equivalent to what designates, in the Proto-Christian martyrological texts, the *prosecutio*, that is the search for and capture of Christians to be sentenced to death by the Roman governmental militia, which included, moreover, regular and irregular troops.

Hypatia was the victim of a brutal power at a time and in a place where, as Chateaubriand wrote, the roles were reversed and "in the race along the slippery slope of the century" Cyril's Christianity was the outdated and retrograde force, the armed wing of conservation and repression. Thus, the way in which Hypatia died still belongs to another role, that of the martyr, also, like the sacerdotal role, certainly not uncommon for the female figure. Martyrdom, together with the option of an ascetic or "virginal" life, both attributed to Hypatia with great emphasis, are fixed characteristics of the "eminent" woman in ancient religious literature. The emergence of this further model allows us to investigate the sources even further, to distinguish between historical testimonies and ideological distortion; ultimately, to interpret them.

While the models of sacrificial virgins were already forged by Roman religiosity, the 5th century was the "period of noble and educated saints", it has been written, "amongst the Pagans no less than amongst the Christians"²²⁸. As a virgin and martyr, Hypatia moves from the Pagan mythology of Damascius – who after mentioning her brilliance (ἀρετή) as a scholar and a teacher describes her intense spiritual and also physical beauty (σφόδρα καλή [...] καὶ εὐειδής) emphasising her *sophrosyne* (σωφροσύνη), chastity, and exalting the fact that "she kept herself a virgin" (διετέλει

---

227 Suidas Y 166, IV, p. 644, 5–6 Adler (Harich-Schwarzbauer 2011, p. 324) see also Philostorgius 8, 9a, 1–2, p. 368 Bleckmann-Stein.
228 Cracco Ruggini 1988, p. 273.

παρθένος)²²⁹ – directly to Christian mythology, with its historiographical expressions, not to mention the hagiographical, such as those found in the *Passion* of Saint Catherine of Alexandria. The "doctrine" is also a martyrological trait, particularly if disclosed to the public (δημοσίᾳ), since Socrates' trial was one of the two great archetypes of Christian trial literature, alongside that of Christ.

---

229 Damascius, *Vita Isidori* fr. *102, p. 77, 9 Zintzen = fr. 43A, p. 128, 7–11 Athanassiadi = Suidas Y 166, IV, p. 644, 18–20 Adler (Harich-Schwarzbauer 2011, p. 247).

Appendix
Hypatia's Sacrifice

The long fragment from Damascius is reported in DAMASCIUS, *Vita Isidori* fr. *104, *105, pp. 79, 25–81, 1–10 Zintzen = fr. 43E, p. 130, 17–22 Athanassiadi = SUIDAS Y 166, IV, p. 645, 12–17 Adler (HARICH-SCHWARZBAUER 2011, pp. 247–248). The passage from Socrates is in VII 15, 5–6, p. 361, 1–9 Hansen (HARICH-SCHWARZBAUER 2011, pp. 188–189). See the brief fragment from PHILOSTORGIUS (8, 9) on p. 111, 3–8 Bidez = 8, 9, pp. 366, 5–368, 2 Bleckmann-Stein (HARICH-SCHWARZBAUER 2011, p. 318). The quotation from John of Nikiu corresponds to LXXXIV, parr. 102–103, p. 102 Charles. See above, part I, chapter "Mortal Envy", Appendix *ad loc.*

That the death of Hypatia was due to literal dismembering, that is to say she was cut to pieces (see both Socrates, μεληδὸν διασπάσαντες, and Suidas, in the passage ascribable to Hesychius: καὶ τὸ σῶμα [...] διεσπάρη, SUIDAS Y 166, IV, p. 644, 5–6 Adler [HARICH-SCHWARZBAUER 2011, p. 324]; see also PHILOSTORGIUS 8, 9a, 1–2, p. 368 Bleckmann-Stein), is suggested by AGABITI, p. 100. It is also considered possible by Enrico Livrea, the expert scholar of 5th-century Egypt in general, and of the case of Hypatia in particular; he also believes that the *diasparagmos* (διασπαραγμός) of Hypatia can be compared to the similar fate of the courtesan Lais of Hyccara, told in Athenaeus and for which see LIVREA 1986, p. 92 (the parallelism with the death of Hypatia was suggested to us *per litteras* by the scholar, whom we wish to thank).

That similar forms of horrendous deaths were not foreign to the mentality of Late Antiquity is also shown by the homophagy reported in the *Bassarica* by Dionysius, fr. 19 Livrea, again *per litteras*. "The memory", writes the scholar, "was kept alive by Orphism, which had one at the centre of its cult. That the 'Christianity' of the *parabalani* was contaminated by similar elements of ferociousness is no surprise; see the similar 'punitive' anti-Pagan monstrosities carried out a little further south in the Panopolite, by the terrible Shenoute, studied by Chuvin"; see LIVREA 1973, pp. 90–93 (text), 127–128 (translation), 26–29 (commentary).

That this type of death was specifically reserved for those guilty of sorcery and magic, according to the edict of the *Codex Theodosianus* 9, 16, 5 *de maleficis et mathematicis et ceteris similibus* already mentioned above, is recalled by TAKÁCS 1995, pp. 60–61. See also WATTS 2006b, p. 335; and the parallel cases of the bishops George and Proterius, mentioned above, part I, chapter "A Three-Handed Game", Appendix *ad loc.*

Of note, in any case, is the evident affinity between the way Hypatia was killed and the way the statue of Serapis was destroyed, which is mentioned by THEODORETUS CYRENSIS 5, 22, p. 321 Parmentier-Scheidweiler (see above, part I, chapter "The Destruction of the Serapeum"). The parallelism is covertly suggested also by John of Nikiu's terming Hypatia's murder the destruction "of the last remains of idolatry in the city" (LXXXIV par. 103, p. 102 Charles), as noticed by WATTS 2017, p. 116 and p. 182, n. 30, who, however, as we have seen above (part I, chapter "Mortal Envy", Appendix *ad loc.*), avoids making explicit what the allusion implies, namely that that of Hypatia was not a casual lynching, but a capital punishment devised as such from the beginning. Whether the parallelism is real or presumed, it in any case indicates the ritual nature of the torment. For a different and interesting interpretation of the affinity between the description of the Serapeum destruction we read in Rufinus and that of Hypatia we find in Socrates Scholasticus and John of Nikiu, see HAASE, cited above, "The Destruction of Serapeum", Appendix.

Whether her heart was also torn out (as with sacrificial victims) we do not know. On the division of the flesh and the excision and scattering of the organs (generally the heart and liver) of the victim of ancient sacrifice see, in any case, amongst others, the paper *Meat and Society, Sacrifice and Creation, Butchers and Philosophy*, read by Bruce Lincoln at the International Conference on *La divisione delle carni* held in Siena in September 1983, later published in LINCOLN.

That Mani died skinned alive in 275 AD, by order of the Persian king Shapur I, is told to us by the same SOCRATES, I 22, p. 68 Hansen. That Hypatia was "only" skinned alive would seem to be suggested by the type of blade – *ostraka* (ὄστρακα), potsherds – available to the sacrificers, and it is thus that not only Gibbon and other modern scholars interpret it as "flayed alive", but also recently, for example THORP. In any case, as summarised by CANFORA 2000, "[...] the scene was that of a human sacrifice carried out for the god of the Christians in one of his churches." See also above, part II, "From Fielding to Gibbon Passing Through the Shadow of a Donkey".

On the *prosecutio* of the Christian martyrs see LANATA; RONCHEY 1999.

The quotation regarding the "noble saints", both Pagan and Christian, from the 5th century is taken from CRACCO RUGGINI 1988, p. 273.

On the models of "sacrificial virgins" expressed in Pagan religious literature, particularly Roman, and the typology of the Late Antique *virgo* see, apart from CRACCO RUGGINI 1988, and BROWN 1988, expecially CONSOLINO, pp. 462–463.

The words of Damascius on the ascetism and the virginity of Hypatia can be read in DAMASCIUS, *Vita Isidori* fr. *102, p. 77, 9 Zintzen = fr. 43A, p. 128, 7–11 Athanassiadi = SUIDAS Y 166, IV, p. 644, 18–20 Adler (HARICH-SCHWARZBAUER 2011, p. 247).

38 The Martyrdom of Hypatia

The triangle between the Christian Church, the Roman government and the Jewish community formed the framework not only of the most ancient narrative on the case of Hypatia, namely that of Socrates Scholasticus, but routinely of those Christian texts of pseudo-legal style designated as "martyrdoms" (*martyria*, μαρτύρια) and that "testify" (μαρτυρέω) the causes and the method of a death sentence considered unjust, of which the executor and the commissioner are the constituted power or the masses, or both. They are known as *Acts of the Martyrs* (*Acta Martyrum*).

The literature of this type, which belongs almost entirely to the 3rd century, often has, in fact, the ultimate intention of attenuating, rather than amplifying, the conflict between Christianity and Roman power. It is not coincidental that in the martyrological texts the same characters and the same final attributions of blame recur; that the political responsibility for the assassinations is ascribed to a culturally "extraneous" and religiously "profane" element – often to the Jews – avoiding censure of the Roman authorities, who are usually portrayed, in the figure of the highest representative, with the traits of indecisiveness already typical of Pilate in the gospel prototype.

In the case of Hypatia, what makes the stereotype of the Pilate-style governor more effective, in the figure and the position of Orestes as presented by Socrates Scholasticus, seems to be the similar intention of moderate Christian opinion in attributing all the blame not so much to the Jews as to the "unholy" Alexandrian clergy, the enemy, on the one hand, of Paganism, and on the other, at least for some of the Byzantine sources, of orthodoxy itself, both religious and political.

To define the conflict between Cyril and Hypatia, historians often speak of "tragedy". Now, the genre of martyrdom in Christian literature is often an application and legal sublimation of the classical dramatic genre, with parts assigned and fixed characters. Such a genre therefore is only apparently objective and written as a chronicle, but it is in reality eminently political and propagandistic.

The conflict between Hypatia and Cyril has traditionally been read in terms of a conflict between religions and between opposing "philosophies" or visions of the world, like a confessional and ideological drama. The protagonist pays with her life for the right to "honourable freedom of speech" (*semne parrhesia*, σεμνὴ παρρησία) which belongs to the Pagan philosopher, and which places her at odds with the Christian bishop, the masculine figure antithetical to her, an aggressive advocate of a populist faith, just as Hypatia is a supporter of elite Hellenism, which brings her, in contrast to Christian radicalism, close to the tolerant pragmatism of the Roman government.

However, this is not true, or it is only partially true. The drama is more concretely and contingently political. In the tragedy of Hypatia, the State power, as personified by Orestes, plays a role not inferior to that of Cyril, and the Jews form the chorus. The elements in conflict are not so much Paganism and Christianity as the ruling classes (local and Roman), the social categories (ancient aristocracy, new ecclesiastical *nomenklatura*) and bellicose ethnic groups, in the climate of instability that accompanies the transfer of powers and the establishment of the "new creed" in the life and urban structures of the Late Roman empire.

It is not after all inaccurate or accidental that Chateaubriand, Wieland, Diodata Saluzzo, and Péguy described the story of Hypatia in terms of martyrdom.

Appendix
The Martyrdom of Hypatia

On the triangle between the Christian Church, the Roman government and the Jewish community as framework of the most ancient narrative of the case of Hypatia see above, part I, chapter "A Three-Handed Game" and Appendix *ad loc.*

On martyrdom in general see LANATA; on the stereotypes, the political aims of the martyrological texts and the need to postdate the majority of the "most ancient" *acta martyrum* to the 3rd century see RONCHEY 1999; RONCHEY 1990, also for the comparison of the martyrological literary genre to the styles of the classical dramatic genre. On the affinity of the narrative scheme concerning the death of Hypatia with that typical of the ancient martyrological texts see RONCHEY 1994.

On Hypatia's "honourable freedom of speech" (*semne parrhesia*, σεμνὴ παρρησία) see above, chapter "Hypatia in All Her States of Being", Appendix, *ad loc.*

On the accounts by Wieland, Diodata Saluzzo, Chateaubriand, and Péguy see part II, chapters "From Fielding to Gibbon Passing Through the Shadow of a Donkey", "Uncontrolled Effects on the Poets", "Miraculous Devotion", with Appendices *ad loc.*

39 A Question of Method

The lesson that the death of Hypatia and her afterlife suggests is therefore also a story method. The story of an event is made up of the sum of the factual data of that event and the transformations, interpolations, manipulations that followed, until they form an integral part of the event itself. The more this is studied, the more this reveals itself as different from the way it has been handed down, the more it is evident that it will never be entirely possible to reconstruct it, because the infiltration of the propaganda began immediately with its very first historical narration.

The event itself, as it happened, can never be truly reconstructed. This is true for modern and even more so for ancient historical events. It is true even more so for events, like those surrounding the story of Hypatia, that maintain vast margins of secrecy or ineffability, of one kind or another, with respect to all the parties involved. But this must not lead to negligence in piecing together the facts as accurately as possible, nor to scepticism on the possibility and necessity of this reconstructive effort, nor cynicism and casualness in reporting it as preferred or as convenient, in explaining the event by twisting it to fit the discussions and the tastes of one's own times.

On the contrary, it is necessary to dissect judgements and prejudices, and to attack the mystery from both sides: on the one hand, from the philological one, by reconstructing it as far as possible in terms of positive facts and exegesis of the sources; and, on the other, from the ideological one, through an analysis of the distortions present in the sources themselves, in the history of the studies that derive from them, and in the literary production they have generated.

In the blurring of the various views of the ancient street murder and of the secret female character, what clearly appears is not so much the end of Paganism as the metamorphosis of Christianity, the evolution, or involution, of its political thinking and necessary critical historiography. The inner reality of Hypatia – as well as the exterior one, whether she was dark-haired and amber-skinned like a true Egyptian, or blonde and pale like some Greeks and as Mitchell represents her – will always remain a mystery to us. Nonetheless, her icon must be restored with the utmost care, because it is essential for our times that we distort it as little as possible.

Such an icon represents in fact the most precious teachings of every story of an intellectual personality in a period of great cultural and political transformation; that is invariably perceived as decadence by some, but seen by others as the start of a new civilisation. The twofold picture of the end of the Roman empire on the one hand, and the start of the Byzantine empire on the other is not, after all, dissimilar to ours, including the ambiguous challenge of a "clash of civilisations" – in this case, the Pagan and the Christian – which in fact was resolved in their integration over the course of the millenium.

Appendix
A Question of Method

That Hypatia was dark-skinned is bizarrely taken for granted by LUMPKIN, and the fact that she was an African woman, not Greek, is shown, according to the author, by her uninhibited behaviour and her freedom of speech; see also the considerations of BERNAL, I, pp. 121–122.

We have deliberately not lingered on Hypatia's fortune in art, a topic that lies outside the confines and the purpose of this book, and also too complex and interesting to be reduced to a brief treatise. The only possible ancient image of Hypatia is, in any case, one on a medallion found at Aphrodisias, now destroyed, reported by HAFNER, according to whom the portrait on the medallion in question derived from a painting. Ari Belenkiy informed us (*per litteras*) that he is working on an essay on the subject.

40 The Eminence of Hypatia

Accurate interrogation of the witnesses and examination of the sources purged of the elements of ideological distortion or conditioned reflexes and clichés completely destroys the rationalist Enlightenment stereotype of the 'Galileo in a dress', of the revolutionary scientist persecuted by the Church for her discoveries.

In the history of philosophy as in that of astronomy, the personage of Hypatia, despite the indisputable prestige of her teaching, appears "as merely another to pass on the torch"[230]. Rather, it was her sacral and charismatic figure and her consequent social prestige and political role that led both to her death – brought about by the glaring and irrational frustration of Cyril, well diagnosed as such by all the sources – and her fame, as a posthumous tool of a propaganda initially Pagan and later Christian.

Hypatia, victim of the Christians, owes her notoriety as much to the Byzantine Church, from which she attained the status of martyr, as to the irreducibility of the Church of Rome in justifying the misdeed of the unbalanced, but from its point of view politically exemplary Cyril. The assassination of Hypatia can be considered collateral damage in the manoeuvre to erode the power of the Roman State, which culminated in the anti-Jewish campaign of the bishop and in the consequent rift with the Augustal prefect and the local elite. It was a false step also with respect to Cyril's own strategy, since it sacrificed a public figure who was neither a public enemy nor a direct political adversary, and who did not belong to any of the categories of confessional competitors of his armed proselytism.

Her power was of another kind. While Hypatia's type of *philosophia* must be included, even before its inclusion in the history of thought, in the relationship, Pagan as much as Christian, between the woman and the sacred, her eminence must be situated in the area of that line of succession of leaders or torchbearers, esoteric if not secret, which according to the testimony of Synesius saw her leading the most important Platonic fraternity of her era, in any case a link in the ancient and unceasing *diadoche* or chain of succession in the initiatory tradition that we call Neoplatonic.

This subterranean stream of Platonism, bound to the pinnacles of secular power, espoused by multiple ecclesiastical intellectual figures, and practically undisturbed by the Greek Church, would continue its underground progress throughout the Byzantine millenium, where we see Hypatia recognised and celebrated in every period and exalted by authors like Psellus, who were in turn members, if not leaders, of that same lineage. Until the twilight of the empire and the school of George Gemistus Plethon in Mystras, the last Platonic circle in Byzantine history and the only one on whose more internal and 'secret' activities we are able to cast a furtive glance, thanks to the critical information of an ex-insider like George of Trebizond. This sort of Proto-Freemasonry, which saw amongst its adepts also high-ranking members of the Christian hierarchies, like Bessarion, remained open above all, as we have said, to

---

230 RIST, p. 224.

women, up to the highest levels of initiation and the maximum resources of power, if not positions at the top like that of Hypatia. It was only with its passage to the West, and its transfusion in the European Platonic academies through the founder of the Mystras school, Gemistus, and his pupils, that the female component, until then vital and illustrious, disappeared.

In the 5th century, therefore, the death of Hypatia did not mark the end of an era, but, as both Diderot and Chateaubriand had realised, marked its beginning. Hypatia died, but she passed on the torch. The intellectual nucleus of which she was erroneously seen as the 'last' exponent is in reality what for eleven centuries the most flourishing Byzantine culture would emerge from; where Paganism would survive not only in its highest form, in philosophical Platonism, but also in the popular Christian culture; where the Olympus of the ancient polytheism would be substituted by the Martyrology and the Synaxarion, the mythological narratives by the hagiographic legends, the jungle of Pagan simulacra by the throng of icons.

The 5th century is not the edge of an abyss, as historians and scholars have often been led to believe by the mistaken perception of the Byzantine millennium as "infinite and protracted decadence", which was also widely linked to Papist propaganda. It was, instead, the beginning of a turnaround, the eve of a rebirth of the ancient *paideia*.

The condemnation of Cyril in the Byzantine sources, compared to his defence in Papal Rome, is the litmus test of the constant aspiration to separation between State and Church that in Byzantium, a secular State although with a State religion, was applied without interruption. The existence in the heart of Europe of a Church State, whose spiritual leader, the Pope, was also the holder of temporal power, was a historical *unicum*. Where this anomaly was not produced, there was no interruption in the ancient culture. The study of the ancient texts continued, together with the manuscript tradition and the transmission of ideas, although these might at times appear to be in conflict with the dominant Christian ideology. The torch that Hypatia carried has not gone out: many other women and men have continued to hand it on.

Through them, the *philosophia* of Hypatia, of Synesius and the ancient *philosophes* of Alexandria, Eclectic or not, would reach our Humanism and Renaissance, and in this way also reach the Enlightenment and those other currents of opinion that broke the conspiracy of silence of the Western Church and made Hypatia the symbol of freedom of thought.

There were distortions and deformations, because in the modern Western world, which has not yet fully comprehended Byzantium, the story of Hypatia was not easily understood in its correct historical terms. It has been actualised and adapted to the times, as history always does, according to the motto – never given enough prominence – of the Italian philosopher Benedetto Croce: that all history is contemporary.

Yet there is one point we can only agree with: whatever Hypatia most resembles, a scholar or a priestess, a self-possessed teacher or an eccentric and transgressive aristocrat; whether she was young or not, whether her pupils fell in love with her or not, whether she discovered something new or not – and it is not to be excluded –, whether the initiatory teaching she imparted so successfully to the restless Hellenic aristocracy did or did not offer the revelation that at a high level Platonic theology incorporated Christian theology and that the improbable dogmas of the latter were to be tolerated by practising the Platonic art of the "noble lie", because it was as useful to the people as any ancient Pagan superstition; whether she was resolute in barring the progress of Church interference in the State and so unmanageable in challenging the strategy of Cyril with her *parrhesia*; whether her death was merely an incident due to the sudden hysteria of an influential Christian prelate benighted by emulation and ambition, and by the momentary disorientation of an Augustal Roman prefect in difficulty because of an imperial power vacuum; in any case, every time that history repeats itself, and it often repeats itself, in the conflict between a Cyril and a Hypatia, one thing is certain: we are and will always be on the side of Hypatia.

Appendix
The Eminence of Hypatia

The quotation is taken from RIST, p. 224, who does not, however, understand either the specific nature of the figure of Hypatia nor the complex and fertile tradition of female knowledge into which her activity as a "teacher" fits, when he writes that the fact of being a woman "increased her fame in an age where the educated woman was comparatively rare" (*ibidem*). Rist is, on the other hand, probably right, from the mere standpoint of the historian of philosophy, when he says that her terrible fate "secured her a posthumous glory which her philosophical achievements would never have warranted" (*ibidem*).

That both social prestige and political role, and the tragic death, should be attributed to Hypatia's sacral and charismatic eminence is underscored in the recent, brief article by ADACHI.

Substantially of the same opinion as Rist is LACOMBRADE 1951, p. 50, who recognises in the output of Synesius the unquestionable imprint of the "revelation of the thinking of those venerated masters that Hypatia disclosed to the elite of her disciples" and therefore, conversely, taking from the first writings of the pupil the mould of the teaching of the mistress, concludes that Hypatia simply imparted the Neoplatonic thinking (with a pre-eminence of Porphyrus on Iamblichus, as we have seen) but did not ever rise to "a general conception of the world, nor create, like any authentic philosopher, an original system": see also LACOMBRADE 1994, coll. 961–963.

It is in any case arbitrary to infer Hypatia's thinking *tout court* from the works of Synesius, as BERETTA 1993, p. 66 does; what is more, the positions of the latter altered as time passed, as noted by LACOMBRADE 1951; in any case, in presenting his *Dion* for Hypatia's approval, Synesius himself implicitly shows that this approval may have been withheld – an eventuality not remote, considering that the dialogue dealt with the training in philosophy and distinguished between the philosophical communication master-pupil, with its eminently rational overtones, and any mystical communication or one based on magical practices. See HARICH-SCHWARTZBAUER 2011, pp. 96–125; TANASEANU-DÖBLER 2008, pp. 229–252; WATTS 2017, pp. 70–71.

With regard to the political exemplarity of Cyril, his ecclesiastical government, as we have seen (see above, part II, chapter "The Catholic Wing"), was praised again by Benedict XVI, who, in the celebrations of October 3rd 2007, commended his "great energy" in the political-ecclesiastical field. This in itself does not mean approving the assassination of Hypatia, but the positive historical judgement on the (successful) Cyrillian strategy of erosion of State power and substitution with temporal ecclesiastical power persists, in line with the entire Papist tradition.

Not even the few scholars who, like Watts, deny the presence of theurgical and ritualistic elements in Hypatia's school (see above, chapter "What Did Hypatia Teach", Appendix *ad loc.*), can deny the 'secret', esoteric, and initiatory, character of the part of her teaching, permeated by the centuries-old Platonic tradition, which was aimed at what WATTS 2017, p. 66, calls the "inner circle of students, to which access was restricted". See also the records of the private meetings in professors' houses, the distinctions between *akroatai* (ἀκροαταί) and *zelotai* (ζηλοταί), and in general the secrecy vow on the "internal" teachings *ibidem*, p. 173, nn. 16–21.

That Hypatia's death did not mark the end of an era, but the start of another one, is not merely an intuition of philosophers and writers (see above, part II, chapters "The Glory of Her Sex and the Wonder of Ours" and "Miraculous Devotion. Chateaubriand, Péguy and the Flourishing of Feminist Literature"): it is a concept that has meandered, although in a minor key, amongst scholars; see also, for example, the words that conclude the essay by LAMIRANDE, p. 489: "Quand on tente de dresser l'arbre généalogique du néoplatonisme, on en vient plutôt à conclure qu'avec Hypatie et Synésios on assiste à un nouveau commencement." Hypatia's murder did not mark the end of Pagan philosophy, as it is still often argued, as it it did not mark the end of Platonic teaching. A *lignée* of teachers continued to make their voice heard in Alexandria throughout the whole 6th century: see WHITBY. The closure of the school of Athens by Justinian in 529 strengthened further the school of Alexandria, which became the most important centre for the teaching of philosophy in the entire Mediterranean: see WATTS 2006a, pp. 111–141 and 232–256. The *diadoche* of Platonism would continue in the prosperous empire of Byzantium for a millenium, and its so called decadence would turn into renaissance in the Constantinopolitan circles.

On the incessant, though subterranean vitality of the esoteric and initiatory thread of Byzantine Platonism see above, chapter "Synesius, Hypatia and *Philosophia*", Appendix *ad loc.*

The type of teaching, the activities, the readings and the esoteric rituals of the Platonic schools of Late Antiquity and Byzantium are inferred not so much from 11th-century testimonies such as that of Michael Psellus, as from the polemical testimony of George of Trebizond, whose information presents, in effect, various points of contact with the encrypted mentions in Synesius' letters. On the polemic of Trapezuntius against Plato in general and Gemistus Plethon in particular, whom he considered the great master of a "noxious" sect, see the synthesis by GARIN, pp. 116–118; the original text of what Trapezuntius says of the rites and the cults of Plethon's school, where astronomy and Neopagan syncretism blended in hymns that the inquisitor himself describes as magical mainly for the "formal elegance, the gentle metrics, the sonority and solemnity of the alliterations" (just like those of Synesius), can be read in GARIN, p. 117; see also MASAI, p. 285, n. 1, for the well-known prayer in which Trapezuntius invokes the intercession of the martyrs "against the Platonists who are re-emerging in Italy." Thus the political circumstances that opposed the Papist and Aristotelian Trapezuntius to what he considered the "great Neopagan plot" against the Roman Catholic religion by the last Byzantine intellectuals emigrated to Italy, represented politically by Bessarion, have allowed the modern scholars to "look through the keyhole" of the last Byzantine Platonic school, which flourished in Mystras in the 15th century, seeing what went on and thus glimpsing the ancient traditions jealously guarded in the Platonic *hetaireiai* (ἑταιρεῖαι) for centuries, or even millennia that had gone before.

The possibility of female initiation up to the highest mystery levels is testified, in this school, at least by Cleopa Malatesta, as mentioned above, chapter "Synesius, Hypatia and *Philosophia*", Appendix *ad loc.*

On the eminent positions of power of the female characters compared with Hypatia by the Byzantine texts, such as the *panhypersebasta* (πανυπερσεβάστη) Irene, daughter of Theodore Metochites, and Eudocia Palaeologina, daughter of Theodore Neocaesarites and second wife of the despot Constantine Palaeologus, son of Andronicus II, both in possession of high ranks at court and with great influence in the political and cultural life of their periods, see *Prosopographisches Lexikon der Palaiologenzeit*, respectively n. 21369, vol. IX, p. 121 (Eudocia), and n. 5972, vol. III pp. 212–213 (Irene). See also above, chapter "Women who Philosophised" and Appendix *ad loc.*

Aftershock: And What If...

> Saint Cyrille fit assassiner Hypathie, etc. Pauvre humanité!
> RÉMY DE GOURMONT

We have tried to reconstruct the series of events that led to the assassination of Hypatia, basing our theories only on the ancient sources and critiquing them briefly, on the basis of knowledge of the various environments that produced them. We have concisely contextualised them in their historical and social scenario, pruning them here and there of the subsequent ideological conceptions that fifteen centuries of historiography have implanted. We have tried to escape the dangers of dialectical schemes – the opposition of Paganism-Christianity, but also the tolerance-intolerance antinomy – and highlighted the inter-connectedness with the various groups of the categories of moderation-integralism and reason-irrationality, or rationalism-irrationalism.

We have ascertained that Hypatia was not, as the stereotype would have it, a champion of philosophical reason in contrast with Christian fideism, but on the contrary the *philosophia* (φιλοσοφία) that she practised had sacral and esoteric-ritual connotations, so that even the simplistic John of Nikiu was not entirely wrong, from his viewpoint, in accusing her of magic[231]. We have learned that the milieu of her pupils and followers was a close network of discreet affiliations and interconnections, and that this also explains, as testified also by Synesius, the "power" (δυναστεία) of Hypatia[232].

Pierre Chuvin, as we have seen, noted that the term used by Damascius/Suidas to describe Hypatia's private receptions (*idia*, ἰδίᾳ), which were the reason for the throng outside her house that so struck Cyril, is the technical term for the audiences granted by a patron to the *clientes*[233]. It is not necessary to trace a clear demarcation, as Chuvin does, between the esoteric element and the patronage aspect[234]. It is on the contrary probable, as we have seen, that during these meetings of Hypatia's "hetaireia", as Syn-

---

[231] See the passage cited earlier ("The Bishop of Nikiu", with Appendix *ad loc.*), produced in JOANNES DE NIKIU LXXXIV, par. 87, p. 100 Charles, and the rigorous comments of Michel Tardieu in CHUVIN-TARDIEU, p. 67.

[232] "You have always had power. May you have it for a long time, and may you put this power to good use", we read in *Ep.* 81 (τῇ φιλοσόφῳ), 17–18, p. 207 Roques: see above ("The Terrible Patriarch of Alexandria" and "The Power of Hypatia", with Appendix *ad loc.*); CAMERON 2016c, pp. 200–201.

[233] As we have seen ("The Power of Hypatia", Appendix *ad loc.*) CHUVIN was, pp. 366–367, the first to speak of the "private sittings" (ἰδίᾳ) held at Hypatia's home, and of the use by Damascius/Suidas of the verb προσαγορεύειν (CHUVIN-TARDIEU, p. 65; on the technical value of προσαγόρευσις inasmuch as it is "the greeting of the client to the patron" see HAAS 1997, pp. 311–312). We have also mentioned ("Mortal Envy" and Appendix *ad loc.*) the official and ceremonial resonance of the term ὠθισμός, with which Damascius indicates the "throng" at the entrance to Hypatia's residence awaiting her πρόοδος, and the use of the same terminology, again by Damascius, in the description of the death of Hypatia (CHUVIN-TARDIEU, pp. 61–62).

[234] Cfr. above, "The Power of Hypatia", Appendix *ad loc.*

esius already defines it, held at her residence, political topics were also discussed. If, in the esoteric sessions designed for the most mature and select acolytes of Hypatia's Platonism, the common philosophical profession went beyond confessional membership, they had to confront issues in which philosophy and politics, especially regarding religious matters, could not be distinguished; thus, when the local elite met with notables and officials sent from Constantinople, strategies and alignments were also determined in city affairs. Which explains why Cyril, when he discovers, noticing the gathering of carriages outside Hypatia's residence, the existence of this circle, and moreover, that its head is a woman, so clearly influential in the political choices of the local aristocracy and even of the authorities themselves, is caught by the furious spasm of φθόνος considered by the sources the trigger for the *klimax* that will lead to her assassination: an "envy" that blends, as we have seen, with a charge of "magic".

We have seen that Cyril was not merely a "fervent" (ἔνθερμος) sectarian, but that he had a *sui generis* rational political strategy, inherited from his predecessor and uncle Theophilus, and that he deliberately pursued it through coherent, although unscrupulous and violent, methods and with a precise aim that Socrates Scholasticus had previously pointed out: "To erode the power of those who exercised it on behalf of the emperor" and "to shape the power of the State beyond the limit allowed to the priestly sphere"[235]. He would, in time, be successful in undermining imperial control over the North African megalopolis, riding the cause of Egyptian nationalism, dogmatically extricating himself from the central Constantinopolitan Church. Christian Egypt, freed from Byzantine political subjugation, and the Coptic Church, bolstered by the Cyrillian doctrinal separatism, would continue to lend support to the West in the political-ecclesiastical struggle between Constantinople and the Roman papacy for centuries[236].

We have thus further clarified the reasons that led the Catholic Church to celebrate the Cyrillian doctrine of the incarnation for fifteen hundred years, and then, at the end of the 19th century, to confer on Cyril the title of Doctor of the Church, *Doctor Incarnationis*[237], denying his guilt in the case of Hypatia against all evidence. This, in contrast with the admissions of the ancient sources, and in particular the Byzantine ecclesiastical sources, which, as we have seen, give unanimous testimonies of Cyril's decisive role and in which the communal condemnation of Cyril's policies derives from the versions of the 5th and 6th centuries, from their influence and from their manuscript tradition[238].

We are in fact certain, if our reading of the sources is precise, that Cyril was responsible for the assassination of Hypatia. Nonetheless, however carefully we analyse the facts, also taking into account the component of entropy and fortuity that almost always interferes with the production of the historical events, as we reconstruct the

---
235 SOCRATES VII 13, 9, p. 358, 13–14 Hansen; VII 7, 4, p. 353, 2–6 Hansen.
236 Cfr. above, "The Terrible Patriarch of Alexandria" and Appendix *ad loc.*
237 *Ibid.*
238 Cfr. above, in particular, "The DNA of the Ancient Tradition" and Appendix *ad loc.*

escalation of violence and the radicalisation of the positions of the two (or more) parts in conflict, we cannot find a real, immediate motive.

Or better, we certainly have more than one motive, but, if we exclude that Platonic philosophy as such was the objective of militant Christianity, as the Enlightenment interpretations of the "excesses of fanaticism" even more radically than the Pagan sources have tried to suggest, and we instead accept that Hypatia's teaching must have been directed at helping the governing class to intellectually and pragmatically digest the process of passage from one religion to another, in the name of a higher Platonic universal belief, we do not find a truly convincing reason for the killing of the great mistress of that sort of Masonry in which the Alexandrian elite (Pagan, Christian and perhaps even Jewish) gathered in order to face the change and safeguard its interests in the passage from one hegemony of cult and thought to another, and in the alternation of the dominant groups at the imperial court of Constantinople[239].

Even if we consider it as collateral damage, as the analysts of the Catholic wing have probably done since the Middle Ages, in Cyril's manoeuvre to erode the power of the Roman State[240], which culminated in the anti-Jewish campaign and then in his quarrel with the Augustal prefect[241], the assassination of Hypatia was, as we have written, a false step with respect to his own strategy. He sacrificed a public personality who effectively acted *super partes*[242] and did not belong to any of the categories of confessional competitors of his armed proselytism[243].

Given that, in one way or another, the ancient sources, aware of the forces in play and chronologically close to the facts, ultimately deliver a concordant diagnosis, attributing the precipitation of the events to Cyril's attack of irrationality, which they describe using the term *phthonos* (φθόνος). An explanation that, as we have seen, undoubtedly has a solid basis in truth. However, this is not sufficient to interpret the historical events on a critical basis, which simply cannot exclude the determination of a *ratio*.

"Jealous of what?", wonders Alan Cameron[244], juxtaposing the accusations of *phthonos* brought against Cyril by two authors "with such different agendas" as the Christian Socrates and the Pagan Damascius. But the answer given is the traditional

---

239 Cfr. above, "What Did Hypatia Teach?" and Appendix *ad loc.*
240 SOCRATES VII 13, 9, p. 358, 13–14 Hansen; VII 7, 4, p. 353, 2–6 Hansen.
241 To quote again CAMERON 2016c, p. 201: "There can be no question that Hypatia's death arose out of the anti-Jewish riots of 415 and the struggle for power between Cyril and Orestes".
242 As we have seen, also CAMERON 2016c, pp. 195–198, has recently insisted on the neutrality of Hypatia's teaching, although he seems to underestimate its substantial and decisive, inasmuch as it was fundamentally tolerant, intellectual Pagan stamp.
243 CAMERON 2016c, p. 202, observes that "as a shrewd politician himself, he is not likely to have imagined that a public lynching would solve the problem". The contrast between the apparent irrationality of the assassination and the political logic of the patriarch is not in our opinion sufficient to presume him to be merely an involuntary or only indirect commissioner, as Cameron suggests, making Hypatia, although with some irony, the "Thomas Becket" of Cyril: see *ibidem.*
244 ID., p. 200.

one ("Cyril was jealous of all the officials [ἄρχοντες] he saw crowding into Hypatia's house", visiting the Pagan philosopher, who moreover was a woman, while he, the bishop, "may not yet have been on the VIP list")[245], and does not supply a motive, as Cameron himself emphasises, for a homicide that could only translate, amongst other things, into "undoubtedly a public-relations disaster"[246].

If we persist in our perhaps vain search for a rationality in what happened, we can attempt an experiment: abandoning the word *phthonos*, "envy", or rather translating it with a more prosaic term, "competition".

Confessional competition (anti-Jewish, if not directly anti-Pagan) first of all, as expressed by all the sources and in particular by the closest from the Coptic standpoint, John of Nikiu. Nevertheless, if Cyril's pogrom against the Jews led to the escalation of violence, as we have seen, the confessional aspect is not the only competition that opposed Cyril to the Jewish community and to its Hellenic protectors gathered around the circle of which Hypatia was the great mistress.

In the province of Egypt, it is said, the mathematics and the poetry, the music and the philosophy of the followers of Plotinus and Porphyry flourished. However, Egypt was not fertile only in intellectuals: it was also, as we have said, rich in grain[247]. The wealthy, well-established and influential Jewish citizens that Cyril's pogrom was meant to eliminate were competitors for the Christian community, not only in religious matters but also, as we mentioned, in the bids for maritime transportation of grain from Alexandria to Constantinople, as attested in the *Codex Theodosianus* by a decree dating from 390[248]. A strategically crucial activity and as such extensively safeguarded, for better or for worse, by the State[249].

Already in past studies[250] the decree issued by Theodosius I, charging the Jewish ship-owners of Alexandria with transporting the rations to the capital[251], was related to Cyril's anti-Jewish policies and in particular the pogrom of 414[252].

---

245 ID., p. 201.
246 ID., 2016c, p. 203.
247 On the grain transported by ship from Alexandria to Constantinople see Haas 1997, p. 42; Fraser, pp. 800–801. As mentioned in Galvão-Sobrinho, chapt. 6, and reported in Watts 2017, p. 158, "it is estimated that during the high season a grain barge entered the Nile canal every twelve seconds".
248 *Codex Theodosianus* 13, 5, 18 (18 February 390), p. 752 Mommsen – Meyer: IMPP. VAL(ENTINI)ANVS, THEOD(OSIVS) ET ARCAD(IVS) AAA. ALEXANDRO P(RAE)F(ECTO) AVGVSTALI; see today Mommsen – Meyer – Krüger – Rougé – Delmaire, pp. 355–356, with updated bibliography.
249 On the safeguards granted to food supplies by the central State, on the meticulous organisation of the transportation of the *annona civica* from Alexandria to Constantinople and on the detailed legislation, not to mention the limits on the *navicularii*, cfr. Carrié, pp. 1078–1080; Sirks, pp. 202–208, 213–216, 226–237; particularly eloquent on the political interests in the shipping of grain from Alexandria, the testimony of the imperial decrees followed by the famine that hit Constantinople in 408 and the consequent protests in the streets, also reported in the *Codex Theodosianus*: 13, 5, 32 (19 January 409), p. 755 Mommsen – Meyer: IMPP. HONOR(IVS) ET THEOD(OSIVS) AA. ANTHEMIO P(RAEFECTO) P(RAETORI)O; 13, 16, 1 (26 April 409), pp. 791–792 Mommsen – Meyer: IMPP. HONOR(IVS) ET THEOD(OSIVS) AA. MONAXIO P(RAEFECTO) V(RBI).
250 See, for example, Jullien, pp. 19–21.

More recently, Sarolta Takács, a scholar very much interested in material history and the political effects of religious phenomena in the ancient and Byzantine world, recalled, in dealing with the events of 415, that the monopoly of maritime grain transport from Egypt to Constantinople had been extended to the Christian Church of Alexandria[253]. Moreover, she adduced a papyrus testimony, where mention is made, in particular, of a Hierax and his son Theon *nauton ekklesias* (ναυτῶν ἐκκλησίας), sailors of the Church[254]. The value of this find and its dating should probably be investigated further[255]. The homonymy between the Hierax mentioned in the papyrus and the pro-Cyrillian agitator at the meetings of the city assembly at the theatre – the teacher of grammar whom John of Nikiu describes with mellifluous admiration[256] – whose killing by the Jews was the origin of the escalation that we described and which would lead to the terrible assassination of Hypatia, is almost certainly a mere coincidence. Lacking a more detailed prosopographical documentation, the emergence of the name amongst the tattered fibres of P. Ross. Georg. III. 6 is merely suggestive, rather than offering a

---

[251] "Les naviculaires alexandrins étaient chargés de conduire le grain jusqu'à Byzance. Ils étaient payés par l'État à raison d'un sou par cent artabas et étaient tenus, sur réquisition des autorités, de fournir leur vaisseaux", summarises JULLIEN, p. 20. The text of the decree reads as follows: "Iudaeorum corpus ac Samaritanum ad naviculariam functionem non iure vocari cognoscitur; quidquid enim universo corpori videtur indici, nullam specialiter potest obligare personam. Unde sicut inopes vilibus que commerciis occupati naviculariae translationis munus obire non debent, ita idoneos facultatibus, qui ex his corporibus deligi poterunt ad praedictam functionem, haberi non oportet inmunes". These Jewish *navicularii* "partageaient avec le duc augustal la responsabilité des accidents possibles et s'appliquaient à amener sans retard la flotte frumentaire à Constantinople", as specified by JULLIEN, *ibidem*, who asks himself: "Les armateurs juifs, qui étaient nombreux, ne voulurent-ils pas se soumettre à la loi de réquisition, ou trouvèrent-ils que le prix payé était insuffisant? La chose est possible et c'est sans doute une raison de ce genre qui expliquerait la loi de Théodose les obligeant au transport de l'annone". But what counts is that "this law offers evidence that the authorities recognized the Jewish community in Egypt, or in Alexandria, as a 'corpus' (synonym of 'collegium')", as illustrated in LINDER, p. 183; evidence also confirmed by other sources, including Synesius himself: *ibidem*, pp. 182–185 and notes.

[252] JULLIEN, pp. 20–21.

[253] TAKÁCS 1995. On the fleet of the Christian Church of Alexandria see above all WIPSZYCKA 1972; cfr. also SIRKS, p. 234.

[254] TAKÁCS 1995, pp. 57–58 and 31–33. The testimony is taken from P. Ross. Georg. III. 6, which Takács quotes on the basis of Zereteli's edition (ZERETELI, pp. 27–31, n. 6, l. 14). The papyrus' fragment has recently been reunited with the fragment P. Hamb. IV 267 and is now published in KRAMER –HAGEDORN, pp. 148–156. On the basis of this edition, the text reads as follows:

καὶ | νῦν κόμισον διὰ Τιμοθέου
καὶ Θέωνος υἱοῦ | Ἱέρακος ναυτῶν ἐκκλησίας
ἀργυρίου κνίδι|ον ἓν ἔχων τάλαντα ἑπτα-
κόσια, γί(νεται) (τάλαντα) ψ, καὶ | ἐπιστολὴν διὰ τ[ου]ῶν αὐτῶν
ναυτῶν

[255] The dating proposed by the editors, the mid-4th century (336–348 A.D.), is based on the comparison with P. Oxy, XXXIV 2729, datable around 350 A.D.: see KRAMER – HAGEDORN, p. 148, n. 1.

[256] JOANNES DE NIKIU LXXXIV, par. 91, p. 101 Charles.

proper identification²⁵⁷. There remains the observation: "Considering that Egypt was still the empire's main grain supplier [...], the economic advantage Christians could reap after the expulsion of Jews becomes clear"²⁵⁸.

In one of the kaleidoscopic transfigurations of the story of Hypatia handed down by the imagination of the poets, the *Superfluous Heroisms* of Maurice Barrès, we see the protagonist barricaded with her acolytes while the "horde of Christian monks" advance like an "immense thundering herd" towards the gardens of the Serapeum. On hearing the distant chime of the bells, the last priestess, ready for martyrdom, is described by Barrès as lifting her hand before the assembly of her faithful Hellenes and "with a low and laboured voice" exhorting them to "swear to love for all time the noble phrases and elevated thoughts, and to renounce life rather than renouncing their independence"²⁵⁹.

We can ask ourselves whether perhaps, amongst those noble phrases and those elevated thoughts that certainly also the genuine Hypatia exchanged during the private meetings with her Alexandrian disciples and followers, a more material concern did not insinuate itself, that a "political" mind (πολιτικήν) such as Hypatia's²⁶⁰ could not ignore: who would be bidding for the tender to transport grain to Constantinople?

---

257 The comment on the text and the updated and comprehensive bibliography are in KRAMER – HAGEDORN, pp. 153–156. The editors moreover compare the testimony to that of a κυβερνήτου πλοίου καθολικῆς ἐκκλησίας τῆς αὐτ[ῆ]ς Ἀλεξανδρείας in P. Münch. III 99, 8, and that of a πλοῖον Θεοδώρου τοῦ ἐπισκόπου ἡμῶν [sic?] in the previously mentioned P. Oxy. XXXIV 2729,7–8. Cfr. also WIPSZYCKA 1972, p. 63.
258 TAKÁCS 1995, p. 58.
259 Cfr. above, "Superfluous Heroisms" and Appendix *ad loc.*
260 DAMASCIUS, *Vita Isidori* fr. *104, p. 79, 12–18 Zintzen = fr. 43E, p. 130, 1–8 Athanassiadi = SUIDAS Y 166, IV, pp. 644, 31–645, 4 Adler (HARICH-SCHWARZBAUER 2011, p. 247).

Bibliography

ADACHI
    H. ADACHI, *Hypatia, a "Pagan" Holy Woman in Late Antiquity*, in T. MINAMIKAWA (ed.), *New Approaches to the Later Roman Empire*, Kyoto: Kyoto University Press, 2015, pp. 123–135

ADAM
    M. ADAM, *Hypatia*, "Die Frau" 37 (1929), pp. 156–165

AGABITI
    A. AGABITI, *Ipazia. La prima martire della libertà di pensiero*, Roma: Enrico Voghera, 1914 (reprint Ragusa: La Fiaccola, 1998)

ALIC
    M. ALIC, *Hypatia's Heritage: A History of Women in Science from Antiquity to the Late Nineteenth Century*, Boston: Beacon Press, 1986 (reprint London: Women's Press, 2001)

Allgemeine Deutsche Biographie
    Allgemeine Deutsche Biographie, hrsg. durch die Historische Kommission bei der Königl. Akademie der Wissenschaften, Leipzig: Duncker & Humblot, 1875–1912, voll. 1–19 (reprint: Berlin: Duncker und Humblot, 1967–1971)

AL-MAS'UDI
    C. BARBIER DE MEYNARD and A. PAVET DE COURTEILLE (eds.), MAÇOUDI, *Les prairies d'or (Murūj al-dhahab)*, voll. I–IX, Paris: Imprimerie Impériale, 1861–1877 (normative edition by C. PELLAT, voll. I–VII, Beirut: Université Libanaise, 1964–1979)

AMANN
    É. AMANN, s.v. *Cyrille d'Alexandrie*, in J. MAHÉ (ed.), *Dictionnaire de Théologie catholique*, vol. III, Paris: Letouzey et Ané, 1938, col. 2477

AMMIANUS MARCELLINUS
    V. GARDTHAUSEN (ed.), *Ammiani Marcellini Rerum gestarum libri qui supersunt*, voll. I–II, Stutgardiae: in aedibus B.G. Teubner, 1967²

ANDRES
    S. ANDRES, *Die Versuchung des Synesios*, München: Piper, 1971

Anthologia Palatina (AP)
    J. IRIGOIN – F. MALTOMINI – P. LAURENS (eds.), *Anthologie grecque, première partie: Anthologie palatine*, vol. IX, Paris: Les Belles Lettres, 2011
    P. WALTZ (ed.), *Anthologie grecque, première partie: Anthologie palatine*, vol. VIII, Paris: Les Belles Lettres, 1974

ARGOV
    E. ARGOV, *Giving the Heretic a Voice: Philostorgius of Borissus and Greek Ecclesiastical Historiography*, "Athenaeum" 89 (2001), pp. 497–524

ARISTOTELES
    J. AUBONNET (ed.), *Aristotle, Politique. Tome I: Introduction – Livres I–II*, Paris: Les Belles Lettres, 1960

ARNAUD
    FR.TH.M. DE BACULARD D'ARNAUD, *Eudoxie*, in *Œuvres de d'Arnaud 9, Nouvelles historiques*, t. III, Paris: Laporte et Maradan, 1803, pp. 181–312

ARNOLD
    G. ARNOLD, *Unparteiische Kirchen- und Ketzerhistorie: vom Anfang des Neuen Testaments biss auf das Jahr Christi 1688*, Franckfurt am Mayn: Bey Thoas Fritschens sel. Erben, 1729².

ASMUS 1907
    R. ASMUS, *Hypatia in Tradition und Dichtung*, "Studien zur verleichenden Literaturgeschichte" 7 (1907), pp. 11–44

Asmus 1911
> R. Asmus, *Das Leben des Philosophen Isidoros von Damaskios aus Damaskos*, Leipzig: Meiner, 1911

Athanasius
> G.J.M. Bartelink (ed.), *Athanase d'Alexandrie. Vie d'Antoine*, Paris: Cerf, 1994 (éd. revue et augmentée 2004)

Athanassiadi
> P. Athanassiadi, *The Chaldean Oracles: Theology and Theurgy*, in P. Athanassiadi – M. Frede (eds.), *Pagan Monotheism in Late Antiquity*, Oxford: Clarendon Press, 1999, pp. 149–184

Aubé
> B. Aubé, s.v. *Hypatie*, in J.-C.-F. Hoefer (ed.), *Nouvelle Biographie Générale depuis les temps les plus reculés jusqu'à nos jours*, t. XXV, Paris: Didot, 1858, coll. 709–713

Averincev
> S.S. Averincev, Поэтика ранневизантийской литературы [*Poetics of Early Byzantine Literature*], Moskva: Soda, 1997² (Italian translation: *L'anima e lo specchio. L'universo della poetica bizantina*, Bologna: Società Editrice il Mulino, 1988)

Azevedo
> M. Azevedo, *Harmonia entre saber e prazer ou a conciliação entre Aspásia e Sócrates*, "Euphrosyne" 31 (2003), pp. 253–270

Badini Confalonieri 1983
> L. Badini Confalonieri, *Sull'*Ipazia *di Diodata Saluzzo Roero: una variante e qualche considerazione*, "Lettere Italiane" 35 (1983), pp. 122–134, later revised and republished with the title *L'alba di Ipazia: un incontro con il poema di Diodata Saluzzo*, in L. Badini Confalonieri, *Il cammino di madonna Oretta. Studi di letteratura italiana dal Due al Novecento*, Alessandria: Edizioni dell'Orso, 2004, pp. 169–179

Badini Confalonieri 2014
> L. Badini Confalonieri, *L'integralista e la storia: Ipazia tra il poema di Diodata Saluzzo e l'*Atenaide *di Franceschinis*, in *Figure di Ipazia*, a cura di G. Sertoli, Roma: Aracne, 2014, pp. 11–36

Bagnall
> R.S. Bagnall, *Egypt in Late Antiquity*, Princeton: University Press, 1993

Bailly
> J.S. Bailly, *Histoire de l'astronomie moderne*, voll. I-III, Paris: De Bure, 1779–1782

Balboni – Bronzini – Brandi
> D. Balboni – G.B. Bronzini – M.V. Brandi, s.v. *Caterina*, in *Bibliotheca Sanctorum*, vol. III, Roma: Città Nuova, 1962, coll. 953–978

Baldi
> D. Baldi (ed.), *Atanasio di Alessandria. Vita di Antonio*, Roma: Città Nuova, 2015

Baldwin
> S.E. Baldwin, *Charles Kingsley*, Ithaca: Cornell University Press, 1934

Bardy 1949
> G. Bardy, s.v. *Catherine*, in A. De Meyer – Ét. Van Cauwenbergh (eds.), *Dictionnaire d'Histoire et de Géographie Ecclésiastiques*, vol XI, Paris: Letouzey et Ané, 1949, coll. 1503–1505

Bardy 1956
> G. Bardy, s.v. *Cyrille d'Alexandrie*, in A. De Meyer – Ét. Van Cauwenbergh (eds.), *Dictionnaire d'Histoire et de Géographie Ecclésiastiques*, vol. XIII, Paris: Letouzey et Ané, 1956, coll. 1169–1177

Barlatier
> P. Barlatier, *Hypatie. Drame antique en deux parties et en vers*, Marseille: Barlatier, 1907

Barnes
> T.D. Barnes, *When Did Synesius Become Bishop of Ptolemais?*, "Greek, Roman, and Byzantine Studies" 27.3 (1986), pp. 325–329

BARNI
G. BARNI, *I martiri del libero pensiero: corso pubblico di lezioni date nella sala del Gran Consiglio di Ginevra [...] e tradotte da G. Frigyesi*, Firenze: Botta, 1869 (photographic reprint Foggia: Bastogi, 1982)
BARONIUS
C. BARONIUS, *Annales ecclesiastici*, Romae: ex Typographia Vaticana, 1602
BARRÈS 1885
M. BARRÈS, *Héroïsmes superflus*, "Tâches d'Encre" Février 1885 (re-published in *Sous l'oeil des barbares*, Paris: Lemerre, 1888)
BARRÈS 1892
M. BARRÈS, *Examen des trois volumes du "Culte du moi"*, Paris: Perrin, 1892
BARRIOLE
A. BARRIOLE, *Hypatie, la lionne de l'apocalypse*, Paris: Pensée universelle, 1987
BARRY
W.D. BARRY, *Roof Tiles and Urban Violence in the Ancient World*, "Greek, Roman, and Byzantine Studies" 37 (1996), pp. 55–74
BARTHÉLEMY
M. BARTHÉLEMY, *La Libre pensée et ses martyrs*, Paris: Librairie de propagande socialiste et anticléricale, 1904
BATIFFOL
P. BATIFFOL, *Quaestiones Philostorgianae*, Paris: Lahure, 1891
BEER
A. BEER, *Hypatia. Tragödie in fünf Akten*, Leipzig: Brockhaus, 1878
BEERS
W.F. BEERS, *Bloody Iuvenalia: Hypatia, Pulcheria Augusta, and the Beginnings of Cyril of Alexandria's Episcopate*, in LAVALLE NORMAN – PETKAS, pp. 67–86.
BELENKIY 2010
A. BELENKIY, *An Astronomical Murder?*, "Astronomy and Geophysics" 51.2 (2010), pp. 9–13
BELENKIY 2016
A. BELENKIY, *The Novatian 'Indifferent Canon' and Pascha in Alexandria in 414: Hypatia's Murder Case Reopened*, "Vigiliae Christianae" 70 (2016), pp. 373–400
BENEDETTO – ISOLA – RUSSO
C. BENEDETTO – S. ISOLA – L. RUSSO, *Dating Hypatia's Birth: a Probabilistic Model*, "Mathematics and Mechanics of Complex Systems" 5.1 (2017), pp. 19–40
BENEDICTUS XVI
http://w2.vatican.va/content/benedict-xvi/it/audiences/2007/documents/hf_ben-xvi_aud_20071003.html
BERARDO
L. BERARDO, *Ipazia o delle ideologie*, in M. GUGLIELMINETTI – P. TRIVERO (eds.), *Il romanticismo in Piemonte: Diodata Saluzzo*, Atti del Convegno di Studi (Saluzzo, 29 settembre 1990), Firenze: Olschki, 1993, pp. 143–154
BERETTA 1993
G. BERETTA, *Ipazia d'Alessandria*, Roma: Editori Riuniti, 1993
BERETTA 2012
G. BERETTA, *Il segno politico di Ipazia nella poesia civile di Pallada*, "Itinera" 4 (2012), pp. 1–19
BERNAL
M. BERNAL, *Black Athena, the Afroasiatic Roots of the Classical Civilization*, New Brunswick, N. J.: Rutgers University Press, 1987
BERNARD 1991
A. BERNARD, *Les sorciers au pays des philosophes*, Paris: Fayard, 1991

BERNARD 2010

    A. BERNARD, *Theon of Alexandria and Hypatia*, in L. GERSON (ed.), *The Cambridge History of Philosophy in Late Antiquity*, vol. I, Cambridge: Cambridge University Press, 2010, pp. 417–436

BERTHELOT – RUELLE

    M. BERTHELOT – C.E. RUELLE (eds.), *Collection des anciens alchimistes grecs*, voll. I–III, Paris: Steinheil, 1887–1888

BIGONI

    G. BIGONI, *Ipazia Alessandrina*, Venezia: Antonelli, 1887

BISMARCK

    O. von BISMARCK, *Über Königtum und Priestertum* (10 März 1873), in *Fürst Bismarcks gesammelte Reden*, vol. II, Berlin: Globus, s.d., pp. 7–8

BLACKBURN

    S. BLACKBURN (ed.), *Oxford Dictionary of Philosophy*, Oxford – New York: Oxford University Press, 2008^2

BLANC

    O. BLANC (ed.), O. DE GOUGES, *Écrits politiques, 1788–1791. Des femmes dans l'histoire*, Paris: Côté-femmes, 1993 (reprint 2007)

BLAUDEAU

    P. BLAUDEAU, *Alexandrie et Constantinople (451–491): de l'histoire à la Géo-Ecclésiologie*, Rome: École Française de Rome, 2006

BLAUFUß – NIEWÖHNER

    D. BLAUFUß – F. NIEWÖHNER (eds.), *Gottfried Arnold (1666–1714). Mit einer Bibliographie der Arnold-Literatur ab 1714*, Wiesbaden: Harrassowitz, 1995

BLOCH

    H. BLOCH, *The Pagan Revival in the West at the End of the Fourth Century*, in A. MOMIGLIANO (ed.), *The Conflict between Paganism and Christianity in the Fourth Century*, Oxford: Clarendon Press, 1963, pp. 193–218

BOUYOUCAS

    P. BOUYOUCAS, *Hypatie ou la mémoire des hommes*, Saint-Laurent: Dramaturges, 2005

BOWERS

    E. BOWERS, *The Black Agathe, or Old Foes with New Faces*, Philadelphia: U.S. Steam-Power and Job Printing Establishment, 1859 (reprint Whitefish, Montana: Kessinger Publishing, 2010)

BOWERSOCK

    G.W. BOWERSOCK, *Parabalani: A Terrorist Charity in Late Antiquity*, in C. BONNET – A. MARCONE (eds.), *Mélanges Leandro Polverini*, "Anabases" 12 (2010), pp. 45–54

BOWRA

    A. BOWRA, *Palladas and the converted Olympias*, "Byzantinische Zeitschrift" 53 (1960), pp. 1–17

BREGMAN

    J. BREGMAN, *Synesius of Cyrene, Philosopher Bishop*, Berkeley: University of California Press, 1982

BRONZINI

    G.B. BRONZINI, *La leggenda di Santa Caterina di Alessandria. Passioni greche e latine*, "Atti dell'Accademia Nazionale dei Lincei. Memorie della Classe di Scienze Morali" 8.9 (1960), pp. 257–416

BROWN 1971

    P. BROWN, *The Rise and Function of the Holy Man in Late Antiquity*, "The Journal of Roman Studies" 61 (1971), pp. 80–101

BROWN 1988

    P. BROWN, *The Body and Society: Men, Women, and Sexual Renunciation in Early Christianity*, London – Boston: Faber & Faber, 1988

BROWN 1992

    P. BROWN, *Power and Persuasion in Late Antiquity*, Madison: University of Wisconsin Press, 1992

Brown 1993
P. Brown, *Il filosofo e il monaco: due scelte tardoantiche*, in A. Momigliano – A. Schiavone (eds.), *Storia di Roma*, III, 1, Torino: Einaudi, 1993, pp. 877–894

Brown 2012
P. Brown, *Through the Eye of a Needle. Wealth, the Fall of Rome, and the Making of Christianity in the West. 350–550 AD*, Princeton: Princeton University Press, 2012

Brucker
J.J. Brucker, *Historia critica philosophiae. 2. Ab initiis Monarchiae Romanae ad repurgatas usque litteras: periodi secundae pars prima*, Leipzig: Breitkopf, 1742 (reprint Hildesheim – New York: Olms, 1975)

Bucci
O. Bucci, *Intolleranza ellenica e libertà romana nel libro XVI del Codice Teodosiano*, in G. Crifò (ed.), *Politica ecclesiastica e legislazione religiosa dopo l'editto di Teodosio I del 360 d.C.*, Atti del VI Convegno Internazionale dell'Accademia Romanistica Costantiniana (Spello – Perugia – Acquasparta – Tuoro – Orvieto, 12–15 ottobre 1983), Città di Castello (Perugia): Accademia Romanistica Costantiniana, 1986, pp. 363–417

Bury
J.B. Bury, *History of the Later Roman Empire from Arcadius to Irene*, voll. I–II, London: MacMillan, 1889

Butler 1902
A.J. Butler, *The Arab Conquest of Egypt and the Last Thirty Years of the Roman Dominion*, Oxford: Clarendon Press, 1902

Butler 1978
A.J. Butler *The Arab Conquest of Egypt and the Last Thirty Years of the Roman Dominion*, second ed. revised and corrected by P.M. Fraser, Oxford: Clarendon Press, 1978

Cacchioli
E. Cacchioli, *La rinascita di Ipazia: i romanzi di Marie-Florence Ehret e Andrée Ferretti a confronto*, in G. Sertoli (ed.), *Figure di Ipazia*, Roma: Aracne, 2014, pp. 117–141

Caetani
R. Caetani, *Hypatia. Azione lirica in tre atti*, Mainz: Schott's Söhne, 1925

Calvino
I. Calvino, *Le città invisibili*, Torino: Einaudi, 1972 (English translation: *Invisible Cities*. London: Vintage, 2009)

Calvo Poyato
J. Calvo Poyato, *El sueño de Hipatia*, Barcelona: Plaza Janés, 2009

Cameron 1965
A. Cameron, *Palladas and Christian Polemic*, "Journal of Roman Studies" 55 (1965), pp. 17–30

Cameron 1990
A. Cameron, *Isidore of Myletus and Hypatia: on the Editing of Mathematical Texts*, "Greek, Roman, and Byzantine Studies" 31 (1990), pp. 103–187

Cameron 1993
A. Cameron, *The Greek Anthology from Meleager to Planudes*, Oxford: Clarendon Press, 1993

Cameron 2013
A. Cameron, *The Life, Work and Death of Hypatia*, in D. Lauritzen – M. Tardieu (eds.), *Le voyage des légendes. Hommages à Pierre Chuvin*, Paris: CNRS, 2013, pp. 65–82

Cameron 2016
A. Cameron, *Wandering Poets and Other Essays on Late Greek Literature and Philosophy*, Oxford – New York: Oxford University Press, 2016

Cameron 2016a
A. Cameron, *Palladas: New Poems, New Date?*, in Cameron 2016, pp. 91–112

CAMERON 2016b
: A. CAMERON, *Poets and Pagans in Byzantine Egypt*, in CAMERON 2016, pp. 147–162

CAMERON 2016c
: A. CAMERON, *Hypatia: Life, Death, and Works*, in CAMERON 2016, pp. 185–203

CAMERON – LONG
: A. CAMERON – J. LONG, *Barbarians and Politics at the Court of Arcadius*, with a contribution by L. SHERRY, Berkeley – Los Angeles – Oxford: University of California Press, 1993

CAMMILLERI
: R. CAMMILLERI, *Ipazia, la "martire" usata come clava contro i cristiani in barba alla storia*, "Il Giornale" 25 April 2010

CANFORA 1986
: L. CANFORA, *La biblioteca scomparsa*, Palermo: Sellerio, 1986

CANFORA 2000
: L. CANFORA, *Un mestiere pericoloso. La vita quotidiana dei filosofi greci*, Palermo: Sellerio, 2000

CANFORA 2010
: L. CANFORA, *Cirillo e Ipazia nella storiografia cattolica*, "Anabases" 12 (2010), pp. 93–102

CANNUYER – HAWKES
: C. CANNUYER – S. HAWKES, *Coptic Egypt: the Christians of the Nile*, London: Thames and Hudson, 2011

CARILE
: A. CARILE, *Giovanni di Nikius, cronista bizantino-copto del VII secolo*, "Felix Ravenna" 121–122 (1981), pp. 103–155

CAROLLA
: P. CAROLLA, *New Fragments of Priscus from Panion in John Malalas? Issues of Language, Style and Sources*, in L. CARRARA – M. MEIER – Chr. RADTKI-JANSEN (eds.), *Die Weltchronik des Johannes Malalas. Quellenfragen*, Stuttgart: Franz Steiner Verlag, 2017, pp. 137–153

CARRIÉ
: J.M. CARRIÉ, *Les distributions alimentaires dans les cités de l'Empire romain tardif*, "MEFRA" 87. 2 (1975), pp. 995–1101

CASSIODORUS – EPIPHANIUS
: W. JACOB – R. HANSLIK (eds.), *Cassiodori-Epiphanii Historia ecclesiastica*, CSEL, 71 Vindobonae: Hoelder – Pichler – Tempsky, 1952

CASSIUS DIO
: E. CARY – B. FOSTER (eds.), *Cassius Dio, Roman History*, I–IX, Loeb Classical Library 175, Cambridge, Mass.: Harvard University Press, 1924 (reprint *ibid.* 1994)

CASTELLI
: B. CASTELLI, *Traicté de la mesure des eaux courantes [...] traduit du Latin en François*, Castres: Bernard Barcouda Imprimeur du Roy, 1664

CAVE
: W. CAVE, *Scriptorum Ecclesiasticorum Historia Literaria*, Genevae: Chonet – De Tournes, 1705[2]

CHADWICK
: H. CHADWICK, *Early Christian Thought and the Classical Tradition: Studies in Justin, Clement, and Origen*, Oxford: Clarendon Press, 2002 (1966[1])

CHALCONDYLAS
: D. CHALCONDYLAS (ed.), *Suidas. Lexicon graecum*, Mediolani: Johannes Bissolus & Benedictus Mangius, 1499

CHATEAUBRIAND 1828
: F.R. DE CHATEAUBRIAND, *Génie du christianisme*, Paris: Gallimard, 1978 (first edition 1828); (English translation *The Genius of Christianity*, by Ch.I. White, Charleston: Kessinger Publishing, 2010)

CHATEAUBRIAND 1832

F.R. DE CHATEAUBRIAND, *Études ou discours historiques sur la chute de l'Empire Romain* (1831), in *Id.*, *Oeuvres complètes*, vol. V, t. II, Paris: Pourrat Frères, 1832

CHOTJEWITZ

P.O. CHOTJEWITZ, *Der Fall Hypatia. Eine Verfolgung*, Hamburg: Europäische Verlagsanstalt, 2002

CHUVIN

P. CHUVIN, *Chronique des derniers païens. La disparition du paganisme dans l'Empire romain, du regne de Constantin à celui de Justinien*, Paris: Les Belles Lettres – Fayard, 2009²

CHUVIN – TARDIEU

P. CHUVIN – M. TARDIEU, *Le "cynisme" d'Hypatie*, *Historiographie et sources anciennes*, in J. Y. EMPEREUR – C. DÉCOBERT (eds.), *Alexandrie médiévale*, vol. III, Le Caire: Institut Français d' Archéologie Orientale, 2008, pp. 59–68

CLAUDEL

P. CLAUDEL, *Oeuvres complètes*, vol. II, Paris: Gallimard, 1950

CLAUS

A. CLAUS, *Ho scholastikos*, Köln: Gerd Wasmund, 1965

CLEMENS ALEXANDRINUS

G.W. BUTTERWORTH (ed.), *Clement of Alexandria, The Exhortation to the Greeks*, Loeb Classical Library 92, Cambridge, Mass.: Harvard University Press, 2012 (first edition Cambridge, Mass. – London: Harvard University Press – Heinemann, 1919)

CLÉVENOT

M. CLÉVENOT, *Les Hommes de la Fraternité, IVe et Ve siècles. Le triomphe de la Croix*, Paris: Fernand Nathan, 1983

Codex Theodosianus

Theodosiani libri XVI cum Constitutionibus Sirmondianis [...] ediderunt TH. MOMMSEN – P.M. MEYER, vol. I, Berlin: Weidmann, 1905

COLAVITO – PETTA

A. COLAVITO – A. PETTA, *Ipazia. Vita e sogni di una scienziata del IV secolo*, Roma: La Lepre, 2009 (first edition: *Ipazia, scienziata alessandrina. 8 marzo 415 d.C.*, Milano: Lampi di Stampa, 2004)

COLOMBI

E. COLOMBI, *La trasmissione dei Padri greci nell'Occidente latino* [forthcoming]

CONAN

J. CONAN, *Synésius de Cyrène fut-il un converti véritable?*, "Augustinianum" 27 (1987), pp. 237–245

CONSOLINO

F.E. CONSOLINO, *Dagli "exempla" ad un esempio di comportamento cristiano: il "De exhortatione virginitatis" di Ambrogio*, "Rivista Storica Italiana" 94.2 (1982), pp. 455–477

COX

P. COX, *Biography in Late Antiquity: A Quest for the Holy Man*, Berkeley: University of California Press, 1983

CRACCO RUGGINI 1979

L. CRACCO RUGGINI, *Potere e carismi in età imperiale*, "Studi Storici" 20.3 (1979), pp. 585–607

CRACCO RUGGINI 1980

L. CRACCO RUGGINI, *Pagani, ebrei e cristiani: odio sociologico e odio teologico nel mondo antico. Discorso inaugurale*, in *Gli Ebrei nell'alto Medioevo*, Settimane di Studio del Centro Italiano di Studi sull'Alto Medioevo 26, Spoleto: presso la sede del Centro, 1980, pp. 15–117

CRACCO RUGGINI 1988

L. CRACCO RUGGINI, *La donna e il sacro, tra paganesimo e cristianesimo*, in R. UGLIONE (ed.), Atti del II Convegno Nazionale di Studi su "La donna nel mondo antico" (Torino, 18–20 aprile 1988), Torino: Regione Piemonte – Assessorato alla Cultura, 1989, pp. 243–275

CRACCO RUGGINI 1989
   L. CRACCO RUGGINI, *Juridical Status and Historical Role of Women in Roman Patriarchal Society*, "Klio" 71.2 (1989), pp. 604–619
CROCE
   B. CROCE, *La storia come pensiero e come azione* (*History as Thought and as Action*), Bari: Laterza, 1938 (English translation B. CROCE, *History as the Story of Liberty*, by S. SPRIGGE, New York: W.W. Norton & Company, 1941, then Carmel, IN: Liberty Fund, 2000)
CROSS
   F.L. CROSS (ed.), *The Oxford Dictionary of the Christian Church*, Oxford: Oxford University Press, 1997³
CYRILLUS ALEXANDRINUS
   W.H. BURNS – P. ÉVIEUX – L. ARRAGON (eds.) *Cyrille d'Alexandrie, Lettres Festales*, vol. I: *Eps.* 1–6, Sources Chrétiennes 372, Paris: Cerf, 1991
DACIER
   A. DACIER, *Des causes de la corruption du goust*, Paris: Rigaud, 1714
DAMASCIUS
   C. ZINTZEN (ed.), *Damascii Vitae Isidori reliquiae*, Hildesheim: Olms, 1967
   P.N. ATHANASSIADI, (ed., transl. and comm.), *Damascius, The Philosophical History. Text with Translation and Notes*, Athenai: Apamea Cultural Association, 1999
DANIEL
   S.H. DANIEL, *John Toland: His Methods, Manners, and Mind*, Montreal: McGill – Queen's University Press, 1984
DANIÉLOU
   J. DANIÉLOU, *Origen*, English translation, Eugene: Wipf & Stock Publishers, 2016 (1941¹)
DAVANTURE
   M. DAVANTURE, *La jeunesse de Maurice Barrès: 1862–1888*, Paris: H. Champion, 1975
DAVIS
   S.J. DAVIS, *The Early Coptic Papacy: The Egyptian Church and its Leadership in Late Antiquity*, Cairo: The American University in *Cairo* Press, 2004
DE ANGELIS
   F. DE ANGELIS, *I giardini di Ipazia e altri racconti*, Roma: CIAS, 1982
DE POL
   R. DE POL, *La* Hypatia *di Fritz Mauthner*, in G. SERTOLI (ed.), *Figure di Ipazia*, Roma: Aracne, 2014, pp. 81–101
DEAKIN 1994
   M.A.B. DEAKIN, *Hypatia and Her Mathematics*, "American Mathematical Monthly" 101 (1994), pp. 234–243
DEAKIN 1995
   M.A.B. DEAKIN, *The Primary Sources for the Life and Works of Hypatia of Alexandria*, Clayton: Monash University, 1995
DEAKIN 2007
   M.A.B. DEAKIN, *Hypatia of Alexandria. Mathematician and martyr*, Amherst, N.Y.: Prometheus Books, 2007
DEAKIN – HUNTER
   M.A.B. DEAKIN – C.R. HUNTER, *Synesios' Hydroscope*, "Apeiron" 27 (1994), pp. 39–43
DELACENSERIE
   É. DELACENSERIE, *La reconstitution des livres perdus de l'*Histoire tripartite *de Théodore le Lecteur*, in E. AMATO (ed.), *Les historiens fragmentaires de langue grecque à l'époque impériale et tardive*, Actes du Colloque international (Université de Nantes 26–28 novembre 2015) [forthcoming]
DELEHAYE
   H. DELEHAYE, *Les martyrs d'Égypte*, "Analecta Bollandiana" 40 (1922), pp. 114–154

DELIA
   D. DELIA, *The Population of Roman Alexandria*, "Transactions of the American Philological Association" 118 (1988), pp. 275–292
DENZINGER – SCHÖNMETZER
   H. DENZINGER – A. SCHÖNMETZER, *Enchiridion symbolorum, definitionum et declarationum de rebus fidei et morum*, Freiburg – Basel – Roma – Wien: Herder, 1997
DESIDERI
   P. DESIDERI, *Dione di Prusa. Un intellettuale greco nell'impero romano*, Messina-Firenze: D'Anna, 1978
DIDEROT
   D. DIDEROT, s. v. *Éclectisme*, in D. DIDEROT – J. LE ROND D'ALEMBERT (eds.), *Encyclopédie, ou Dictionnaire raisonné des sciences, des arts et des métiers, par une Société de gens de lettres*, Paris: Briasson – David – Le Breton – Durand, 1755, vol. V, p. 282 a – b (anastatic reprint Parma: Franco Maria Ricci, 1970, vol. XIV, pp. 3 – 19)
DIEHL
   C. DIEHL, *Figures byzantines*, Paris: A. Colin, 1908
DIONIGI ORFEI
   E. DIONIGI ORFEI, *Del poema d'Ipazia, ossia delle Filosofie, mandato alla luce dalla Marchesa Diodata Saluzzo Roero*, "Giornale Arcadico di Scienze, Lettere ed Arti" 36 (October, November and December 1827), pp. 286 – 295
DODDS
   E.R. DODDS, *Pagan and Christian in an Age of Anxiety*, Cambridge: Cambridge University Press, 1965
DONOVAN
   S. DONOVAN, *Hypatia. Mathematician, Inventor, and Philosopher*, Minneapolis: Compass Point Books, 2008
D'OSORIO
   L. D'OSORIO, *Hypathia, arpenteur de l'absolu*, Paris: Harmattan, 2005
DOYSON
   D. DOYSON, *Cities of God. Communist Utopias in Greek Thought*, New York – Oxford: Oxford University Press, 1992
DRAPER
   J.W. DRAPER, *History of the Intellectual Development of Europe*, New York: Harper & Brothers, 1863 (reprint Memphis: General Books, 2012)
DUCHESNE
   L. DUCHESNE, *Histoire ancienne de l'Église*, voll. I-III, Paris: Fontemoing, 1910²
DUPIN
   L. ELLIES DUPIN, *Nouvelle Bibliothèque des auteurs ecclésiastiques*, vol. IV, Paris: à Mons, aux dépens des Huguetan, 1691²
DURRELL
   L. DURRELL, *Clea*, London: Faber & Faber, 1960
DZIELSKA 1991
   M. DZIELSKA, *Ipazia e la sua cerchia intellettuale*, in M. SALAMON (ed.), *Paganism in the Later Roman Empire and in Byzantium*, Kraków: Jagiellonian University Press, 1991, pp. 45 – 60
DZIELSKA 1993
   M. DZIELSKA, *Hypatia z Aleksandrii*, Kraków: Jagiellonian University Press, 1993
DZIELSKA 1995
   M. DZIELSKA, *Hypatia of Alexandria*, English translation by F. LYRA, Cambridge, Mass.: Harvard University Press, 1995
ECO 2000
   U. ECO, *Baudolino*, Milano: Bompiani, 2000

Eco 2010
  U. Eco, *Ipazziammo!*, "l' Espresso" 30th April 2010
Ehret
  M.F. Ehret, *Hypatie, fille de Théon*, Mont de Marsan: Atelier des Bridsants, 2001
Elli
  A. Elli, *Storia della Chiesa Copta*, I. *L'Egitto romano-bizantino e cristiano*, Cairo – Jerusalem: Franciscan Centre of Christian Oriental Studies, 2003
Engels
  D. Engels, *Zwischen Philosophie und Religion: Weibliche Intellektuelle in Spätantike und Islam*, in D. Groß (ed.), *Gender schafft Wissen, Wissenschaft Gender. Geschlechtsspezifische Unterscheidungen und Rollenzuschreibungen im Wandel der Zeit*, Kassel: Kassel University Press, 2009, pp. 97–124
Erskine
  A. Erskine, *Culture and Power in Ptolemaic Egypt: the Museum and Library of Alexandria*, "Greece and Rome" 42 (1995), pp. 38–48
Eschenbacher
  W. Eschenbacher, *Fritz Mauthner und die deutsche Literatur um 1900. Eine Untersuchung zur Sprachkrise der Jahrhundertwende*, Bern: Peter Lang, 1977
Escolan
  P. Escolan, *Monachisme et église. Le monachisme syrien du IVe au VIIe siècle: un monachisme charismatique*, Paris: Beauchesne, 1999
Etymologicum Magnum
  Etymologicum Magnum seu Lexikon sapientissime vocabulorum origine indagans [...] recensuit et notis variorum instruxit Th. Gaisford, Oxonii: e Typographeo Academico, 1848
Eunapius
  I. Giangrande (ed.), *Eunapii Vitae sophistarum*, Romae: Typis Publicae Officinae Polygraphicae, 1956
  M. Civiletti (transl. and comm.), *Eunapio, Vite di filosofi e sofisti*, Milano: Bompiani, 2007
Evagrius Scholasticus
  A. Hübner (ed.), *Evagrius Scholasticus, Historia Ecclesiastica*, Turnhout: Brepols, 2007
Évrard
  É. Évrard, *À quel titre Hypatie enseigna-t-elle la philosophie?*, "Revue des Études Grecques" 90 (1977), pp. 69–74
Fabricius
  A. Fabricius, *Bibliotheca Graeca*, voll. I-XIV, Hamburgi: sumptu Christiani Liebezeit, typis Spiringianis, 1705–1728
Feldman
  L.H. Feldman, *Jew and Gentile in the Ancient World: Attitudes and Interactions from Alexander to Justinian*, Princeton, NJ: Princeton University Press, 1992
Fernandez
  G. Fernandez, *La muerte de Hipatia*, "Erytheia" 62 (1985), pp. 269–282
Ferretti
  A. Ferretti, *Renaissance en Paganie*, Montreal: L'Hexagone, 1987
Fielding
  H. Fielding, *A Journey from this World to the Next* (1743), London: Cooke, [1798]
Fincher
  J. Fincher, *Hypatia's Sisters? Gender and the Triumph of Knowledge in Nonnus' Dionysiaca*, in LaValle Norman – Petkas, pp. 151–169
Flacius
  Mathias Flacius, *Ecclesiastica historia, integram Ecclesiae Christi ideam* [...] *secundum singulas centurias perspicuo ordine complectens* [...], Basileae: per Ioannem Oporinum, 1559–1574

FLAUBERT
    G. FLAUBERT, *Bouvard et Pécuchet*, Paris: A. Lemerre, 1881
FLEURY
    C. FLEURY (ed.), *Histoire ecclésiastique*, Paris: Emery – Saugrain – Pierre Martin, 1722–1738
FLICHE – MARTIN
    A. FLICHE – V. MARTIN (eds.), *Histoire de l'Église, depuis les origines jusqu'à nos jours*, vol. IV, Paris: Bloud & Gay, 1948
FLICHE – MARTIN – FRUTAZ
    Storia della Chiesa, cominciata da A. FLICHE e V. MARTIN, ed. it. a cura di A.P. FRUTAZ, vol. IV, Torino: S.A.I.E., 1961
FORSTER
    E.M. FORSTER, *Alexandria. A History and a Guide*, Alexandria: Whitehead Morris, 1922 (third edition Gloucester, Mass.: P. Smith, 1968)
FOURIKIS
    N. FOURIKIS, *Hypatia's Feud*, Denver, CO: Outskirts Press, 2011
FOURNEL
    V. FOURNEL, s.v. *Dacier, Anne Lefèvre*, in J.Chr.F. HOEFER (ed.), *Nouvelle biographie générale depuis les temps les plus reculés jusqu'à nos jours, avec les renseignements bibliographiques et l'indication des sources à consulter*, vol. XI, Paris: Didot, 1855, coll. 757–764
FOWDEN 1978
    G. FOWDEN, *Bishops and Temples in the Eastern Roman Empire, A.D. 320–434*, "Journal of Theological Studies" 29.1 (1978), pp. 53–78
FOWDEN 1982
    G. FOWDEN, *The Pagan Holy Man in Late Antique Society*, "Journal of Hellenic Studies" 102 (1982), pp. 33–59
FOWDEN 1986
    G. FOWDEN, *The Egyptian Hermes: a Historical Approach to the Late Pagan Mind*, Cambridge: Cambridge University Press, 1986
FRANCESCHINIS
    F. M. FRANCESCHINIS, *L'Atenaide*, Padova: Tipografia della Minerva, 1822–1823 (1837²)
FRANDON
    I.-M. FRANDON, *L'Orient de Maurice Barrès*, Genève-Lille: Droz-Giard, 1952
FRASER
    P.M. FRASER, *Ptolemaic Alexandria*, Oxford: Clarendon Press, 1972
FREND
    W.H.C. FREND, *The Rise of the Monophysite Movement. Chapters in the History of the Church in the Fifth and Sixth Centuries*, Cambridge: Cambridge University Press, 1972
GAJERI
    E. GAJERI, *Ipazia: un mito letterario*, Roma: La Meridiana, 1992
GALI
    R. GALI, *Hypatia y la eternidad*, Madrid: Es Editiones, 2009
GALVÃO-SOBRINHO
    C.R. GALVÃO-SOBRINHO, *Doctrine and Power: Theological Controversy and Christian Leadership in the Later Roman Empire*, Berkeley: University of California Press, 2006
GARCÍA
    O. GARCÍA, *El jardin de Hipatia*, Madrid: Espasa, 2009
GARIN
    E. GARIN, *Il platonismo come ideologia della sovversione europea*, in E. HORA – E. KESSLER (eds.), *Studia Humanitatis. Ernesto Grassi zum 70. Geburtstag*, München: W. Fink, 1973, pp. 114–120

GARZYA

A. GARZYA, *Introduzione*, in A. GARZYA (ed.), *Sinesio, Opere. Epistole, Operette, Inni*, Torino: UTET, 1989, pp. 9–34.

GAUDEMET

J. GAUDEMET, *Politique ecclésiastique et législation religieuse après l'édit de Theodose I de 380*, in G. CRIFÒ (ed.), *Politica ecclesiastica e legislazione religiosa dopo l'editto di Teodosio I del 360 d.C.*, Atti del VI Convegno Internazionale dell'Accademia Romanistica Costantiniana (Spello – Perugia – Acquasparta – Tuoro – Orvieto, 12–15 ottobre 1983), Città di Castello (Perugia): Accademia Romanistica Costantiniana, 1986, pp. 1–22

GAUTIER

T. GAUTIER, *Rapport sur les progrès de la poésie*, in S. USTAZADE – S. DE SACY – TH. GAUTIER – P. FÉVAL – ÉD. THIERRY (eds.), *Rapport sur le progrès des lettres depuis vingt-cinq ans*, Paris: Hachette – Imprimerie impériale, 1868, pp. 67–141

GEBREMEDHIN

F. GEBREMEDHIN, *Life-giving Blessing. An Inquiry into the Eucharistic Doctrine of Cyril of Alexandria*, Uppsala: Acta Universitatis Upsaliensis – Stockholm: Almqvist & Wiksell, 1977

GEFFCKEN

J. GEFFCKEN, *Der Ausgang des griechisch-römischen Heidentums*, Heidelberg: Winter, 1920

GENTZ – WINKELMANN

G. GENTZ – F. WINKELMANN, *Die Kirchengeschichte des Nicephorus Callistus Xanthopoulos und ihre Quellen*, Berlin: Akademie Verlag, 1966

GERTZ

S. GERTZ, '*A Mere Geometer'? Hypatia in the Context of Alexandrian Neoplatonism*, in LAVALLE NORMAN – PETKAS, pp. 133–150

GIBBON

E. GIBBON, *The History of the Decline and Fall of the Roman Empire*, edited by D. WOMERSLEY, London – New York: Penguin Books, 1995 (first ed. 1776–1789)

GIORGIADÈS – LACKANY

P. GIORGIADÈS – R. LACKANY, *Une Martyre païenne: la mort d'Hypatie*, Alexandria: Les Publications de l'Atelier, 1982

GIORELLO

G. GIORELLO, *Senza dio. Del buon uso dell'ateismo*, Milano: Longanesi, 2010

GÓMEZ DE LIAÑO

I. GÓMEZ DE LIAÑO, *Hipatia, Bruno, Villamediana: tres tragedias del espiritu*, Madrid: Siruela, 2008

GONZÁLEZ SUÁRES 2002

A. GONZÁLEZ SUÁRES, *Hipatia (¿355?-415 d. de C.)*, Madrid: Otro, 2002

GONZÁLEZ SUÁRES 2012

A. GONZÁLEZ SUÁRES, *Hipatia: otra hija del Nilo*, "Devenires. Revista de Filosofia y Filosofia de Literatura" 11 (2012), pp. 16–32

GOUILLARD

J. GOUILLARD, *L'hérésie dans l'empire byzantin des origines au XIIe siècle*, "Travaux et Mémoires" 1 (1965), pp. 299–324

GOUJET

C.-P. GOUJET, *Dissertation sur Hypacie, où l'on justifie Saint Cyrille d'Alexandrie sur la mort de cette Sçavante*, in *Continuation des Mémoires de littérature et d'histoire*, par le P. DESMOLETS, t. V, Paris: Nyon fils, 1749, pp. 138–187

GOULET-CAZÉ

M.O. GOULET-CAZÉ, *L'arrière-plan scolaire de la Vie de Plotin*, in L. BRISSON – M.O. GOULET – CAZÉ – D. O' BRIEN (eds.), *Porphyre. La vie de Plotin*, Paris: Vrin, 1982, pp. 231–327

GREGORAS
    L. SCHOPEN (ed.) *Nicephori Gregorae Byzantina Historia*, voll. I–II, Bonn: Weber, 1829–1830
    J.L. van DIETEN – F. TINNEFELD (eds., transl. and comm.), *Nikephoros Gregoras, Rhomäische Geschichte, Historia Rhomaike*, voll. I-VI, Stuttgart: A. Hiersemann, 1973–2007
GREGORY
    T.E. GREGORY, s.v. *Parabalani*, in A.P. KAZHDAN (ed.), *Oxford Dictionary of Byzantium*, vol. III, New York – Oxford: Oxford University Press, 1991, p. 1582
GREYDANUS
    S.D. GREYDANUS, *Agora: An Atheist Sets the Record Straight*, "National Catholic Register" 28 May 2010
GRIFFITH
    S. GRIFFITH, *Arabic Christianity in the Monasteries of 9th Century Palestine*, Northampton: Galliard, Variorum Reprints, 1992
GRINSTEIN – CAMPBELL
    L.S. GRINSTEIN – P.J. CAMPBELL, *Women of Mathematics: A Bibliographic Sourcebook*, New York: Greenwood Press, 1987
HAAS 1997
    C. HAAS, *Alexandria in Late Antiquity. Topography and Social Conflict*, Baltimore – London: Johns Hopkins University Press, 1997
HAAS 2002
    C. HAAS, *John Moschus and Late Antique Alexandria*, in C. DECOBERT – J.Y. EMPEREUR (eds.), *Alexandrie médiévale*, vol. II, Cairo: I.F.A.O., 2002, pp. 47–59
HAASE
    M. HAASE, *The Shattered Icon: An Alternative Reading of Hypatia's Killing (Socrates,* Hist. eccl. *7.15.5–7, John of Nikiu,* Chron. *84.100–103, and Rufinus,* Hist. eccl. *11.23)*, in LAVALLE NORMAN – PETKAS, pp. 87–117
HADOT
    I. HADOT, *Le problème du néoplatonisme alexandrin: Hieroclès et Simplicius*, Paris: Études Augustiniennes, 1978
HAFNER
    G. HAFNER, *Drei Bildnis Medaillons aus Aphrodisias*, "Revue d'Histoire de l'Art" 22 (1998), pp. 27–35
HAHN 2004
    J. HAHN, *Gewalt und religiöser Konflikt: Studien zu den Auseinandersetzungen zwischen Christen, Heiden, und Juden im Osten des Römischen Reiches (von Konstantin bis Theodosius II)*, Berlin: Akademie Verlag, 2004
HAHN 2008
    J. HAHN, *The Conversion of the Cult Statues: The Destruction of the Serapeum 392 AD and the Transformation of Alexandria into the "Christ Loving City"* in J. HAHN – S. HEMMEL – U. GOTTER (eds.), *From Temple to Church: Destruction and Renewal of Local Cultic Topography in Late Antiquity*, Leiden: Brill, 2008, pp. 335–363
HARICH-SCHWARZBAUER 2002
    H. HARICH-SCHWARZBAUER, *Erinnerungen an Hypatia von Alexandria: zur fragmentierten Philosophinnenbiographie des Synesios von Kyrene*, in B. FEICHTINGER – G. WÖHRLE (eds.), *Gender Studies in den Altertumswissenschaften: Möglichkeiten und Grenzen*, Trier: Wissenschaftlicher Verlag Trier, 2002, pp. 97–108
HARICH-SCHWARZBAUER 2011
    H. HARICH-SCHWARZBAUER, *Hypatia: die spätantiken Quellen: eingeleitet, kommentiert und interpretiert*, Bern – Berlin – Bruxelles et al.: P. Lang, 2011
HARING
    N.M. HARING, *The Character and Range of Influence of St. Cyril of Alexandria on Latin Theology*, "Medieval Studies" 12 (1950), pp. 1–19

HARTLEY
    A.J. HARTLEY, *The Novels of Charles Kingsley*, Folkestone: Hour-Glass, 1977

HEDSTROM – DARLENE
    BR. HEDSTROM – L. DARLENE, *Redrawing a Portrait of Egyptian Monasticism*, in D. BLANKS – M. FRASSETTO – A. LIVINGSTONE (eds.), *Medieval Monks and Their World, Ideas and Realities: Studies in Honor of Richard Sullivan*, Leiden: Brill, 2006, pp. 11–34

HENRY
    P. HENRY, *Étude sur Hypatie*, unedited, mentioned in "Revue Belge de Philologie et d'Histoire" 18.1 (1939), p. 286

HERCHER
    R. HERCHER (ed.), *Epistolographi Graeci*, Paris: Didot, 1873 (photographic reprint Amsterdam: Hakkert, 1965)

HERNÁNDEZ DE LA FUENTE
    D. HERNÁNDEZ DE LA FUENTE, *Sobre la figura de Hipatia en las fuentes literarias y en Ágora*, in A.J. QUIROGA (ed.), *Texto, traducción, !acción! El legado clásico en el cine*, Almería: Círculo Rojo, 2018, pp. 115–123

HERRIN
    J. HERRIN, *Mathematical Mysteries in Byzantium: the Transmission of Fermat's Last Theorem*, "Dialogos" 6 (2000), pp. 21–44

HILLMAN
    J. HILLMAN, *La giustizia di Afrodite – Aphrodites' justice*, Italian translation by S. RONCHEY, Capri: La Conchiglia, 2008

HOCHE
    R. HOCHE, *Hypatia, die Tochter Theons*, "Philologus" 15 (1860), pp. 435–474

HOLMES 1973
    G.S. HOLMES, *The Trial of Doctor Sacheverell*, London: Eyre Methuen, 1973

HOLMES 1976
    G.S. HOLMES, *The Sacheverell Riots: the Crowd and the Church in Early Eighteenth Century London*, "Past and Present" 72.1 (1976), pp. 55–85

HOLMES 1986
    G.S. HOLMES, *Politics, Religion and Society in England, 1679–1742*, London: Hambledon Press, 1986

HOPPE
    E. HOPPE, *Mathematik und Astronomie in klassischen Altertum*, Heidelberg: C. Winter, 1911 (reprint Wiesbaden: Sändig, 1966)

HUBBARD
    E. HUBBARD, *Hypatia*, East Aurora, NY: *Roycrofters*, 1901

HUNGER
    H. HUNGER, *Die hochsprachliche profane Literatur der Byzantiner*, vol. I, München: Beck, 1978

IRMSCHER
    J. IRMSCHER, *Pallas und Hypatia (Zu Anthologia Palatina 9, 40)*, in B. GEROV – V. VELKOV – V. TAPKOVA – ZAIMOVA (eds.), Actes de la VIème Conférence Internationale des Études Classiques des Pays Socialistes (Plovdiv, 24–28 aprile 1962), Sofija: Académie Bulgare des Sciences, 1963, pp. 313–318

JACOBACCI
    R. JACOBACCI, *Women of Mathematics*, "Arithmetic Teacher" 17.4 (1970), pp. 316–324

JAMES
    H. JAMES, *The Bostonians*, London – New York: MacMilland & Co., 1886

JAMESON
    A.B. JAMESON, *Sacred and Legendary Art*, voll. I–II, London: Longmans, Green & Co., 1874

JAMESON – EASTLAKE
    A.B. JAMESON – L. EASTLAKE, *The History of Our Lord in Art*, London: Longmans, Green & Co., 1892

JAMESON – HURLL
: A.B. JAMESON, *Sacred and Legendary Art*, with additional notes by E.M. HURLL [...], voll. I-II, Boston-New York: Houghton & Mifflin, 1904

JÄGER 1956
: W. JÄGER, s.v. *Hypatia* in *Die Religion in Geschichte und Gegenwart*, vol. III, Tübingen: J. C. B. Mohr, 1956³, col. 502

JÄGER 1961
: W. JÄGER, *Early Christianity and Greek Paideia*, English translation, Cambridge, Mass.: Belknap Press of Harvard University Press, 1961

JOANNES DE NIKIU
: R.H. CHARLES (transl. and comm.), *The Chronicle of John, Bishop of Nikiou*, translated from Hermann Zotenberg's Ethiopic text, London – Oxford: published for the Text and Translation Society by Williams & Norgate, 1916 (reprint Merchandville, NJ: Evolution, 2007)
: H. ZOTENBERG (ed. and transl.), *Chronique de Jean, évêque de Nikiou, texte éthiopien publié et traduit*, Paris: Imprimerie nationale, 1883 (reprint Paris: Hachette Livre, 2014)

JOHNSTON
: S. Iles JOHNSTON, *Sosipatra and the Theurgic Life: Eunapius* Vitae Sophistarum *6.6.5 – 6.9.24*, in J. RÜPKE – W. SPICKEMANN (eds.), *Reflections on Religious Individuality: Greco-Roman and Judaeo-Christian Texts and Practices*, Berlin: De Gruyter, 2012, pp. 99 – 118

JUGIE
: M. JUGIE, s.v. *Cirillo*, in *Enciclopedia Cattolica*, vol. II (1950), col. 1716

JULIANUS APOSTATA
: G. ROCHEFORT (ed.), *Oeuvres complètes de l'empereur Julien*, t. II, Paris: Les Belles Lettres, 1963

JULLIEN
: L. JULLIEN, *Les Juifs d'Alexandrie dans l'Antiquité*, Alexandrie: Éditions du Scarabée, [1944]

KAÇAR
: T. KAÇAR, *Iskenderiye kilisesinde siddet geleneği ve Hypatia'nin ölümü* [*The Tradition of Violence of the Alexandrian Church and the Death of Hypatia*], "Toplumsal Tarih Dergisi" 14.79 (2000), pp. 54 – 57

KALDELLIS
: A. KALDELLIS, *The Works and Days of Hesychios the Illoustrios of Miletos*, "Greek, Roman, and Byzantine Studies" 45 (2005), pp. 381 – 403

KASHER
: A. KASHER, *The Jews in Hellenistic and Roman Egypt. The Struggle for Equal Rights*, Tübingen: Mohr, 1985

KAZHDAN – RONCHEY
: A. KAZHDAN – S. RONCHEY, *L'aristocrazia bizantina*, postscript by L. Canfora, Palermo: Sellerio, 1999²

KETTENBURG
: K. VON DER KETTENBURG, *Julianus Apostata. Tragödie*, Berlin: in der Salfeldschen Buchhandlung, 1812

KIESEWETTER
: J.Chr. KIESEWETTER, *Hipparchum Theonas, doctamque Hypatiam, in Mathesi celebres. Dissertatione Historico-Mathematica* [...] *exhibet* [...], Jena: Krebs, 1689

KINGSLEY
: C. KINGSLEY, *Hypatia, or New Foes with an Old Face*, voll. I-II, London: E. A. Weeks & Company, 1853 (reprint London – New York: Everyman's Library, 1968)

KLAVER
: J.M.I. KLAVER, *The Apostle of the Flesh: A Critical Life of Charles Kingsley*, Leiden – Boston: Brill, 2006

KLEIN
: R. KLEIN, *Die Ermordung der Philosophin Hypatia: Zum Kampf um die politische Macht in Alexandria*, in F.B.J. WUBBE – G. CRIFÒ – ST. GIGLIO (eds.), *Atti dell'Accademia Romanistica Costantiniana*, XI Convegno Internazionale in onore di Felix B.J. Wubbe, Napoli: Edizioni Scientifiche Italiane, 1996, pp. 509 – 524; reprinted in R. KLEIN – R. VON HAEHLING – K. SCHERBERICH (eds.), *Roma versa per aevum: ausgewählte*

Schriften zur heidnischen und christlichen Spätantike, Hildesheim-Zürich-New York: Georg Olms Verlag, 1999

KLINE

M. KLINE, *Mathematical Thought from Ancient to Modern Times*, New York: Oxford University Press, 1972

KNORR

W. KNORR, *Textual Studies in Ancient and Mediaeval Geometry*, Boston: Birkhäuser, 1989

KOPALLIK

J. KOPALLIK, *Cyrillus von Alexandrien. Eine Biographie, nach den Quellen gearbeitet*, Mainz: Kirchheim, 1881

KRAMER

C. KRAMER, *Holy Murder. The Death of Hypatia of Alexandria. A Story where Good is Cloaked beneath a Pagan's Cape and Evil Wears a Bishop's Crown*, West Conshohocken, PA: Infinity Publishing, 2006

KRAMER – HAGEDORN

B. KRAMER – D. HAGEDORN (eds.), *Griechische Papyri der Staats- und Universitatsbibliothek Hamburg (P. Hamb. 4)*, Stuttgart – Leipzig: Teubner, 1998

KRISCHER

T. KRISCHER, *Ein Zeugnis zur Geschichte der Impetustheorie*, "Hermes" 122 (1994), pp. 381–383

KRUMBACHER

K. KRUMBACHER, *Geschichte der byzantinischen Literatur*, voll. I-II, München: Beck, 1897²

KUNST

H. KUNST, *Geschichte der Legenden der heiligen Katharina von Alexandria und der heiligen Maria Ägyptiaca*, Halle: M. Niemeyer, 1890

LA CALPRENÈDE

G. de Costes de LA CALPRENÈDE, *Faramond où l'Histoire de France*, tt. I-VII, Paris: Sommaville, 1661–1670, completed by P. d'Ortigue de VAUMORIÈRE (tt. VIII–XII); definitive posthumous edition tt. I-XII, Paris: Sommaville et al., 1664–1670

LA SPISA

P. LA SPISA, *Fra storia e allegoria: Ipazia in un romanzo egiziano contemporaneo*, in G. SERTOLI (ed.), *Figure di Ipazia*, Roma: Aracne, 2014, pp. 229–254

LABRIOLLE

P. DE LABRIOLLE, *La réaction païenne. Étude sur la polémique antichrétienne du Ier au VIIe siècle*, Paris: L'artisan du livre, 1934 (photographic reprint Paris: Cerf, 2005)

LACOMBRADE 1951

C. LACOMBRADE, *Synésios de Cyrène hellène et chrétien*, Paris: Les Belles Lettres, 1951

LACOMBRADE 1954

C. LACOMBRADE, *Autour du meurtre d'Hypatie*, "Pallas" 2 (1954), pp. 18–28

LACOMBRADE 1972

C. LACOMBRADE, *Hypatie: le mythe et l'histoire*, "Bulletin de la Société Toulousaine d'Études Classiques" 16 (1972), pp. 5–20

LACOMBRADE 1994

C. LACOMBRADE, s.v. *Hypatia*, in Reallexikon für Antike und Christentum, vol. XVI (1994), coll. 956–967

LACOMBRADE 1995

C. LACOMBRADE, *Hypatie. Un singulier "revival" du cynisme*, "Byzantion" 65 (1995), pp. 529–531

LACOMBRADE 2001

C. LACOMBRADE, *Hypatie, Synésios de Cyrène et le patriarcat alexandrin*, posthumous edition by N. AUJOULAT (ed.), "Byzantion" 71 (2001), pp. 404–421

LA CROZE

M. Veyssière de LA CROZE, *Histoire du Christianisme des Indes*, La Haye: Vaillant & Prevost, 1724

LAMBROPOULOU

V. LAMBROPOULOU, Ὑπατία ἡ Ἀλεξανδρινὴ φιλόσοφος [*Hypatia, the Alexandrian Philosopher*], "Platon" 29 (1977), pp. 65–78 (with a summary in French)

LAMIRANDE

E. LAMIRANDE, *Hypatie, Synésios et la fin des dieux. L'histoire et la fiction*, "Studies in Religion/Sciences religieuses" 18 (1989), pp. 467–489

LAMPROS

S. LAMPROS, Παλαιολόγεια καὶ Πελοποννησιακά [*Palaiologeia kai Peloponnesiaka*], voll. I-IV, Athenai: V.N. Gregoriades, 1926–1930

LANATA

G. LANATA, *Gli atti dei martiri come documenti processuali*, Milano: Giuffrè, 1973

LAPATZ

F. LAPATZ, *Lettres de Synésius, traduites pour la première fois et suivies d'études sur les derniers moments de l'hellénisme*, Paris: Didier et Cie, 1870

LASTEYRIE

C.-P. de LASTEYRIE, *Vie d'Hypatie, femme célèbre, professeur de philosophie dans le deuxième siècle* [sic] *à l'école d'Alexandrie*, in *Sentences de Sextius, philosophe pythagoricien*, Paris: Pagnerre, 1843, pp. 273–304

LAVALLE NORMAN – PETKAS

D. LAVALLE NORMAN – A. PETKAS (eds.), *Hypatia of Alexandria: Her Context and Legacy*, Tübingen: Mohr Siebeck, 2020

LECONTE DE LISLE

Oeuvres de Leconte de Lisle, édition critique par E. PICH, vol. I: *Poèmes antiques*, Paris: Les Belles Lettres, 1977 (first ed. 1847, second ed. 1874)

LENKOWSKI

S. LENKOWSKI, *Hypatia i jej epoka*, "Kwartalnik Klasyczny" 3 (1930), pp. 473–489

LEONARD

V. LEONARD, *The Ideal (Bleeding?) Female: Hypatia of Alexandria and Distorting Patriarchal Narratives*, in LAVALLE NORMAN – PETKAS, pp. 171–192

LEOPARDI

G. LEOPARDI, *Storia della astronomia dalla sua origine fino all'anno MDCCCXII*, ed. A. Massarenti, appendix by L. Zampieri, Milano: La vita felice, 1997

LEWIS

T. LEWIS, *The History of Hypatia, A Most Impudent School-Mistress of Alexandria: Murder'd and Torn to Pieces by the Populace, in Defence of Saint Cyril and the Alexandrian Clergy. From the Aspersions of Mr Toland*, London: T. Bickerton, 1721

LEWY – TARDIEU

H. LEWY – M. TARDIEU, *Chaldaean Oracles and Theurgy. Mysticism, Magic, and Platonism in the Later Roman Empire*, Paris: Études Augustiniennes, 2011^3

LIÉBAERT

J. LIÉBAERT, *Saint Cyrille d'Alexandrie et la culture antique*, "Mélanges de Science Réligieuse" 12 (1955), pp. 5–21

LIEBESCHÜTZ

J.H.W.G. LIEBESCHÜTZ, *Why did Synesius become Bishop of Ptolemais?*, "Byzantion" 56 (1986), pp. 180–195

LIGIER

H. LIGIER, *De Hypatia philosopha et eclecticismi Alexandrini fine* (Thèse de Doctorat, Université de Dijon), Dijon: Chassel, 1879

LINCOLN
    B. LINCOLN, *Meat and Society, Sacrifice and Creation, Butchers and Philosophy*, "L'Uomo" 9 (1985), pp. 9–29

LINDER
    A. LINDER (ed.), *The Jews in Roman imperial legislation* (translation of *Ha-Yehudim yeha-Yahadut be-ḥuḳe ha-ḳesarut ha-Romit*), Detroit, Mich.: Wayne State University Press – Jerusalem: Israel Academy of Sciences and Humanities, 1987

LIVREA 1973
    H. LIVREA (ed.), *Dionysii Bassaricon et Gigantiadis Fragmenta*, Romae: in aedibus Athenaei, 1973

LIVREA 1986
    E. LIVREA, *Studi cercidei (P. Oxy. 1082)*, Bonn: Habelt, 1986

LIVREA 1987
    E. LIVREA, *Il Poeta ed il Vescovo. La questione nonniana e la storia*, "Prometheus" 13 (1987), pp. 97–123

LIVREA 1995
    E. LIVREA, *I gynaikeia rhake di Ipazia [Hypatia's menstrual cloths]*, "Eikasmos" 6 (1995), pp. 271–273; reprinted in E. LIVREA, *Da Callimaco a Nonno. Dieci studi di poesia ellenistica*, Firenze: D'Anna, 1995, pp. 129–132

LIVREA 1997
    E. LIVREA, *AP 9.400: iscrizione funeraria di Ipazia?*, "Zeitschrift für Papyrologie und Epigraphik" 117 (1997), pp. 99–102

LIVREA 2000
    E. LIVREA (ed.), *Nonno di Panopoli, Parafrasi del Vangelo di S. Giovanni: Canto B*, Bologna: Centro Editoriale Dehoniano, 2000

LIZZI TESTA
    R. LIZZI TESTA, *Ascetismo e predicazione urbana nell'Egitto del V secolo*, "Atti dell'Istituto Veneto di Scienze, Lettere ed Arti" 141 (1982–1983), pp. 139–145

LONGFELLOW
    K. LONGFELLOW, *Flow Down like Silver: Hypatia of Alexandria*, Belvedere, California: Eio Books, 2009

LÓPEZ MARTÍNEZ
    M. P. LÓPEZ MARTÍNEZ, *"Había una mujer en Alejandría que se llamaba Hipatia": su presencia en Ágora de Amenábar*, "Asparkía. Investigación feminista" 25 (2014), pp. 202–222

LOUKAKI
    M. LOUKAKI, Σκολαστικός. *Remarques sur le sens du terme à Byzance (IVe–XVe siècles)*, "Byzantinische Zeitschrift" 109 (2016), pp. 41–72

LOUTH
    A. LOUTH, *The Literature of the Monastic Movement*, in F. YOUNG – L. AYRES – A. LOUTH (eds.), *The Cambridge History of Early Christian Literature*, Cambridge: Cambridge University Press, 2004, pp. 373–381

LOVASCIO
    D. LOVASCIO, *Occasioni mancate: Ipazia nella letteratura italiana contemporanea*, in G. SERTOLI (ed.), *Figure di Ipazia*, Roma: Aracne, 2014, pp. 165–198

LUCCHESI
    N. LUCCHESI, *Autorità femminile nella filosofia antica: da Diotima a Ipazia*, in Atti dei Seminari Piero Treves (Venezia 1995–1996), Venezia: Fondazione Scientifica Querini Stampalia, 1999, pp. 15–30

LUCK
    G. LUCK, *Palladas: Christian or Pagan?*, "Harvard Studies in Classical Philology" 63 (1958), pp. 455–471

LUDOVICI
    M.A. LUDOVICI, *Lysistrata, or Woman's Future and Future Woman*, London – New York: K. Paul, Trench, Trubner – E.P. Dutton, 1925

LUMPKIN

B. LUMPKIN, *Hypatia and Women's Rights in Ancient Egypt*, in I. VAM SERTIMA (ed.), *Black Women in Antiquity* [= "Journal of African Civilization" 5.6 (1984)], New Brunswick: Transaction Press, 1988², pp. 155–156

LUPUS

C. LUPUS, *Ad Ephesinum concilium variorum patrum epistulae*, Lovanii: typis Hieronymi Nempaei, 1682

LUZI 1972

M. LUZI, *Ipazia* (1969), Milano: All'insegna del Pesce d'Oro, 1972

LUZI 1977

M. LUZI, *Il messaggero*, "L'Approdo Letterario" 77–78 (1977), pp. 18–50

LUZI 1978

M. LUZI, *Libro di Ipazia*, introduzione di G. Pampaloni, con una nota di G. Quiriconi, Milano: Biblioteca Universale Rizzoli, 1978

MAAS

E. MAAS [ed.], *Commentariorum in Aratum reliquiae*, Berlin: Weidmann, 1898 (reprint 1958)

MAEGER 1995

A. MAEGER, *Amo(r) ergo sum: über die Macht der Liebe. Die Philosophie der Hypatia und ihre Bedeutung*, Hamburg: A. Maeger, 1995

MAEGER 1999

A. MAEGER, *Hypatia: die Dreigestaltige*, Hamburg: A. Maeger, 1999²

MAEGER 2002

A. MAEGER, *Hypatia: Heilige oder Hexe? Neue Indizien zur Hypatia-Forschung*, Hamburg: A. Maeger, 2002

MALALAS

I. THURN (ed.), *Ioannis Malalae Chronographia*, Corpus Fontium Historiae Byzantinae (CFHB), Series Berolinensis 35, Berlin: De Gruyter, 2000

E. JEFFREYS – M. JEFFREYS – R. SCOTT (eds. and transl.), *The Chronicle of John Malalas*, Melbourne: Melbourne Australian Association for Byzantine Studies, 1986

L. DINDORF (ed.), *Ioannis Malalae Chronographia*, Corpus Scriptorum Historiae Byzantinae (CSHB), Bonnae: Impensis ed. Weberi, 1831

MALEVILLE

G. MALEVILLE, *Histoire critique de l'Éclectisme, ou des Nouveaux Platoniciens*, voll. I–II, London: [s.n.], 1766

MANGASARIAN

M.M. MANGASARIAN, *The Martyrdom of Hypatia and Other Lectures*, Cabin John, Ma.: Wildside Press, 2013

MARCEL

J. MARCEL, *Hypatie ou la fin des dieux*, Montreal: Leméac, 1989

MARCIANO-JACOB

C. MARCIANO-JACOB, *Hypatia – Un phare dans la nuit*, Montreal: Lys, 2008

MARINUS

H.D. SAFFREY – A.PH. SEGONDS (eds., transl., and comm.), *Marinus, Proclus ou sur le bonheur*, Paris: Les Belles Lettres, 2001

MARROU 1956

H.I. MARROU, *A History of Education in Antiquity*, English translation, New York: Sheed and Ward, 1956

MARROU 1963

H.I. MARROU, *Synesius of Cyrene and Alexandrian Neoplatonism*, in A. MOMIGLIANO (ed.), *The Conflict between Paganism and Christianity in the Fourth Century*, Oxford: Clarendon Press, 1963, pp. 126–150

MARTELLI 2011

M. MARTELLI (ed.), *Pseudo-Democrito, Scritti alchemici con il commentario di Sinesio*, Paris – Milano: S.É.H.A. – Arché, 2011

MARTELLI 2016
M. MARTELLI, *Synésius l'Alchimiste*, in R. GOULET (ed.), *Dictionnaire des philosophes antiques*, vol. VI, Paris: Éditions du CNRS, 2016, pp. 676–678

MARTIN
A. MARTIN, *Les premiers siècles du christianisme à Alexandrie: essai de topographie religieuse (IIIe-Ve siècles)*, in "Revue des Études Augustiniennes" 30 (1984), pp. 211–225

MARTINDALE
J.R. MARTINDALE, *The Prosopography of the Later Roman Empire*, vol. II: *AD 395–527*, Cambridge: Cambridge University Press, 1980

MARTINEZ MAZA
C. MARTINEZ MAZA, *Hipatia: la estremecedora historia de la ùltima gran filosofa de la Antigüedad y la fascinante ciudad de Alejandrìa*, Madrid: Esfera de los Libros, 2009

MASAI
F. MASAI, *Pléthon et le platonisme de Mistra*, Paris: Les Belles Lettres, 1956

MASPÉRO
J. MASPÉRO, *Histoire des patriarches d'Alexandrie depuis la mort de l'empereur Anastase jusqu'à la réconciliation des Églises jacobites (518–613)*, posthumous edition by A. FORTESCUE – G. WIET (eds.), Paris: Édouard Champion, 1923

MASSON
O. MASSON, *Theoteknos, Fils de Dieu*, "Revue des Études Grecques" 110 (1997), pp. 618–619

MAUTHNER
F. MAUTHNER, *Hypatia. Roman aus Altertum*, Stuttgart: Cotta'schen Buchhandlung Nachfloger, 1892; anastatic reprint La Vergne, 2010

MCALISTER
L. Lopez MCALISTER (ed.), *Hypatia's Daughters: Fifteen Hundred Years of Women Philosophers*, Bloomington, Ind.: Indiana University Press, 1996

MCGUCKIN
J.A. MCGUCKIN, *St. Cyril of Alexandria. The Christological Controversy. Its History, Theology and Texts*, Leiden – NewYork – Köln: Brill, 1994

MCKENZIE
J. MCKENZIE, *The Architecture of Alexandria and Egypt, 300 BC – 700 AD*, New Haven – London: Yale University Press, 2007

MCKENZIE – GIBSON – REYES
J. MCKENZIE – S. GIBSON – A.T. REYES, *Reconstructing the Serapeum in Alexandria from the Archaeological Evidence*, "Journal of Roman Studies" 94 (2004), pp. 73–121

MEINARDUS 1999a
O.F.A. MEINARDUS, *Two Thousand Years of Coptic Christianity*, Cairo – New York: The American University in Cairo Press, 1999

MEINARDUS 1999b
O.F.A. MEINARDUS, *Das ägyptische jungfräuliche Dreigestirn: Damiana, Katharina, Hypatia*, "Kemet" 8.2 (1999), pp. 42–47

MÉNAGE
G. MÉNAGE, *Historia mulierum philosopharum*, Lugduni: apud Anissonios, Joan. Posuel & Claudium Rigaud, 1690 (English translation: G. MÉNAGE, *A History of Women Philosophers*, by B.H. ZEDLER, New York – London: University Press of America, 1984)

MÉNARD
L. MÉNARD, *Rêveries d'un païen mystique*, Paris: A. Lemerre, 1876 (1886²)

MENZIO
M.R. MENZIO, *Senza fine*, in M.R. MENZIO, *Spazio, tempo, numeri e stelle*, Torino: Bollati Boringhieri, 2005, pp. 81–106

MERELLO
> I. MERELLO, *Ipazia in terra di Francia*, in G. SERTOLI (ed.), *Figure di Ipazia*, Roma: Aracne, 2014, pp. 103–116

MEYER
> W.A. MEYER, *Hypatia von Alexandria: ein Beitrag zur Geschichte des Neuplatonismus*, Heidelberg: G. Weiss, 1886

MIESEL
> S. MIESEL, *Agora-phobia: The True Story of Hypatia*, "Ignatius Insight" 24 September 2010

MILES
> R. MILES, *The Women's History of the World*, New York: Salem House, 1988

MINARDI
> C. MINARDI, *Re-Membering Ancient Women: Hypatia of Alexandria and her Communities*, Dissertation, Georgia State University, 2011 <https://scholarworks.gsu.edu/english_diss/67/>

MISSALE ROMANUM
> *Missale Romanum ex decreto Sacrosancti Oecumenici Concilii Vaticani II instauratum, auctoritate Pauli PP. VI promulgatum, Ioannis Pauli PP. II cura recognitum*, editio typica tertia, Città del Vaticano: Libreria Editrice Vaticana, 2002

MOGENET – TIHON
> T. MOGENET – A. TIHON (eds.), *Le "Grand Commentaire" de Théon d'Alexandrie aux Tables faciles de Ptolémée*, Studi e Testi 215, Città del Vaticano: Biblioteca Apostolica Vaticana, 1985

MOLINARO
> U. MOLINARO, *A Christian Martyr in Reverse: Hypatia 370–415 A.D.: A Vivid Portrait of the Life and Death of Hypatia as Seen through the Eyes of a Feminist Poet and Novelist*, "Hypatia" 4.1 (1989), pp. 6–8

MOMMSEN – MEYER – KRÜGER – ROUGÉ – DELMAIRE
> *Code Théodosien 1–15; Code Justinien; Constitutions sirmondiennes*, texte latin T. MOMMSEN, P. MEYER, P. KRÜGER; traduction J. ROUGÉ, R. DELMAIRE; introduction et notes R. DELMAIRE; avec la collaboration de O. Huck, F. Richard et L. Guichard; Paris: Cerf, 2009

MONETI CODIGNOLA
> M. MONETI CODIGNOLA, *Ipazia muore*, Milano: La Tartaruga, 2010 (first edition, under the pseudonym C. Contini: *Ipazia e la notte*, Milano: Longanesi, 1999)

MONTI 1797a
> *Il Fanatismo e La Superstizione. Poemetti due del cittadino Vincenzo Monti ferrarese*, Venezia: Presso A. Curti Q. Giacomo, l'anno 1797, primo della Libertà Italiana [1797, the first year of Italian Freedom]

MONTI 1797b
> *Il Pericolo, canto del cittadino Vincenzo Monti ferrarese*, Genova: nella stamperia Francese e Italiana degli amici della libertà, l'anno I della Libertà Ligure [1797]

MORÉRI 1674
> L. MORÉRI, s.v. *Hypatia*, in *Le Grand Dictionnaire historique ou le Mélange curieux de l'Histoire sacrée et profane* [...], Lyon: J. Girin – B. Rivière, 1674, p. 162

MOSCHUS
> *Ioannes Moschus, Pratum spirituale*, in J.P. MIGNE, *Patrologia Graeca* 83.3, coll. 2851–3112

MOUSOUROS
> M. MOUSOUROS (ed.), *Epistolae diversorum philosophorum. Oratorum. Rhetorum sex et viginti* [...], Venetiis: apud Aldum [Manutium], 1499

MURALT
> E. DE MURALT, *Essai de Chronographie Byzantine*, Saint Pétersbourg – Bâle – Genève: Eggers et Cie – H. Georg, 1855–1871 (photographic reprint Paris 1963)

MÜLLER
> K. MÜLLER (ed.), *Fragmenta Historicorum Graecorum*, IV, Paris: Didot, 1851

MYRSILIDES

B.A. MYRSILIDES, Βιογραφία τῆς φιλοσόφου ἑλληνίδος Ὑπατίας, ἐρανισθεῖσα ἐκ ἀρχαιοτάτων χριστιανῶν ἱστορικῶν πηγῶν καὶ τῆς παραδόσεως ἐν τοῖς ἐρείπιοις τῆς Μικρῆς Ἀσίας πρὸ τῆς καταστροφῆς καὶ τῶν σφαγῶν τοῦ 1922, Athenai: Typois A.E.E. Adelphoi P. Palaiologou & Sia, 1926
(German translation: B.A. MYRSILIDES, *Biographie der hellenischen Philosophin Hypatia: Exzerpiert aus ältesten christianischen historischen Quellen und der Überlieferung in den Trümmern [...] vor der Katastrophe und dem Gemetzel von 1922*, translation, introduction and commentary by A. MAEGER, Hamburg: A. Maeger, 2002)

NERI

M. NERI, *In cerca di Ipazia*, Firenze: Angelo Pontecorboli, 2016

NERVAL

G. DE NERVAL, *Les filles du feu*, Paris: Michel Lévy Frères, 1856[2] (published posthumously)

NESSELRATH

H.-G. NESSELRATH (ed.), *Dion von Prusa: Der Philosoph und sein Bild*, Tübingen: Mohr Siebeck, 2009

NEUGEBAUER

O. NEUGEBAUER, *A History of Ancient Mathematical Astronomy*, vol. II, Berlin – Heidelberg – New York: Springer, 1975

NEWMAN

J.H. NEWMAN, *Historical Sketches*, voll. I-III, London: Longmans, Green & Co., 1906–1909

NONNUS PANOPOLITANUS

P. CHUVIN (ed. and transl.), *Nonnos De Panopolis, Les Dionisiaques*, tome III: *Chants VI–VIII*, Paris: Les Belles Lettres, 1992

NUFFELEN

P. VAN NUFFELEN, s.v. *Socrates scholasticus*, in Gr. DUNPHY (ed.), *Encyclopedia of the Medieval Chronicle*, Leiden: Brill, 2010, also available as Brill Online: <http://referenceworks.brillonline.com/entries/encyclopedia-of-the-medieval-chronicle/socrates-scholasticus-EMCSIM_02331>

O' MEARA

D. O' MEARA, *Pythagoras Revived: Mathematics and Philosophy in Late Antiquity*, Oxford: Clarendon Press, 1989

OGILVIE

G. Stuart OGILVIE, *Hypatia: A Play in Four Acts*, London: W. Heinemann, 1894

OGILVIE

M.B. OGILVIE, *Women in Science: Antiquity through the Nineteenth Century*, Cambridge, MA: The MIT Press, 1986

OPPIANUS

A.W. MAIR (ed.), *Oppian of Cilicia, Halieutica*, Loeb Classical Library, Cambridge, Mass.: Harvard University Press, 1928

ORACULA CHALDAICA

E. DES PLACES (ed.), *Oracles chaldaïques, avec un choix des commentaires anciens*, Paris: Les Belles Lettres, 1971

OSER

L.M. OSER, *Women in Mathematics*, Cambridge, Mass. – London: The MIT Press, 1974

PACK

R. PACK, *A Romantic Narrative in Eunapius*, "Transactions of the American Philological Association" 83 (1952), pp. 198–204

PALLADIUS

A.-M. MALINGREY – P. LECLERQ (eds.), *Palladius, Dialogus de vita beati Ioannis Chrysostomi*, Sources Chrétiennes 341, Paris: Cerf, 1988

Papaconstantinou
   A. Papaconstantinou, *Historiography, Hagiography, and the Making of the Coptic Church of the Martyrs in Early Islamic Egypt*, "Dumbarton Oaks Papers" 60 (2006), pp. 65–86
Parsons
   E.A. Parsons, *The Alexandrian Library. Glory of the Hellenic World*, Amsterdam – London – New York: The Elsevier Press, 1952
Pascal
   C. Pascal, *Figure e Caratteri*, Milano: Sandron, 1908
Patlagean
   E. Patlagean, *Lingue e Confessioni religiose fra Oriente e Occidente*, in A. Momigliano – A. Schiavone (eds.), *Storia di Roma*, III, 1, Torino: Einaudi, 1993, pp. 975–989
Pecout – Greiner
   C. Pecout – V. Greiner, *Hypathie*, Marcinelle: Dupuis, 2010
Pedraza
   P. Pedraza, *La perra de Alexandría*, Madrid: Club Diogénes-Valdemar, 2003 (2009^2)
Péguy
   C. Péguy, *Oeuvres en prose 1898–1908*, Paris: Gallimard, 1959 (first edition 1898–1908)
Penella
   R.J. Penella, *When Was Hypatia Born?*, "Historia" 33 (1984), pp. 126–128
Perl
   T. Perl, *Math equals: biographies of women mathematicians + related activities*, Menlo Park, California: Addison – Wesley Pub. Co., 1978
Petau
   Συνεσίου ἐπισκόπου Κυρήνης Ἅπαντα τὰ εὑρισκόμενα. *Synesii episcopi Cyrenes Opera quae extant omnia*, nunc primum Graecè & Latinè coniunctim edita, subsidio & liberalitate reuerendiss. episcoporum & cleri vniuersi Franciae regni. Interprete Dionysio Petauio [...], Lutetiae: Typis Regiis apud Cl. Morellum via Iacobaea, ad insigne Fontis, 1612
PG
   Patrologiae cursus completus [...] *omnium Ss. Patrum, doctorum scriptorumque ecclesiasticorum, sive Latinorum sive Graecorum* [...] *Series Graeca*, accurante J.-P. Migne [...], Lutetia Parisiorum: apud J.-P. Migne, 1856–1866 <https://www.roger-pearse.com/weblog/patrologia-graeca-pg-pdfs/>
Philipsborn
   A. Philipsborn, *La compagnie d'ambulanciers "parabalani" d'Alexandrie*, "Byzantion" 20 (1950), pp. 185–190
Philostorgius
   J. Bidez (ed.), *Philostorgius, Kirchengeschichte*, 8, 9, revised by F. Winkelmann, Leipzig: Hinrich, 1913^1 (Berlin: Akademie Verlag, 1972^2; ibid., 1981^3); reprint Berlin – Boston: De Gruyter, 2013^3
   Recent critical edition, German translation and commentary: B. Bleckmann – M. Stein (eds.), *Philostorgios Kirchengeschichte*, voll. I–II, Paderborn: F. Schoeningh, 2015
   French translation: É. des Places (ed.), *Philostorge, Histoire ecclésiastique*, Sources Chrétiennes 564, Paris: Cerf, 2013
   English translation: Ph.R. Amidon (ed.), *Philostorgius, Church History. Writings from the Greco* [sic] *Roman World*, Atlanta: Society of Biblical Literature, 2007; E.W. Walford, London: Henry G. Bohn, 1855 <http://www.ccel.org/ccel/pearse/morefathers/files/philostorgius.htm>
Photius
   R. Henry (ed.), *Photius, Bibliothèque*, voll. I–IX, Paris: Les Belles Lettres, 1959–1991
Phrangopoulos
   Th.D. Phrangopoulos, *Hypatia*, Athens: Ekdoseis Hermeias, s.d.

PIGANIOL

A. PIGANIOL, *L'empire chrétien (325–395)*, in A. PIGANIOL – G. GLOTZ (eds.), *Histoire romaine. Tome IV. Deuxième partie*, Paris: Presses Universitaires de France, 1972², pp. 160–161

PIUS XII

PIUS PP. XII, *Litt. enc.* Orientalis Ecclesiae *de Sancto Cyrillo Patriarcha Alexandrino, saeculo exeunte quinto decimo a piissimo eius obitu, [Ad venerabiles Fratres Patriarchas, Primates, Archiepiscopos, Episcopos aliosque locorum Ordinarios, pacem et communionem cum Apostolica Sede habentes]*, 9 aprilis 1944, "Acta Apostolicae Sedis" 36 (1944), pp. 129–144

PLOTINUS

P. HENRY – H.R. SCHWYZER (eds.), *Plotini opera*, vol. II: *Enneades 4–5*, Oxford: Clarendon Press, 1977
English translation: A.H. ARMSTRONG (ed.), *Plotinus Enneads*, vol. V: *Ennead 5*, Loeb Classical Library 444, Cambridge, Mass.: Harvard University Press, 1984

POMEROY

S. POMEROY, *Pythagorean Women: Their History and Writings*, Baltimore: The John Hopkins University Press, 2013

POUDERON

B. POUDERON, *Théophane, témoin de l'Épitome d'histoires ecclésiastiques de Théodore le Lecteur ou de Jean Diacrinoménos?*, in E. AMATO (ed.), *Les historiens fragmentaires de langue grecque à l'époque impériale et tardive*, Actes du Colloque international (Université de Nantes 26–28 novembre 2015) [forthcoming]

POZZI 2014a

R. POZZI, *La città e la donna nel* Libro di Ipazia *di Mario Luzi*, in G. SERTOLI (ed.), *Figure di Ipazia*, Roma: Aracne, 2014, pp. 143–163

POZZI 2014b

R. POZZI, *Notizie di Ipazia dalla Spagna d'oggi*, in G. SERTOLI (ed.), *Figure di Ipazia*, Roma: Aracne, 2014, pp. 215–228

PRAECHTER 1916

K. PRAECHTER, s.v. *Hypatia*, in *Paulys Real-Encyclopädie der classischen Altertums-wissenschaft* [...], vol. IX, Stuttgart: J.B. Metzler, 1916, coll. 242–249

PRAECHTER 1920

K. PRAECHTER, *Die Herrschaft des Neuplatonismus*, par. 84: *Die alexandrinische Schule*, in F. ÜBERWEG, *Grundriss der Geschichte der Philosophie des Altertums*, ed. by K. PRAECHTER, vol. I: *Die Philosophie des Altertums*, Berlin: E.S. Mittler, 1920¹¹, p. 660

PRATT

H. PRATT, *Favola di Venezia*, "L'Europeo" 21–22 (3 giugno 1977) – 51 (23 dicembre 1977);
Corto Maltese. Sirat Al Bunduqiyyah, Milano: Milano Libri, 1979

PROSOPOGRAPHISCHES LEXICON DER PALAIOLOGENZEIT

E. TRAPP (ed.), *Prosopographisches Lexikon der Palaiologenzeit*, unter Mitarbeit von R. Walther und H.-V. Beyer, Wien: Verlag der Österreichischen Akademie der Wissenschaften, 1976-

PROUST

M. PROUST, *À l'ombre des jeunes filles en fleur*, Paris: Gallimard, 1944²

PSELLUS

K.N. SATHAS (ed.), Μεσαιωνική Βιβλιοθήκη, vol. V, En Benetia – En Parisiois: Typois tou Phoinikos – Maisonneuve, 1876 (reprint Hildesheim: G. Olms, 1972)

U. CRISCUOLO (ed.), *Michele Psello, Autobiografia (Encomio per la madre)*, Napoli: D'Auria, 1989

J. WALKER (transl.), *Michael Psellos: the Encomium of his Mother*, "Advances in the History of Rhetoric" 8 (2005), pp. 239–313

RAMAKRISHNAN

T.D. RAMAKRISHNAN, *Francis Itty Kora*, Kottayam, Kerala: DC Books, 2009

Renan
    E. Renan, *Nouvelles études d'histoire religieuse*, Paris: Calmann Lévy, 1857
    English translation *Studies in Religious History*, Miami, Florida: Hardpress Publishing, 2012
Rensi
    E. Rensi, *Ipazia. La prima martire della libertà di pensiero*, in Agabiti, pp. 6–38
Reuss
    J. Reuss, *Matthäus – Markus – und Johannes-Katenen nach den handschriftlichen Quellen untersucht*, Münster i. W.: Aschendorff, 1941
Richardson
    R. Richardson, *The Star Lovers*, New York: Macmillan, 1967
Richeson
    A.W. Richeson, *Hypatia of Alexandria*, "National Mathematics Magazine" 15.2 (1940), pp. 74–82
Rist
    J.M. Rist, *Hypatia*, "Phoenix" 19 (1965), pp. 214–225
Rome 1936
    A. Rome (ed.), *Commentaires de Pappus et de Théon d'Alexandrie sur l'Almageste*, vol. II: *Théon d'Alexandrie, Commentaire sur les livres 1 et 2 de l'Almageste*, Studi e Testi 72, Città del Vaticano: Biblioteca Apostolica Vaticana, 1936
Rome 1943
    A. Rome (ed.), *Commentaires de Pappus et de Théon d'Alexandrie sur l'Almageste*, vol. III: *Théon d'Alexandrie, Commentaire sur les livres 3 et 4 de l'Almageste*, Studi e Testi 106, Città del Vaticano: Biblioteca Apostolica Vaticana, 1943
Roncaglia
    M. Roncaglia, *Histoire de l'Église copte*, voll. I–IV, Beyrouth: Dar al-Kalima, 1966–1973
Ronchey 1990
    S. Ronchey, *Indagine sul martirio di San Policarpo. Critica storica e fortuna agiografica di un caso giudiziario in Asia Minore*, Introduzione di G. Clemente, Roma: Istituto Storico Italiano per il Medioevo, 1990
Ronchey 1994
    S. Ronchey, *Ipazia, l'intellettuale*, in A. Fraschetti (ed.), *Roma al femminile*, Roma: Laterza, 1994, pp. 213–258
Ronchey 1995
    S. Ronchey, *Filosofa e martire: Ipazia tra storia della chiesa e femminismo*, in R. Raffaelli (ed.), *Vicende e figure femminili in Grecia e a Roma*, Atti del Convegno (Pesaro, 28–30 aprile 1994), Ancona: Commissione per le Pari Opportunità della Regione Marche, 1995, pp. 449–465
Ronchey 1999
    S. Ronchey, *Gli atti dei martiri tra politica e letteratura*, in A. Momigliano – A. Schiavone (eds.), *Storia di Roma*, III, 2, Torino: Einaudi, 1999, pp. 781–825
Ronchey 2001
    S. Ronchey, *Hypatia the Intellectual*, in A. Fraschetti (ed.), *Roman Women*, Chicago: University of Chicago Press, 2001, pp. 160–189. English version of Ronchey 1994
Ronchey 2010
    S. Ronchey, *Ipazia. La vera storia*, Milano: Rizzoli, 2010
Roques 1982
    D. Roques, *Synésios, évêque et philosophe*, "Revue des Études Grecques" 95 (1982), pp. 465–467
Roques 1995
    D. Roques, *La famille d'Hypatie (Synésios, epp. 5 and 16 G.)*, "Revue des Études Grecques" 108 (1995), pp. 128–149
Roques 1998
    D. Roques, *Theoteknos, "Fils de Dieu"*, "Revue des Études Grecques" 111 (1998), pp. 735–756

Rougé 1987

J. Rougé, *Les débuts de l'épiscopat de Cyrille d'Alexandrie et le Code Théodosien*, in Cl. Mondésert (ed.), *Alexandrina: hellénisme, judaïsme et christianisme à Alexandrie. Mélanges offerts au P. Claude Mondésert*, Paris: Cerf, 1987, pp. 341–349

Rougé 1990

J. Rougé, *La politique de Cyrille d'Alexandrie et le meurtre d'Hypatie*, "Cristianesimo nella Storia" 11.3 (1990), pp. 485–504

Rufinus

Rufinus, *Historia Ecclesiastica*, in E. Schwartz – Th. Mommsen – Fr. Winkelmann (eds.), *Eusebius Werke*, vol. II, 2, Berlin-Boston: De Gruyter, 2011² (first edition: Th. Mommsen [ed.], *Die lateinischen Übersetzung des Rufinus*, Leipzig: J.C. Hinrichs, 1909)

Rufus

C.B. Horn – R.R. Phenix Jr. (eds.), *John Rufus, The Lives of Peter the Iberian, Theodosius of Jerusalem, and the Monk Romanus*, Atlanta: Society of Biblical Literature, 2008, pp. 2–281

Ruprechter

W. Ruprechter, s.v. *Mauthner, Fritz*, in W. Killy (ed.), *Literaturlexikon*, second edition (digital), vol. VIII, Berlin: Directmedia, 2005

Russell 1947

B. Russell, *A History of Western Philosophy and Its Connection with Political and Social Circumstances from the Earliest Times to the Present Day*, London: George Allen and Unwin, 1947

Russell 1925

D.W. Russell, *Hypatia or Woman and Knowledge*, New York: Kegan Paul, Trench & Trubner, 1925

Russell 2007

N. Russell, *Theophilus of Alexandria*, London – New York: Routledge, 2007

Saffrey

H.D. Saffrey, s.v. *Hypatie d'Alexandrie*, in R. Goulet (ed.), *Dictionnaire des philosophes antiques*, t. IV, *De Labeo à Ovidius*, Paris: CNRS éditions, 2005, p. 817

Saluzzo Roero

D. Saluzzo Roero, *Ipazia ovvero delle filosofie*, voll. I–II, Torino: Chirio e Mina, 1827

Salvatore

A. Salvatore, *Pensare come Ipazia:* Flow Down Like Silver *di Ki Longfellow*, in G. Sertoli (ed.), *Figure di Ipazia*, Roma: Aracne, 2014, pp. 199–214

Sauvage

F. Sauvage, *Hypatie, drame en un acte*, "La Nouvelle Revue" 33 (March-April 1905), pp. 49–66

Schaefer 1902

F. Schaefer, *St. Cyril of Alexandria and the Murder of Hypatia*, "The Catholic University Bulletin" 8 (1902), pp. 441–453

Schäfer 1997

P. Schäfer, *Judeophobia. Attitudes toward the Jews in the Ancient World*, Cambridge, Mass. – London: Harvard University Press, 1997

Scheidegger Laemmle

S. Scheidegger Laemmle, *Starring Hypatia: Amenábar's Agora and the Tropology of Reception*, in LaValle Norman – Petkas, pp. 209–237

Scherr

J. Scherr, *Hypatia*, in *Menschliche Tragikomödie*, Leipzig: Otto Wigand, 1874, pp. 115–137

Schmitt

T. Schmitt, *Die Bekehrung des Synesios von Kyrene. Politik und Philosophie, Hof und Provinz als Handlungsräume eines Aristokraten bis zu seiner Wahl zum Metropoliten von Ptolemais*, München – Leipzig: K. G. Saur, 2001

SCHREK
    D.J.E. SCHREK, *Hypatia van Alexandria*, "Euclides" 21 (1945–46), pp. 164–173
SCHUBERT
    H. VON SCHUBERT, *Hypatia von Alexandrien in Wahrheit und Dichtung*, "Preussische Jahrbücher" 124 (1906), pp. 42–60
SCHWARTZ
    E. SCHWARTZ (ed.), *Acta Conciliorum Oecumenicorum*, voll. I–IV. Strassburg – Berlin: De Gruyter, 1914–40, t. II: *Concilium Universale Chalcedonense*, vol. I: *Acta Graeca. Pars I. Epistularum collectiones. Actio prima*, Berlin: De Gruyter, 1932 (reprint Berlin-Boston: De Gruyter 2011)
SEIBER
    J. SEIBER, *Early Byzantine Urban Saints*, Oxford: British Archaeological Reports, 1977
SERTOLI
    G. SERTOLI, *Ipazia nell'Inghilterra vittoriana: Charles Kingsley*, in G. SERTOLI (ed.), *Figure di Ipazia*, Roma: Aracne, 2014, pp. 37–52
SHANZER
    D. SHANZER, *Merely a Cynic Gesture?*, "Rivista di Filologia e di Istruzione Classica" 113 (1985), pp. 61–66
SHAW 2011
    B.D. SHAW, *Sacred Violence and Sectarian Hatred in the Age of Augustine*, Cambridge: Cambridge University Press, 2011
SHAW 1985
    G. SHAW, *Theurgy: Rituals of Unification in the Neoplatonism of Iamblichus*, "Traditio" 41 (1985), pp. 1–28
SIMONUTTI
    L. SIMONUTTI, *Deism, Biblical Hermeneutics and Philology*, in W. HUDSON – D. LUCCI – J.R. WIGELSWORTH (eds.), *Atheism and Deism Revalued: Heterodox Religious Identities in Britain, 1650–1800*, Farnham, Surrey, England – Burlington, Vermont: Ashgate, 2014, pp. 45–62
SIRKS
    A.J.B. SIRKS, *Food for Rome: the Legal Structure of the Transportation and Processing of Supplies for the Imperial Distributions in Rome and Constantinople*, Amsterdam: Gieben, 1991
SOCRATES SCHOLASTICUS
    G.C. HANSEN (ed.), *Socrates Scholasticus, Kirchengeschichte*, mit Beiträgen von M. ŠIRINJAN, Berlin: Akademie Verlag, 1995
SOLDAN – HEPPE
    W.G. SOLDAN – H. HEPPE (eds.), *Geschichte der Hexenprozesse*, Stuttgart: Cotta, 1880, voll. I–II, (photographic reprint Essen: Athenaion, 1990)
SOPHRONIUS HIEROSOLIMITANUS 1
    SOPHRONIUS HIEROSOLIMITANUS, *Vita Cyri et Ioannis*, in J.P. MIGNE, *Patrologia Graeca*, 87.3, coll. 3677–3689
SOPHRONIUS HIEROSOLIMITANUS 2
    SOPHRONIUS HIEROSOLIMITANUS, *Alia vita acephala Sanctorum Martyrum Cyri et Ioannis*, in J.P. MIGNE, *Patrologia Graeca*, 87.3, coll. 3689–3696
SOPHRONIUS HIEROSOLIMITANUS 3
    SOPHRONIUS HIEROSOLIMITANUS, *Laudes in SS. Cyrum et Ioannem*, in J.P. MIGNE, *Patrologia Graeca*, 87.3, coll. 3387–3421
SOZOMENUS
    G.Chr. HANSEN (ed.), *Sozomenus, Kirchengeschichte*, Berlin – Boston: De Gruyter, 1995 (= J.P. MIGNE, *Patrologia Graeca*, 67, coll. 1452 ff.)
SPETZIERIS
    K. SPETZIERIS, *Εἰκόνες ἑλλήνων φιλοσόφων εἰς Ἐκκλησίας. Συμπληρωματικὰ στοιχεῖα*, "Epistemonike

Epeteris tes Philosophikes Scholes tou Panepistemiou Athenon" ("Annuaire Scientifique de la Faculté de Philosophie de l'Université d'Athènes"), 24 (1973 – 1974), pp. 418 – 420

SPINDELER

A. SPINDELER, s.v. *Hypatia*, in *Lexikon für Theologie und Kirche*, vol. VI, Freiburg i. Br.: Herder, 1961, col. 707

STEPHANUS

Ἐκκλησιαστικῆς ἱστορίας Εὐσεβίου τοῦ Παμφιλίου ἐπισκόπου [...] βιβλία 10 [...] *Ecclesiasticae Historiae Eusebii Pamphili lib. 10. Eiusdem de vita Constantini lib. 5. Socratis lib. 7. Theodoriti episcopi Cyrensis lib. 5. Collectaneorum ex historia eccles. Theodori Lectoris lib. 2. Hermii Sozomeni lib. 9. Euagrii lib. 6*, Lutetiae Parisiorum: ex officina Roberti Stephani regiis typis, 1544

STOPPA

A. STOPPA, *Ipazia e la rete d'oro*, in A. STOPPA, *Sette universi di passione*, Colledara: Andromeda, 2004, pp. 20 – 34

Synaxarium Alexandrinum

I. FORGET (ed. and transl.), *Synaxarium Alexandrinum*, Louvain: Secrétariat du Corpus Scriptorum Christianorum Orientalium, 1922

SYNESIUS

J. LAMOUREUX – N. AOUJOULAT (eds., transl. and comm.) *Synésios de Cyrène, Opuscules*, vol. III, t. VI, Paris: Les Belles Lettres, 2008

D. ROQUES (ed. and transl.), *Synésios de Cyrène, Correspondance: Lettres I – CLVI*, (t. I: *Epistles* I-LXIII, t. II: *Epistles* LXIV-CLVI), à partir du texte établi par A. GARZYA, Paris: Les Belles Lettres, 2003 (tom. II: epistles I – LXIII; tom. III: epistles LXIV – CLVI)

A. GARZYA (ed.), *Sinesio, Opere. Epistole, operette, inni*, Torino: UTET, 1989

C. LACOMBRADE (ed.), *Synésios de.Cyrène, Hymnes*, Paris: Les Belles Lettres, 1978

English translation: A. FITZGERALD (ed.), *The Letters of Synesius of Cyrene*, Oxford: Oxford University Press, 1926 (reprint Charlottesville, VA: University of Virginia 1994)

SUIDAS

A. ADLER (ed.), *Suidae Lexicon*, voll. I-V, Stuttgart: Teubner, 1928 – 1938 (reprint 1989 – 1994), see also *Suda Online: Byzantine Lexicography*, <http://www.stoa.org/sol-entries/upsilon/166>

SWEET

M. SWEET, *The Story of the Death of Hypatia*, Bloomington, Indiana: AuthorHouse, 2007

SWINBURNE

A.C. SWINBURNE, *Hymn to Proserpine (After the Proclamation in Rome of the Christian Faith)*, in ID., *Poems and Ballads*, 1st series, London: Savill and Edwards, 1866, pp. 77 – 84

TAKÁCS 1992

S. TAKÁCS, *Roman Politics and the Cult of Isis and Sarapis*, Ann Arbor: University Microfilm International, 1992

TAKÁCS 1994

S. TAKÁCS, *The Magic of Isis Replaced or Cyril of Alexandria's Attempt at Redirecting Religious Devotion*, "Poikila Byzantina" 13 (1994), pp. 489 – 507

TAKÁCS 1995

S. TAKÁCS, *Hypatia's Murder. The Sacrifice of a Virgin and Its Implications*, in K.B. FREE (ed.), *The Formulation of Christianity by Conflict Through the Ages*, New York: Mellen Press, 1995, pp. 47 – 62 (reprint in G. NAGY [ed.], *Greek Literature*, vol. VIII, New York – London: Routledge, 2002, pp. 397 – 412)

TANASEANU-DÖBLER 2008

I. TANASEANU-DÖBLER, *Konversion zur Philosophie in der Spätantike: Kaiser Julian und Synesius von Kirene*, Stuttgart: Steiner, 2008

TANASEANU-DÖBLER 2012

I. TANASEANU-DÖBLER, *Synesios und die Theurgie*, in H. SENG – L.M. HOFFMANN (eds.), *Synesios von Kyrene: Politik-Literatur-Philosophie*, Turnhout: Brepols 2012, pp. 201–230

TANNERY 1880

P. TANNERY, *L'article de Suidas sur Hypatie*, "Annales de la Faculté des Lettres de Bordeaux" 2 (1880), pp. 197–201 (reprinted in J.L. HEIBERG. – H.G. ZEUTHEN [eds.], TANNERY, *Mémoires Scientifiques*, vol. I, Toulouse – Paris: Privat – Gauthier-Villars, 1912)

TANNERY 1896

P. TANNERY, *Sur la religion des derniers mathématiciens de l'Antiquité*, "Annales de Philosophie Chrétienne" 34 (1896), pp. 26–36 (reprinted in J.L. HEIBERG. – H.G. ZEUTHEN [eds.], TANNERY, *Mémoires scientifiques*, vol. II, Toulouse – Paris: Privat – Gauthier-Villars, 1912)

TANNERY – HENRY

P. TANNERY – C. HENRY (eds.), *Oeuvres de Fermat*, Paris: Gauthier – Villars, 1891

TARDIEU

M. TARDIEU, *La Gnose valentinienne et les Oracles Chaldaïques*, in B. LAYTON (ed.), *The Rediscovery of Gnosticism*, Proceedings of the International Conference on Gnosticism at Yale (New Haven, Connecticut, March 28–31, 1978), vol. I: *The School of Valentinus*, Leiden: Brill, 1980, pp. 194–237

TERUEL 2011

P.J. TERUEL, *Filosofía y ciencia en Hipatia*, Madrid: Gredos, 2011

TERUEL 2012

P.J. TERUEL, *Ipazia d'Alessandria come anello della grande tradizione filosofica greca*, "Itinera" 4 (2012), pp. 20–45

THEODORETUS CYRENSIS

L. PARMENTIER – F. SCHEIDWEILER (eds.), *Theodoret, Kirchengeschichte*, Berlin: Akademie Verlag, 1954

THEOPHANES

C. DE BOOR (ed.), *Theophanis Chronographia*, vol. I, Leipzig: Teubner, 1883

THESLEFF

H. THESLEFF (ed.), *The Pythagorean Texts of the Hellenistic Period*, Âbo: Âbo Akademi, 1965

THORP

J. THORP, *In search of Hypatia / À la recherche d'Hypatie*, being the Canadian Philosophical Association Presidential Address for 2004, https://www.acpcpa.ca/cpages/presidential-address

THULARD

A. THULARD, *Ipazia: reinterpretazioni teatrali e romanzesche francesi del ventesimo secolo*, "Itinera" 4 (2012), pp. 92–113

TIHON

A. TIHON, *Le Petit commentaire de Théon d'Alexandrie aux Tables faciles de Ptolémée: histoire du texte, édition critique, traduction*, Studi e Testi 282, Città del Vaticano: Biblioteca Apostolica Vaticana, 1978

TILLEMONT

L.S. Le Nain De TILLEMONT, *Mémoires pour servir à l'histoire ecclésiastique des six premiers siècles*, voll. I-XVI, Paris: chez Charles Robustel, 1693–1712

TISSONI

R. TISSONI, *Considerazioni su Diodata Saluzzo (con un'appendice di lettere inedite ad Alessandro Manzoni)*, in G. IOLI (ed.), Atti del Convegno "Piemonte e letteratura 1789–1870" (San Salvatore Monferrato, 15–17 October 1981), Torino: Regione Piemonte, s.d., vol. I, [1983], pp. 145–199

TOLAND

J. TOLAND, *Hypatia: Or, the History of a most beautiful, most vertuous, most learned and every way accomplish'd Lady; who was torn to Pieces by the clergy of Alexandria to gratify the Pride, Emulation, and Cruelty of their Archbishop Cyril, commonly but undeservedly stil'd Saint Cyril*, in J. TOLAND, *Tetradymus, Part III*, London: J. Brotherton & W. Meadows, 1720 (reprint in D.BERMAN [ed.], "Atheism in Britain", vol. II, Bristol: Thoemmes Press, 1996), pp. 101–136

TOMMASEO 1828
N. TOMMASEO, *Saluzzo (Diodata). Ipazia*, "Antologia" 24 (January-March 1828), pp. 146–153 (article signed K.X.Y.), then in TOMMASEO 1840, pp. 354–357
TOMMASEO 1840
N. TOMMASEO, *Dizionario estetico*, Venezia: Co' Tipi del Gondoliere, 1840 (Firenze: Le Monnier, 1867[4])
TORCUTTI
M.C. TORCUTTI, *L'Ipazia filo-drammatica di G. Stuart Ogilvie*, in G. SERTOLI (ed.), *Figure di Ipazia*, Roma: Aracne, 2014, pp. 53–80
TOULOUSE
S. TOULOUSE, s.v. *Synésios de Cyrène*, in R. GOULET (ed.), *Dictionnaire des philosophes antiques*, vol. VI, Paris: Éditions du CNRS, 2016, pp. 639–676
TRABAL SVALUTO-FERRO – RIVERA GARRETAS
L. TRABAL SVALUTO-FERRO – M.-M. RIVERA GARRETAS, *Auctoridad científica autoridad feminina: Hipatia*, Madrid: Horas y horas, 1998
TRENT
B. TRENT, *Remembering Hypatia: A Novel of Ancient Egypt*, Lincoln, Nebraska: iUniverse, 2005
TURNEBUS
Συνεσίου ἐπισκόπου Κυρήνης Περὶ βασιλείας, εἰς τὸν αὐτοκράτορα Ἀρκάδιον. Διών, ἢ περὶ τῆς καθ'αὑτὸν διαγωγῆς [...], *Synesij episcopi Cyrenes De regno ad Arcadium imperatorem. Dion, siue de suae vitae ratione. Caluitij laudatio. De prouidentia, seu aegyptius. Concio quaedam panegyrica. De insomnijs, cum Nicephori Gregorae explicatione. Eiusdem Synesij epistolae. Ex bibliotheca regia*, Parisijs: ex officina Adriani Turnebi typographi regij, 1553
UFFELMAN 1979
L.K. UFFELMAN, *Charles Kingsley*, Boston: Twayne, 1979
UFFELMAN 1986
L.K. UFFELMAN, *Kingsley's* Hypatia: *Revisions in Context*, "Nineteenth-Century Literature" 41 (1986), pp. 87–96
URBAINCZYK
T. URBAINCZYK, *Socrates of Constantinople*, Ann Arbor: University of Michigan Press, 1997
URSELLI
T. URSELLI, *Ipazia. La nota più alta*, Milano: Sedizioni, 2012
VALESIUS
Socratis Scholastici et Hermiae Sozomeni historia ecclesiastica Henricus VALESIUS Graecum textum coll. mss. codicibus emendavit, Latine vertit, et adnotationibus illustravit, excudebat Antonius Vitre, Parisiis 1668
VAQUERIZO
E. VAQUERIZO, *La última noche de Hipatia*, Madrid: Alamut, 2009
VARE – PTACEK
E.A. VARE – G. PTACEK, *Mothers of Invention. From the Bra to the Bomb: Forgotten Women & Their Unforgettable Ideas*, New York: William Morrow & Company, 1988
VASILEV
A.A. VASILEV, *History of the Byzantine Empire. 324–1453*, English translation, voll. I-II, Baltimore, Maryland: Project Muse 2014 (first edition vol. I-II, Madison, Wisconsin: University of Wisconsin, Studies in the Social Sciences and History, 1928–1929)
VIGANÒ
A. VIGANÒ, *Ipazia e le formiche nell'agorà di Amenábar*, in G. SERTOLI (ed.), *Figure di Ipazia*, Roma: Aracne, 2014, pp. 255–264
VINCENZI
M. VINCENZI, *Il sogno di Ipazia*, ed. by F. Verdinelli, s.l.: Mondo digitale, 2010

VINZENT
    M. VINZENT, *Oxbridge in der ausgehenden Spätantike oder: Ein Vergleich der Schulen von Athen und Alexandrien*, "Zeitschrift für antikes Christentum" 4.1 (2000), pp. 49–82
VIVIEN
    R. VIVIEN, *Les cahiers de Renée Vivien. Fragments d'un journal inédit* (1893), posthumous edition, "Les Écrits nouveaux" 9.2 (1922), pp. 51–64
VOGT 1985
    J. VOGT, *Das unverletzliche Gut: Synesios und Hypatia* (1972), in ID., *Begegnung mit Synesios, dem Philosophen, Priester und Feldherrn. Gesammelte Beiträge*, Darmstadt: Wissenschaftliche Buchgesellschaft, 1985, pp. 84–91
VOGT 1994
    J. VOGT, s.v. *Cyril of Alexandria*, in *Lexikon für Theologie und Kirche*, vol. II, Freiburg i. Br.: Herder 1994³, coll. 1368–1370
VOGT – SCHRAMM
    J. VOGT – M. SCHRAMM, *Synesius vor dem Planisphaerium*, in K. GAISER (ed.), *Das Altertum und jedes neue Gute. Festschrift für Wolfgang Schadewaldt zum 15. März 1970*, Stuttgart – Berlin – Köln – Mainz: Kohlhammer, 1970, pp. 264–311
VOLLKOMMER
    R. VOLLKOMMER, s. v. *Bryaxis*, in *Kunstlerlexikon der Antike*, Hamburg: Nikol, 2007, pp. 122–125
VOLTAIRE 1736
    Fr.M. Arouet de VOLTAIRE, *Examen important de Milord Bolingbroke ou le tombeau du fanatisme* (1736), in *Oeuvres complètes de Voltaire: Nouvelle édition*, vol. XXVI, Paris: Didot 1879, pp. 283–290 = W.H. BARBER (ed.), *Les œuvres complètes de Voltaire*, vol. 62: 1766–1767, Oxford: Voltaire Foundation – Taylor Institution, 1987, pp. 334–335
VOLTAIRE 1765
    Fr.M. Arouet de VOLTAIRE, *Lettre XIV. À M. Covelle, citoyen de Genève, par M. Baudinet*, in *Questions sur les miracles* (1765), in *Oeuvres complètes de Voltaire: Nouvelle édition*, vol. XIX, Paris: Didot, 1860, pp. 382–383 = N. CRONK – C. MERVAUD (eds.), *Les œuvres complètes de Voltaire*, vol. 60 D: *Collection des lettres sur les miracles*, Oxford: Voltaire Foundation, 2018, pp. 312–313
VOLTAIRE 1768
    Fr.M. Arouet de VOLTAIRE, *Examen du discours de l'empereur Julien contre la secte des Galiléens* (1768), in *Œuvres complètes de Voltaire: Nouvelle édition*, vol. 28, Paris: Hachette, 1894
VOLTAIRE 1770
    Fr.M. Arouet de VOLTAIRE, *De la paix perpétuelle* (Londres, 1770), in N. CRONK – C. MERVAUD (eds.), *Les œuvres complètes de Voltaire*, vol. 70 B: *Writings of 1769* (IIb), Oxford: Voltaire Foundation, 2016
VOLTAIRE 1772
    Fr.M. Arouet de VOLTAIRE, *Questions sur l'Encyclopédie, par des Amateurs*, 9e partie, nouvelle édition, soigneusement revue, corrigée et augmentée, Genève: Cramer, 1772 = *Œuvres complètes de Voltaire: Nouvelle édition*, vol. XIII, Paris: Didot, 1860 = N. CRONK – C. MERVAUD (eds.), *Les œuvres complètes de Voltaire*, vol. 42 A: *Questions sur l'Encyclopédie, par des amateurs*, 6 (*Gargatua – Justice*), Oxford: Voltaire Foundation, 2011
VOLTAIRE 1777
    Fr.M. Arouet de VOLTAIRE, *Histoire de l'établissement du Christianisme* (1777), in *Oeuvres complètes de Voltaire: Nouvelle édition*, vol. VI, Paris: Didot, 1876, pp. 582–616 = N. CRONK – C. MERVAUD (eds.), *Les œuvres complètes de Voltaire*, vol. 79 B: *Religious works of 1776*, Oxford: Voltaire Foundation, 2014, pp. 381–524
VONA
    C. VONA, s.v. *Cirillo di Alessandria*, in *Bibliotheca Sanctorum*, vol. III, Roma: Città Nuova, 1962, coll. 1308–1316

WAERDEN
   B.L. VAN DER WAERDEN, *Science Awakening*, English translation by Arnold Dresden with additions of the author, New York: John Wiley & Sons, 1963
WAITHE
   M. E. WAITHE (ed.), *A History of Women Philosophers*, vol. I: *Ancient Women Philosophers. 600 B.C. – 500 A.D.*, Dordrecht – Boston – Lancaster: Nijoff, 1987
WALRAFF
   M. WALRAFF, *Die Kirchenhistoriker Sokrates. Untersuchungen zu Geschichtsdarstellung, Methode und Person*, Göttingen: Vandenhoeck & Ruprecht, 1997
WATTS 2006a
   E.J. WATTS, *City and School in Late Antique Athens and Alexandria*, Berkeley – Los Angeles – London: University of California Press, 2006
WATTS 2006b
   E.J. WATTS, *The Murder of Hypatia. Acceptable or Unacceptable Violence?*, in H.A. DRAKE (ed.), *Violence in Late Antiquity. Perception and Practices*, Aldershot, England – Burlington, Vermont: Ashgate, 2006, pp. 333–342
WATTS 2010
   E.J. WATTS, *Riot in Alexandria: Tradition and Group Dynamics in Late Antique Pagan and Christian Communities*, Berkeley – Los Angeles – London: University of California Press, 2010
WATTS 2011
   E.J. WATTS, *Doctrine, Anecdote, and Action: Reconsidering the Social History of the Last Platonists (c. 430-c. 550 CE)*, "Classical Philology" 106 (2011), pp. 226–244
WATTS 2013
   E.J. WATTS, *Damascius's Isidore: Collective Biography and a Perfectly Imperfect Philosophical Exemplar*, in M. DZIELSKA – C. TWARDOWSKA (eds.), *Divine Men and Women in the History and Society of Late Hellenism*, Kraków: Jagiellonian University Press, 2013, pp. 159–168
WATTS 2017
   E.J. WATTS, *Hypatia. The Life and Legend of an Ancient Philosopher*, Oxford: Oxford University Press, 2017
WATTS 2020a
   E.J. WATTS, *Athens, Educational Reform, and the Future of Philosophy*, in I. Tanaseanu-Döbler – L. von Alvensleben (eds.), *Athens II: Athens in Late Antiquity*, Tübingen: Mohr Siebeck, 2020, pp. 247–258
WATTS 2020b
   E.J. WATTS, *Hypatia and her Eighteenth-Century Reception*, in LAVALLE NORMAN – PETKAS, pp. 193–207
WAUGH
   E. WAUGH, *Officers and Gentlemen*, London: Chapman & Hall, 1955
WERNSDORF
   J.C. WERNSDORF, *Dissertationes Academicae de Hypatia philosopha Alexandrina I–IV*, Vitembergae: Schlomach, 1747–1748
   J.C. WERNSDORF, I. *De Hypatia philosopha Alexandrina*
   J.C. WERNSDORF – R.E.Chr. SCHEFFLER, II. *De Hypatia philosopha Alexandrina speciatim de ejus caede*
   J.C. WERNSDORF – C.B. ACOLUTHUS, III. *De Hypatia philosopha Alexandrina speciatim de causis caedis ejus*
   J.C. WERNSDORF – A.L.Fr. DRECHSEL, *Dissertatio Academica IV. De Hypatia philosopha Alexandrina speciatim de Cyrillo episcopo in causa tumultus Alexandrini caedisque Hypatiae contra Gothofr. Arnoldum et Io. Tolandum defenso*
WESSEL
   S. WESSEL, *Socrates's narrative of Cyril of Alexandria's Episcopal Election*, "Journal of Theological Studies" 52 (2000), pp. 98–104
WHITBY
   M. WHITBY, *John of Ephesus and the Pagans: Pagan Survivals in the Sixth Century*, in M. SALAMON (ed.),

Paganism in the Later Roman Empire and in Byzantium, Byzantina et Slavica Cracoviensia 1, Kraków: Jagiellonian University Press, 1991, pp. 111–131

WHITFIELD

B.J. WHITFIELD, *The Beauty of Reasoning: A Reexamination of Hypatia of Alexandra* [sic], "The Mathematics Educator" 6 (1995), pp. 14–21

WIELAND

C.M. WIELAND, *Sämmtliche* [sic] *Werke*, vol. XIII: *Supplemente*, t. I: *Die Natur der Dinge – Moralische Briefe*, Leipzig: Goschen, 1798 (photographic reprint Hamburg 1984)

WILCKEN 1905

U. WILCKEN, *Zur Ägyptischen Prophetie*, "Hermes" 40 (1905), pp. 544–560

WILKEN 1971

R.J. WILKEN, *Judaism and the Early Christian Mind: A Study of Cyril of Alexandria's Exegesis and Theology*, New Haven: Yale University Press, 1971 (reprint Eugene, Oregon: Wipf & Stock, 2004)

WILLIAMS

F.J. WILLIAMS, *Callimachus: Hymn to Apollo, a Commentary*, Oxford – New York: Clarendon Press – Oxford University Press, 1978

WIPSZYCKA 1972

E. WIPSZYCKA, *Les ressources et les activités économiques des églises en Égypte du IVe au VIIIe siècle*, Bruxelles: Fondation Égyptologique Reine Elisabeth, 1972

WIPSZYCKA 1992

E. WIPSZYCKA, *Le nationalisme a-t-il existé dans l'Égypte byzantin?*, "Journal of Juristic Papyrology" 22 (1992), pp. 83–128

WIPSZYCKA 2015

E. WIPSZYCKA, *Alexandrian Church. People and Institutions*, "Journal of Juristic Papyrology", Supplement 25, Warsaw: Warsaw University – Raphael Taubenschlag Foundation, 2015

WOLF 1735

J.C. WOLF, *Mulierum Graecarum, quae oratione prosa usae sunt, fragmenta et elogia Graece et Latine* […], *accedit Catalogus foeminarum sapientia artibus scriptisve apud Graecos Romanos aliasque gentes olim illustrium*, Hamburgi: apud Vandenhoeck, 1735

WOLF 1879

S. WOLF, *Hypatia die Philosophin von Alexandrien: ihr Leben, Wirken und Lebensende nach den Quelleschriften dargestellt*, Program des k. k. Ober-Gymnasiums in Czernowitz in dem Herzogtume Bukowina für das Schuljahr 1881, Wien: in Kommission bei Alfred Hölder, 1879 (reprint London: British Library Reference Division Reprographic Section, 1978)

WYDER

W. WYDER, *Women Philosophers in the Ancient Greek World: Donning the Mantle*, "Hypatia" 1.1 (1986), pp. 21–62

XANTHOPOULOS

Nicephorus Callistus XANTHOPOULOS, *Historia ecclesiastica, libri VIII–XIV*, in J.P. MIGNE, *Patrologia Graeca*, 146

ZANETTI

U. ZANETTI, *L'Église copte*, "Seminarium" 26.3 (1987), pp. 352–363

ZERETELI

G. ZERETELI (ed.), *Papyri russischer und georgischer Sammlungen (P. ross.-georg.)*, vol. III: *Spätrömische und byzantinische Texte*, t. 1: *Briefe*, Tiflis: Universitätslithographie, 1929

ZIEDAN

Y. ZIEDAN, *Azâzîl*, Cairo: Dar El Shourouk, 2009

ZITELMANN

A. ZITELMANN, *Hypatia*, Weinheim – Basel: Beltz & Gelberg, 1988

Index of Names

Abrotelia, Pythagorean philosopher   180
Acacius of Constantinople, patriarch   28
Achilles Tatius, rhetorician   27
Adachi, H.   208
Adam, M.   119
Adler, A.   5–11, 18, 20, 30, 32, 45, 48, 51–54, 56, 59, 98, 151, 153, 155, 174, 178, 180, 182, 189, 192 f., 195–199, 216
Aedesia, Neoplatonic philosopher   180
Aedesius, duke of Thebaid   59, 61, 195
Aeneas of Gaza, Neoplatonic philosopher   158
Aeschylus, tragedian   36
Agabiti, A.   73, 84 f., 87, 133, 135, 198
Alcibiades, statesman   22
Alexander the Great, king of Macedonia   42
Alic, M.   182
al-Maqrizi, historian   17
al-Mas'udi, historian   13, 17
Alpers, K.   9
Amann, É.   86
Amenábar, A.   129, 193
Amidon, P.R.   10
Ammianus Marcellinus, historian   8, 12, 16, 154
Ammonius, follower of Cyril of Alexandria   32, 46, 48–50, 53, 67, 95, 158, 194
Ammonius Saccas, Neoplatonic philosopher   164
Andres, S.   128
Andronicus II Palaeologus, Byzantine emperor   210
Anna Komnene, historian   180
Anne, queen of Great Britain   76, 124, 134
Anthemius, minister of Theodosius II   61
Anthony of Thebaid, saint   23
Antoninus, Iamblichan teacher   16, 21, 159, 164
Apollonius of Perga, mathematician   109, 157
Apollonius the Stoic, scholar   180, 182
Aratus of Soli, poet and philosopher   178
Archilochus, poet   183
Archimedes of Syracuse, mathematician   163
Arethas of Caesarea, scholar   175
Argov, E.   10
Arignote, Pythagorean philosopher   180
Aristotle, philosopher   7, 45, 48, 67, 109, 151, 188
Arius, theologian   52, 137, 139, 147
Armstrong, A.H.   153
Arnold, G.   78, 89, 91 f.
Arria, Neoplatonic philosopher   180

Asclepigenia of Athens, Neoplatonic philosopher   180, 183
Asmus, R.   10, 20, 71 f., 106, 112, 135
Aspasia of Miletus, hetaera   181, 183
Athanasius of Alexandria, theologian   27, 52, 137, 139, 145
Athanasius, pupil of Hypatia   8, 147, 156
Athanassiadi, P.   5–7, 10 f., 18, 20, 30, 32, 45, 48, 51–54, 56, 59, 61, 151, 155, 157, 159, 161, 164 f., 189, 192 f., 195, 197–199, 216
Athenaeus of Naucratis, rhetorician   180, 198
Athenais Eudocia, Byzantine empress   72
Atticus of Constantinople, patriarch   46, 49
Aubé, B.   92 f.
Aubonnet, J.   48
Augustine of Hippo, theologian   170
Augustus, Roman emperor   17
Aujoulat, N.   157, 160, 162, 166, 168, 171, 173, 175–177, 179
Aurelian, Roman emperor   154
Averincev, S.S.   44, 170
Azevedo, M.   183

Baculard d'Arnaud, F.-T.-M. de   72
Badini Confalonieri, L.   96–99, 103, 112
Bagenal, F.   135
Bagnall, R.S.   148
Bailly, J.S.   114, 117
Balboni, D.   112
Baldi, D.   27
Baldwin, S.E.   102
Barbier de Meynard, C.   17
Bardy, G.   86, 112, 146, 148
Barlatier, P.   123 f.
Barna da Siena, painter   112
Barnes, T.D.   170
Barni, G.   84, 87
Baronius, Caesar, cardinal   77, 83, 85, 141
Barrès, M.   121–123, 125, 216
Barriole, A.   129
Barry, W.D.   82
Barthélemy, M.   123 f.
Basil of Caesarea, theologian   147, 193
Basil of Seleucia, theologian   41
Baudrillart, A.-H.-M.   145
Beer, A.   106
Beers, W.F.   61

Belenkiy, A.   55, 204
Benedetto, C.   133, 135, 154, 206
Benedict XVI, pope   84, 87, 208
Berardo, L.   98
Beretta, G.   8, 111, 113, 143, 153, 161f., 190, 208
Berkeley, G.   11, 78
Bernal, M.   204
Bernard, A.   37, 161
Berthelot, M. P. E.   176
Bessarion of Nicaea, scholar and statesman   205, 209
Bidez, J.   5, 10, 52, 56f., 138f., 149, 154, 174, 179, 195, 198
Bigoni, G.   8, 59, 61, 73, 84, 87
Bismarck, O. von   104–106
Blackburn, S.   182
Blanc, O.   72
Blaudeau, P.   147
Blaufuß, D.   91
Blaze de Bury, A.H.   123
Bleckmann, B.   5, 10, 52f., 56f., 138f., 149, 154, 174, 179, 195f., 198
Bloch, E.   15
Bloch, H.   17, 91
Borghese, Scipione, cardinal   70
Bouyoucas, P.   129
Bowers, E.   103
Bowersock, G.W.   44
Bowra, A.   111
Brandi, M.V.   112
Bregman, J.   165, 170–172, 179, 185, 187f.
Bréhier, L.   86
Bronzini, G.B.   109, 112f.
Brown, P.   1, 33f., 36, 156, 182, 199
Brucker, J.J.   55, 67
Bruno, Giordano, philosopher   75, 87f., 124, 192
Bryaxis, sculptor   13, 16
Bucci, O.   15
Burns, W.H.   43
Bury, J.B.   80–82
Butler, A.   17, 40, 80
Butterworth, G.W.   16

Cacchioli, E.   113
Caetani, R.   84, 87, 169
Callimachus of Cyrene, scholar and poet   36, 108
Calvino, I.   128
Calvo Poyato, J.   129
Cameron, A.   16, 20, 33, 37, 43, 48, 54, 111, 152f., 161–163, 165, 171, 176f., 183, 211, 213f.

Cammilleri, R.   193
Campanella, Tommaso, philosopher   87
Campbell, P.J.   163
Canfora, L.   10, 17, 49, 52, 56f., 85f., 89, 91f., 102, 139, 199
Cannuyer, C.   148
Caravaggio (Michelangelo Merisi), painter   112
Carducci, G.   84, 87
Carile, A.   40
Carlyle, T.   100
Carolla, P.   10, 138, 140
Carrié, J.M.   214
Cary, E.   43
Cassiodorus, Flavius Magnus Aurelius, scholar and statesman   139
Cassius Dio Cocceianus, Lucius Claudius, historian and statesman   41, 43
Castelli, B.   163
Castiglioni, Branda da, cardinal   112
Catherine of Alexandria, saint   95, 99, 108–110, 112f., 115, 148, 164, 197
Cavari, O.   87
Cave, W.   92f., 102
Celestine I, pope   24, 146
Chadwick, H.   193
Chalcondylas, Demetrius, scholar   74, 77
Charles, R.H.   38, 40, 43, 53, 58f., 109, 186, 190, 195, 198, 211, 215
Chateaubriand, F.-R. de   37, 114f., 117f., 196, 201f., 206, 209
Chicago, J.   119
Choniates, Nicetas, historian and statesman   175
Chotjewitz, P.O.   129
Chuvin, P.   16f., 21, 32, 36, 40, 48, 54f., 58, 87, 135, 143, 149–152, 154–156, 166, 179, 182, 187–189, 198, 211
Civiletti, M.   15
Claudel, P.   110, 113f.
Claudianus, Claudius, poet   15
Claus, A.   9
Clement of Alexandria, theologian   13, 16, 143, 193
Clévenot, M.   119
Colavito, A.   129
Colombi, E.   139
Conan, J.   170
Consolino, F.E.   199
Constantine I, Roman emperor   12, 24, 34, 89, 108f., 141, 174, 192
Constantine Palaeologus, Byzantine despot   180, 184, 210

Constantius II, Roman emperor   174, 177
Contini, C.   129
Cox, P.   36
Cracco Ruggini, L.   36, 43, 182, 196, 199
Crates of Thebes, Cynic philosopher   153
Criscuolo, U.   183
Croce, B.   133, 135, 206
Cronk, N.   68
Cross, F.L.   102, 147
Curie, M.   1
Cyril of Alexandria, theologian   16, 23–28, 32, 36–46, 48–57, 59–61, 65, 68f., 71–81, 83–87, 89–98, 101–104, 106, 109, 117f., 123, 125f., 128, 134, 137–146, 148, 150, 163f., 167, 185f., 188–196, 200, 205–208, 211–215
Cyrus, saint   24, 27

Dacier, A.   69, 71f., 94, 180
Daia, Maximinus, Roman emperor   108f.
Damascius, Neoplatonic philosopher   5–7, 10f., 18, 20f., 30, 32, 40, 45, 48, 51–54, 56f., 59, 61, 65, 75f., 91, 93f., 111, 114, 134, 136–138, 140f., 143, 149–153, 155, 157, 159, 161, 163f., 177f., 180, 188f., 192–199, 211, 213, 216
Damiana, Neoplatonic philosopher   180
Damo, Pythagorean philosopher   180
Daniel, S.H.   78
Daniélou, J.   193
Darlene, L.   27
Davanture, M.   123
Davis, S.J.   17, 28
Deakin, M.A.B.   113, 153, 161–163, 177
De Angelis, F.   129
De Boor, C.   10, 138, 140
Déforis, J.-P.   109f.
Delacenserie, É.   139
Delehaye, H.   112
Delia, D.   50
Delmaire, R.   214
De Muralt, E.   61
Denzinger, H.   147
De Plinval, G.   86
De Pol, R.   104, 106
Descartes, R.   162
Desideri, P.   36
Desmolets, P.-N.   90, 92
Des Places, É.   10, 173, 176f.
Diderot, D.   6f., 11, 19, 51, 54f., 65–68, 71, 90, 137, 206
Diehl, C.   61

Dindorf, L.   56
Diocletian, Roman emperor   24
Diogenes Laertius, biographer and philosopher   153, 180
Dionigi Orfei, E.   94, 98
Diophantus of Alexandria, mathematician   73, 119, 157, 162
Dioscorus of Alexandria, bishop   144
Diotima of Mantinea, prophetess and philosopher   180
Dodds, E.R.   147
Donovan, S.   119
D'Ortigue de Vaumorière, P.   72
D'Osorio, L.   129
Doyson, D.   153
Draper, J.W.   163
Drechsel, A.L.F.   78, 92
Duchesne, L.   26, 89, 91, 148
Dupin, L.E.   91
Durrell, L.   82
Dzielska, M.   8, 16, 20, 22, 28, 43, 55, 61, 85, 87, 111, 113, 135, 143, 152–156, 163f., 166, 171f., 178f., 183, 188f.

Eastlake, C.   109, 112
Echecratia, Pythagorean philosopher   180
Eco, U.   84, 87, 128
Ehret, M.F.   128
Elli, A.   148
Ellies du Pin, L.   91
Engels, D.   119
Epiphanius Scholasticus, historian   139
Erasmus of Rotterdam, scholar and philosopher   167
Erskine, A.   154
Eschenbacher, W.   106
Escolan, P.   27
Estienne, Robert, scholar   74, 77
Euclid, mathematician   109
Eudocia, Aelia, Byzantine empress   72, 180
Eudocia Palaeologina, Neoplatonic philosopher   180f., 184, 210
Eunapius of Sardis, Neoplatonic philosopher   12–16, 20f., 23, 27, 45, 159, 180
Euoptius, brother of Synesius of Cyrene   128, 135, 156, 165, 168, 170f.
Eusebius of Nicomedia, theologian   147
Eustathius of Cappadocia, Neoplatonic philosopher   15, 20, 27
Eustratius of Nicaea, theologian   148

Eutyches, theologian 28
Evagrius Scholasticus, historian 15
Évieux, P. 43
Évrard, É. 152, 154, 158, 164

Fabia Aconia Paulina, philosopher 180
Fabricius, J.A. 68, 73, 89 f., 92, 114
Feldman, L.H. 43
Fermat, P. 77, 157, 163
Fernandez, G. 129
Ferretti, A. 112, 128, 158, 163
Fielding, H. 57, 79, 82, 154, 199, 202
Fincher, J. 36 f.
Fitzgerald, A. 11, 33, 87, 135, 152, 154, 156, 165 f., 170 f., 176, 179, 184, 188
Flacius Illyricus, Matthias, historian and theologian 74, 77, 83
Flaubert, G. 116, 121, 124
Flavian of Constantinople, patriarch 144
Fleury, C. 67 f.
Fliche, A. 83, 86
Forget, I. 43
Forster, E.M. 80, 82, 149, 154
Foster, H.B. 43
Fourier, J.B.J. 125
Fourikis, N. 129
Fournel, V. 71
Fowden, G. 17, 36, 164 f., 177 f.
Franceschinis, F.M. 95 – 99
Frandon, I.M. 123
Fraser, P.M. 27, 102, 214
Frederick I, king of Prussia 91
Frend, W.H.C. 28, 43, 147 f.
Frutaz, A.P. 86

Gajeri, E. 67, 71 f., 78, 82, 87, 91 f., 106, 111, 113, 117 f., 120, 126, 128, 135, 145, 148, 184, 188
Galilei, Galileo, astronomer 87
Gali, R. 129
Galvão-Sobrinho, C.R. 214
García, O. 129
Garibaldi, G. 84
Garin, E. 209
Garzya, A. 8, 158, 164 f., 172, 176, 188
Gaudemet, J. 15
Gautier, T. 125 f.
Gebremedhin, E. 148
Geffcken, J. 20
Gemina, Neoplatonic philosopher 180
Gemistus Plethon, George 209

Gemistus Plethon, George, Neoplatonic philosopher 8, 142, 175, 177, 179, 205 f., 209
Gentz, G. 140
George of Cappadocia, bishop of Alexandria 43, 198
George of Trebizond, scholar 148, 177, 205, 209
Gertz, S. 21
Giangrande, G. 12, 14 – 16, 23, 27, 159
Gibbon, E. 14, 17, 57, 79 f., 82, 92, 137, 141, 143, 154, 199, 202
Gibson, S. 16
Giorello, G. 46, 49
Giorgiadès, P. 128
Gómez de Liaño, I. 88
González Suáres, A. 129
Gouges, O. de 69, 72, 118 f.
Gouillard, J. 148
Goujet, C.-P. 90, 92
Goulet-Cazé, M.-O. 155, 177
Gregoras, Nicephorus, scholar 85, 170, 179 – 181, 184
Gregory of Nazianzus, theologian 147, 193
Gregory of Nyssa, theologian 86, 147, 193
Gregory, T.E. 44
Greiner, V. 129
Greydanus, S.D. 193
Griffith, S.H. 148
Grinstein, L.S. 163
Grotius, Hugo, scholar 72, 108, 111
Guaita, S. de 123
Guiducci, A. 113

Haas, C. 16 f., 27, 36, 48, 56, 143, 177, 188, 199, 211, 214
Haase, M. 16, 199
Hadot, I. 164
Hafner, G. 204
Hagedorn, D. 215 f.
Hahn, J. 17
Hansen, G.C. 5 f., 9, 11, 14 f., 17, 19 f., 22 f., 27, 32, 34 f., 42 f., 45 – 53, 55, 104, 106, 137, 139, 164, 178, 185, 189, 195, 198 f., 212 f.
Hanslik, R. 139
Harich-Schwarzbauer, H. 5 – 8, 11, 18 – 20, 22 f., 30, 32, 34 f., 42, 44 – 54, 56 f., 59, 61, 98, 111, 119, 138 f., 149 – 151, 153 – 155, 157, 161, 174, 176, 179, 182, 189, 192, 194 – 199, 216
Haring, N.M. 143
Hartley, A.J. 102
Hawkes, S. 148

Hedstrom, B.   27
Henry, C.   163
Henry, P.   85, 153
Henry, R.   10, 157, 161, 180, 182
Henry VIII, king of England   100, 103
Heppe, H.   82
Heraiscus, Neoplatonic philosopher   20
Hercher, R.   156
Herculian, pupil of Hypatia   135, 156, 160, 166 f., 170, 176, 179, 181, 184
Hernández de la Fuente, D.   129
Herrin, J.   161
Hesychius of Miletus, historian   5 f., 10 f., 20, 51, 53 f., 56, 65, 73, 98, 117, 136–138, 140, 153, 156, 161, 172, 196, 198
Hierocles of Alexandria, Neoplatonic philosopher   158, 164
Hilarion, saint   121, 123
Hillman, J.   37
Hipparchia, Cynic philosopher   20, 149, 151–153, 180
Hipparchus, Pythagorean philosopher   135
Hoche, R.   8, 56, 68, 82, 98, 135, 153, 155
Holmes, G.S.   78
Homer, poet   51 f., 54, 69, 71, 122, 168, 183
Honorius, Roman emperor   51
Hoppe, E.   177
Horn, C.B.   15
Hubbard, E.   107
Hunger, H.   10
Hunter, C.R.   162
Hurll, E.M.   110, 112
Huss, Jan, theologian   87, 124

Iamblichus, Neoplatonic philosopher   159, 164 f., 208
Irene panhypersebasta, Neoplatonic philosopher   180, 184, 210
Irigoin, J.   15
Irmscher, J.   111
Isidore of Pelusium, saint   20, 90, 92, 176
Isola, S.   154
Italus, John, scholar and philosopher   175

Jacobacci, R.   163
Jacob, W.   139
Jäger, W.   86, 193
James, H.   115, 118
Jameson, A.B.   109 f., 112, 118
Jeffreys, E.   53, 56 f., 138 f., 150, 154, 174

Jeffreys, M.   53, 56 f., 138 f., 150, 154, 174
Joan of Arc, saint   108
John Chrysostom, theologian   17, 28
John of Nikiu, historian   35, 38–41, 43, 46, 49, 53–55, 57–59, 79, 137, 140 f., 143, 145, 160, 166, 186, 190, 192, 195 f., 198 f., 211, 214 f.
John Paul II, pope   28
John Rufus, historian   15
John, saint and martyr under Diocletian   24, 27, 36,
Johnston, S. Iles   21
Jugie, M.   83, 85
Julia Domna, Roman empress   180
Julian the Apostate, Roman emperor   48, 67, 72, 79, 82, 155, 159
Jullien, L.   214 f.
Justinian I, Byzantine emperor   5, 36, 52, 56, 109, 138, 149, 209
Juvenal, poet   180

Kaçar, T.   43
Kaldellis, A.   10
Kasher, A.   43
Kassia, poet   180
Kazhdan, A.   9
Kettenburg, K. von der   72
Kiesewetter, J.C.   68, 77
Kingsley, C.   100, 102–104, 106, 114, 123, 128, 134, 141
Klaver, J.M.I.   102
Klein, R.   61, 143
Kline   163, 179
Kramer, C.   129, 215 f.
Krischer, T.   162
Krüger, P.   214
Krumbacher, K.   183
Kunst, H.   112

La Bella, V.   73
Labriolle, P. de   86, 156
La Calprenède, G. de Costes de   72
Lackany, R.   128
Lacombrade, C.   21, 48, 135, 143, 152–155, 161 f., 164, 166, 168, 170–174, 176, 179, 185, 187 f., 193, 208
La Croze, M.V. de   91
Lais of Hyccara, hetaera   198
Lambropoulou, V.   119
Lamirande, É.   102, 128, 209
La Motte, A.H. de   71 f.

Lamoureux, J.   157, 160, 162, 166, 168, 171, 173, 175–177, 179
Lampros, S.P.   179
Lanata, G.   199, 202
Lapatz, F.   135
La Spisa, P.   129
Lasteyrie, C.P. de   123
Lasthenia of Mantinea, Platonic philosopher   180
Laurens, P.   15
Leclerq, P.   17
Leconte de Lisle, C.M.R.   125 f., 149, 154
Le Fèvre, T.   72
Lenkowski, S.   85
Leopardi, G.   69, 72
Leo the Mathematician, scholar   178
Leonard, V.   20, 153
Leo XIII, pope   28, 84, 87
Lewis, T.   75 f., 78
Lewy, H.   165
Liébaert, J.   83, 85, 148
Liebeschütz, J.H.W.G.   170
Ligier, H.   67 f., 135
Lincoln, B.   199
Linder, A.   215
Livrea, E.   21, 36, 111, 152, 198
Lizzi Testa, R.   156
Loisy, A.   89
Longfellow, K.   129
Long, J.   16, 20, 152 f., 165, 176 f., 183
López Martínez, M.P.   129
Louis XIV, king of France   89
Loukaki, M.   9
Louth, A.   27
Louÿs, P.   100, 102
Lovascio, D.   128
Lucchesi, R.   182
Lucian of Samosata, rhetorician   54
Luck, G.   111
Ludovici, M.A.   118
Lumpkin, B.   204
Lündstrom, S.   15
Lupus, C.   98
Luzi, M.   127 f.
Lydus, John, scholar and statesman   156
Lysis, Pythagorean philosopher   135

Maas, E.   178
Mademoiselle B.   92, 175
Maeger, A.   119
Mair, A.W.   37

Malalas, John, historian   40, 52 f., 56 f., 138 f., 149 f., 154, 174, 178
Malatesta, Cleopa, despina of Mystras   179, 210
Maleville, G.   68
Malingrey, A.M.   17
Maltomini, F.   15
Mangasarian, M.M.   107
Manzoni, A.   95
Marcel, J.   128
Marciano-Jacob, C.   129
Marinus of Neapolis, Neoplatonic philosopher   20, 183
Marrou, H.I.   31 f., 100, 102, 155, 165, 191, 193
Martelli, M.   176
Martin, A.   56
Martindale, J.R.   61
Martinez Maza, C.   129
Martin, V.   83, 86
Martin V, pope   112
Masaccio (Tommaso di Ser Giovanni Cassai), painter   112
Masai, F.   209
Masolino da Panicale (Tommaso di Cristoforo Fini), painter   112
Maspéro, J.   145, 148
Masson, O.   8
Mauthner, F.   104, 106, 114, 123
Maximus of Ephesus, Neoplatonic philosopher   72, 180, 183
McAlister, L.L.   182
McGuckin, J.A.   27
McKenzie, J.   16, 56
Meinardus, O.F.A.   28, 112 f., 148
Ménage, G.   69, 71 f., 92, 111, 180, 182
Menander, comedist   183
Ménard, L.   121, 123
Menzio, M.R.   129
Mercati, A.   83
Merello, I.   67 f., 117, 123 f., 126
Mervaud, C.   68
Metochites, Theodore, scholar and statesman   167, 170, 175, 180, 184, 210
Meyer, P.M.   12, 15, 44, 49, 60–62, 174, 177, 214
Meyer, W.A.   8, 68, 111, 135, 155
Miesel, S.   193
Migne, J.P.   140, 187
Miles, R.   119
Minardi, C.   119
Mitchell, C.W.   100, 203
Mogenet, T.   161, 178

Molinaro, U.   119
Mommsen, T.   12, 15 f., 44, 49, 60 – 62, 104, 174, 177, 214
Moneti Codignola, M.   129
Montale, E.   133
Monti, V.   69 f., 73, 95
Moréas, J.   123
Moréri, L.   85 f.
Moschus, John, hagiographer   21
Müller, K.   10
Mündler, O.   112
Muraro, L.   113
Musurus, Marcus, scholar   74, 77
Myia, Pythagorean philosopher   180
Myrsilides, B.A.   113

Neocaesarites, Theodore, statesman   210
Neri, M.   88
Nerval, G. de   14, 17
Nesselrath, H.-G.   36
Nestorius, theologian   24 f., 28, 98, 144 – 146, 164
Neugebauer, O.   8, 162
Newman, J.H.   101, 103, 134
Nicaeus, young friend of Synesius   33
Nicetas of Heraclea, scholar   148
Nicholas of Cusa, philosopher   192
Nietzsche, F.   86
Niewöhner, F.   91
Nonnus of Panopolis, poet   36 f.
Nuffelen, P. van   9

Ogilvie, G. Stuart   103
Ogilvie, M.B.   163
Olympius, pupil of Hypatia   135, 156, 170, 176
Olympus, Iamblichan teacher   15 f., 26, 159, 164, 174, 206
O' Meara, D.   161
Oppian, poet   37
Orestes, augustal prefect of the diocese of Egypt   26 f., 31 f., 34 f., 38, 40 f., 43, 45 – 49, 51, 56, 59, 61, 72 f., 83, 86 f., 89, 91, 96, 102, 109, 119, 140, 143, 145, 190, 194, 200, 213
Origen, theologian   143, 158, 164, 193
Oser, L.M.   119, 163

Pack, R.   21
Palladas of Alexandria, poet   12, 15, 26, 72, 108, 111, 128, 150, 152
Palladius of Galatia, ascetical writer   17
Papaconstantinou, A.   28

Parini, G.   95
Parmentier, L.   16, 198
Parsons, E.A.   17
Pascal, C.   56, 84, 87
Patlagean, E.   23, 26 f., 41, 43 – 45, 48
Paul of Tarsus, saint   19, 22
Paul VI, pope   28, 112
Pavet de Courteille, A.   17
Pecout, C.   129
Pedraza, P.   129
Péguy, C.   37, 114 – 117, 119, 121, 125, 201 f., 209
Pellat, C.   17
Penella, R.J.   153 f., 172
Peonius, addressee of Synesius's *De dono*   168, 171, 176
Perl, T.   163
Petau, D.   77
Peter the Reader, follower of Cyril of Alexandria   51, 55, 57, 65, 79, 89 – 92, 123, 195
Petta, A.   129
Phenix jr., R.R.   15
Philipsborn, A.   44
Philochorus of Athens, historian   180, 182
Philolaus, young friend of Synesius   33
Philometor, cousin of Sosipatra   20
Philoponus, John, theologian   17, 158, 162
Philostorgius, historian   5, 10, 52 f., 56 f., 59, 91, 111, 136 – 140, 143, 149, 154, 161, 164, 174, 178 f., 195 f., 198
Philostratus, rhetorician   180
Photius, scholar   10, 52, 73, 138 – 140, 142, 146, 157, 161, 164, 170, 179 f., 182
Phrangopoulos, T.D.   128
Piero della Francesca, painter   109
Piganiol, A.   177
Pilate, Pontius, governor of Judaea   200
Pius VI, pope   70
Pius XII, pope   84, 87
Plato, philosopher   7, 22, 109, 117 f., 122, 125, 128, 150 f., 157, 164, 188, 209
Plotinus, philosopher   1, 6, 22, 30, 85, 123, 135, 153, 159, 164, 177, 180, 214
Plutarch, biographer and philosopher   11
Plutarch of Athens, Neoplatonic philosopher   164, 183
Politian (Agnolo Ambrogini), scholar   167
Pomeroy, S.   182
Porphyry, Neoplatonic philosopher   30, 159, 164, 173, 177, 214
Portia, Stoic philosopher   180

Pouderon, B.   139
Pozzi, R.   128 f.
Praechter, K.   104, 106, 135, 145, 148, 152 f., 165
Pratt, H.   128
Proclus, Neoplatonic philosopher   20, 67, 164, 178, 183
Proterius of Alexandria, bishop   43, 198
Proust, M.   125, 149, 154
Psellos, Michael, historian and statesman   167, 170, 175, 179, 181, 183 f., 190, 205, 209
Ptacek, G.   119
Ptolemy, Claudius, astronomer   157, 178
Ptolemy I Soter, king of Egypt   154
Pulcheria, Byzantine empress   59, 61, 145

Ramakrishnan, T.D.   128
Renan, E.   67, 123
Rensi, E.   83, 85
Reuss, J.   148
Reyes, A.T.   16
Richardson, R.   113
Richeson, A.W.   163
Rist, J.M.   100, 102, 139, 152 f., 155, 164, 177, 205, 208
Rivera Garretas, M.-M.   129
Rochefort, G.   155
Rome, A.   157, 161, 178
Roncaglia, M.   148
Ronchey, S.   9, 50, 98, 166, 182, 187, 199, 202
Roques, D.   6, 8, 11, 26, 31, 33, 87, 135, 151, 154, 156 f., 160, 162, 165–173, 176, 179, 181, 184 f., 187 f., 211
Rougé, J.   27, 39 f., 44, 46, 49 f., 61, 86 f., 143, 179, 189, 193, 214
Ruelle, C.E.   176
Rufinus, Tyrannius, historian   15 f.
Ruprechter, W.   106
Russell, B.   81 f., 118, 137
Russell. D.W.   115, 118
Russell, N.   17
Russo, L.   154

Sacheverell, H.   76, 78
Saffrey, H.D.   48, 183
Saluzzo Roero, D.   20, 94 f., 98, 125, 201, 202
Salvatore, A.   129
Sand, G.   2, 110, 114
Sappho, poet   183
Sara, Pythagorean philosopher   180
Sathas, K.N.   181, 183

Sauvage, F.   123
Savoia-Carignano, M.T.L. di, princess of Lamballe   118
Schaefer, F.   83, 85
Schäfer, P.   43
Scheidegger Laemmle, S.   135
Scheidweiler, F.   16, 198
Scherr, J.   118
Schiller, J.C.F. von   69, 72
Schmidt, J.A.   77
Schmitt, T.   8, 170
Schönmetzer, A.   147
Schopen, L.   181, 184
Schramm, M.   163
Schrek, D.J.E.   163
Schubert, H. von   102, 106, 135
Schwartz, E.   15 f., 44
Schwyzer, H.R.   153
Scott, R.   53, 56 f., 138 f., 150, 154, 174
Segonds, A.Ph.   183
Seiber, J.   156
Sertoli, G.   102 f.
Shanzer, D.   153
Shaw, G.   43, 165
Shenoute of Atripe, saint, hegumen of the White Monastery   61, 144, 198
Simonutti, L.   78
Sirks, A.J.B.   214 f.
Socrates, philosopher   22, 82, 181, 183, 185, 189
Socrates Scholasticus, historian   5 f., 9, 14 f., 17, 19 f., 22 f., 27, 32, 34, 36, 40 f., 43, 45 f., 50 f., 72, 74, 77, 83, 85, 89, 92, 95, 104, 106, 114, 137 f., 143, 164, 185, 195–200, 212 f.
Soldan, W.G.   82
Sophronius of Jerusalem, bishop   24, 27
Sosipatra of Ephesus, Neoplatonic philosopher   180, 183
Sozomenus, Salminius Hermias, historian   15
Spetzieris, K.   113
Spindeler, A.   86
Sprigge, S.   133, 135
Staël, Madame de (Necker, A.-L. Germaine, Baroness de Staël-Holstein)   95
Stein, M.   5, 10, 52 f., 56 f., 138 f., 149, 154, 174, 179, 195 f., 198
Stoppa, A.   129
Suidas, scholar   5–11, 18, 20, 30, 32, 37, 45, 48, 51–54, 56, 59, 61, 65, 71, 73 f., 76 f., 85, 89, 98, 136–138, 140, 146, 149–151, 153–157, 161 f.,

174, 178–180, 182, 185, 188 f., 192 f., 195–199, 211, 216
Sweet, M.   129
Swinburne, A.C.   67
Syrianus, Neoplatonic philosopher   164, 183

Tailhade, L.   123
Takács, S.A.   17, 26–28, 43, 49, 66 f., 198, 215 f.
Tanaseanu-Döbler, I.   165, 170, 176, 208
Tannery, P.   10, 61, 158, 161, 163
Tardieu, M.   16, 40, 54 f., 58, 87, 135, 143, 149 f., 152, 155 f., 165 f., 179, 182, 187 f., 211
Tarrent, V.   115
Teruel, P.J.   129
Theano, Pythagorean philosopher   180 f., 183
Themistoklea, Pythagorean philosopher   180
Theodora, Byzantine empress   36
Theodora, Neoplatonic philosopher   180
Theodoret of Cyrus, theologian   13, 16, 41, 139, 198
Theodosius II, Byzantine emperor   51, 56, 59, 61, 95, 145, 180
Theodosius I, Roman emperor   8, 12, 15, 34, 147, 168, 174, 192 f., 214
Theon of Alexandria, mathematician   5 f., 8 f., 52, 72, 79, 109, 111, 117, 127, 140, 153 f., 156 f., 159, 161 f., 174 f., 177 f., 215
Theophanes the Confessor, historian   138, 140
Theophilus of Alexandria, bishop   12–17, 23 f., 26, 28, 42, 44, 52, 58 f., 96 f., 102, 121, 137, 167, 189, 193, 195, 212
Thesleff, H.   135
Thorp, J.   102, 113, 136, 156, 165, 199
Thulard, A.   128
Thurn, I.   53, 56 f., 138 f., 150, 154, 174, 178
Tihon, A.   161, 178
Tillemont, L.S. Le Nain de   90, 92, 95, 98, 141
Tissoni, R.   98
Toland, J.   74–78, 87, 92, 100, 114, 134
Tommaseo, N.   95, 98
Torcutti, M.C.   103
Toulouse, S.   165, 177
Trabal Svaluto-Ferro, L.   129
Trajan, Roman emperor   41
Trent, B.   129
Turnèbe, A.   77
Tymicha, Pythagorean philosopher   180

Uffelman, L.K.   102

Urbainczyk, T.   9
Urselli, T.   129

Valens, Roman emperor   175, 177
Valois, Henri de, scholar   89, 91, 114
Vanini, Giulio Cesare (Lucilio), philosopher   87, 124
Vaquerizo, E.   129
Vare, E.A.   119
Vasilev, A.A.   171
Veyssière de La Croze, M.   91
Viganò, A.   129
Vignier, C.   123
Vincenzi, M.   129
Vinzent, M.   155
Vivien, R.   115, 118 f.
Vogt, J.   86, 163, 172
Vollkommer, R.   16
Voltaire (François-Marie Arouet)   68 f., 71 f., 92, 137, 180
Vona, C.   148

Waerden, B.L. van der   163
Waithe, M.E.   163
Walford, E.W.   10
Walker, J.   183
Walraff, M.   9
Waltz, P.   111
Watts, E.J.   9–11, 15 f., 20–22, 26 f., 32, 40, 43, 48–50, 54 f., 57 f., 71, 77 f., 92, 140, 143, 147, 153, 155, 159, 161 f., 164 f., 170–172, 177 f., 183, 187–189, 194, 198, 208 f., 214
Waugh, E.   80, 82
Weber, M.   91
Wernsdorf, J.C.   68, 78, 92
Wessel, S.   27
Whiston, W., mathematician   78
Whitby, M.   209
White, C.I.   61, 94, 100, 104, 115, 117, 121
Whitfield, B.J.   163
Wieland, C.M.   79, 82, 201 f.
Wilamowitz, U. von   86, 167, 177
Wilcken, U.   12, 15
Wilken, R.L.   43
Williams, F.J.   36
Winkelmann, F.   15 f., 140
Wipszycka, E.   26, 29, 215 f.
Wolf, J.C.   69, 72, 180, 182
Wolf, S.   68, 135, 153
Wyder, W.   182

Xanthopoulos, Nicephorus Callistus 138, 140
Xerxes the Great, king of Persia 36

Yeats, W.B. 80

Zanetti, U. 28
Zedler, B.H. 71
Zeno, Byzantine emperor 28
Zereteli, G. 215

Ziedan, Y. 128
Zintzen, C. 5–7, 10f., 18, 20, 30, 32, 45, 48, 51–54, 56, 59, 61, 151, 155, 157, 159, 161, 164, 189, 192f., 195, 197–199, 216
Zitelmann, A. 128
Zonaras, John, historian 148
Zotenberg, M.H. 40
Zuckerman, C. 61

www.ingramcontent.com/pod-product-compliance
Lightning Source LLC
Chambersburg PA
CBHW080408230426
43662CB00016B/2355